South East
Trail Running

Mark Rainsley

   www.pesdapress.com

First published in Great Britain 2021 by Pesda Press
Tan y Coed Canol
Ceunant
Caernarfon
Gwynedd
LL55 4RN

© Copyright 2021 Mark Rainsley

Maps by Bute Cartographics
Contains Ordnance Survey data © Crown copyright and database right 2021

ISBN: 9781906095819

The Author has asserted his rights under the Copyright, Designs
and Patents Act, 1988, to be identified as Author of this Work.
All rights reserved. No part of this publication may be reproduced, stored in a retrieval
system, or transmitted, in any form or by any means, electronic, mechanical, photocopying,
recording or otherwise, without the prior written permission of the publisher.

Printed and bound in Poland, www.hussarbooks.pl

Introduction

With thanks to Susie Allison.

'I just felt like running.'
Forrest Gump, *Forrest Gump* (1994)

This book is about running for fun in beautiful places. Each route has been selected for its inspirational scenery and runnable terrain. The range of routes is deliberately diverse; these runs follow rivers and coastlines, go up hills and along ridges, cross open heathland and weave through leafy woodlands. The selected routes come highly recommended and include many of South East England's most enjoyable and inspiring trails. But this is not a definitive collection. These runs are intended to open people's eyes to the region's potential and to act as a springboard for further personal explorations of South East England's trails.

Downland Trail, Butser Hill (Route 11)

Contents

INTRODUCTION 3
About the Author	6
Why Trail Running?	7
How to Use This Book	9
Getting Started	13
Skills Development	17
Outdoor Access	21
Enjoy	22

ISLE OF WIGHT 23
1 The Needles	25
2 The Tennyson Trail	29
3 St Catherine's Oratory	33
4 Appuldurcombe House	37
5 The Devil's Chimney	41
6 Bembridge Down	45

HAMPSHIRE 49
7 Hurst Castle	51
8 Beaulieu Heath	55
9 Burley	59
10 Coopers Hill and Hampton Ridge	63
11 Queen Elizabeth Country Park	67
12 Old Winchester Hill	71
13 The Clarendon Way	77
14 Selborne	83
15 Highclere Castle	87

BERKSHIRE 91
16 Combe Gibbet	93
17 Windsor Castle	97
18 Greenham Common	103
19 Lough Down	107
20 Goring to Avebury	111
21 Winter Hill	117

OXFORDSHIRE 121
22 The Uffington White Horse	123
23 Chimney Meadows	127
24 Blenheim Palace	131
25 Wittenham Clumps	135
26 Grim's Ditch	139
27 Watlington Hill	143

BUCKINGHAMSHIRE AND HERTFORDSHIRE 147
28 Turville	149
29 Chequers	153
30 Wendover Woods	157
31 Tring Park	161
32 Ivinghoe Beacon	167
33 Dunstable Downs	171
34 Hatfield House	175
35 Lee Valley	179

ESSEX 183
36 Epping Forest	185
37 Hatfield Forest	189
38 Hadleigh Castle	193
39 The Broomway	197
40 The Dengie Peninsula	201
41 Dedham Vale	205

KENT 209
42 The White Cliffs of Dover	211
43 The Reculver Towers	217
44 Folkestone Warren	221
45 The Wye Downs	225
46 Maidstone to Hollingbourne	229
47 Knole Park	233
48 The Eden Valley	239

Old Winchester Hill (Route 12)
Photo: Chris Eden

EAST SUSSEX 245

49 Camber Castle	247
50 Hastings Country Park	251
51 Seven Sisters and Beachy Head	255
52 Ashdown Forest	259
53 Ditchling Beacon	263

WEST SUSSEX 267

54 Devil's Dyke	269
55 Cissbury Ring and Chanctonbury Ring	273
56 Petworth Park	277
57 Black Down	281
58 Thorney Island	285
59 Petersfield to Amberley	289

SURREY 295

60 The Devil's Punch Bowl	297
61 St Martha's Hill	303
62 The Hurtwood and Leith Hill	307
63 Box Hill	313
64 Reigate Hill	319
65 Happy Valley	323

APPENDICES 329

Resources	329
Mapping	329
Access	330
Running clubs	330
Trail races	331
Training, coaching and guiding	331
New route ideas	331
Acknowledgements	332
Index	333

5

About the Author

Mark Rainsley

Mark Rainsley lives and works in Dorset. As a keen trail runner (and also kayaker, surfer and mountain biker), he has explored every corner of the wild and wonderful South East, in all its moods and seasons. He has been known to survive the occasional ultra-marathon, but largely he runs sensible distances, purely for the joy of exploring the landscape. He is the author of *South West Trail Running*.

Mark took on the challenge of researching the South West's and then the South East's trail-running potential as a means of recovering physically and mentally from major surgery to correct a genetic heart defect. This seems to have worked; he recently celebrated his 50th birthday by completing a 50-mile trail run. He hopes that this book demonstrates that these wonderful places are accessible to all runners, and that this book offers useful information and maybe even a bit of inspiration.

Why Trail Running?

Moving fast and light through, and engaging with, the landscape is what trail running is all about. All that is required is just you and a pair of running shoes! Trail runners leave roads and traffic behind in search of the quieter and wilder, sometimes hidden, paths and tracks that criss-cross the outdoors. Leafy woodland, meandering river banks, winding ridges, dramatic sea cliffs, lonely saltmarshes, open heathland; South East England has all of these and all are fantastic places to run.

Trails are everywhere
The beauty of trail running is that it combines the speed and ease of running on roads with fresh air and wide-open spaces. Trails enable runners to move quickly over ground that might otherwise be too rough or boggy for a speedy passage. Trails enable runners to explore all across South East England; from the inner reaches of suburban woodlands to isolated high ridges and remote coastline.

Trails are for everyone
Trail running is a simple activity which is accessible to everyone wishing to give it a go. Great off-road running trails are found anywhere and everywhere, in cities and towns as well as in the countryside. Anyone can take up trail running. Many trails are easily tackled by the most novice of runners and just as many trails will delight experienced runners seeking new challenges. Trail running is an activity that fits and grows with the experience and skill of the individual runner.

Mottistone Down (Route 2)

Why Trail Running?

Definition of a running trail

A trail is simply a path or a track. Some are boggy or muddy, some are stony or sun-baked ... but all are easier on the joints and (in this author's humble opinion!) far more interesting and enjoyable than running along roads. The routes in this book all have public access. Most follow footpaths or bridleways. Many utilise unsurfaced roads such as farm access tracks. Some are on Access Land, where you may roam freely. Tarmacked paths and roads do inevitably feature from time to time, but only when there is no alternative way to approach or complete a great trail run.

Guidebook scope and purpose

This guidebook sets out to describe trail runs right across South East England, including several islands; all are enjoyable, many are sublime! The routes presented here are selected to showcase the available spectrum of trail-running experiences to be found in each of the South East's diverse regions, and to present physical challenges ranging from mild to superhuman. Inevitably, the choice of routes reflects the author's prejudices; for example, I love coastal running, I love running across open heathland, I love running through landscapes which tell a story of geology, history or prehistory and I especially love running along Southern England's incredible chalk ridgetops.

Many of the routes are easily-accessible trails close to towns, cities and popular holiday destinations. These runs range from short, straightforward circuits to longer, half-day outings. The remaining routes take runners into the heart of South East England's wilder landscapes; these absolutely do exist! The selection process has inevitably required compromise as there just isn't space for every great trail-running route in the region. Some routes require some road running and at the other end of the spectrum some routes have short unrunnable sections, usually where extreme gradient is involved. Running on rougher terrains does require skill and experience. The routes in this book have been selected to cover a wide range of running terrain so that runners can develop their ability in whichever direction they want; to run further, to climb higher, tackle trickier ground or navigate more complex terrain. Developing these skills opens up a whole new world of opportunities for exploring the rich and varied landscapes of South East England.

Disclaimer

Every effort has been made to ensure that the information supplied is accurate. However, mistakes happen and trails are subject to change. The author welcomes updates / corrections.

As with any activity, trail runners must accept responsibility for their own actions, stay within their own limits and avoid harming other people or property. The author, publisher and distributor of this book do not recognise any liability for any injury or damage to person or property arising from the use of this guide.

How to Use This Book

This book is for reading in the armchair at home or for storing in the car glovebox. It has been designed so that the turn-by-turn route description and map can be photocopied and taken on the run. Each route is laid out in the same format.

Quick reference

This section lists the length of the route in kilometres and miles as well as the cumulative ascent (height gain) in metres and feet. Distances are given to the nearest 0.5km for routes under 10km and to the nearest kilometre for routes over 10km. Ascent is given to the nearest 25m. A mixture of computer, GPS and paper mapping has been used to calculate distance and ascent. Although every effort has been made to supply accurate information, it is inevitable that there will be inconsistencies with readers' own plots and GPS tracks. Ascent calculations are liable to vary much more than distance, especially along coasts. Relevant maps are listed along with the start (and end) point(s) of the route with grid references and postcodes. The grid reference gives the precise location of the start of the route. The postcode is approximate and is provided to help Satnav users reach the correct general area; rural postcodes cover a much larger area than urban postcodes. Each route is rated to indicate the level of navigation required, the roughness of the terrain underfoot and the likelihood of getting wet feet.

South Downs Way near Ditchling Beacon (Route 53)

How to Use This Book

Rating system

Three aspects of the route are rated to set appropriate expectations. The rating is based on the section of the route which requires the highest level of navigation, has the roughest terrain and the highest probability of wet or muddy feet.

Navigation ●○○	These routes are relatively easy to follow, usually with full or partial way-marking or signposts.
Navigation ●●○	Some care is needed to stay on the described route as there are multiple junctions without waymarkers or signs. Some routes are graded ** if they are technically easy to navigate but in a remote area where the consequences of getting lost could be serious. Map and compass are advisable.
Navigation ●●●	These routes cross remote regions where the consequences of getting lost are serious. A map, compass and the ability to use both are required in addition to the route description. The route may not always follow obvious land features. The path may not always be obvious on the ground and may depend upon the season and weather conditions.

Terrain ●○○	Smooth paths or tracks which are easy to run. There may be a few short rougher patches.
Terrain ●●○	Fairly easy to run but stones, tree roots or uneven path sections merit care at times.
Terrain ●●●	These routes are almost entirely runnable provided sufficient attention is paid to foot placement. They may be rocky, boggy or generally uneven. A few routes have sections where walking is unavoidable. This grading also encompasses routes where there are repeated very steep climbs.

Wet Feet ●○○	On a dry day, wet or muddy feet are unlikely. There may be occasional and avoidable muddy puddles or patches of shallow mud.
Wet Feet ●●○	Damp or muddy feet are likely, particularly in autumn and winter. During drier spells, puddles and muddy patches can often be avoided. In normal conditions streams can be crossed by jumping or on stepping stones.
Wet Feet ●●●	Wet or muddy feet are inevitable due to unjumpable stream or river crossings and / or boggy areas.

How to Use This Book

Map

The route maps are based on Ordnance Survey mapping with the scale varied in order to fit the whole route onto the page. They are intended to be complementary to, not substitutes for, Ordnance Survey or other published maps.

Route description

The route description is divided into two parts; a scene-setting preamble followed by functional, turn-by-turn instructions. The numbering in the description matches the numbers on the route maps.
Compass directions given in the route directions are intended to be used as a *rough indication* alongside the map, not for precise navigation!

Types of trail

All of the routes in this book have legal access. However, it is important to understand the distinctions between the different kinds of trails used. In the route descriptions, the following language is used:

Path: if the word 'path' is used alone, it describes a trail which is not a footpath, bridleway or byway (see below). If marked on the OS map it will be as short black dashes.

Footpath: this word is used to describe a trail marked on Ordnance Survey maps as footpath, i.e. a public right of way. These are marked by a line of short dashes – red on 1:50K Landranger maps, Green on 1:25K Explorer maps. In practice, footpaths can range from a narrow trail to a wide track.

Bridleway: this word is used to describe a trail marked on Ordnance Survey maps as a bridleway, i.e. a public right of way. These are marked by a line of long dashes – red on Landranger maps, green on Explorer maps. In practice, bridleways can range from a narrow trail to a wide track. If the route description says, 'bridleway path', this simply indicates that the bridleway is narrow; if it says 'bridleway track' it simply indicates that the bridleway is wide.

Byways: this word is used to describe a trail marked on Ordnance Survey maps as a byway, i.e. a public right of way. These are marked by a line of red crosses on Landranger maps and a line of green crosses on Explorer maps. Byways are (in theory) driveable, so tend to be relatively wide. Many have firm or tarmacked surfaces. Unsurfaced byways are often heavily rutted from use by off-road vehicles and liable to flooding. Some byways are marked on maps by a line of 'T' dashes: these are Restricted Byways, where motor vehicles are not allowed.

Permissive: if a footpath, bridleway or byway is described as 'permissive', this means that the landowner has 'allowed' access and that it could potentially be withdrawn.

Access Land: if an area is described as 'Access Land', this means that you are allowed to run freely within it, without restriction (see page 21).

Lane / road: the word 'lane' is used to describe a tarmacked public highway where cars may be encountered, but traffic is usually light. The word 'road' is used to describe busier highways.

How to Use This Book

Signage (Route 22)

Trip planning

This section outlines the logistics involved in running this route. Driving directions and parking information may be supplied. Where public transport is important in shuttling a route, details will be provided. Conveniently located shops, pubs or cafés may be mentioned. Any particular local conditions requiring consideration will be mentioned in this section.

Useful websites for trip planning are listed in the resources section at the back of the book.

Other routes

Every runner is different, so this section aims to help those looking for longer, shorter or just plain different routes, as well as runners staying in the area for more than one day.

Events

The Events section is a non-comprehensive list of trail races held on the route or in the local area. Distances for events can be given in either kilometres or miles, depending upon whatever format the organiser uses. More detailed event listings can also be found at websites such as *www.tra-uk.org*, *www.runnersworld.co.uk*, *www.runabc.co.uk*, *www.findarace.com*, *www.100marathonclub.org.uk*, *www.fellrunner.org.uk* and *www.sleepmonsters.com*.

Getting Started

Running is one of the simplest and most satisfying activities you can do; just head out of the door and put one foot in front of the other. There are just a few things it may be helpful to think about first.

Why run?

People run for all sorts of reasons. Some view running as just a means to an unexciting end: becoming fitter, losing weight, achieving performance targets. Trail runners soon come to understand that the activity is greater than the sum of its parts. Your experiences along the trails will help you in maintaining mental wellbeing. They will help you to achieve a sense of mindfulness. You will have fun. You will share adventures and bond with your buddies. You will immerse yourself in beautiful and engaging landscapes and learn how to 'read' the story they tell of nature, geology, prehistory and history. You will become more resilient and now when the printer jams or the photocopier breaks at work, it won't be an apocalyptic scenario. You will become a happier person*.

If all of this is accompanied by side-effects such as stronger muscles, improved cardiovascular fitness and speedier performance, then that's just great.

First steps

Those who have tried road running and found it uncomfortable (or developed injuries) will be pleased to hear that trail running – even in the driest conditions, when the ground is baked hard – is much less stressful on joints and muscles than road running.

All of the routes in this book are just as well walked as jogged or run (or walk-jog-run, the author's preferred style), so *there is no fitness barrier to getting started*. Just get out there and give them a go! Start off by only running the downhills. Even the world's best runners walk steep uphill sections. As with any activity, it is sensible to start small and gradually increase the effort required. Check the suitability of a route by looking at the distance, ascent (height gain) and profile chart (steep or gradual climbs?) given in the route description.

Steady progress

Increase activity levels gradually to give both your muscles and brain time to adapt to the demands of running on trails. Running on uneven trails engages a wider range of muscles than running on smooth roads and pavement. On slippery or rocky trails, the brain needs to work quickly to pick the most secure foot placements. There is an abundance of information on running-specific training and technique available from medical professionals and running coaches as well as from books and magazines.

Footwear

Well-fitting shoes suitable for the terrain are essential for enjoyable and injury-free running. The fundamentals of choosing the right footwear are comfort and grip. Comfort depends on the way the shoe fits, stabilises, supports and cushions the runner's foot. The correct shoe is a very individual decision.

* Possibly via some truly miserable and masochistic moments!

Getting Started

Shoe manufacturers use differently-shaped lasts and have a range of ideas about the ideal amount of stability, support and cushioning. Specialist running shops can analyse your running gait, advise on these differences and suggest appropriate footwear.

Road shoes usually have the most stability, support and cushioning. They have a smoother sole which will give adequate grip in dry conditions for well-constructed paths and tracks. On uneven terrain this can make it more difficult to place feet accurately.

Fell shoes have comparatively little cushioning and an exaggerated knobbly sole which helps runners stay secure on steep wet grass. They can be an uncomfortable choice on anything harder than earth or grass paths, particularly during longer runs.

Further still along the 'little cushioning' spectrum are so-called 'barefoot' running shoes. Their minimalist soles are controversially claimed to reduce injury supposedly caused by padded soles. These are definitely an acquired taste.

Unsurprisingly, trail shoes are usually the best compromise for trail running. These have a rugged sole giving better grip, making each step much more secure, particularly on wet days. Many models have waterproof and breathable Gore-Tex membranes, expensive but well worth considering if you will be tackling muddy or boggy conditions.

Clothing

There is plenty of technical clothing available from specialist running shops. Synthetic materials are recommended as cotton takes a long time to dry and can rub badly when wet. Multiple thin layers are more flexible for regulating temperature than one thick layer. Zip-neck tops are good for the same reason. Ankle socks are better at preventing stones and dirt from entering shoes than low cut trainer liners. Well-fitting underwear is essential for both men and women; for women this means a high impact-level sports bra.

Weather can be fickle. Hence, lightweight and breathable waterproofs are an important element of the runner's wardrobe. Hats and gloves should be carried in colder weather. Runners must wear enough to stay warm. It can be tempting to wear less clothing on the assumption that running will help keep the body warm. However, in wet, cold conditions thinly-clad runners are prone to developing hypothermia, particularly when they tire.

High-visibility reflective clothing is a must, even if (as with the routes in this guidebook) road time will be a small proportion of your run. Those worried about fashion sensibilities may be interested to know that a number of manufacturers now utilise modern materials which reflect light extremely efficiently despite being conventionally coloured (i.e. not Day-Glo).

What to carry?

For short routes there is little need to carry anything at all. For longer routes, especially those in remote areas, food, water and additional clothing are the basic extras. It is most comfortable to carry these in a lightweight rucksack or bumbag designed especially for runners and sold in specialist running or outdoor shops.

It is important to stay well-fed and hydrated. While out on routes lasting several hours, runners should aim to eat a small amount regularly. What to eat is a matter of personal preference. Muesli bars, sandwiches,

Getting Started

Suggested kit list

	WEAR (CONDITIONS DEPENDENT)	CARRY (CONDITIONS DEPENDENT)
SHORT RUNS	SHOES	(ROUTE DESCRIPTION)
	SOCKS	(MAP AND COMPASS)
	SHORTS OR LEGGINGS	(MOBILE PHONE)
	SUPPORTIVE UNDERWEAR	(MONEY)
	SHORT- OR LONG-SLEEVED TOP	(FOOD)
	(CAP)	(WATER)
	(WARM LAYER)	
	(WIND OR WATERPROOF TOP)	
	(HAT, NECK BUFF AND GLOVES)	
	(SUNSCREEN)	
LONGER RUNS	AS ABOVE	LIGHTWEIGHT RUCKSACK OR BUMBAG
		ROUTE DESCRIPTION
		MAP AND COMPASS
		MOBILE PHONE
		MONEY
		FOOD
		WATER
		(EXTRA WARM LAYERS)
		(WATERPROOF BOTTOMS)
		FIRST AID KIT
		WHISTLES
		SURVIVAL BAG
		HEAD TORCH
		(SUNSCREEN)
OVERNIGHT CAMPING RUNS: FASTPACKING	AS ABOVE	LIGHTWEIGHT RUCKSACK (25L IS GOOD)
		ROUTE DESCRIPTION
		MAP AND COMPASS
		MOBILE PHONE
		MONEY
		FOOD
		WATER
		EXTRA WARM LAYERS INCLUDING FULL LENGTH LEGGINGS
		WATERPROOF TOP AND BOTTOMS
		FIRST AID KIT
		WHISTLES
		SURVIVAL BAG
		HEAD TORCH
		(SUNSCREEN)
		TENT OR BIVVY BAG
		STOVE, PAN, FUEL AND LIGHTER / MATCHES
		FOAM OR INFLATABLE SLEEPING MAT
		SLEEPING BAG
		(TOTAL WEIGHT 4–7 KG)

Getting Started

jelly babies, malt loaf and gloopy energy gels are just some of the foods popular with experienced runners. Drink when thirsty. The amount of fluid needed varies between individual runners and also depends upon the conditions. Water, squash or energy drink can be carried in either a bottle or a bladder and hose.

Map, compass and the ability to use both are essential for some of the routes. A mobile phone is recommended for safety reasons. A basic first aid kit containing at least a crepe bandage, wound dressing and a few sticking plasters is recommended, as are a lightweight survival bag and whistle. Headtorches weigh very little and prove their worth more often than anticipated.

Use common sense when packing for a run. Running with a week's supply of muesli bars, three litres of water and five spare tops will not be much fun. On the other hand, omitting waterproofs and a spare warm layer could lead to a wet, cold and exhausting epic. Go fast and light ... and well prepared.

Hypothermia

Hypothermia is a serious medical condition which occurs when a person's core body temperature drops abnormally low. Look out for stumbles, mumbles and fumbles – key signs of the onset of hypothermia – and make sure these are addressed immediately by putting on more clothes and heading for home. Another key sign of hypothermia is a loss of awareness and judgement – something for solo runners to be mindful of.

Ticks

Ticks are a serious danger to trail runners. Ticks can carry Lyme Disease, a life-threatening condition. Even wearing long sleeves and leggings, ticks are liable to sneak in and find a spot to bite. Always do a full body check as soon as possible after running in potentially tick-infested areas such as heathland or forest where deer graze. All of the South East outside London is assessed as 'High Risk' according to Bristol University's 'Big Tick Project'. See their risk map for more details: *www.bigtickproject.co.uk*.

The NHS-recommended removal method is to grab the tick as close to the skin as possible using tweezers, then extract by pulling straight up gently. See a GP immediately if a target-shaped rash or flu-like symptoms develop.

Skills Development

Trail running technique

There is a real joy and satisfaction to running fast over uneven ground. This is a skill that can be learnt through conscious thought and experience. Running on trails requires concentration and can be mentally tiring. It is important to adapt speed to the terrain and to stay within personal limits. Looking ahead and 'reading the trail' to choose the best foot placement is the key to moving swiftly. There may be uneven ground, tree roots, muddy puddles, soft boggy areas, patches of gravel or larger rocks. The skill lies in selecting the clear area among gravel, varying stride length between tree roots, pushing off firm earth rather than soft bog and landing a footstep precisely on top of a rock instead of slipping awkwardly off its side.

Navigation

The routes in this book range from city centre parks and landscaped estates to hilly areas and remote marshland. They cover the whole spectrum from runs where going off-route is no problem at all to those where getting lost could be serious.

Confident navigation is essential for progressing to the more remote routes included in this guidebook. Each route is graded to indicate the level of navigation required. Confident navigation comes through practice and the ratings system is intended to help development of the required skills.

The route descriptions should be read and used in conjunction with maps. Basic map reading starts by relating the hills, valleys and features such as rivers, buildings and boundaries seen on the ground to the contour lines and symbols marked on the map. Orientate your map to the direction of travel so that the features line up with those on the ground. While moving, keep a mental tick list of features on the map which must be passed in order to reach the next key point on the route. Get into the habit of memorising your tick list and consulting the map only at key points. It helps enormously to know where you are all of the time, rather than spending time figuring out the location from scratch at every stop.

The level of navigation required often changes dramatically with weather conditions. A straightforward trot over moorland to a trig point may require counting paces and following a compass bearing when the cloud rolls in.

Navigators must constantly challenge their own assumptions. Look for features that disprove an identified location. It is all too easy to make features fit with the map and inadvertently 'confirm' an incorrect location. Estimate the width and height of a feature as well as the distance to it before consulting the map. Map measurements should corroborate the estimations. If not, alarm bells should ring!

Developing an awareness of distance and timing is very useful. Try identifying features at varying distances – say, 100m, 500m and 1km – and timing how long it takes to run to each of them. Try timing the same distances on rougher terrain.

No times are given for the routes in this book as running time varies so much from person to person. Keep a record of how long each route takes and work out a personalised version of Naismith's Rule. This rule of thumb is used by hillwalkers to calculate the length of time a route will take, based on its distance and total ascent. The standard Naismith's Rule allows one hour for every 5km plus one minute for each 10m of

Skills Development

height gained. For runners, a good starting point is to assume one hour for every 10km plus one minute for each 10m height gain. Rougher terrain will increase the time taken, often very significantly.

Almost all of the routes in this book use paths and tracks that are clear and easy to follow independent of the weather conditions. Some follow fainter paths and need a higher level of navigation. Path recognition is key to finding the way on less distinct routes. Developing an eye for traces of previous usage is helpful. Look out for clues such as slightly polished rocks, aligned patches of bare earth and broken, stunted or different types of vegetation. Paths often disappear into boggy or stony areas and reappear on the far side. Humans tend to follow fence lines and head to obvious features. In summertime, even usually clear paths may become overgrown and tricky to identify.

Basic navigational techniques such as orientating (also known as setting) the map, pacing, timing and following a compass bearing can be taught through courses and by studying books (e.g. *Mountain and Moorland Navigation* by Kevin Walker). A theoretical knowledge of navigation is not enough. Good navigation only comes through practice. One excellent way of learning and improving navigation skills is the sport of orienteering.

Phone apps

Paper maps are still the best and surest way to develop navigational skills and to understand your position and route in relation to the wider landscape. However, there are numerous mapping apps which can help. For example, there are several free apps which give your OS grid reference, allowing rapid confirmation of your position when unsure. A number of compass apps are useful for when you want to quickly orientate yourself or confirm your direction of travel. The author frequently uses Viewranger, which allows you to download OS mapping for your location but requires a subscription for the full features.

All of these apps should be strictly viewed as just a back-up to physical map and compass; mostly obviously because mobile phones fail, run out of battery or lose signal … but more importantly because over-reliance on technology will inhibit your development of navigational skills and awareness.

Measuring distance and height

Grid squares are always 1km

OS Landranger 1:50,000 2cm = 1km, 10m contour interval

OS Explorer 1:25,000 4cm = 1km, 10m contour interval

Harvey Superwalker 1:25,000 4cm = 1km, 15m contour interval

Conversion to imperial units:

10km is approximately 6 miles

10m is approximately 33ft

Skills Development

Naismith's rule

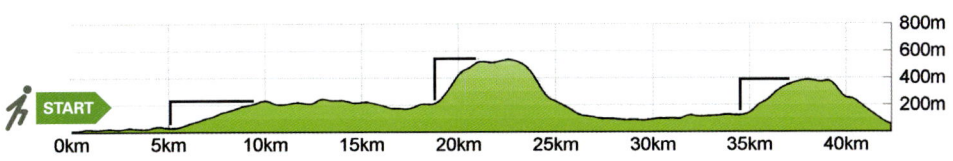

For runners a good starting point is to assume one hour for every 10km plus one minute for each 10m height gain.

EXAMPLE:
approx. 40km run = 4 hours
three climbs total 750m = +75 mins
total estimate = 5 hours 15 mins

Six figure grid references

On an OS map each 1km square has a four-figure reference (look for the blue grid numbers).
Divide each square into ten units.
Count along then up the square to find your location to within a 100m.square.

EXAMPLE:
Tennyson's Monument is in the grid square 3285;
dividing that square into tenths the monument is five tenths along and three tenths up
so the grid reference is SZ 325 853

Skills Development

Headon Hill bivvy (Route 1)
Photo: Andy Levick

Fastpacking

What is fastpacking? It's the zone of overlap between backpacking and trail running. It describes a means of accessing some amazing mini-adventures. Fastpackers move fast and light through the landscape, carrying the minimum gear to sleep and eat. You sleep wherever you wind up when the sun sinks and the stars come out. When dawn rises you quickly pack up, head off again and cover as much ground as your legs will allow; running, jogging, walking.

The key to this being practical is travelling lightweight. This author tends to carry a 2-season down sleeping bag, inflatable mattress and Gore-Tex bivvy bag. These weigh under two kilos, can be laid out quickly – literally wherever you stop on the trail – and offer decent protection and comfort outside the winter months. Carrying cooking gear and evening meals etc. is possible, but a non-purist approach is to utilise pubs and other eateries along your route … eat well, sleep rough!

Where do you sleep? There is no legal right to camp as you please in England and the frequently cited advice of 'get permission from the landowner' is in reality almost always impractical. However, careful judgement and discretion in terms of location and timing (choose somewhere quiet and out of sight, arrive late and leave early), coupled with absolute respect for the environment (there should never be any trace that you were ever there) will get you a long way.

Outdoor Access

Rights and responsibilities

The routes in this book follow trails, commons, heaths and parkland where you are legally entitled to run. However, your right to enjoy these outdoor places comes with responsibilities. Adopt a minimum impact approach and leave these trails as it would be good to find them. This definitely means not dumping your gel wrappers on the trail and it may well mean carrying out other people's litter! Mesh rucksack side-pockets are particularly handy for this.

The Countryside Code

The Countryside Code is worth repeating here, as it sums up the approach that mindful and environmentally sensitive trail runners should be taking:

Respect - Protect - Enjoy

Respect other people:
- consider the local community and other people enjoying the outdoors
- leave gates and property as you find them and follow paths unless wider access is available

Protect the natural environment:
- leave no trace of your visit and take your litter home
- keep dogs under effective control

Enjoy the outdoors:
- plan ahead and be prepared
- follow advice and local signs

The full version, with advice on each section, is of course available online.

Access Land

Access Land is a splendid thing, created in 2000 by the CRoW (Countryside and Rights of Way) Act. On Access Land, you have a right of access on foot for various forms of open air recreation, including trail running. Note that camping is not included. Access Land can be identified using Ordnance Survey Explorer maps, where it is coloured pale yellow. Up-to-date maps can also be found on the Natural England website. If you find yourself unsure (or in dispute) about Access Land, call the Open Access Call Centre on 0845 100 3298.

Most enclosed fields and farmyard areas will not be Access Land. The CRoW Act exempts the following areas from becoming Access Land: land ploughed or drilled within the previous year, land within 20 metres of a dwelling, parks, gardens and golf courses.

River Crouch Estuary (Route 40)

Enjoy

Have fun! Above all, this book is intended to encourage runners to get out and explore the South East's amazing and diverse landscapes and trails. There are a great many hours of trail running contained within these pages (several years' worth, in the case of the author!). Some are easy, some are tough. Sometimes the weather will cooperate and sometimes it will hurl horizontal rain. Sunny day trail runs make the world feel a better place, but a hard run through foul weather can paradoxically be even more satisfying. Going running is always the right decision – there is no such thing as a bad run.

Isle of Wight

Despite being a compact 20 by 35 kilometres in size, the Isle of Wight offers truly fantastic potential for trail running adventures; its complex geology has produced spectacular coastal cliffs, steep-sided interior hills and long snaking ridge tops. About half of the island comprises the Isle of Wight Area of Outstanding Natural Beauty, and truth be told, the remainder isn't too shabby. All of this is densely criss-crossed by an impressive network of well-marked trails. Enjoy the routes suggested here, or just run free.
Getting here takes a little more effort than is typical within the South East, due of course to the barrier formed by the Solent. Don't be deterred, however. Take the ferry across for a trail running weekend (or longer) on the island and you will be rewarded by inspiring panoramic views, ineffable sunrises and sunsets ... and resentful thighs.

Gore Cliff (Route 3)

The Freshwater Way

The Needles

Headon Hill
Photo: Claire Pinder

1 The Needles

Distance		21km (13 miles) **Ascent** 475m (1,560ft)
Map		OS Landranger 196 OS Explorer OL29
Navigation	●●●	Mostly following the waymarked IOW Coastal Path.
Terrain	●●●	Grass, roads, heathland, marshland, concrete promenades, several very steep ascents
Wet feet	●●●	The marshland can flood in exceptionally high tides
Start / Finish		Yarmouth Ferry Terminal PO41 0PH / SZ 353 897

A demanding tour of Isle of Wight highlights

Looking for a single run which encapsulates the Isle of Wight's engaging variety of landscapes and running surfaces? This classic loop is precisely that. The first third includes too many hard surfaces, but the Solent views compensate. The crux challenge is climbing the steep hills either side of Alum Bay, with excellent views of the famous Needles rocks. This serrated ridge of white chalk juts out to sea with an iconic striped lighthouse perched at the end. After you turn your back on the Needles, you enjoy an exhilarating run along the ridge of Tennyson Down, with the sea over 100 metres vertically below on your right (tip: stay left). The highest point is marked by the Tennyson Monument; this granite cross commemorates poet Alfred, Lord Tennyson. After descending to the sea at Freshwater Bay, you head inland and cross from the English Channel to the Solent via a smidgeon of suburbia, followed by the peaceful estuary of the River Yar.

1 The Needles

Route description

START From the ferry terminal, cross the bus station to the A3054 and follow this across the Yar Bridge. When the A3054 bends left (inland) 400m after the bridge, instead turn right onto the Isle of Wight Coastal Path. The IOWCP follows woods along the shore for 500m before heading uphill into Fort Victoria Country Park. After another 1.5km, the IOWCP turns inland following Monk's Lane. ❶ Follow Monk's Lane 500m to the entrance to Linstone Chine Holiday Village, and turn right into the 'village' following IOWCP signage. Signs direct you along tracks through the 'village' around three corners, past Brambles Farm and out onto the A3054 (Colwell Road). ❷ Turn right onto Colwell Road and follow it for 450m to the junction with Colwell Chine Road. Turn right onto this and follow it 450m to the seafront. ❸ Turn left and follow the IOWCP for 2km along the seafront (tarmac, but you can run along some of the beach if the tide is out). At Widdick Chine, just before a landslip bars the way, the IOWCP is directed inland up steep steps to Cliff Road. ❹ Turn right onto Cliff Road and follow it uphill for 300m to a left bend, where the IOWCP turns off on the right. Take the IOWCP, which leads uphill onto Headon Hill. Head W following the footpath

The Needles

along the top of the hill, and zigzag downhill on the footpath to Alum Bay Chine, bearing right at the only junction. ❺ When you reach the bottom of Alum Bay Chine, turn right down this ravine, and follow it until you reach steep steps on the left. Ascend these into The Needles Landmark Attraction (amusement park). Bear left through the park to the entrance and re-join the IOWCP. Ascend towards the Needles along a tarmac road and footpath. ❻ At the top, follow signs to the Needles viewpoint, before ascending onto the ridge top and following the IOWCP for 4.5km E along the ridge to Freshwater Bay. ❼ When you hit the road at Freshwater Bay, turn right towards the beach beside a toilet block. After 80m you reach the large Albion Hotel. Turn left onto Coastguard Lane which is opposite the hotel, and follow this to its end where it becomes a footpath. After 600m it reaches Blackbridge Road. ❽ Turn left onto Blackbridge Road, after 120m turn off right onto Easton Lane. After 400m, leave Easton Lane by a gate on the right and follow this footpath for 500m to Stroud Road. Turn right and cross the roundabout to Hooke Hill (opposite road). ❾ Turn right immediately onto the footpath behind the large supermarket building and follow this through Afton Marsh to The Causeway (lane at the head of the River Yar Estuary). ❿ Turn right and immediately left again onto the bridleway following the estuary. Follow this for 3km back into Yarmouth.

Trip planning

Yarmouth is the stepping-off point for the ferry from Lymington, so it is possible to run this as a day trip from the Mother Country.

If you have a car, there is a paying car park alongside the ferry terminal, alternatively hide it in a side street.

Yarmouth is well served with shops, pubs and cafés. Along the route, you should be able to grab emergency refreshments at beach kiosks. Freshwater Bay has a number of beachfront eateries which are a challenge to keep running past*.

An after-run visit to the Needles Battery is recommended; the National Trust manage this nineteenth century fort, which has tunnels leading through the cliffs to amazing views of the Needles and was (improbably) the site of a space rocket testing facility.

Tennyson Down

The Needles

Other routes

The loop can be tightened to about 13km by starting from Golden Hill Country Park. From the car park off the A3054 Colwell Road at PO40 9SJ / **SZ 338 879**, backtrack to Colwell Road, turn left (W) and join the route at ❷ after 450m. Upon reaching the roundabout

Alum Bay

*It's true! Last time we broke every trail running rule by stopping for tea and ice cream.

The Needles

at ⑨, turn left (W) along School Green Road for 330m until you see a road on the right signposted for the primary school. Take this and continue N past the school into the Country Park, following a bridleway past Golden Hill Fort to the car park.

If you want to avoid hills, the Yar Estuary is a lovely 7.5km loop. After crossing the Yar Bridge outside Yarmouth, turn left onto Gasworks Lane and follow the signposted Freshwater Way S along footpaths to All Saint's Church. Turn left here onto The Causeway to reach ⑩.

East of Yarmouth, the IOWCP (after a short road section) follows a great section of rugged Solent coast above crumbling cliffs, before heading inland to loop around the Newtown River. Well worth exploring.

River Yar

Totland Bay

Events

The Needles Half Marathon follows a loop similar to this and is the centrepiece of the annual Isle of Wight Festival of Running, usually held in June. In the same week, the Freshwater 5K and the Tapnell 10K offer milder challenges within West Wight.

Ryde Harriers organise the West Wight Three Hills, the three hills in this 8-mile race being Headon Hill, Tennyson Down and Golden Hill. West Wight Sports and Community Centre's Chilly Hilly is a 10-mile slog around a similar circuit.

Visiting the Isle of Wight

To reach 'The Island', you are beholden to two ferry companies*; Wightlink and Red Funnel. Red Funnel only operate the route between Southampton and East Cowes; this is the longest of the crossings but the views of the Solent are fine and more crucially, it's the cheapest; recommended if you are bringing a car. Wightlink make shorter crossings; Portsmouth to Fishbourne, Portsmouth to Ryde and Lymington to Yarmouth.

Getting around the Isle of Wight is easy enough without a car; a web of bus routes connects all corners.

*Hovertravel, a third company, link Portsmouth and Ryde by hovercraft. However, it's absurdly noisy and the author dislikes flying.

2 The Tennyson Trail

Descent to Freshwater Bay

2 The Tennyson Trail

Distance	22km (14 miles)	Ascent	575m (1,890ft)
Map	OS Landranger 196 OS Explorer OL29		
Navigation	●●● Route-finding doesn't get easier, just follow the geography		
Terrain	●●● Undulating chalk byways, sometimes stony or grassy, long gradual ascents		
Wet feet	●●● The chalk slickens in the wet		
Start	Clatterford Road, Carisbrooke PO30 1NQ / SZ 484 882		
Finish	Alum Bay New Road PO39 0JD / SZ 307 854		

Ridge running par excellence

The Tennyson Trail traces a direct route from the heart of the island to the Needles, following an undulating ridge. It is of course named after Victorian Poet Laureate Alfred Lord Tennyson (*'Into the valley of death, rode the six hundred ...'*), who lived at Farringford House in Freshwater Bay for four decades, walking these trails for inspiration. The route (mostly a byway) is untechnical to run and simple to follow, but the experience adds up to rather more than the sum total of this. Starting in the town of Newport within sight of Carisbrooke Castle (Charles I was imprisoned here, awaiting his trial in 1649), you climb onto the central spine of the island, and follow this west. After reaching the route's highest point in Brighstone Forest, you emerge from the shadows and glades to quite amazing seaward views ... on both sides! Enjoy these (and the numerous prehistoric burial mounds you run among) as the trail dips and rises, before descending to

The Tennyson Trail

Freshwater Bay. You then need to steel yourself to leave the beach behind and climb steeply (following part of Route 1 in reverse), to the Tennyson Monument which caps enormous chalk cliffs. Eventually, you run out of island at the Needles and the fun is sadly over.

Route description

START Head to the Waverley pub which is on the roundabout at the NE end of Clatterford Road. Turn left at the pub onto the B3401. Follow this for 150m and then turn left on Nodgham Lane. After 100m turn right (uphill) onto a byway (Down Lane). ❶ The byway is mostly straight and is easy to follow; all notable junctions are signposted, keep following 'Tennyson Trail'. The byway ascends Bowcombe Down and stays on or close to the ridge top. 5km from the start, Brighstone Forest is entered. ❷ After another 3.5km, the byway descends to cross a lane (Lynch Lane) to a parking area. ❸ The byway passes through a gate signposted for the National Trust Mottistone Estate and ascends Mottistone Down, before descending steeply again. The B3399 road is crossed, 2.8km after Lynch Lane. ❹ The byway ascends Brook Down and follows

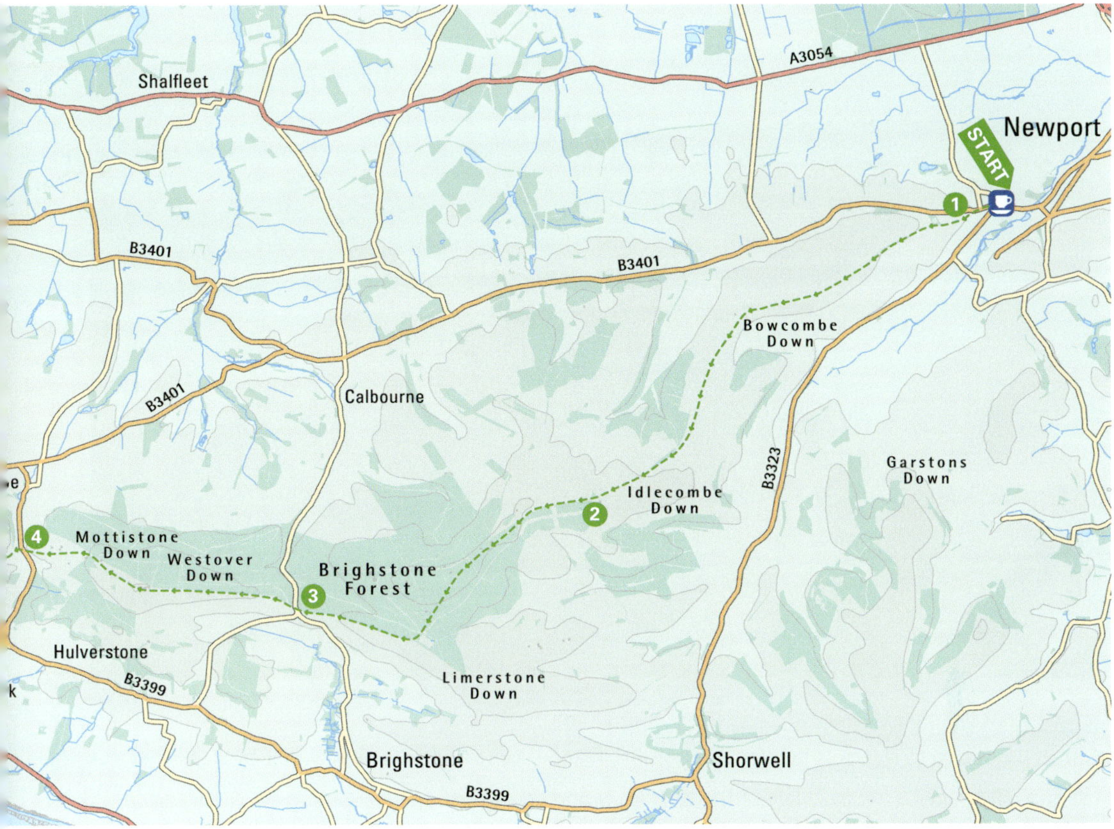

The Tennyson Trail

the ridge top, before descending through a golf course towards Freshwater Bay. The A3055 coast road is reached, 4.5km after the B3399. ❺ Follow this downhill into Freshwater Bay and continue on Gate Lane (road following the beach), passing the Albion Hotel on your left. 80m past the hotel, a footpath track leads off on the left beside a toilet block, signposted 'Fort Redoubt'; take this. ❻ Follow the footpath track 350m to the coast (alternatively take the short cut: a short distance along the lane, go through a gate on the right and ascend across the field). Follow the coastal footpath for 4.5km uphill and across Tennyson Down via the Tennyson Monument, and then across West High Down to the Needles viewpoint (this is signposted off the main footpath). ❼ Locate the road leading downhill from the Coastguard Cottages; the footpath follows alongside this down to the bus stop outside The Needles Landmark Attraction (amusement park).

Trip planning

Although much of the route is a byway, motor vehicles have been banned from the Tennyson Trail since 2006. Leaving a car at the start is no problem, park roadside. It's simple to return to Newport after your run; you finish at the bus stop for the Number 7 'Needles Breezer' service, which deposits you right back at your start point. If you abort your run and finish earlier, the

Brighstone Forest

2 The Tennyson Trail

Mottistone Down

Number 12 service to Newport helpfully calls at Brighstone, Mottistone and Freshwater Bay.

Post-run refreshments are available at the Needles Landmark Attraction where there are cafés and snack stalls (candyfloss is an energy food, right?).

For a bit of culture, explore Carisbrooke Castle before or after your run (English Heritage) and if you somehow have excess energy left, head back to the National Trust's Mottistone Estate to walk the gardens.

Other routes

An excellent simple loop starts from the parking area on Lynch Lane PO30 4JH / **SZ 420 845** and heads E into Brighstone Forest along the Tennyson Trail for 1km and then further E to the viewpoint on Limerstone Down, before returning W for 4km along the bridleways which run parallel just north of the TT, before returning east on the TT over Mottistone Down.

Brighstone Forest is Forestry Commission land where you could get lost for a long while exploring the tracks.

Events

A number of events are based around the Needles; see Route 1.

St Catherine's Oratory

St Catherine's Oratory

3 St Catherine's Oratory

Distance	9.5km (6 miles)	**Ascent**	300m (985ft)
Map	OS Landranger 196 OS Explorer OL29		
Navigation ●●○	Well signposted, but plenty of junctions to keep track of		
Terrain ●●●	Steep grassy ascents, rooty paths		
Wet feet ●●○	Damp socks from the grass …		
Start / Finish	Blackgang Viewpoint car park PO38 2JB / SZ 490 767		

Magnificent vistas from the Isle of Wight's southern hinterland

No warm-up allowed here; you are storming directly to the 240m summit of St Catherine's Down. Painful as this ascent is, it's over quickly and you can catch your breath while absorbing a breathtaking 360° vista encompassing the entire island and beyond. The strange 'space rocket' building atop the summit is St Catherine's Oratory, Britain's second oldest lighthouse* and locally dubbed 'the Pepperpot'. From here, you head inland to explore some of the least frequented downland in South East England. The Hoy Monument was apparently erected to commemorate an 1814 visit by the Tsar of Russia, although just as likely it served as an over-phallic status-signifier for the landowner whose name it carries, as with all of these hilltop monuments.

The final stage of this run follows one of the highlights of the Isle of Wight Coastal Path, an airy run along the rim of cliffs 150m above St Catherine's Point Lighthouse. This lighthouse marks the southernmost point of the Isle of Wight, so you run with the sea beneath, ahead and behind you …

* *Dating from the 14th century; the oldest is Roman and can be glimpsed within the walls of Dover Castle during Route 42.*

3 St Catherine's Oratory

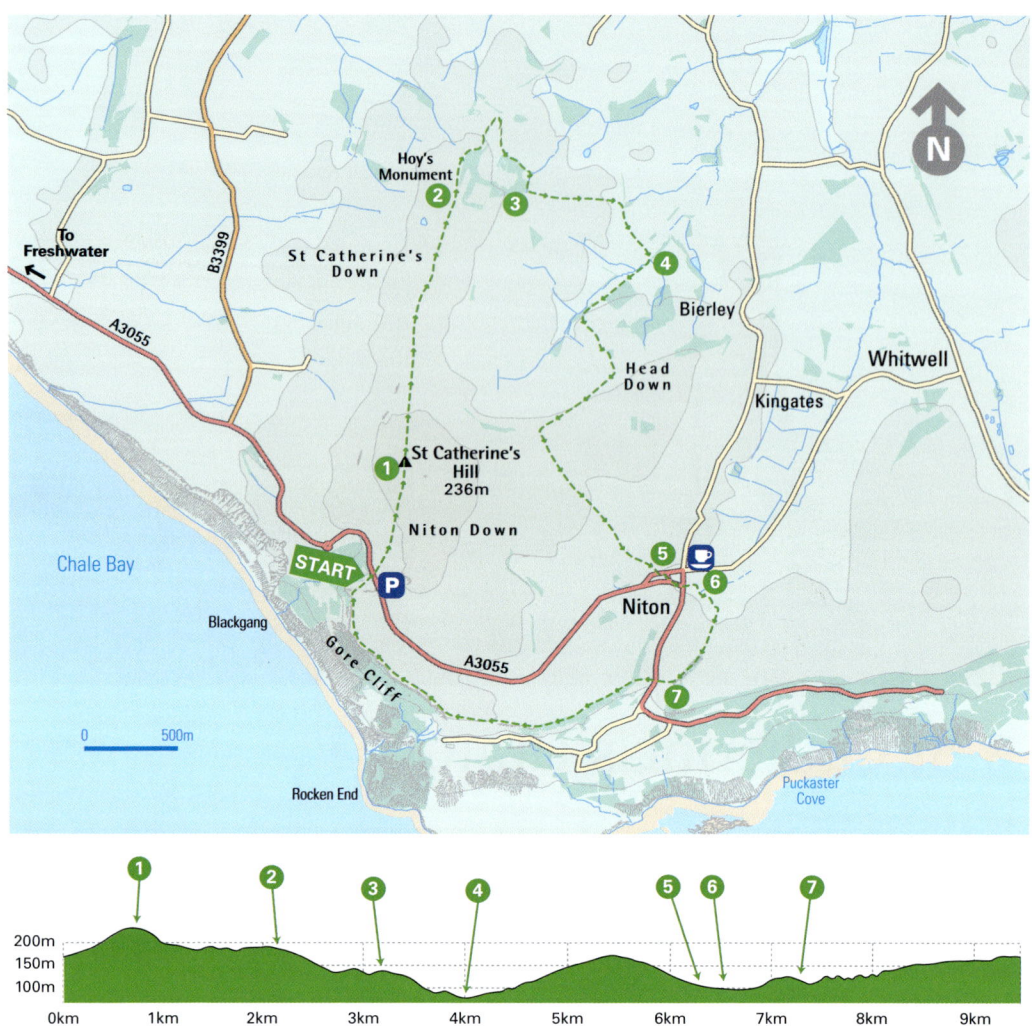

Route description

START From the car park, cross the A3055 / Blackgang Road and ascend the steps to the footpath signposted 'St Catherine's Oratory'. Ascend steeply uphill on the footpath to the Oratory (looks like a rocket ship). ❶ Descend N following the path along the fence towards the ridge of St Catherine's Down. After 500m a junction of bridleways is reached, continue N and pass through a gate to follow the bridleway and then a path along the top of the ridge towards Hoy's Monument (obvious tall column). ❷ Just before reaching the Monument, a bridleway leads off downhill on the left, take this. Three bridleways join from the left in quick succession on the way downhill, keep bearing right at these junctions and then cross a field to reach a footpath track (Dolcoppice Lane). Turn sharp right (S) onto this track and follow it 150m to the entrance of The Hermitage (mansion). Take the footpath which leads off on the left around The Hermitage, reaching a bridleway track after 250m. ❸ Turn left (downhill) onto the bridleway track and follow it to a T junction with another bridleway. Turn right (downhill), after 100m the bridleway bears right (uphill), but continue downhill following a footpath along the field boundary which leads to the valley

St Catherine's Oratory

floor and crosses a stream after 200m. ❹ Turn right onto the footpath leading up the valley (SW). After 450m it bends left and climbs across fields to a stile at the base of Head Down (steep hill). Footpaths are signposted in three directions up the hill, take the right-hand footpath and ascend. At the top of Head Down, a T junction with a bridleway track (Crocker Lane) is reached. Turn left onto this and then immediately right onto the bridleway track (Bury Lane) leading SE. Descend on this to Niton village. ❺ When you reach Church Street, turn left onto this, then directly after turn right onto the road with the 'No Entry' sign. This leads to Blackgang Road, turn left onto this and follow it to the White Lion Inn. ❻ Continue directly ahead crossing High Street and take the footpath signposted 'St Lawrence'. This winds around several corners before reaching a five-way junction. Take the footpath to the right signposted 'Barrack Shute' and follow this for 475m S until you reach a junction with the signposted 'Coastal Path' footpath. ❼ Turn right (W) and follow the Coastal Path for 2km (crossing the A3055 and then following the rim of big cliffs) back to the start. When you see a screen of trees leading uphill from the Coastal Path at a junction with a footpath, turn right up this footpath to reach the car park after 150m.

Trip planning

Blackgang Viewpoint car park charges from March to October.

There is a grocer's shop in Niton, which you'll spot en route. Niton's post-run dining choices are the pub (The White Lion) or the Fields Café, which as the name implies serves local produce.

A stroll from Niton to St Catherine's Point Lighthouse is recommended after your run. It's no longer possible to tour the lighthouse, but the southern tip of the Isle of Wight is a great place from which to watch time and tide flow past, especially at sunset.

Hoy's Monument

Gore Cliff

Head Down

St Catherine's Down

St Catherine's Oratory

St Catherine's Point

Other routes

A web of footpaths and bridleways crisscross the downland (much of which is Access Land); be our guest and explore further!

The IOWCP to the east of this section is great. It continues along the cliff before descending steeply to the coast proper, where it undulates along the small eroding cliffs which form the base of the Undercliff, a series of ancient (and recent) landslips. Ventnor is reached after about 6km.

To the west, the IOWCP descends by road past the theme park at Blackgang Chine, before following a level (and borderline monotonous) course along identikit cliffs for over 13km until a final climb above chalk cliffs into Freshwater Bay.

Events

The Great NorthSouth R#n finishes at St Catherine's Point, having crossed 19.6 miles of hills from Egypt Point, the northern tip of the Isle of Wight. The event is confusingly advertised as, *'leisurely'.*

The Isle of Wight Area of Outstanding Natural Beauty

All of the routes in this chapter are wholly or partly within the Isle of Wight AONB. The AONB covers 189km^2, just under half of the island. Included within it are the chalk ridge that crosses the island's centre, the steep greensand and chalk hills along the south coast and the southern and western cliffs (the Tennyson Heritage Coast). Trail runners exploring the AONB will quickly appreciate that what is remarkable here is that these are recognisably typical South East landscapes, but that they are amazingly undeveloped and unspoiled.

4 Appuldurcombe House

Appuldurcombe House

4 Appuldurcombe House

Distance		14km (8.5 miles)	Ascent	400m (1,350ft)
Map		OS Landranger 196 OS Explorer OL29		
Navigation	●●○	Mostly simple navigation with signposted trails following the landscape		
Terrain	●●●	Not-too-technical rooty and grassy trails, but two harsh ascents		
Wet feet	●●○	Various boggy or muddy sections		
Start / Finish		Appuldurcombe House English Heritage car park PO38 3HA / SZ 542 801		

A grand sweep around the Isle of Wight's south-eastern skyline

Starting from the ghostly shell of Appuldurcombe House – once the grandest house on the Isle of Wight – what you see is precisely what you get; you are going to run around the entire surrounding skyline. This is one of the many awesome things about trail running; you can glance at a whole landscape, and know that soon, you'll have tamed it. Or vice versa.

This circuit entails a couple of long (even, seemingly endless) ascents and some rather speedier descents. On the whole though, your morning will be spent bounding along fairly level ridgetops, soaking up grand views. The ridge along the eastern skyline is comprised of St Martin's Down, Shanklin Down, Luccombe Down, Bonchurch Down and finally St Boniface Down, the highest point on the island at 241m (neither ridgetop drops below 200m). You descend via a glorious dry valley which conveniently bypasses most of

4 Appuldurcombe House

Ventnor, and then climb through a golf course onto the western skyline; Week Down, Stenbury Down and Appuldurcombe Down. The latter is topped by the Worsley Monument, signifying that the descent back to the grounds of the House is about to commence ...

Route description

START Follow the footpath track N from the car park, past Appuldurcombe Farm. After 220m the track bends left, but the footpath continues ahead across a field, stay on it until it merges with a bridleway and you reach a large estate gate. Pass through the gate and immediately turn right (NE) onto a bridleway. ❶ Follow the bridleway 400m downhill to cross a lane (Redhill Lane) and continue following it for another 900m, ignoring any side turns and passing through a donkey sanctuary, to reach a road (B3327). Cross this and take the footpath track 30m to the right. ❷ The footpath leaves the track on the right and ascends SE across several fields before reaching a pond (unmapped as of 2020) after 800m, below a small covered reservoir. Pass to the left of the pond and ascend further on the footpath to reach a junction of multiple

Appuldurcombe House 4

footpaths and bridleways. Take the bridleway signposted 'V46 Ventnor and Shanklin'. ❸ Follow the bridleway, which contours around St Martin's Down while gradually ascending. After 1km it reaches the top and turns SE along the ridgetop (the summit trig point of Shanklin Down is seen just across a stile, worth a quick out-and-back detour). ❹ Follow the bridleway along the ridgetop, it bears S along Luccombe Down and after 1.7km it merges with a track leading WNW–ESE, in front of a wire fence. Turn sharply left (ESE) onto this track (it's a footpath) and follow it 200m to a parking area. ❺ Follow the wire fence past the parking area towards the sea and turn right onto a footpath which follows the fence WSW along the top of a steep slope. After 650m a gate is reached (below a communication mast). ❻ Pass through and turn left (SW) off the fence

St Boniface Down

Shanklin Down local

footpath to follow the footpath leading steeply downhill. After 200m turn off the footpath (closed ahead as of 2020) to follow the track zigzagging downhill into the valley. When you reach the valley floor, take the footpath which leads along the right-hand (N) edge and follow this downhill until it emerges at a road (B3327 Ocean View Road). ❼ Turn right (W) and follow the road for 200m until you see a tarmac bridleway ascending steeply on the right, follow this for 200m to reach a road (B3327 Newport Road). Cross the road, turn left (downhill) and follow it for 90m to where Steephill Down Road turns off on the right, take this. Follow Steephill Down Road 210m to its end where it becomes a bridleway track. Take the footpath which turns off right, steeply uphill. ❽ Ascend following the footpath into and through a golf course on Rew Down. After 1km the footpath joins with a bridleway path, turn right onto this and follow it NW and then N along the ridgetop (it briefly becomes a byway). After 1.9km the bridleway passes around a communication tower and then bears left (downhill) at a gate in front of two more towers. Turn off right onto the footpath here. ❾ Follow the footpath around the hillside for 400m and then turn right onto the footpath leading towards a prominent monument (the Worsley Monument). At the monument, continue on the footpath which leads steeply downhill for 400m before reaching a T junction with a bridleway. ❿ Turn right (NE) and follow the bridleway 300m downhill to the crossroads in front of the estate gate you passed through earlier. Turn right to pass through the gate again, and retrace your steps 700m along the footpath back to the car park.

Trip planning

The car park is free, located at the end of Appuldurcombe Road and signposted off St John's Road which leads north out of Wroxhall. An alternative start point (missing Appuldurcombe House) is the free National Trust car park at the top of St Boniface Down; park at the end of Down Lane PO38 1YL / **SZ 573 786**. This would start the route at ❺.

Appuldurcombe House

Visiting Appuldurcombe House before/after running is recommended; there is no downside, it's free. Also alongside the car park is the Isle of Wight Owl and Falconry Centre, a possible diversion for family while you escape to the hills?

Wroxall is nearby and boasts a pub and a supermarket. However, Ventnor sea front is surely the place to go for post-run relaxation; soaking your toes in the sea is the perfect wind-down. Although you are spoilt for food and drink choices, the author's pick is the Ocean Blue Quay where you can eat a Full English while sitting alongside a paddling pool featuring a giant topographical map of the Isle of Wight.

Other routes

Route 5 slightly overlaps this route, offering a shorter but more severe alternative. You could of course combine both routes into an arduous but rewarding figure of eight. Be careful what you pray for, though … The ridges at either side of the valley could be tackled in isolation, for a shorter outing. Beyond that, the possibilities are quite literally endless. An amazingly dense array of trails surrounds these hills, and crosses between them. Explore, explore, explore.

Events

One of the founder members of the Fell Running Association lives on the Isle of Wight. Hence, the Isle of Wight Fell Running Championship Series has been going for over a quarter of a century. Three (rather savage) races are held over two days, with the longest and toughest (The Wroxall Round) covering similar ground to this route, naturally with more distance and ascent.

Appuldurcombe House

Although gutted inside, the house is still impressive with its Baroque façade. What's really worth knowing about the place however, is the Worsley Scandal. In 1782, Sir Richard Worsley, seventh Baronet of Appuldurcombe, sued his friend George Bisset for 'damaging the purity' of his wife, Seymour. Bisset was fined only a shilling after it was revealed in court that – as he was Seymour's twenty-eighth lover – that ship had already sailed. Adding to Worsley's humiliation, a poem about the scandal became a bestseller. Worsley erected the tall obelisk on Appuldurcombe Down, which was reduced by lightning to the emasculated stump which this route passes. Some metaphors are too obvious. English Heritage open the grounds from Sunday to Friday, April until September. Regarding wandering around at other times, I couldn't comment.

Worsley Monument on Appuldurcombe Down

5 The Devil's Chimney

St Boniface Down

Distance	11km (7 miles)	Ascent	425m (1,400ft)
Map	OS Landranger 196 OS Explorer OL29		
Navigation ●●●	Well signposted, but plenty of route-finding needed		
Terrain ●●●	Varied grassy, rooty, rocky, narrow trails, tarmac. One crazy-steep climb		
Wet feet ●●○	Coastal path tends to get muddy		
Start / Finish	Car park at end of Down Lane PO38 1YL / SZ 573 786		

Challenging traverse of the Isle of Wight's steepest landscapes

This is the toughest of the Isle of Wight routes in this book; choose this one for relentless climbs, precarious paths and an exhilarating array of landscapes, all packed into a modest distance. You will tick off the highest point on the island at St Boniface Down (241m), the jungly interlude of The Landslip and the claustrophobic steps ascending a cleft in the cliffs known as the Devil's Chimney. Despite being squeezed around the seaside resorts of Shanklin and Ventnor, these trails feel wild and untamed. Which style of running do you prefer? The open heathland high on top, the rooty Undercliff paths or the mountain goat trail which clings to the steep down and woodland behind Ventnor?

5 The Devil's Chimney

Route description

🚶 **START** From the car park, follow paths leading N, which soon join with the bridleway leading N along the ridge top of Luccombe Down. After 1.5km, you reach a stile in the hedgerow to your right, leading to the trig point on top of Shanklin Down. Cross the stile to the trig point. ❶ Descend Shanklin Down by the footpath leading NE. After 500m you reach a T junction with a footpath leading E-W, turn right (downhill) and follow this for 900m to pass a church and reach the A3055 road. Cross the road and follow it to the right for 30m to join a footpath lane leading off left. ❷ Follow the footpath lane 400m downhill (it merges with a residential lane, Vaughan Way) to reach a T junction with Priory Road. Turn right (E) and head 150m to the end of Priory Road, then turn right again onto Luccombe Road (signposted as the Isle of Wight Coastal Path). ❸ Ascend along Luccombe Road for 800m to where it ends and merges into a footpath track. Continue S following the IOWCP. After 600m and 700m footpaths lead left (steeply downhill) to the sea at Luccombe Chine (a worthwhile out-and-back excursion, but the paths have been closed due to landslips for years up to 2020). 1km after Luccombe Chine, a junction is reached, turn right (uphill) to follow the footpath

The Devil's Chimney

marked 'V65c Devil's Chimney'. ❹ Ascend steeply on the footpath, via stairs and then a narrow cleft in a cliff (the 'Devil's Chimney') At the top of the 'Chimney', turn right and follow the path along the clifftop for 200m to reach Bonchurch Landslip car park, beside the B3055 Bonchurch Road. Cross the road and take the footpath heading SW signposted 'V109 Bonchurch and Ventnor'. ❺ Follow this narrow footpath along the steep hillside above the town of Ventnor. After 1km it enters woodland and becomes narrow / precarious, then after 1.8km it emerges on a road (B3327 Mitchell Avenue). Turn right (W) and follow the pavement for 400m to the entrance to Ventnor Industrial Estate. Cross the entrance and take the footpath leading up steps on the right. ❻ After ascending on the footpath for 100m you reach a junction of footpaths, take the right-hand footpath and follow this up the valley floor. After 600m you reach the end of the valley floor, turn left off the footpath and follow the zigzagging track which ascends steeply onto St Boniface Down. ❼ When you reach the mast tower at the top, bear right to pass through the gate onto the footpath leading ENE along the fence. After 800m you reach the end of the fence, and the car park is a short distance uphill to your left (N).

Devil's Chimney
Photo: Chris Eden

Trip planning
Parking is simple and free at the National Trust car park where you start. If you wanted to start your run with the ascent of St Boniface Down, park roadside along Mitchell Avenue PO38 1DS / **SZ 562 778** and pick up the route at ❻, just past Ventnor Industrial Estate.
Ventnor is your best bet for RnR afterwards; see Route 4.

Other routes
The IOWCP to the north or south of this section isn't much recommended, as it plods along an interminable concrete esplanade through Shanklin and Ventnor.

Shanklin

Above Ventnor

Woods above Ventnor

5 The Devil's Chimney

The Landslip

Events

The Isle of Wight Fell Running Championship Series is held on St Boniface Down; see Route 4.

The Isle of Wight Coastal Path

Most of these routes utilise sections of the Isle of Wight Coastal Path. This offers a 113km / 70-mile yomp around the Island, with around 2,100 metres of ascent. The only chink in its course is the short passenger ferry between West and East Cowes, where most folk start and finish. The IOWCP offers a splendid challenge for trail runners, with the option of tackling the whole thing in a multi-day fastpacking challenge or just cherry-picking sections using Wight's excellent public transport links. It must be noted that much of the route treads tarmac; the initial section from East Cowes diverts far inland on roads around the Osbourne House Estate (Queen Victoria died twelve decades ago, and we're still not allowed to run across her lawn?) and the seaside resorts of Ryde, Sandown and Shanklin are fronted by shin-destroying concrete promenades. Although there are great stretches of trail between these towns, the best part of the IOWCP is the western and southern two-thirds between Shanklin and West Cowes.

Want to run the IOWCP in an organised event? The Isle of Wight Challenge offers options from 25km to 106km, with the longer distance available in two stages, if wanted. The LDWA also hold a Challenge Event, the (self-explanatory) 24 Hour Round the Island. XNRG no longer organise their 113km Round the Island Ultra; nevertheless, the author feels compelled to mention it as his name once briefly appeared on the leader board, mid-event … until they recounted the timings and realised their mistake!

6 Bembridge Down

Bembridge Windmill

Distance	8.5km (5.5 miles)	**Ascent**	200m (650ft)
Map	OS Landranger 196 OS Explorer OL29		
Navigation	●●○ Excellent signposting, not too many junctions to negotiate		
Terrain	●●○ Grass, stones, mud, tarmac, a bit of everything really.		
Wet feet	●●○ Prone to dampness, on account of passing through a marsh		
Start / Finish	Car park beside Culver Haven Inn, Culver Down Road PO36 8QT / SZ 634 856		

Mild trails around Wight's easternmost hill

Looking for a manageable outing with plenty of variation, interesting things to see and wonderful views (and a café and pub at the finish line)? This is that run, a lovely jaunt around a corner of Wight which is less frequented than it should be.

The band of chalk that runs right across the centre of the island from the Needles rocks meets the sea again when Bembridge Down terminates abruptly at Culver Cliff. Culver Cliff isn't quite the easternmost tip of the Isle of Wight, but its strategic significance (overlooking the approaches to Portsmouth and the Solent) has long been recognised and it is adorned with Victorian and Second World War fortifications. The Yarborough Monument is also here (these tall obelisks are almost a legal requirement for Isle of Wight hills), commemorating a founder of the Royal Yacht Squadron at Cowes.

6 Bembridge Down

Bembridge Down overlooks the marshland of the River Yar Estuary, and a run past this wetland (part of the RSPB Brading Marshes reserve) is a sharp contrast to the chalk upland. Look out for egrets, lapwing and Cetti's warbler. After ascending to the Isle of Wight's oldest windmill, you return along the coast path, backed by a glorious panorama of the beach and reefs extending seawards from the eastern tip of the island. If you are an early bird, this is a fantastic place and way to experience sunrise!

Route description

START From the car park, head past the Culver Haven Inn to where the Isle of Wight Coastal Path crosses the lane. Turn left (SW) onto this footpath, and descend along it. After 1km you reach a pair of metal gate posts, turn right (NW) and head 50m to the field boundary. ❶ Turn right again and follow the footpath leading uphill along the field boundary. After 140m, the footpath crosses into another field and crosses this field diagonally (NW) to the far corner. Follow the footpath downhill along the rim of a dry valley to reach a road (B3395 Sandown Road). ❷ Turn right onto the road and follow it for 40m to a

Bembridge Down

footpath on the opposite side, signposted 'BB31'. Follow this permissive footpath along a field for 700m to its end. ❸ When you leave the field, turn right onto a footpath and follow this E through a marsh. After 250m a junction of footpaths is reached, bear left following the sign marked 'BB20 Bembridge'. This footpath crosses several open fields before passing through marshland (Brading Marshes RSPB) and then ascending a hill to a prominent windmill. ❹ The footpath reaches a T junction with a bridleway, beside the windmill; turn right (downhill) onto this. After 300m and as the bridleway starts to ascend, take the footpath leading off on the left. After 100m on the footpath, cross the B3395 Sandown Road and continue for 330m on the footpath to reach a lane (Hillway Road). ❺ Turn left and follow the lane uphill for 90m to where a footpath turns off on the right. Take this and follow it for 400m to reach the IOWCP. ❻ Turn right onto the IOWCP and follow this footpath around Whitecliff Bay, passing a holiday park, and then uphill onto Culver Down. After you reach the Yarborough Monument at the top, cross the fence and turn left to return to the car park.

Ascending Culver Down

Sandown Bay

Brading Marsh

Trip planning

The car park is free, located just past the Culver Haven Inn near the end of Culver Down Inn. If there is no space here, there are five other parking areas dotted along the hilltop road.

The Culver Down Inn welcomes muddy trail shoes, and just across the road you have the option of faster food at the (open air) Culver Café.

Bembridge Fort is easy to miss when you drive past, dug low-lying into the ridgetop of Bembridge Down. This hexagonal Victorian fort is being restored and is only open for guided tours, arranged beforehand via the National Trust website. The Yarborough Monument was moved 1km along the hill to build the fort! The National Trust also own Bembridge Windmill (passed on the route), which can be visited.

Other routes

This decent extension doubles the length of the loop and allows you to enjoy the grassy dunelands of the Duver, the wonderful old houseboats lining Bembridge Harbour and Foreland, the easternmost point of Wight; At ❸, ignore the right turn and continue N on footpaths, via a short section heading E on the B3395 Carpenters Road, until you reach an E–W byway (Attrill's Lane). Turn right (E) onto this and follow it to the IOWCP. Turn right onto the IOWCP and follow to the finish.

6 Bembridge Down

Events

The Bembridge 5 and the Soup Run are events organised by Bembridge Youth and Community Centres, respectively covering 5 and 6 trail and road miles on similar ground to this route.

The Duver Dash is part of the annual Isle of Wight Festival of Running and involves a 5km ... well, 'dash' around the dunes and beach.

The geology of South East England

The great and varied trail running to be found across South East England is directly related to the underlying geology. A glance at the geological map used here* shows this pretty clearly.

The bands of chalk which fan across the map form the classic landscape of the region, chalk downlands (and gleaming white cliffs!). Chalk is comparatively resistant, hence the prominent hills of the Isle of Wight's central ridge, the Hampshire and Berkshire Downs, the Chiltern Hills and the North and South Downs. These distinctive long ridges are all outcrops of the same sheet of chalk, known by geologists as 'The Chalk'. It formed on a warm shallow ocean floor during the Late Cretaceous epoch (100–66 million years ago). The Chalk sinks from view between the Chilterns and North Downs (known as a syncline) and resurfaces to form a dome joining the North and South Downs (known as an anticline, specifically the Wealden Anticline) ... except, of course, that the dome of chalk isn't there. It has eroded away completely, with the only trace being the North and South Downs' steep scarps facing one another across the Weald. The Weald is the area between the North and South Downs, extending from Hampshire to Kent. As the numbers on the map indicate, the surface consists of three bands which get successively more ancient as you head towards the centre, spanning the Early Cretaceous epoch (145–100 mya). The outside rim of the Weald is a layer of Upper Greensand, a form of sandstone containing the greenish mineral glauconite. This forms the Greensand Ridge which (in Surrey) underlies some of the highest hills in the South East. The next Weald layer heading inwards is clay, this soft material forming the more gently rolling hills of the Low Weald. The centre of the Weald's eroded dome is hard sandstone ('Hastings Sand' on the map), which gives us the notably ridged hills of the High Weald.

Essex and the New Forest both have similar and relatively 'young' geology, formed from clay, silt, sand and gravel deposited on a seabed during the Paleogene period (66–23 mya). This material is fairly easily eroded as the sediment has not been fully cemented into rock, meaning that the hills of these areas are low with mild gradients.

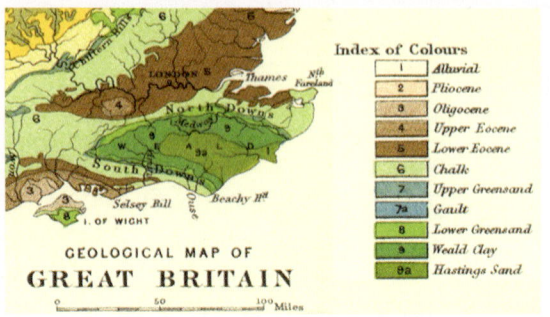

South East geology – Wikimedia Commons

*The map is Victorian, but geology doesn't change very quickly.

Hampshire

Hampshire's geology offers a choice of enticing trail running landscapes; the low-lying Hampshire Basin to the south, where the underlying clay gives rise to the heath and woodland of the New Forest, or the rolling chalk hills which swathe the rest of the county. The largest county in South East England, Hampshire contains two national parks and an Area of Outstanding Natural Beauty. The New Forest National Park includes ancient forest and heath but also incorporates the shingle and marsh of the Solent coast, the South Downs National Park spreads eastwards from Winchester, and the less-visited North Wessex Downs AONB hides trail running gems like the Highclere Estate. The Clarendon Way across the Test Valley is included as a reminder that Hampshire's beauty is not confined to these more protected areas.

Kingston Great Common (Route 9)

Keyhaven Marshes

Hurst Castle

Hurst Castle and Lighthouse

7 Hurst Castle

Distance		13km (8 miles)	Ascent	25m (80ft)
Map		OS Landranger 196 OS Explorer OL22		
Navigation	●●●	Few route options, mostly following the coast		
Terrain	●●●	Completely flat firm trails, gruelling section along loose pebbles at the end		
Wet feet	●●●	Firm well-draining trails		
Start / Finish		Saltgrass Lane, Keyhaven SO41 0TQ / SZ 302 909		

Simple trails snaking through Solent saltmarsh and shingle spit

This outing explores a beautiful corner of the Solent. Despite flat and easy trails, interest is maintained by the flora and fauna of the nature reserves you pass through, by views of the sea and Isle of Wight, and by the sprawling bulk of Hurst Castle. You run right around the brackish lagoons and marshland which comprise the Lymington-Keyhaven Nature Reserve; outside the sea wall, the tidal mud flats and channels extending towards Hurst Castle are the Keyhaven and Pennington Marshes Reserve. All manner of avian life is encountered here (especially in winter) and you'll have to weave around the occasional 'twitcher' and associated tripod and spotting scope. On the author's most recent run, the lack of aforementioned equipment didn't prevent him from enjoying close encounters with lapwings, terns, egrets and a kestrel. The final part of this run is optional but recommended nonetheless! The curving shingle spit leading to Hurst Castle will test your calves, but the destination is worth the grind. The English Channel surges

7 Hurst Castle

and breaks as it squeezes through the narrow entrance to the Solent, watched over by the castle and lighthouse. You can of course then run the 3km back along the beach, but the ferry across the harbour back to Keyhaven is our recommended means of finishing … why not?

Route description

START Cross the Saltgrass Lane from the parking area and follow the footpath NE along the coast leading towards Keyhaven. Follow the footpath around the harbour in Keyhaven and across the bridge. ❶ When the lane continues ahead but the footpath turns right to follow the coast, continue ahead on the lane (signposted 'cycle path to Lymington'). The lane becomes a byway, continue ahead (ignoring any footpaths turning off) until the byway ends at a parking area and lane (Lower Pennington Lane). ❷ Continue ahead on the lane for 350m to a sharp left turn; go around this, then 70m after the turn, take the footpath leading off on the right. ❸ Follow the footpath for 275m until it joins a lane (Lower Woodside), continue ahead on the lane. After 400m a footpath turns off on the right, 50m after a left

Hurst Castle

Oxey Marsh

bend. Take this footpath. ❹ Follow the footpath 50m to a tidal creek, where the footpath splits. Take the right-hand footpath, following the S shore of the creek. Continue following this footpath along the shore for 5km back to Keyhaven. Continue past Keyhaven retracing your former route to the start point. ❺ Cross Saltgrass Lane to the footpath on the raised bank behind and follow it to the footbridge beside where the lane bends right. Cross the footbridge and ascend onto the shingle bank (Hurst Beach). Turn left (SE) and follow the bank to the castle and lighthouse. ❻ If you run right around the castle, be careful on the seaward edge when the tide is high. You now have the choice of taking the ferry back into Keyhaven (13km route) or retracing your steps along Hurst Beach (16km route).

Trip planning

The suggested parking spot is on Saltgrass Lane, about 1km west of Keyhaven. There is plenty of space to park along the road by the waterside (note that this can flood during exceptionally big tides) or just around the corner past the footbridge. There is also a pay car park in Keyhaven itself on Keyhaven Road SO41 0TP / SZ 306 914.

The ferry slipway

At the end of this route, the ferry (runs late March to October) will take you back to Keyhaven for a few pounds. Obviously, this is an unnecessary and effete luxury (saving you a 3km run on shingle), but it is a great way to round off your exploration of the Keyhaven marshes. The castle is well worth a visit before you hop on the ferry, and (should you need any further encouragement to do some history) has a small café inside.

7 Hurst Castle

Hurst Castle

The Gun Inn in Keyhaven is beside the car park and can feed and water you, under new management after being infamous for its misanthropic landlord. For all other needs, it's only a short drive to Milford on Sea.

Other routes
There are simple ways to shorten this run; taking the footpath on the right at ❷ will lop about 3km off, while finishing at ❺ will avoid the 3km shingle slog.
East of this route is a tarmac section along the Solent Way (see page 58) before reaching Route 8.

Hurst Castle
A visit to Hurst Castle at the end of your run is recommended; English Heritage charge admission. Henry VIII built the original fort, to keep the French out (naturally). In the following century, King Charles I was imprisoned here, en route to the Isle of Wight. The castle was hugely expanded through the eighteenth and nineteenth centuries, as the French again became our enemy of choice. The expanded castle is an example of a 'Palmerstonian folly', named after the then-Prime Minister; a perceived threat of French invasion in the 1860s (which never came remotely close to happening) lead to a massively expensive fortress-building programme around Britain. Over a dozen fortifications were built around the Solent alone; including the Needles Battery (Route 1) and Bembridge Fort (Route 6). During the World Wars, the castle was again used to defend the Solent.

Beaulieu Heath

Beaulieu Heath

8 Beaulieu Heath

Distance		16km (10 miles)	**Ascent**	125m (400ft)
Map		OS Landranger 195 OS Explorer OL22		
Navigation	●●●	Partly across open heathland requiring a compass, waymarked Solent Way towards end		
Terrain	●●○	Rooty forest trails, rough heathland		
Wet feet	●●●	Some very boggy stretches, outside summer		
Start		Brockenhurst Railway Station SO42 7PU / SU 302 021		
Finish		Lymington Pier Railway Station SO41 5SB / SZ 333 954		

Forest to Solent

Leading from the heart of the New Forest at Brockenhurst to the sea at Lymington, this is a great route; beautiful, varied and constantly engaging. It did however take the author two separate attempts to complete it; the first was curtailed by a painful night-time root / ankle interaction. The start leads through woodlands, emerging from the trees onto the eerie open vistas of Beaulieu Heath. After picking a course across the Heath, the Solent Way is joined, making for easy route-finding through farmland to the ferry terminal. It is a simple and fast shuttle back to the start, courtesy of the railway.

Beaulieu Heath has seen four millennia of human activity, evidenced by clues in the landscape such as burial mounds. From 1942 to 1959 it was used as an RAF airfield; the runways are still clearly discernible

8 Beaulieu Heath

in the bracken to the north of this route. Today Beaulieu Heath is the preserve of lizards, butterflies and well-camouflaged ground-nesting birds. The presence of moisture-loving plants such as sundews and bog myrtle should tell you something about the ground underfoot …

Route description

START Turn right (S) out of the railway station onto the A337 and cross the level crossing. After 50m turn left onto Mill Lane (B3055) and follow this for 225m until you reach a track on the right leading S between signs for Mulberry and Reynolds Cottages. Turn right and follow the track until it reaches a lane (Church Lane). Turn left onto the lane and follow it 230m to a bridleway signposted on the left, opposite a house drive. ❶ Turn left onto the bridleway and follow it SSE through Roydon Woods Nature Reserve. After 1.2km ignore a bridleway turning off to the right, and after 1.7km take the bridleway turning off left (E).

Beaulieu Heath

2 Cross a stream (Lymington River) by a footbridge and after another 300m, bear right at a junction of bridleways. After 1km you pass the entrance to Dilton Gardens (a house) and reach a T junction. Turn right (S) and then immediately left (E) onto a bridleway track passing through Little Dilton Farm. Follow the bridleway for 500m to its end at a gate opening onto Beaulieu Heath. **3** Pass through the gate and go onto the open heathland. Take the faint path leading SE, after 100m it joins a N-S track. Turn R (S) and follow this track for 300m until you spot a small path on the left leading SE across the heathland. **4** Follow this path roughly SE, after 1.1km you reach a left turn to cross a small stream (Crockford Stream). Cross the stream and then follow rough paths paralleling the stream for 500m SE until you reach the B3054 road at Crockford Bridge. **5** Cross the road and follow rough paths (track on OS map does not exist!) paralleling Crockford Stream (E) through woodland and gorse. After 700m a crossroads is reached, turn right (S) and descend to cross Crockford Stream. Ascend to the edge of Norley Inclosure. **6** Turn left onto the rough path leading ESE (downhill). Follow it to cross Crockford Stream again and continue 500m (crossing a second small stream) to reach woodland on Broom Hill. Pass through the woodland until you reach a path leading S. **7** Follow paths roughly S for 1km until you reach the heathland's southern tip, the junction of Norleywood Road and Lymington Road at the village of East End. **8** Follow Lymington Road (signposted 'Lymington 4') for 160m to a footpath sign on the left, just after crossing a bridge. Take the footpath and follow it for 800m through woods to a crossroads where a field opens out on the left. **9** Turn right (W) at the crossroads onto the Solent Way footpath (marked with a tern symbol on signs). Follow the Solent Way for 4km along a series of footpaths and lanes. When you reach a T junction with Monument Lane, turn left off the Solent Way and descend 200m steeply to a car park. Lymington Pier Railway Station is just across the car park.

Crockford

Fishing pool

Entering Sowley Copse

Lymington

Sowley Copse

Beaulieu Heath

Trip planning

Running on Beaulieu Heath is inadvisable from March to July, due to ground-nesting birds on the heathland; see page 66.

There is pay parking beside Brockenhurst Railway Station. It is also possible to park roadside for free, if you venture into the village's quiet side streets. To return to the start, you could leave a car at the large car park beside Lymington Railway Station but it's hard to see why you wouldn't make use of the train; they run every half hour or so and the journey only takes 15 minutes.

It is only a short walk into the centre of Brockenhurst from the railway station, to find shops and services. As the author has eaten at the Buttery Tearoom on every single one of the many times that he has visited Brockenhurst, he is unfortunately unable to inform you about any of the other options.

Other routes

There are worse ways to spend a morning than just freely exploring the expanses of Beaulieu Heath, perhaps starting from the car park on Hatchet Lane SO42 7WE / **SU 369 016** at lovely Hatchet Pond in the north-east corner.

When the birds are nesting (see above), it is possible (although uninspiring) to bypass Beaulieu Heath by road: continue ahead from ❷, do not turn off left. You reach a lane, follow this S to the village of Boldre. Turn left and follow this lane along its winding course to the village of East End at ❽. A map will certainly help.

Thinking bigger ... the Isle of Wight is just a short ferry trip away (you literally end your run at the terminal) and you could consider joining this with Route 1 for a fantastic New Forest / Isle of Wight combo weekend.

Events

Oakhaven Hospice have run a half marathon and a 10-mile race (the Oakhaven Ten) on and around Beaulieu Heath.

New Forest Runners organise the long-running New Forest Ten, ten miles on and off road from Brockenhurst. Beyond Events organise the New Forest Trail, which has 10km, 16km and half marathon options. The New Forest Marathon (which includes 5km, 10km, half and full marathon routes) is a major event starting and finishing at Brockenhurst. In 2020, Covid-19 caused the event to be moved to Wimborne in Dorset (i.e. outside the New Forest) but it is expected to return to its original location.

The Solent Way

The Solent Way leads around the northern shores of the Solent (not always on the coast) for 96km / 60 miles between Milford on Sea and Emsworth in Chichester Harbour. Parts of Routes 7 and 8 are along the SW, and it ends near the start of Route 58. The route involves a fair amount of tarmac and passes through large urban areas such as Southampton and Portsmouth, but also includes pleasant footpaths paralleling the Beaulieu River Estuary between Buckler's Hard and Beaulieu as well as some fine trails along lonely sea walls. A few ferry journeys are required to join up the whole thing. Guides can be downloaded from the Hampshire County Council website. The SW is marked on OS maps and signposted by an arrow with an image of a tern imposed on it.

The disused railway

9 Burley

Distance	14km (9 miles)	Ascent	175m (575ft)
Map	OS Landranger 195 OS Explorer OL22		
Navigation ●●●	Map and compass strongly recommended, numerous trails and zero waymarking		
Terrain ●●●	Forest trails, sandy heathland paths, some tarmac		
Wet feet ●●●	Some sections become particularly squelchy in the wet		
Start / Finish	Woods Corner car park BH24 4HW / SU 219 041		

New Forest trail running 101

This lovely route is the perfect introduction to the New Forest, giving a sampling of classic New Forest landscapes and scenery, while never straying too far from the picture-postcard village of Burley. The first part passes through a succession of both enclosure and natural woodlands, where the many diverging paths will make you glad you installed that compass app on your phone. The second part is all about the New Forest's heathlands; after ascending Vereley Hill, you pick a route south along low hills, eroded sandy gullies and the occasional bog. Downhill on your right is Kingston Great Common National Nature Reserve (effectively a large swamp), uphill on the left are Castle Hill Iron Age hillfort and Burley Beacon, home of the Bisterne Dragon (don't worry, it was apparently slain by a valiant knight). The final part follows 'Castleman's Corkscrew', a now disused railway line so-named because of its winding route. A short steep climb and you are back in Burley. With its half-timbered buildings, thatched cottages and freely wandering

9 Burley

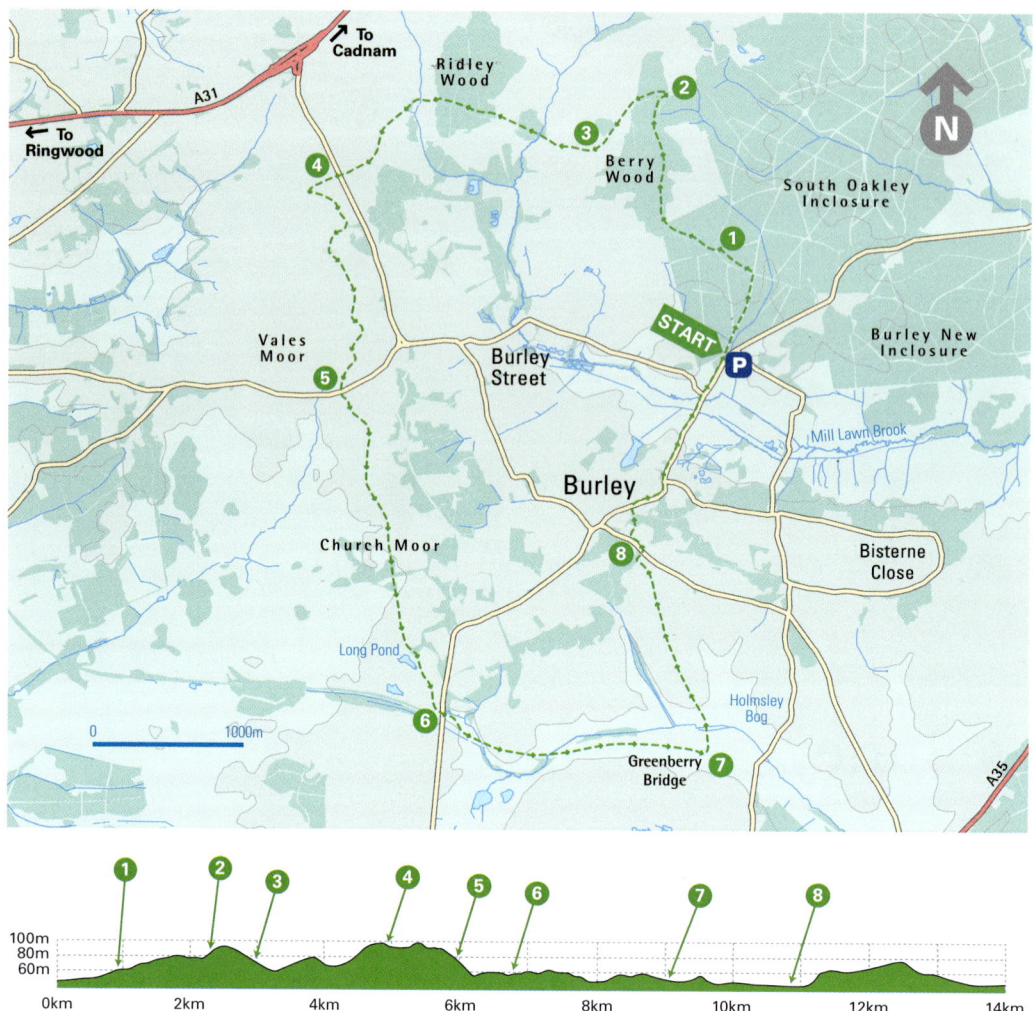

ponies, Burley is the dictionary definition of twee ... yet, the witchcraft shops indicate that the village is more edgy than first impressions suggest! This is the legacy of 'White Witch' Sybil Leek who lived here in the 1950s, walking the streets with a jackdaw on her shoulder.

Route description

START Pass through the gate at the back of the car park into the woods and follow the track heading NNE (signposted as a cycle trail). After 580m, a crossroads is reached; turn left and follow this track for 250m before taking the second track on the left. ❶ 60m along this track, a path leads off through a gate on the right. Turn right and follow this path through the woods heading roughly NW. After 400m the path divides into multiple indistinct paths; bear right to keep on the path which leads N through Berry Wood. The path becomes a track and about 1.2km from the gate you emerge from the woods at an open heath (Berry Beeches). ❷ Take the path leading back into woods, bearing off immediately on the left. Follow this uphill (WSW) for 250m until you emerge from woods onto high ground and open heath. Follow the tracks

Burley

which lead SW towards the buildings (Turf Croft) you can see 800m away, but after 500m take a right turn leading downhill to cross a stream via a footbridge. ❸ Continue ahead (WNW) along this path through two successive woods (Ridley Green and Ridley Wood) before descending to cross another stream (Mill Lawn Brook). Follow the path uphill (SW) to cross a lane at the top of the hill (Vereley Hill). ❹ Continue ahead for 240m until you find a path on the left leading back SE towards Vereley Hill car park. Just before, and at the car park, various paths lead roughly S along the hill top; choose one and follow it. After 500m, the paths merge and descend to Broad Bottom. Continue ahead (S) and cross a lane after 700m. ❺ Continue following paths roughly S. After 2km you pass Long Pond on your right, after another 400m you reach a lane (Pound Lane) beside a bridge crossing a disused railway. ❻ Cross the lane to Burbush car park and descend from the car park onto the disused railway. Turn left (E) and follow the disused railway for 1.7km to a crossroads at Greenberry Bridge (the bridge is gone but brick walls remain). ❼ Climb out of the railway cutting by taking the left turning and follow tracks uphill (NNW) onto Turf Hill. After 1.4km, Burley car park is reached. ❽ Pass through Burley car park to Wilverley Road. Turn left onto this and follow it 125m to Burley Primary School. Take the track on the right just before the school, and follow it 200m to Church Lane. Turn left onto this and follow it 60m to Chapel Lane. Turn right (NE) onto Chapel Lane and follow it for 1.3km back to the start.

Trip planning

This route is inadvisable from March to July, due to ground-nesting birds on the heathland; see page 66. Woods Corner car park is free and usually fairly quiet. If you want to start somewhere more central to Burley, then Burley car park BH24 4BB / **SU 214 028** on Wilverley Road ❽ fits the bill and is also free, but is usually busy.

Ridley Green

Berry Wood

Vereley Hill

Long Pond

Burley

Within Burley, there are various pubs and cafés to choose from, once you've finished shopping for broomsticks and pointy hats at 'A Coven of Witches'. For splendid cream teas, head a little out of the village along Station Road to The Old Station Tea Rooms, which is exactly what the name suggests, on the disused railway.

Other routes

'Castleman's Corkscrew', the disused railway, is a useful all-weather alternative. From Burley it is 8km east to Brockenhurst (Route 8) and 8km west to Ringwood.

If you continue directly ahead (NNE) on the very first track, you get swallowed by the vast area of inclosures (planted woodland) that covers the heart of the forest. Keeping track of where you are in this deep, dense forest is a challenge, expect to encounter ewoks, gingerbread houses and teddy bear's picnics.

With some precarious route-finding across the heathland and through Burley New Inclosure, it is possible to extend this route right around Burley. From Burley car park ❽ head east along Wilverley Road until a crossroads where you continue directly ahead along a track, and thereafter follow the trails you encounter, keeping the houses in sight on your left. Depending on how lost or bog-fast you get, this extends the route by at least 4km.

Events

Maverick Race's New Forest race is based from Burley and has route choices of 6km, 17km and 24km.

The LDWA's New Forest Challenge is an 18- or 26-mile loop around the forest. The author has completed it when it started and finished at Burley (including some really boggy sections!), it is currently run from Minstead, near Lyndhurst.

The New Forest

The New Forest, created by William the Conqueror in 1079 as a private hunting ground, is a distinctive and unique landscape in which to run. The New Forest SSSI covers nearly 300km^2, comprising of huge areas of deciduous woodland (146km^2) broken up by a patchwork of sandy heath, pasture and bog (151 km^2), sprawled across low-lying hills between quaint *olde worlde* villages. This is the largest area of unplanted flora in lowland Britain. Another 84km^2 of the New Forest is fenced tree plantations called inclosures or enclosures, dating from the Napoleonic era's shipbuilding needs. Around 2,000 wild deer live in the forest, alongside 5,000 New Forest ponies which are privately owned, despite wandering freely (even in village centres). 'Commoners' are families traditionally permitted to graze horses, cattle and pigs. Overseeing the administration of the forest is the archaic 'Court of Verderers'.

The New Forest National Park, created in 2005, encompasses a larger area than the SSSI at 566km^2, including the Solent coast. Routes 7, 8, 9 and 10 are within the National Park.

Coopers Hill and Hampton Ridge

Windmill Hill
Photo: Graham Bland

10 Coopers Hill and Hampton Ridge

Distance		13km (8 miles)	Ascent	225m (740ft)
Map		OS Landranger 184, 195 OS Explorer OL22		
Navigation	●●○	Clear paths and trails, but no signage		
Terrain	●●○	Some technical paths, mostly wide gravelled tracks		
Wet feet	●●●	Some streams to jump or ford, really muddy and boggy in winter		
Start / Finish		Godshill Cricket car park SP6 2LN / SU 181 150		

The New Forest's quiet northern reach

This is an exploration of the New Forest's hilly north, including its remotest part (i.e. furthest from any road). The route was born out of the author's experience running the Heartbreaker Marathon years ago. The marathon repeatedly criss-crosses the main track through this area and I wanted to delve deeper into this less-visited corner of the national park. Be careful what you wish for! Although much of the route is on firm tracks, included here (quite deliberately) are stream crossings, muddy firebreaks and sticky mires. You will mutter rude words at various points, but focus on the challenge and enjoy the solitude; for much of the time, it'll be just you and the ponies. A more tangible reward is the final stride along Hampton Ridge, which is fairly elevated by New Forest standards and is perhaps its best viewpoint.

Wild and undeveloped as this area seems, it was used as a bombing range during the Second World War. The obvious trace is the bomb shelter passed (note the 'V' for Victory in the brickwork), but the keen-eyed

10 Coopers Hill and Hampton Ridge

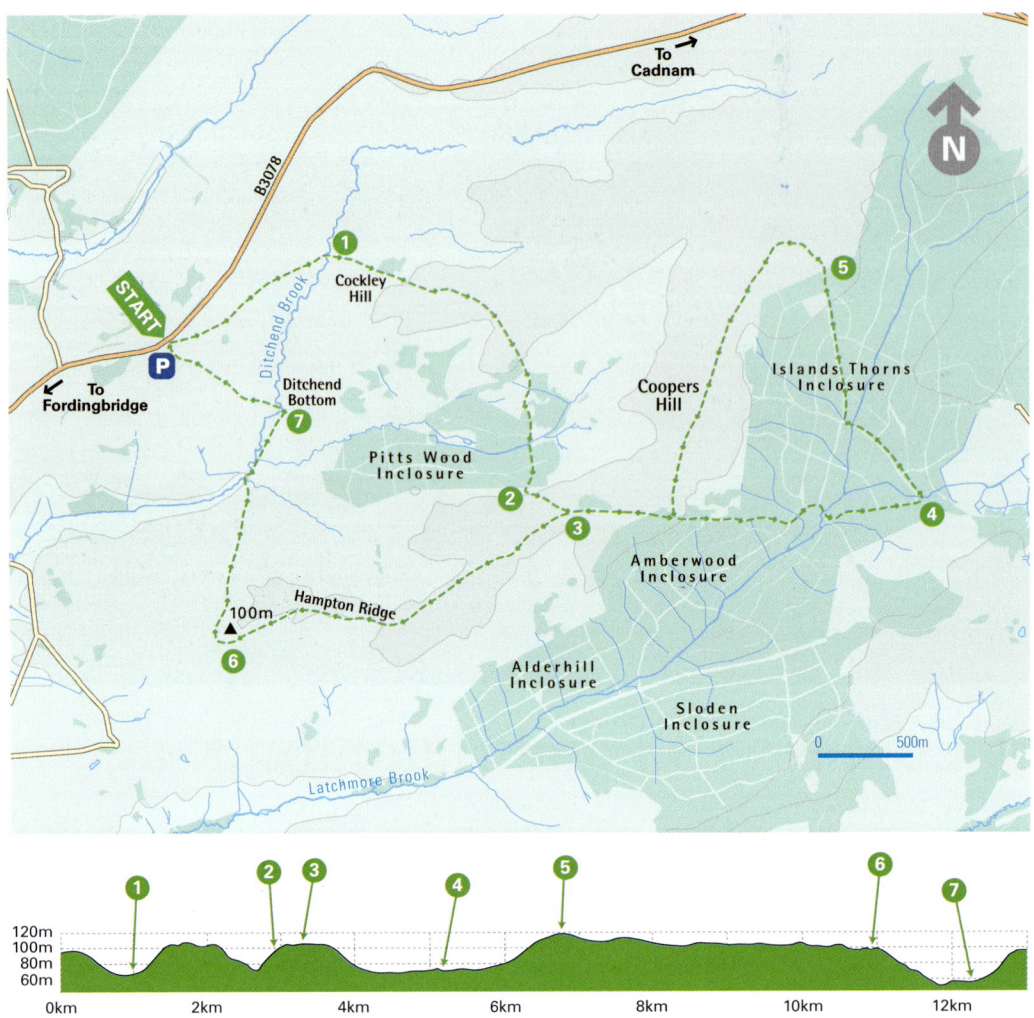

will also spot craters and the huge concrete arrow (formerly an illuminated target marker) hidden in the heather on Hampton Ridge.

Wear your waterproof trail shoes.

Route description

START Take the path leading ENE from the cricket field (furthest left path, looking away from the road). Follow this downhill for 750m until it reaches a gravelled track. ❶ Turn right onto the track and follow it for 2km up Cockley Hill and then through woods (Pitts Wood Inclosure), ignoring any turn-offs. ❷ After you climb out of the woods and reach a crossroads, turn left (ESE) and follow this track 350m to where it merges with a wide gravelled track (with cycle route signs). ❸ Follow this track E into woods (Amberwood Inclosure), ignoring all turn-offs. 1.4km after the junction you cross a stream (Latchmoor Brook) by a bridge and then the track bends sharp left; continue on the track past the first track leading into the woods on the left (beside a cycle path marker) and then take the second track on the left, 500m

Coopers Hill and Hampton Ridge

after the bridge. ❹ Jump or ford the stream to reach the track and then follow the track for 600m NW to Latchmoor Brook; cross this. Directly after Latchmoor Brook is a crossroads, turn right and follow this firebreak uphill (N), ignoring any side turns, until you reach the edge of the woods. ❺ Continue ahead on the track for 300m (crossing several small paths) until you reach a T junction with the cycleway track. Turn left (SSW) and follow the track for 1.5km until you reach the edge of woods (Amberwood Inclosure), just after a small brick building (WWII bombing range shelter). The track bends right, follow it for 2.6km (retracing your earlier steps for the first 500m) along the ridge top (Hampton Ridge) until you see a trig point on the right. ❻ Directly after the trig point, turn off the track sharp right (N) onto the path leading downhill. Follow this N until you reach valley floor, then follow the stream (Ditchend Brook) upstream for 400m along the grassy bank until you reach a path crossing the river. ❼ Turn left (WNW) onto the path; jump or ford the river and follow the path uphill to the car park.

Amberwood Inclosure

Ditchend Brook

Hampton Ridge

Trip planning

From March to July, the off-piste parts of this route are inadvisable due to nesting birds; see 'Access in the New Forest' below.

Godshill Cricket car park is on the B3078 Roger Penny Way, just over 3km east of Fordingbridge. Like the numerous roadside car parks in the area (some listed below in 'Other routes') it is free and has plenty of space. Don't leave food unattended or the ponies will have it (actual author experience), not good for them or your lunch plans.

Godshill Ridge

The Fighting Cocks Pub is a few hundred metres from the start, in the village of Godshill. On the menu is local venison, if you like the idea of sampling the wildlife you encountered while running. Otherwise, the town of Fordingbridge has all shops and services.

Make sure that you close gates when entering or leaving inclosures (planted woodland), these are to keep animals such as ponies out.

Coopers Hill and Hampton Ridge

Other routes

This route can be easily shortened to 7km by turning sharp right (WSW) at ❸ and skipping straight to Hampton Ridge.

Between March and July, you can still run the main gravel tracks; start from Ashley Walk car park SP6 2LH / **SU 185 155**, located 800m further along Roger Penny Way from Godshill Cricket car park. The main track leading from the car park joins the route at ❶. At ❸ you reach an intersection of tracks where you have the choice of heading 3km SW to Frogham car park SP6 2JA / **SU 177 129** via Hampton Ridge, 4km NE to Telegraph Hill car park SP5 2PX / **SU 228 166** or 3km E via Amberwood Inclosure to Fritham car park SO43 7HL / **SU 231 141**. It's all good!

Windmill Hill
Photo: Graham Bland

Cockley Hill

Events

As noted above, the Heartbreaker Marathon's route crosses this area repeatedly, following the central gravel track. The marathon and accompanying half marathon start nearby at Sandy Balls: no sniggering please, nor should you snigger at the fact that the route described here passes through Burnt Balls. Totton Running Club's New Forest Stinger is a 5- or 10-mile race starting from Fritham (just east of this route).

Access to the New Forest

The New Forest National Park has 325km of footpaths, bridleways and byways; a small amount given its size. The good news is that there is actually open access to roughly half of the National Park, around 30,000 hectares. This is Crown Land, administered by Forestry England. New Forest Crown Lands are marked as Access Land on OS Maps (see page 21) although the public access rights date from 1925 and were unchanged by the 2000 CRoW Act. Wild camping is not permitted on the Crown Lands.

From the start of March to the end of July, the public (i.e. you) are requested to avoid rough trails on the New Forest's open heathlands and to keep to the main gravel paths. This is to protect ground-nesting birds (curlew, lapwing, redshank and snipe) in breeding season. This means that routes 8, 9 and 10 are all inadvisable at this time of year. See the respective routes for alternative suggestions.

Queen Elizabeth Country Park

Queen Elizabeth Forest

11 Queen Elizabeth Country Park

Distance		14km (9 miles)	Ascent	425m (1410ft)
Map		OS Landranger 197 OS Explorer OL8		
Navigation	●●●	Mostly waymarked trails		
Terrain	●●●	Easy wide tracks, some technical paths, brutal ascent of Butser Hill		
Wet feet	●●●	Easy to dodge the mud, some slippery chalk in the wet		
Start / Finish		Queen Elizabeth Country Park Visitor Centre PO8 0QE / SU 718 185		

Easy forest trails and an epic ascent

Queen Elizabeth Country Park is a great place to dip your toes into trail running, with waymarked routes exploring varied scenery and no shortage of space in which to escape the crowds (564 hectares of it). What that doesn't mean though, is that the going is easy! The park spans two steep hills on the South Downs ridge, with the A3 intruding rather rudely in between. What is presented here, are two of the park's sharply contrasting waymarked trails joined into one long outing; the less hardy can just choose one or the other. The first part covers the 8km Long Woodland Trail which loops for 8km around 244m War Down, exploring the heavily forested part of the park. After a long gradual ascent at the start, the going is more moderate and the trails vary from wide forestry tracks to narrow paths weaving through the undergrowth. Agoraphobes will prefer this to the second part ...

Queen Elizabeth Country Park

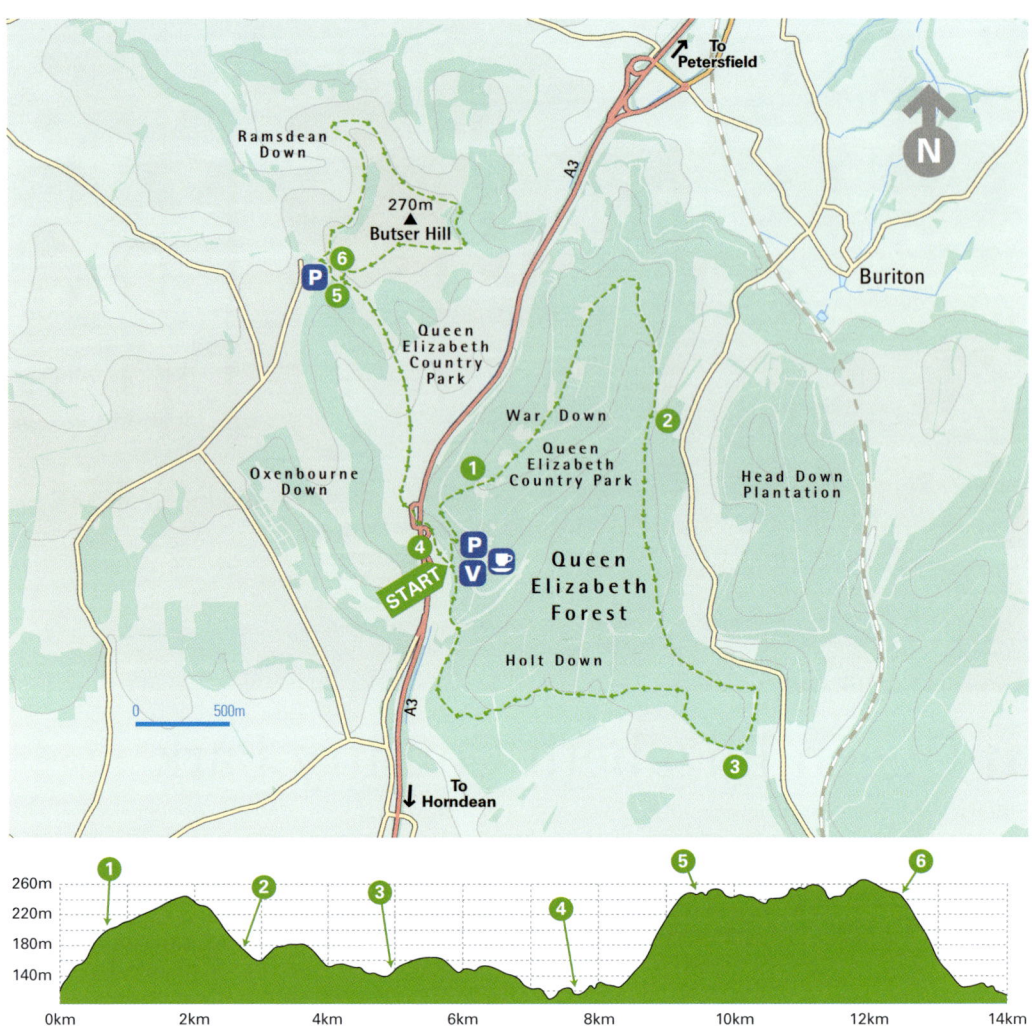

The second part crosses the A3 to ascend the open downland of 270m Butser Hill, the highest point on the entire South Downs ridge. It's a long and remorseless ascent that you'll probably never forget(!), but once up there, you'll be rewarded by stunning views to the Isle of Wight and beyond, as you traverse around Butser Hill National Nature Reserve following the 2.7km Downland Trail.

Route description

START To the left (E) of the visitor centre entrance are a wide set of steps. Ascend these and turn left to follow the Long Woodland Trail, marked by 'purple footprint' signs, which you will follow for the next 8km. The LWT zigzags uphill through the woods to reach a car park and play area after 650m. ❶ Pass through the car park and then follow the wide track gradually uphill leading NE. After 1.2km it passes through a clearing and picnic area, before bending around to the S and commencing an extended downhill stretch. ❷ After nearly 1km of descent, the South Downs Way crosses. Shortly after this, a footpath joins from the left, then the route ahead splits; follow the LWT signs to take the left turn-off and ignore the

Queen Elizabeth Country Park

Butser Hill ascent

bridleway to the right. After 1km the track reaches a crossroads and becomes a footpath, continue ahead. After another 650m a T junction is reached, turn right (S) to reach the forest boundary after 350m. ❸ Follow the LWT path along the edge of the forest for 350m until you see a path on the right leading back into the woods. Turn right (N) onto this path. After 140m a T junction is reached where you turn left (W), then continue ahead on a path following LWT signs, crossing several tracks, until after 1.6km you reach a T junction at the edge of the woods above the A3. Turn right and follow this track N back to the visitor centre. ❹ Pass the visitor centre and continue through the car park to its exit. Follow the South Downs Way bridleway beside the road. After passing under the A3, the SDW turns left to cross the road and then leads steeply up Butser Hill. Ascend and enjoy. ❺ When the SDW levels out at the top of Butser Hill, turn right (N) off the SDW onto a footpath and follow this 100m to the building with the conical roof. After passing this, join the Downland Trail by turning right. The DT is a path leading around the hillside, occasionally marked by posts with red stripes. Follow the obvious path and ignore any offshoots heading downhill. For the first 800m, the DT contours around Rake Bottom (steep-sided valley), then it bends sharply right to contour along the E side of the hill. After 1km the DT passes through a wood (Whiteland Copse) before emerging onto open downland; choose any of several paths leading back W towards the SDW. ❻ Turn left onto the SDW and descend Butser Hill back to pass under the A3 and reach the visitor centre.

Whiteland Copse

Queen Elizabeth Country Park

Trip planning

Queen Elizabeth Country Park is reached by following signs off the A3, coming south after Petersfield or north after Havant. Entrance to the park is free, however parking certainly isn't. The car park is open from 8am to 8pm daily. There is also a paying car park at the top of Butser Hill, at the end of Limekiln Lane GU32 1QN / SU 711 199. Yes, it is possible to bypass the epic climb and just run around the Downland Trail.

The visitor centre can sell you a map of the trails in the park, as well as a leaflet outlining the Forest Wayfaring Course for orienteering. There is also a canteen-style café, grandly called the Beechwood Kitchen.

Other routes

As noted above, it is simple to divide this into either an 8km trail run (the Long Woodland Trail), finishing at ❹, or a 6km trail run starting at ❹, ascending Butser Hill and following the Downland Trail. There is also the 3km Short Woodland Trail to consider. All are shown on the map which can be bought at the visitor centre. There is open access within the park, so don't feel constrained by these routes, explore away!

The South Downs Way passes through the park; Butser Hill is actually its highest point! From Butser Hill it is 4km west (partly on roads) to join up with Route 12 around Old Winchester Hill. The SDW to the east of the park forms a long and defined ridge and is described in Route 59. The Hangers Way (see page 86) which is also part of Route 59, terminates at the park.

Long Woodland Trail

Rake Bottom

Events

Queen Elizabeth parkrun is held every Saturday morning, following a route around the forest to the south of the visitor centre.

The Butser Hill Challenge, an event run by Run Events, has been going since 1978. It's a 5-mile Grade B fell race, involving a truly demented, three successive ascents of the hill. There are shorter races for youngsters on the same day.

Second Wind Running organise the Queen Elizabeth Spring Marathon & Half, with the route largely within the park. Maverick Race hold the Dark Series at the park, a night trail race with 5, 10 and 15km distances.

Old Winchester Hill

12 Old Winchester Hill

Distance		29km (18 miles)	Ascent	575m (1850ft)
Map		OS Landranger 185, 196 OS Explorer OL3		
Navigation	●●○	Following waymarked routes, but stay alert		
Terrain	●●○	Chalk, mud, grass, tarmac, several long ascents		
Wet feet	●●○	Chalky mud, dairy farms with associated stinky mud		
Start / Finish		Old Winchester Hill NNR car park GU32 1HN / SU 645 214		

Glorious solitude in a rural backwater

Despite having ridden the length of the South Downs Way many times, only recently did the author realise that (following the bridleway options) he'd been missing one of the National Trail's highlights! 130m Old Winchester Hill has commanding views, being the centrepiece of a glorious rolling landscape of downs, farm, and copse. Despite the name, the hill is a long way from Winchester, located above the valley of the River Meon, a bubbling chalk stream. The hilltop (which is both a National Nature Reserve and an SSSI) is ringed with the walls of an Iron Age hillfort, with the summit trig point obscured between two Bronze Age burial mounds.

Old Winchester Hill is a lovely spot, but you really have to earn it as it comes at the end of this long and demanding route. The route uses four long-distance trails to explore the Hampshire wilds; the South Downs Way, the Monarch's Way, the Wayfarer's Walk and the Meon Valley Trail. Expect a fair bit of mud (why can't those farmers keep their fields tidy?) and a fair few uphill bits, but one thing you won't see a whole lot of, is people.

12 Old Winchester Hill

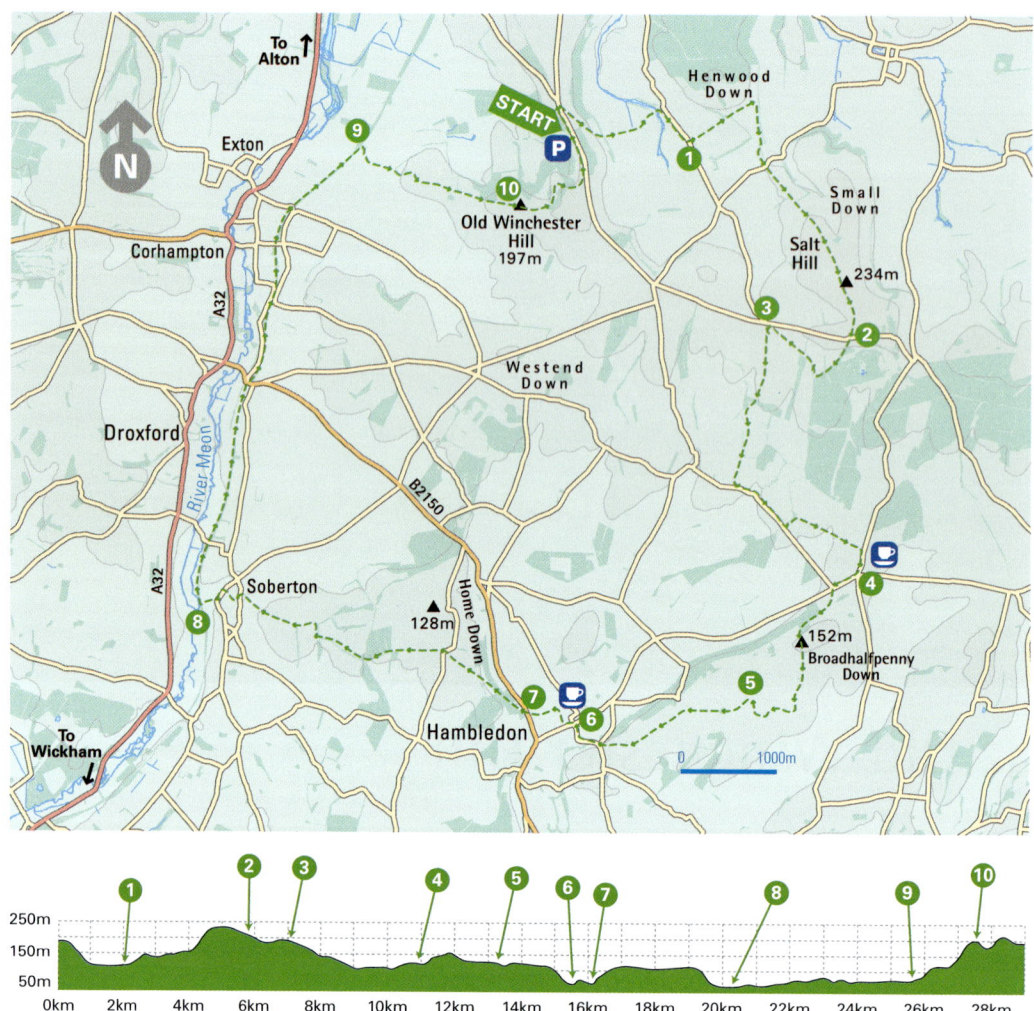

Route description

START From the car park, follow the South Downs Way along the lane for 200m N to a junction, where the SDW is signposted off on the right, through a gate. Turn right and follow the SDW bridleway steeply downhill and past Whitewool Farm to reach a lane after 1.3km. Turn right and follow the lane 480m to where the SDW bridleway is signposted off on the left. ❶ Turn left, follow the SDW bridleway uphill for 860m to a T junction with a byway track. Turn right (S) and follow the SDW byway for 3.4km; you cross a lane, then steeply ascend Wether Down, then descend to cross a second lane (Droxford Road). ❷ Cross the lane to continue ahead (SW) on the byway track (leaving the SDW). Follow the byway for 500m to where it ends at a lane. Turn right (N) onto the lane and follow it 280m. It turns into a rough track; when the track bends right, take the byway signposted off on the left. Follow the byway 480m to reach a lane (Droxford Road). ❸ Immediately on the left when you reach the lane is a bridleway signposted for the Monarch's Way (disks show a ship above an oak tree), take this and follow it S. You will follow the waymarked MW for the next 8.4km to the village of Hambledon. First you descend 1.9km on a bridleway and footpath to a lane,

Old Winchester Hill

you turn left (E) onto the lane and follow it 700m before turning off left to follow a footpath around three fields to another lane (Hyden Farm Lane), where you turn right to reach the Bat and Ball pub. ❹ From the Bat and Ball pub, turn right (SW) and follow the road (East Street) for 280m to where a footpath is signposted off on the left. Take this footpath and follow it uphill, through woods and over Broadhalfpenny Down. Follow the track (Dogkennel Lane) which leads S from the top of Broadhalfpenny Down. After 350m it bends right beside buildings, turn off left to follow the footpath track which continues S. After 500m, a track leads off on the right, just before the footpath track descends steeply. Turn right onto this track and follow it W, bearing right when it forks, to a pond just before Glidden Farm. ❺ Take the footpath track which turns off left (W) at the pond. Follow it ahead across fields, ignoring side-turns, to reach Stud Farm and then a lane (Speltham Hill). Turn right onto the lane and follow it steeply downhill into the village of Hambledon. ❻ In Hambledon, turn left (W) onto West Street and follow it 120m to where Vicarage Lane turns off right. Turn right and follow this lane 170m to a T junction with a footpath track. Turn left and follow the footpath track 320m

Salt Hill

Meon Valley Trail

Monarch's Way

and through houses to a road (B2150, Green Lane). Cross the road to take the footpath which is a short distance to the right. ❼ This footpath is the Wayfarer's Walk (disks show the letters 'WW'), which you will follow for 4.2km to reach the Meon Valley Trail. Follow the WW footpath steeply uphill through woods, across a lane (East Hoe Road), then W across and along a succession of fields before descending steeply to reach a second lane (Chalk Hill). Cross the lane and continue downhill, turning left onto a lane (West Street) which leads you downhill, bearing right at a junction, to reach a disused railway bridge leading to the River Meon. ❽ Ascend steps onto the disused railway, this is the Meon Valley Trail which you will follow N for 5.5km; after passing beneath two bridges, the MVT is diverted off the railway track and then back on again at Droxford, after this count three more bridges passing overhead; at the third bridge, the SDW joins the MVT. Continue another 1km to where the SDW leaves the MVT and crosses underneath it, heading E (right of the MVT). ❾ Descend from the MVT onto the SDW bridleway (the bridleway immediately takes a sharp turn right to the S) and follow it for 1.3km to a junction where the SDW footpath continues ahead (steeply uphill), while the SDW bridleway turns right (S). Follow the footpath steeply to the summit of Old Winchester Hill. ❿ Either continue ahead for 1.5km following the SDW back to the car park, or follow the narrow path which branches off left of the SDW and contours around the steep hillside at a lower level.

Old Winchester Hill

South Downs Way mud

Trip planning

Old Winchester Hill NNR car park is free, located by following Old Winchester Hill Lane uphill from West Meon. For food and drink, there are various options dotted around the villages. Given that most will approach the start through West Meon, it's worth mentioning The Beech Café, which is vegetarian and vegan. You pass more than one pub along the route, should you be in danger of dehydrating; most accessibly, The Bat and Ball at ④ and The Vine in Hambledon ⑥.

If for whatever reason you have to cut short your run before the end, it's worth noting that there isn't a whole lot of public transport hereabouts. Buses run along the Meon Valley, but you'd need a taxi to get back to the car park. If unsure whether you can complete this, check bus times and perhaps start from Droxford on the Meon Valley Way between ⑧ and ⑨.

Other routes

For a short run, you could do far worse than simply run across and around Old Winchester Hill from the car park. Having crossed the hill, the Monarch's Way branches off on the right, offering an alternative route back to the road; a 6km loop.

The long-distance trails which this route utilises can of course be explored further. The South Downs Way to the east joins Route 11 after 4km, much of which is on roads. To the west, the 20km of the SDW to Winchester is naturally worth exploring, but is one of the least geographically defined sections of the National Trail, i.e. it meanders a bit aimlessly! The Wayfarer's Walk is outlined in Route 16. The Meon Valley Trail is just 17.7km, following the disused railway from Wickham to West Meon; what you see in this route is what you get all along. The Monarch's Way is something else again; 1006km / 625 miles, passing through

Old Winchester Hill

nineteen counties ranging from the North Midlands through the South West and finally reaching the sea at Brighton. It follows the route used by Charles II in 1651 as he retreated from Parliament's forces; he must have been quite the trail runner.

Events

Rural Running Events organise the River Meon Marathon which combines the Meon Valley Trail with a circuit of Old Winchester Hill. They have also organised half marathon and shorter events hereabouts.

National Trails in the South East

- **England Coast Path** – under construction (see page 220)
- **North Downs Way** – Farnham to Dover, 246km / 153 miles (see page 232)
- **Thames Path** – Thameshead to Thames Barrier, 296km / 184 miles (see page 120)
- **Ridgeway** – Avebury to Ivinghoe Beacon, 140km / 87 miles (see page 115)
- **South Downs Way** – Winchester to Eastbourne, 160km / 100 miles (see page 294)

Other selected long-distance trails in the South East

- **Capital Ring** – Woolwich foot tunnel to Woolwich foot tunnel, 126km / 78-mile loop (see page 327)
- **Chiltern Way** – 215km / 134-mile loop, 138km of extensions (see page 156)
- **Clarendon Way** – Salisbury to Winchester, 42km / 26 miles (see Rt 13)
- **Downs Link** – St Martha's Hill to Shoreham-by-Sea, 59km / 37 miles (see page 306)
- **Essex Way** – Epping to Harwich, 132km / 82 miles (see page 208)
- **Green Chain Walk** – Thamesmead to Nunhead Cemetery, 64km / 40 miles (see page 327)
- **Greensand Way** – Haslemere to Hamstreet, 174km / 108 miles (see page 312)
- **Hangers Way** – Alton to Queen Elizabeth Country Park, 34km / 21 miles (see page 86)
- **Icknield Way Trail** – Thetford to Chinnor, 274km / 170 miles (see page 170)
- **Isle of Wight Coastal Path** – 113km / 70-mile loop (see page 44)
- **London Loop** – Erith to Coldharbour, 233km / 145 mile-loop (see page 327)
- **Saxon Shore Way** – Hastings to Gravesend, 262km / 163 miles (see page 254)
- **Serpent Trail** – Haslemere to Petersfield, 108km / 67 miles (see page 284)
- **Solent Way** – Milford on Sea to Emsworth, 97km / 60 miles (see page 58)
- **Stour Valley Path** – Newmarket to Cattawade, 97km / 60 miles (see page 208)
- **Sussex Border Path** – Emsworth to Rye, 222km / 138 miles (see page 288)
- **Test Way** – Inkpen Hill to Eling Quay, 71km / 44 miles (see page 96)
- **Three Castles Path** – Winchester to Windsor, 99km / 61 miles (see page 102)
- **Three Forests Way** – 94km / 58-mile loop (see page 192)
- **Vanguard Way** – Croydon to Newhaven, 106km / 66 miles (see page 258)
- **Wayfarers Walk** – Inkpen Hill to Emsworth, 141km / 88 miles (see page 96)
- **Wealdway** – Gravesend to Eastbourne, 134km / 83 miles (see page 258)

Further information and additional trails from www.ldwa.org.uk.

12 Old Winchester Hill

Broadhalfpenny Down

The Clarendon Way | 13

King's Somborne

13 The Clarendon Way

Distance		40km (25 miles)	Ascent	725m (2380ft)
Map		OS Landranger 184, 185 OS Explorer 130, 131, OL32		
Navigation	● ● ●	Mostly waymarked throughout		
Terrain	● ● ●	Mild gradients, tarmac, farmland, rutted byways, rooty paths		
Wet feet	● ● ●	Some byway sections become hellishly muddy in the wet		
Start		Salisbury Cathedral SP1 2EJ / SU 142 296		
Finish		Winchester Cathedral SO23 9LS / SU 481 293		

An epic cross-country cathedral-to-cathedral adventure

The Clarendon Way links Salisbury and Winchester Cathedrals* via the beautiful Test Valley and makes for an excellent off-road marathon challenge. If you are wondering whether you can tackle this adventure unsupported, you'll be reassured to know that public transport links make the shuttle back fairly easy, and also allow the possibility of bailing out about halfway. The CW explores an area outside of Hampshire and Wiltshire's national parks and AONBs, yet the scenery is somehow none the worse for it.
What will you see along the way? Endless long and often straight footpaths, bridleways and byways offer up fine views; of Salisbury Cathedral, the traces of Clarendon Palace (a former royal hunting lodge), rolling farmland, chalk streams and rivers, some steep downlands, a few forgotten villages and chalk meadows

*It also neatly links the guidebooks South West Trail Running and South East Trail Running!

13 The Clarendon Way

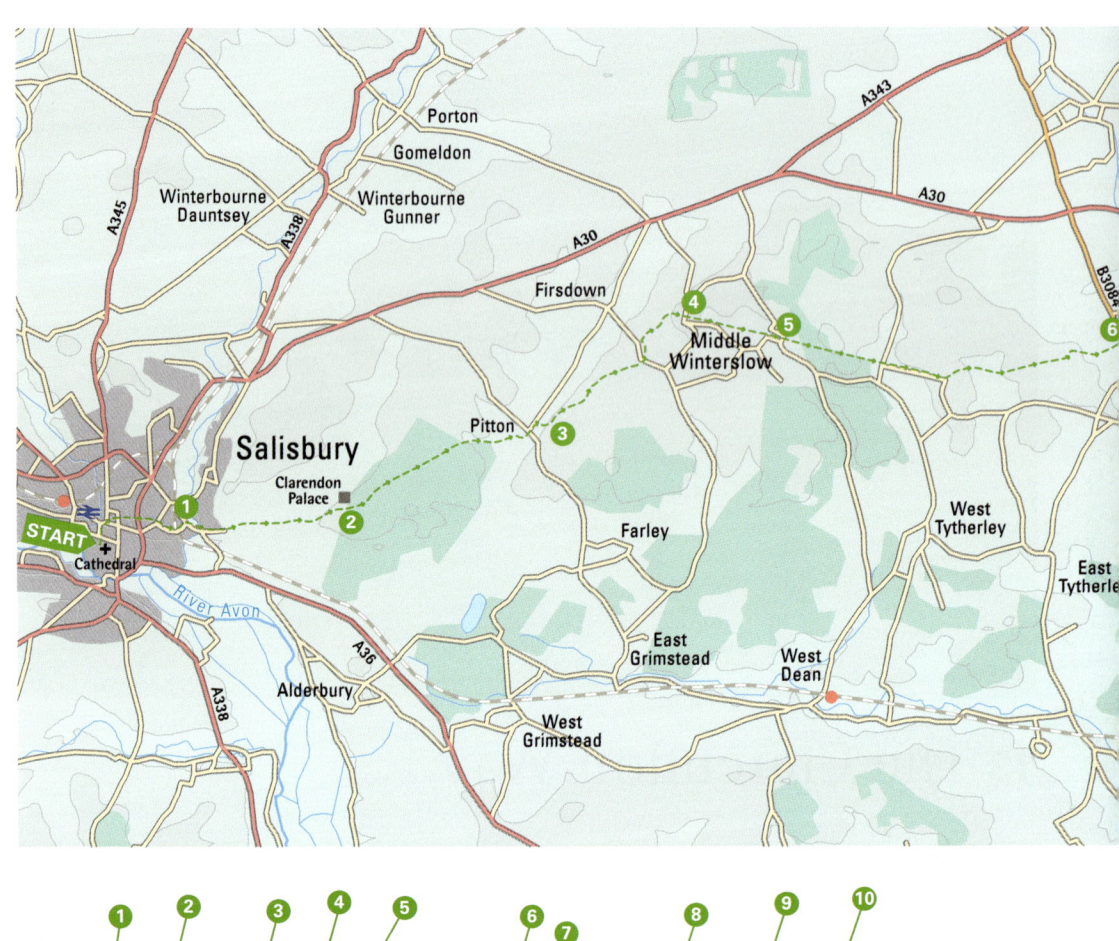

in a country park. The Farley Mount Monument is the most notable landmark; a pyramidal tower erected, rather ridiculously, in honour of someone's horse. The final section is admittedly a bit drab, a long tarmac descent into Winchester.

Route description

The Clarendon Way is mostly well-signposted, with vertical 'Clarendon Way' signs and disks featuring a helmet design. This route mostly follows the CW, but deviates in the final section.

START Starting from the front entrance (W end) of Salisbury Cathedral, head N across the green to pass under an archway and join High Street. After 350m (end of the pedestrianised precinct), New Canal Street leads off on the right, turn right to follow this E. Continue ahead, it becomes Milford Street and passes under the A36 road after 550m. It ascends to a roundabout, take the right turn here for Shady Bower (a road). Follow Shady Bower for 500m until you see Milford Mill Road leading off on the right.

1 Turn right onto Milford Mill Road. Follow the road for 300m. After crossing the River Bourne, Milford

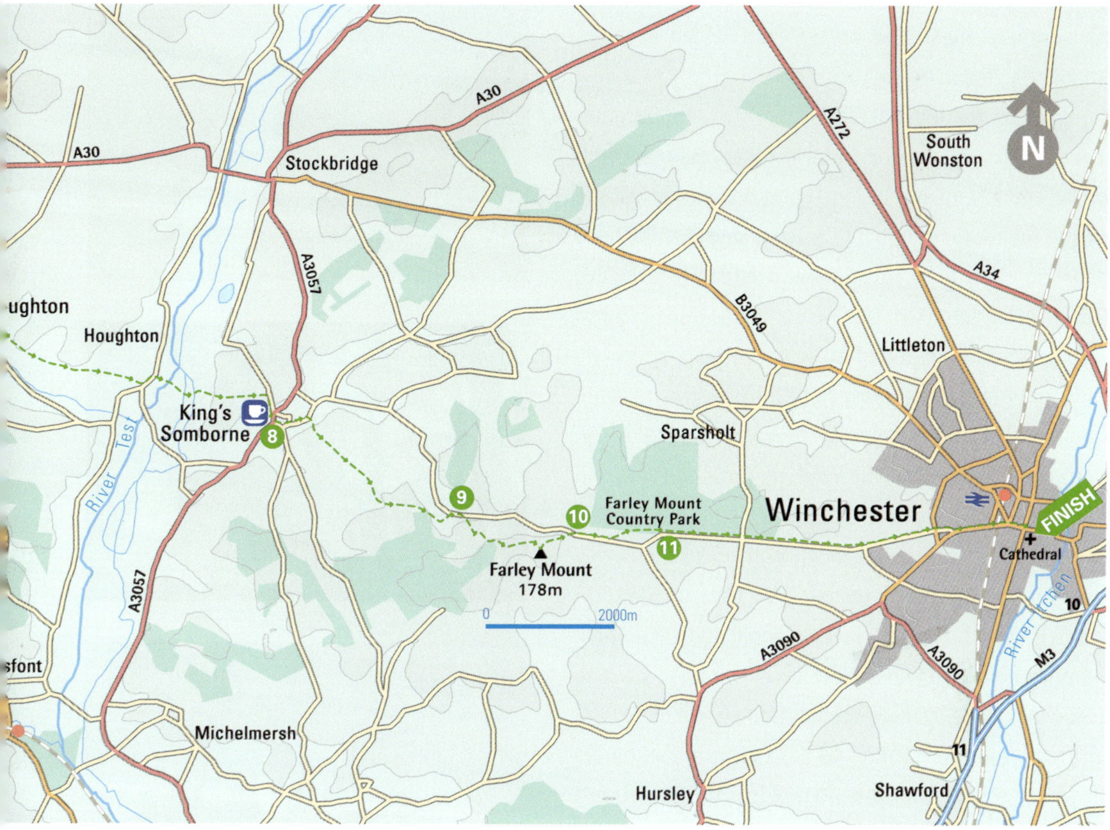

The Clarendon Way

Mill Road turns right, but Queen Manor Road continues ahead (E). Continue E on Queen Manor Road, which becomes a byway track after 280m. The byway track ends after 480m at Ranger's Lodge Farm, pass through this to join a footpath continuing E. Follow the footpath which crosses a field and steeply ascends King Manor Hill (remains of Clarendon Palace are now on your left). ❷ Continue ahead on the footpath, which enters woods and then reaches a fork of footpaths; take the left-hand footpath and follow it for 2.2km through woods and then downhill to reach a lane (Slate Way). Turn left and follow the lane into the village of Pitton across a crossroads (becomes High Street) for 400m until you see a footpath signposted off on the right, just before a church. Turn right onto the footpath and follow it 150m to a lane (The Green). Turn left onto the lane and follow it NE. After 100m, a bridleway path leads off on the right, take this (if you reach a parking area, you've overshot slightly). ❸ Follow the bridleway for 250m to where it joins a byway track, turn right onto this and follow it uphill. At the top of the hill after 410m, a footpath leads off to the left; take this footpath and follow it 1.2km to reach a lane (The Street). Cross the lane and continue on the footpath which heads N past a church (ignore a succession of right turns) to join a byway track after 800m. Continue ahead on the byway track, which feeds into a lane (Roman Road) after 500m.

Salisbury Cathedral

The Clarendon Way

4 Continue ahead ESE on the lane, which becomes Middleton Road. After 400m, a lane (The Causeway) forks off on the left, take this lane. The lane becomes a track, after 450m look for two footpaths branching off on the left, take the right-hand one which leads E. Follow the footpath uphill to reach a lane (The Flashett) and turn right onto this. Follow it ahead (it becomes Gunville Hill) for 200m to where it bends right at a bus stop in front of a patch of grass. Cross the grass to Mill Lane and immediately turn right into a byway (Easton Common Hill). **5** Follow the byway track 1.7km ESE until you reach a lane (The Warren). Cross the lane and follow the lane (Buckholt Lane) which continues ahead. After 1km the lane bends sharp right, take the byway track which turns off on the left here, through Buckholt Farm. Follow the byway track downhill and then uphill onto Broughton Down, before descending steeply and following a lane to reach a road (Romsey Road, B3084) in Broughton after 3.1km. **6** Turn right onto Romsey Road and follow it for just 40m before turning off left into Queenwood Road. Follow this for 250m to High Street, turn left onto this and then immediately off right into Rectory Lane. Follow Rectory Lane 260m to where it ends at a stream. Cross the stream and follow

Beacon Hill

Clarendon Way

Farley Mount monument

the track ahead to a crossroads of footpaths. Turn right to follow the footpath leading SSE. **7** Follow the footpath track for 3.2km (it becomes Faithfulls Drove, permissive track) to reach a road. Turn left onto the road and follow it for 220m to where a footpath track leads off on the right. Cross the road and take this footpath track. Follow it E for 2.4km, crossing the River Test and Park Stream, then ascending steeply before turning right (S) and descending steeply (parallel to a lane, Cow Drove Hill) to the village of King's Somborne. **8** Cross the A3057 road at the bottom of the hill, to Old Vicarage Lane (20m to the right). Follow Old Vicarage Lane for 200m to where it ends, cross onto Winchester Road which parallels it and follow this for another 300m until you see a footpath signposted on the right. Turn right and follow the footpath uphill. After 1.9km it merges with a byway and keeps ascending, it then descends and reaches a lane after 3.3km. **9** Don't go onto the lane, instead turn right to follow the bridleway path which heads SE across fields and ascends Beacon Hill. At the top it reaches a T junction, turn left to follow a permissive path E. 500m from the junction, look for a footpath leading off 150m on the right to Farley Mount Monument (white pyramidal building). Go see, then return to the permissive path. After another 500m, the path reaches a parking area leading to a lane. **10** ***Note that from this point, the route described here sometimes differs from the signposted CW route.*** Turn right onto the lane and then immediately turn off left onto the path

The Clarendon Way

River Test

just before the 'Farley Mount Country Park' sign. The path leads to a car park; continue through this and then a gate into the Country Park. Follow the path leading E along the uphill side of the meadow and through trees for 450m to a second car park, then bear left to follow the path leading diagonally downhill (NE) across a second meadow. 350m from the second car park and at the bottom of the slope, a junction of trails is reached.

Farley Mount Country Park

Take the track which leads ahead, bearing E for 500m across the downhill edge of a third meadow to reach a lane. ⑪ Continue ahead on the lane 6.5km into Winchester! The lane becomes Sarum Road, which heads downhill into Winchester and joins the B3040 Romsey Road after 4.1km. Romsey Road ends at a roundabout, continue ahead here beneath a town gate onto High Street. Follow High Street downhill for 350m (pedestrianised) to the Buttercross Monument (ornate monument opposite Café Nero) and turn right here under an arch onto The Square. This leads to the green in front of Winchester Cathedral's west entrance.

Trip planning

The easiest way to shuttle back to the start is via train. Whether you shuttle beforehand (leaving a vehicle at Winchester) or after (leaving a vehicle at Salisbury) will depend upon the direction you are arriving from, and time considerations. Salisbury Railway Station SP2 7NH / SU 136 301 is a 1km walk from the cathedral; follow Mill Road from the station car park and aim for the 123m spire. Winchester Railway Station SO23 8TJ / SU 477 299 is passed in the last kilometre of this route, turn left (N) at the roundabout

The Clarendon Way

at the end of Romsey Road and follow this to Station Road. There is a car park on Station Road, opposite the station. The train journey should take less than an hour and a half, changing trains at either Basingstoke or Southampton Central.

If driving, it takes 45 mins to an hour each way between the two cathedrals. Parking close to them is not easy, definitely go early if this is your plan.

If you elect to finish early, it's possible to escape by bus from Broughton (after about 20km) or King's Somborne (after about 25km). The number 16 bus will get you to Winchester in less than an hour, but check times as there is a limited service at weekends. It's probably easier to do this and then take the train back to Salisbury, than to head to Salisbury by bus; this latter option involves more than one bus route, changing at Stockbridge.

Broughton Down

Signage

There is a post office on the route at Pitton which sells snacks. Carry plenty of water for the wilds; the author didn't on his last effort and his poorly thought through hydration plan was to call in at either the Greyhound Inn in Broughton or the Crown Inn in King's Somborne; both were closed.

Other routes

If you just want to run half the distance, start or finish at Broughton ❻. See above for details of how to shuttle this. Farley Mount Country Park SO21 2JG / **SU 414 292** near ❿ outside Winchester is the place to head if you just want to stretch your legs for a short run.

Grand as your arrival at Winchester Cathedral is, it does lack sea views. You may wish to consider continuing through the city to follow the superb South Downs Way National Trail (see page 294) for another 160km to Beachy Head. Alternatively, you could head to Windsor following the Three Castles Path (see page 102). A third escape route from Winchester is offered by the Itchen Navigation Heritage Trail. This follows the (very attractive) valley of the River Itchen along restored weirs and locks for 16km / 10 miles south to Woodmill near Southampton. Shuttling back by public transport is fairly simple.

Events

The Clarendon Marathon was the author's first experience of the CW. It is precisely what it sounds like, with some bits added to the CW to make up the full 26.2 miles. The organisers suggest that it is, *'tough and challenging but possibly one of the most scenic races you'll ever enter'*. There is also a half marathon which ends at Broughton with a shuttle bus service, a Relay Marathon and a 5-mile 'Mini' event, starting from Farley Mount Country Park. It's a great event.

Atop the Zigzag Steps

14 Selborne

Distance	10km (6 miles)	Ascent	250m (820ft)
Map	OS Landranger 186 OS Explorer OL33		
Navigation	●●●	Numerous unmapped trails on Selborne Common	
Terrain	●●●	Dirt trails, several steep ascents	
Wet feet	●●●	Horses tend to churn the trails up somewhat	
Start / Finish	Car park behind the Selborne Arms GU34 3JR / SU 742 335		

Gilbert White's trails

Gilbert who? Gilbert White was an eighteenth-century vicar who is regarded as the first ecologist and naturalist. He scientifically observed and recorded the flora and fauna around his home at Selborne for four decades before publishing *The Natural History of Selborne* in 1789. White's writings (which have never been out of print since) inspired Darwin in the following century.

This route is another example of trail running having greater dimensions than just being a way to work up a sweat at weekends. The trails and hills are of course present and correct (211m Selborne Hill and 210m Noar Hill to be precise), offering a worthwhile physical challenge. However, running this landscape also immerses you in the natural world that White experienced; the steep Zig-Zag Path cut in 1753 by White's brother to ascend Selborne Hill; the beech, oak and ash woodland on Selborne Common where butterflies

Selborne

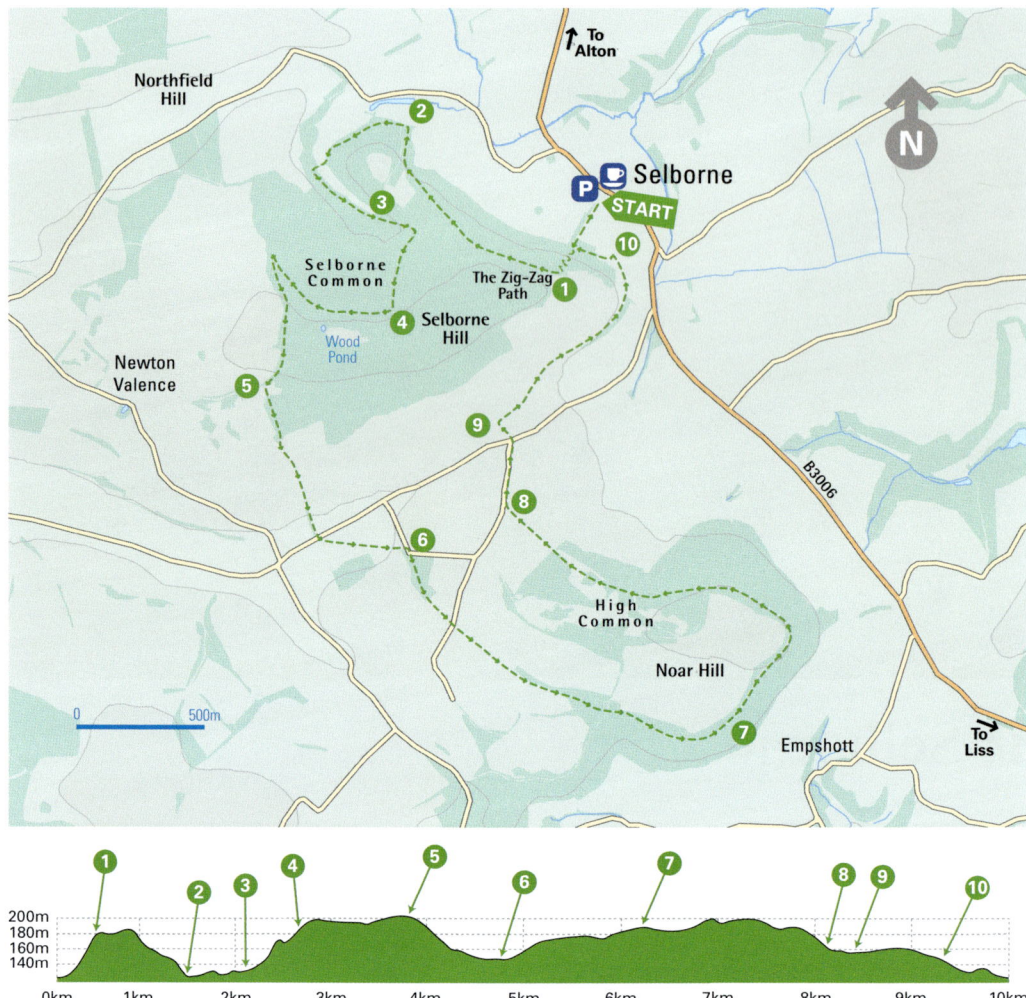

thrive; the wild meadows such as Coneycroft Valley, where orchids proliferate; the open Hampshire skies where White was the first to observe swifts mating on the wing.

Selborne and Noar Hills are part of the Hangers, a line of hills marking the eastern fringe of the Hampshire Downs where they meet the Weald; a hanger is a long wooded steep slope. This area is within the South Downs National Park.

Route description

START Take the footpath which leads out of the back of the car park, behind the toilet building. After 210m you reach a crossroads of footpaths; go straight ahead (steeply uphill) following the Zig-Zag Path. ❶ When you reach the top of the Zig-Zag Path, turn right and follow the path which leads along the top of the hillside. After 400m this begins to slope downhill. Continue ahead, ignoring other paths, until the path ends at a T junction after 500m, at the bottom of the hill. ❷ Turn left and follow the path W along the edge of the woods. After 400m you reach a treeless field at the bottom of a narrow valley (Dell Field).

Selborne 14

Cross the valley following the path, then turn left to follow the path up the valley. ❸ At the end of the field, the path goes through a gate and ascends steeply, continue climbing on the path. When you reach the top of the steep section (another gate), turn right and follow the path leading S (still uphill). Keep following this for 300m, ignoring a path which crosses, until it ends at a T junction with an E–W path. ❹ Turn right (W) and follow the path. It bends N and after 600m reaches a N–S bridleway. Turn sharply left (S) onto the bridleway and follow this for 500m to a junction of multiple footpaths and bridleways. ❺ Of the two signposted bridleways, take the left-hand choice, which leads S (steeply downhill). Follow this bridleway track (Green Lane) for 700m downhill to a lane. Cross the lane and take the footpath which heads to the left (E) across a field for 350m to reach another lane (ignore the path which leads S to a wood after just 120m). ❻ Turn right onto the lane, which bends left after just 20m. Do not follow the lane around the bend, instead continue ahead (SSE) onto the bridleway track which leaves the lane at the corner. After 300m the bridleway track ends at a lane, cross the lane and take the footpath which continues ahead (beside a partridge sculpture!). After

Leaving Selborne

The Zigzag Steps

The Zigzag Steps

700m the footpath reaches a six-way junction, go straight ahead on the bridleway. This leads around the side of a hill (Noar Hill), forking after 400m; take the left-hand (uphill) of the two bridleways. ❼ Stay on this bridleway as it bends around the edge of the hill, bearing right at a fork after 1km. After 1.8km the bridleway leaves the woods and reaches a lane. Turn right onto this lane. ❽ Follow the lane for 250m N to a T junction with another lane. Cross this lane and take the footpath opposite. Follow the footpath for 70m along a field edge to where a footpath leads off right; turn right to take this (signposted Hangers Way). ❾ Follow the footpath NE along field edges. It becomes a track and then joins a lane (Selborne Common) after 900m. Follow the lane until you see a footpath sign and a small set of steps on the left. ❿ Turn left onto this footpath and follow this uphill for 160m to the bottom of the zigzag steps; turn right here (opposite the steps) to return to the car park.

Trip planning

Parking behind the Selborne Arms is free, however it's a small car park so don't leave it too late in the day. Eating in the Selborne Arms saves you a journey after your run, although there are various other cafés and suchlike to consider along the street.

14 Selborne

Noar Hill

Selborne Common and Noar Hill are both SSSIs; the former managed by National Trust and the latter being a Hampshire and Isle of Wight Wildlife Trust nature reserve.

While in Selborne, consider learning a bit more about Gilbert White; his house and garden 'The Wakes' can be visited. The house also incorporates the Oates Collections, about the doomed Polar explorer Captain Oates (*"I am just going outside and may be some time"*). If further culture is required, the novelist Jane Austen lived just down the road at Chawton and her house is also open to the public.

Other routes

Selborne Common is managed by the National Trust and has open access, so explore at your leisure. There is further information and some short route suggestions on their website. The NT also manage the Lythes meadows and woods which stretch north-east to Coombe Wood on the far side of the road in Selborne; for a 4km loop follow the Hangers Way until it meets / becomes a byway track, then turn right onto this to return. There are numerous trails to explore and extend your run around Noar Hill, for example the byway around Goleigh Farm. Following the Hangers Way 6km south from Noar Hill will bring you to 244m Wheatham Hill, a great viewpoint.

The Hangers Way

The Hangers Way is relatively short, as long-distance trails go; 34km / 21 miles from Alton to Queen Elizabeth Country Park. It is recommended as an engaging long outing. The HW roughly follows the line of the Hangers scarp, along its way passing parts of Routes 11, 14 and 59. The signage is a disk with a green arrow featuring a tree on a slope. The HW is marked on OS maps, and detailed guides can be downloaded from the Hampshire County Council website.

15 Highclere Castle

Highclere Castle

Distance	21km (13 miles) **Ascent** 400m (1,280ft)
Map	OS Landranger 174, 185 OS Explorer 144, 158
Navigation ●●●	Easy to follow and obvious trails
Terrain ●●●	Mostly on stony tracks and rooty paths, some tarmac, mild climbs
Wet feet ●●●	A few muddy bits in the wet
Start / Finish	Beacon Hill parking area RG20 9LJ / SU 462 577

Downton Abbey!

This is a great exhilarating run! Fast trails, varied scenery, open vistas. It roughly follows the perimeter and skyline of the Highclere Estate, better known as the filming location of the *Downton Abbey* TV series and movie. This lovely corner of the North Wessex Downs Area of Outstanding Natural Beauty is generally ignored by folk whizzing through unawares on the A34; the author is ashamed to admit that he did the same for many years, until the research for this book.

The route passes through the parkland and woods around Highclere Castle, home for centuries of the Carnarvon family. This spectacular nineteenth-century Italianate mansion should look pretty familiar, on account of its TV fame. You then climb (via seasonally open estate tracks) onto the main Hampshire Downs ridge and follow the Wayfarer's Walk along it in a big arc back towards the start. There's nothing here not to like. Maybe they could shift the A34 though.

15 Highclere Castle

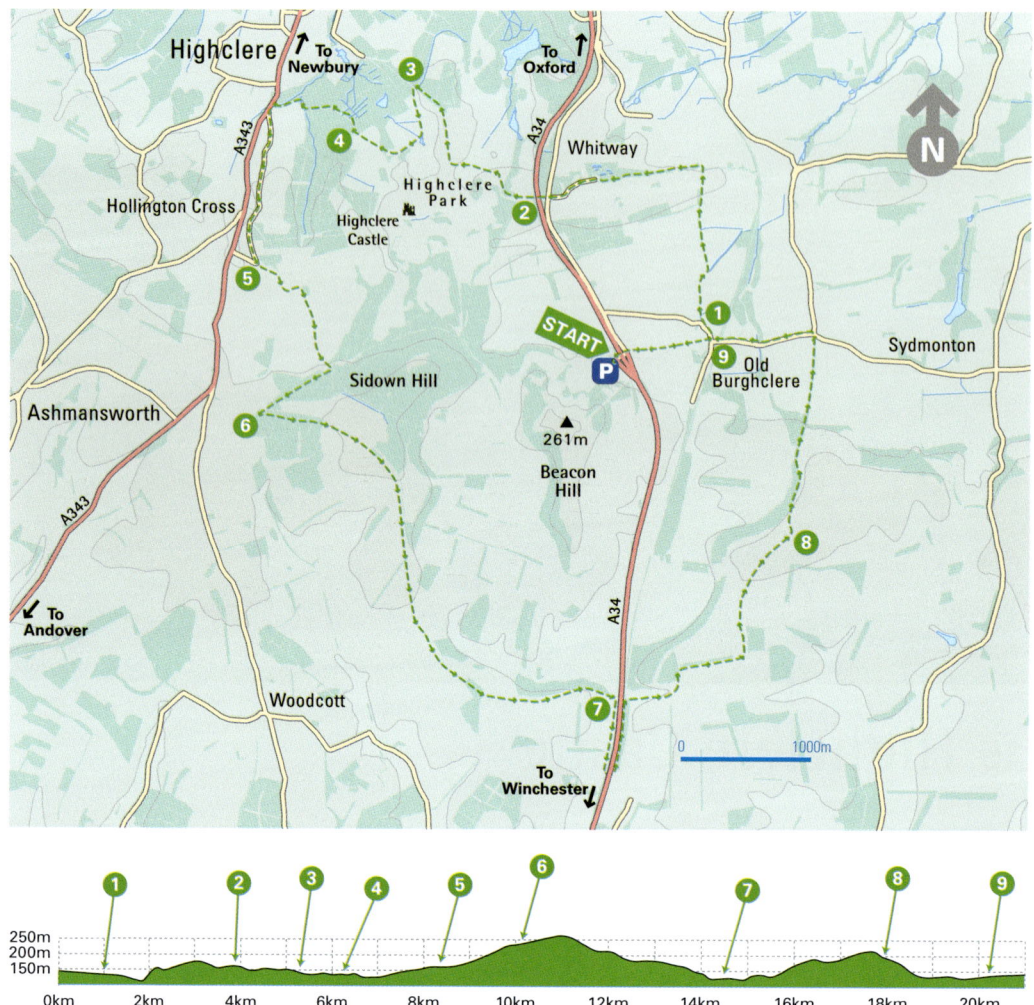

Route description

START From the parking area, cross the A34 by the road bridge you came in on. After the bridge, continue directly ahead and across the road you reach, to take the footpath which is signposted ahead (E). Follow this footpath 600m E along a field and then past a church to reach a tarmac track and then a crossroads. Turn left onto a lane and follow this for 180m to a sharp left bend. A byway track continues ahead (N) here, take this. ❶ Follow the byway for 1.3km uphill. When you reach a crossroads of byways, turn left (W) and follow this byway for 800m (still uphill) to where it joins a lane. Continue ahead on the lane for 600m, passing a crossroads with another lane and crossing the A34, to reach the entrance gates for the Highclere Estate. ❷ Pass through the gates and continue ahead on the tarmac footpath track. After 700m you reach a crossroads, turn right here (as instructed by estate signs). Follow this tarmac footpath track N for 800m. When you enter trees, look for a footpath track signposted off the track on the left, and take this. ❸ Follow the footpath track for 600m back S, until you reach the Carnarvon Mausoleum (a chapel building). Follow the footpath leading past this building on its right-hand (N) side, through

Highclere Castle

the cemetery and across the field behind. Avoid the more obvious path heading W across the field, the footpath exits the field on its N edge, look for the footpath signposts to get the correct exit. ④ Follow the footpath through woods and then along a field until it emerges after 800m at a road (the A343). Turn left onto the road and then immediately turn off left again, onto a lane (Highclere Street). Follow the lane for 1.2km S until you reach a sharp right bend. ⑤ Leave the lane and continue straight ahead here on the estate track. ***Between August Bank Holiday and Easter Bank Holiday, this track (the 'Grotto Lodge Summer Walk') is closed. You will have to continue 160m to the end of Highclere Street, cross the A343 to the footpath opposite, follow the footpath 140m to a lane, turn left onto the lane and follow it 1.3km uphill, then turn off left onto a byway (Wayfarer's Walk) which will bring you to ⑥ after 1.6km.*** Follow the estate track uphill, around two sharp bends. When you reach a T junction with another track, turn right (uphill) and climb on this track to reach a crossroads (beside Grotto Lodge) after 1.8km. ⑥ Turn left (E) onto the byway track, signposted as the Wayfarer's Walk. Follow the byway for 4.3km; at first it climbs, then there is a long gradual descent to the A34.

Near Old Burgclere

Highclere Park

Grotto Lodge Summer Walk

⑦ When the byway ends at the A34, turn right (S) following signs 600m to a tunnel under the A34, pass through the tunnel, then turn back N and follow the permissive path 600m alongside the A34 to re-join the WW. This turns right (E) and is now a bridleway path (ignore the footpath continuing N). Follow the WW bridleway uphill. After 2.2km, a bridleway path leads downhill on the left, take this (leaving the WW). ⑧ Descend steeply on the bridleway path. After 1.6km, it ends at a crossroads with lanes. Turn left onto the lane (signposted Burghclere) and follow it for 800m to a sharp right bend. ⑨ Continue straight ahead through a gate onto the footpath track ahead; this is the first footpath you ran on, follow it back to the start.

Trip planning

The car park is simply a free roadside area, directly off the A34 if coming from the south. The junction is signposted for Beacon Hill and Highclere Castle. Coming from the north, turn off at the junction signposted for Burghclere and then follow signs for Beacon Hill.

The nearest food can be found at Burghclere in the Carnarvon Arms; the pub building was once the estate's coach house. Should you be interested, they cater to shooting parties and the menu includes things like 'Paignton Crab brûlée on sourdough bread', whatever that is. Otherwise, Tot Hill Services are located beside

15 Highclere Castle

the A34 turn-off for Burghclere; here, you can dine beneath the golden arches.
Visits to Highclere Castle itself have to be pre-booked, on the limited days when it is open to the public. The route here follows public rights of way that should always be open, although a short section follows an estate track which is closed in the colder months; see the route description for the simple diversion.

Other routes

It's not really practical to shorten this loop, given the limited public access within the estate. However, there are various ways to extend it. The Highclere Castle website has a downloadable guide to the trails open to the public within the estate, and several offer interesting diversions off the route described here. The most challenging is to run up 261m Beacon Hill from the start car park ... although perhaps save this for the end, to burn off excess energy!

See page 96 for more information about the great Wayfarer's Walk long-distance trail.

Wayfarer's Walk

Events

Newbury AC organise the Highclere Castle 10K, based from the castle grounds. The event facilities are listed online as, *'toilets, on-site parking, refreshments, stunningly beautiful scenery'*.

The Hampshire Hobbit is a trail marathon and half marathon organised by Basingstoke and Mid Hants AC. The race route is mostly based to the south-east of this route, but overlaps the Wayfarer's Walk bit.

The North Wessex Downs Area of Outstanding Natural Beauty

North Wessex Downs isn't an actual place name, but when the AONB was created this umbrella term was invented to sum up 1,730km^2 of interlinked chalk uplands in south-central England, which on the map describe a vast letter 'C'. The top arm of the C reaches into Oxfordshire and Berkshire (the Lambourn Downs, Berkshire Downs and Sinodun Hills, including Routes 19, 20, 22 and 25), the bottom arm into Hampshire (the North Hampshire Downs, location of Routes 15 and 16). The back of the C is in Wiltshire, described in this book's companion volume *South West Trail Running* (the Marlborough Downs, Pewsey Downs and Savernake Forest, including Routes 61, 62, 63, 64, 65 in that book).

The downs within the AONB are generally characterised by long, undulating ridges with steep scarp faces to the north, although exceptions exist like the isolated Sinodun Hills and the expansive downland of the Ridgeway near Goring Gap. What is consistent across the AONB is the relatively small number of visitors outside a handful of popular beauty spots. The author and his friends have enjoyed many runs here in the heart of Southern England, where the hills were ours alone.

Berkshire

The largely green 'Royal County of Berkshire' offers a wide range of trail running environments. The 'Royal' title is due to the presence of Windsor Castle; Royal forests and parks approaching the world's largest inhabited castle make up a notable proportion of Berkshire's east. The River Thames delineates much of the county's northern border, beauty spots include Winter Hill and Goring Gap. The Berkshire Downs, covering much of Berkshire's western half, are within the North Wessex Downs Area of Outstanding Natural Beauty. The Berkshire Downs are represented in this chapter by the highest point in South East England, Walbury Hill, as well as an epic route along the ancient Ridgeway. To the south, along the River Kennet valley, Greenham Common is a remarkable natural and historical landscape.

Snow Hill (Route 17)

Combe Gibbet

Summer Hill

16 Combe Gibbet

Distance	11km (7 miles)	Ascent	225m (705ft)
Map	OS Landranger 174 OS Explorer 158, 131		
Navigation	● ● ●	Clear and obvious signposted tracks	
Terrain	● ● ●	Stony and rutted tracks, one long but mildly angled ascent	
Wet feet	● ● ●	Propensity for long-lasting muddy puddles	
Start / Finish	Combe Gibbet car park RG17 9EL / SU 370 620		

On top of South East England

The Combe Gibbet of the title is a literal gibbet, which you pass at the start of this outing. It looms tall over a Neolithic Long Barrow (60m long!) on steep-sided Inkpen Hill, with expansive views across Berkshire, Wiltshire and Hampshire. The gibbet is a replica of the original, which was constructed in 1676 for the execution (in chains) of George Broomham and Dorothy Newman, lovers who had murdered Broomham's wife and son. As you run past, spoil your enjoyment of the largest area of pristine chalk downland in Berkshire by visualising their rotting cadavers, being picked apart by crows.

This is a fairly simple run, following wide estate tracks and long obvious paths. The author didn't meet a soul once he left the main ridge, just sheep. Climbing back atop the ridge is an extended gradual grind, but you'll make it. This brings you (via a short road section) to Walbury Hill, which at 297 metres (974 feet) happens to be not just the highest point in Berkshire, but the highest in South East England and

Combe Gibbet

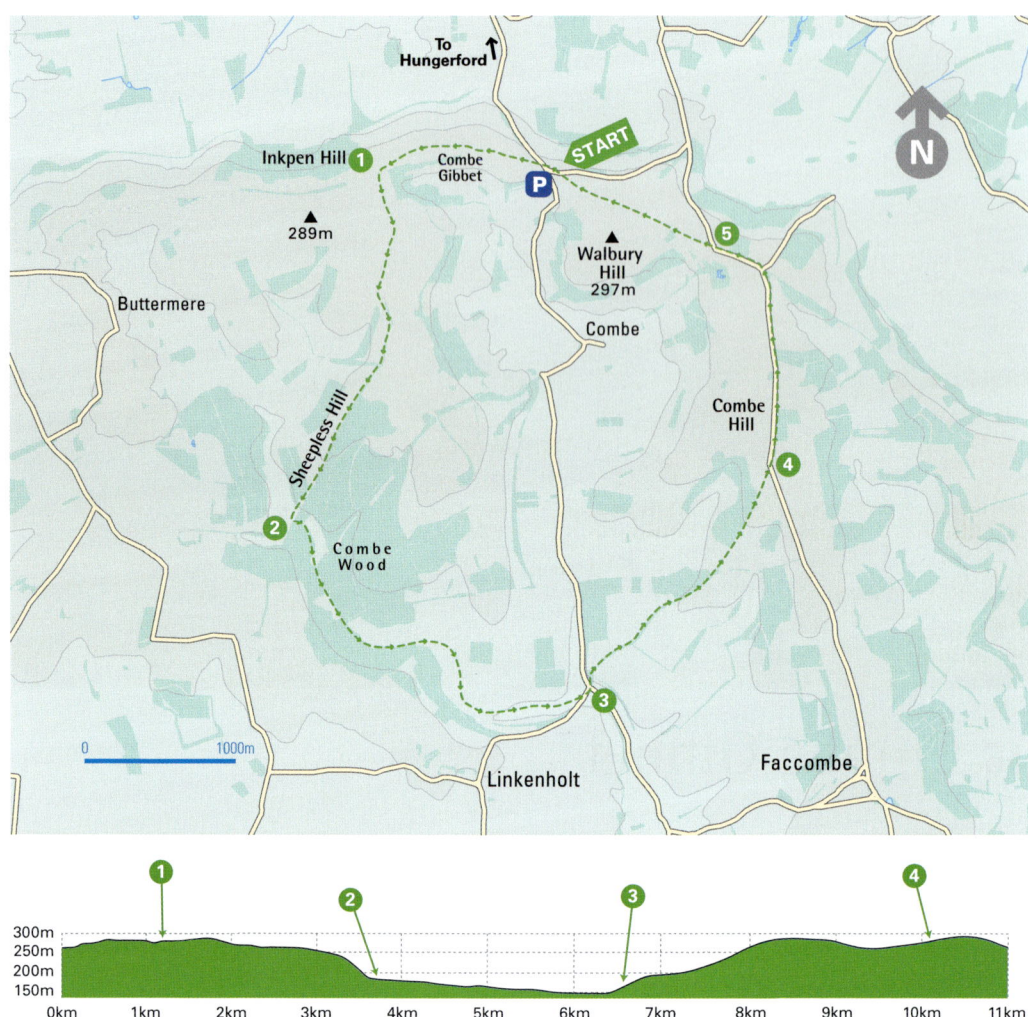

the highest chalk hill in Britain. The summit plateau's views are obscured by hedges and the earthworks of Walbury Camp, the largest Iron Age hillfort in Berkshire. It's only when you emerge from the holloway (sunken lane) leading from the hillfort, that the horizon expands once more and you are reminded of the rather awesome fact that you're running 200m above the River Kennet valley.

Route description

START Leave the car park by crossing the road junction and heading W (uphill) along the byway track towards Combe Gibbet (the prominent wooden gallows). Follow the byway past the gallows and for another 700m to a junction of tracks. **1** Turn left (S) onto the bridleway and follow it S along field edges. After 900m the bridleway reaches a gate. Do not descend here, stay on the bridleway which contours around the rim of the hill. It then passes alongside woodland and descends steeply to reach a five-way junction, 2.5km after turning S. **2** Take the first track on the left, and follow this bridleway track along the winding valley floor for 2.7km until you reach a lane. Turn left onto the lane and follow it 75m to a

Combe Gibbet 16

Descending Walbury Hill

T junction with another lane. Cross this lane and continue straight ahead on the byway track leading uphill. ❸ Follow the byway track NE for 2km until it ends at a lane on the hill top. ❹ Turn left onto the lane (N, towards the communications mast) and follow it. After 1.3km, bear left at a junction. After another 300m, the lane bends right at a parking area. Continue straight ahead onto the byway track. ❺ Follow the byway track over Walbury Hill for 1.2km to reach the start car park. The summit trig point is 200m along a track from the byway, over a small stile on the left, 700m past the lane; this is private land, however.

Trip planning
Combe Gibbet car park is easily located by following lanes for 2km south of the village of Inkpen … just keep going uphill. It is free but small and can fill up quickly. At such times, try Walbury Hill car park RG17 9ED / **SU 380 615** which is located 1km east along the ridge; annoyingly you have to drive down the hill and right back up again.
Nourishment can be found close by in Inkpen village, where there is the Honesty Coffee Shop (yummy local produce on sale) and the Crown and Garter pub. There is also a corner shop in Kintbury but beyond is nothing but desolation and wasteland in any direction; joking aside, West Berkshire is notably devoid of services, possibly because the region is parcelled up into vast private estates. Hungerford is the place to go for anything else; the author quite likes The Tutti Pole café on High Street.

Other routes
The Berks, Bucks and Oxon Wildlife Trust (BBOWT) publish the downloadable 17km 'Inkpen Wild Walk' which ascends Inkpen Hill from Kintbury.

Combe Gibbet

The Kennet and Avon Canal is a short distance north; for a pleasant tow path run, any section between Hungerford and Newbury is good to go. More details about the K&A can be found in *South West Trail Running*.

The start point of this route is also the start point of both the Wayfarer's Walk and Test Way long-distance trails; see below.

View from Inkpen Hill

Events

The Gibbet Challenge is a 10km race taking in Combe Gibbet and Walbury Hill, via the steeper north slopes ... gulp! It is part of the Run West Berks series of events which also includes the Kintbury 5 (miles), about 5km north of this route.

The Combe Gibbet to Overton Race is a classic 16-mile point to point race organised by Overton Harriers. The route follows the Wayfarer's Walk for most of the way.

Walbury Hill

The Wayfarer's Walk and the Test Way

Two long distance routes have their start points at Inkpen Hill:

The **Wayfarer's Walk** extends 141km / 88 miles to Emsworth in Chichester Harbour. The first section crosses Walbury Hill and then follows similarly spectacular, elevated ridgetop tracks east, crossing Pilot Hill (highest point in Hampshire at 286m) before passing through Route 15 to reach Watership Down (yes, the place with the bunnies) near Kingsclere; all making for a superb c. 25km run. The WW then veers south, intersecting with Route 12 en route to its finish point at the seaside, which happens to be the start point of Route 58. Second Wind Running organise the Wayfarers 100k, which follows the WW as far as Portsmouth.

The **Test Way** leads directly south from Inkpen Hill, reaching Eling Quay near Southampton after 71km / 44 miles. The first half to Westdown follows footpaths over mild downland. The TW then descends into the River Test valley, closely following this pristine chalk river including long flat sections along a disused railway line. Andover Trail Events' Testway Ultra utilises the TW, with 40- and 50-mile options.

Maps and detailed descriptions of both the WW and TW are available online.

17 Windsor Castle

17 Windsor Castle

Distance		28km (17.5 miles) **Ascent** 250m (780ft)
Map		OS Landranger 175 OS Explorer 160
Navigation	●●●	Map recommended, signage is missing for much of the route
Terrain	●●●	Roots, mud, grass, forest tracks, far too much tarmac
Wet feet	●●●	Squelchy patches usually dodge-able
Start		Crowthorne Railway Station RG45 6GY / SU 822 637
Finish		Windsor and Eton Central Railway Station SL4 1RH / SU 966 769

Through Royal forests and parks, to visit the Queen

When first told that a great long trail run threads right through East Berkshire's suburbia, the author was sceptical. Yet there really is such a trail! Following a section of the Three Castles Path, it is possible to run for hours through forest, heath and parkland, right up to the doors of Windsor Castle. The key to this is the Crown Estate stretching south-west of Windsor, a massive 31km² of land which has been spared from the developers.

Swinley Forest is the first hefty chunk of Her Majesty's property which you run through, via long, straight and eerily empty plantation tracks. This is followed by Swinley Park, a continuation of the same theme. The halfway point is an utterly surreal interlude where you run across the track of Ascot Racecourse, before you plunge into landscaped Windsor Great Park, our monarch's front garden. To give some idea of the scale, it's

17 Windsor Castle

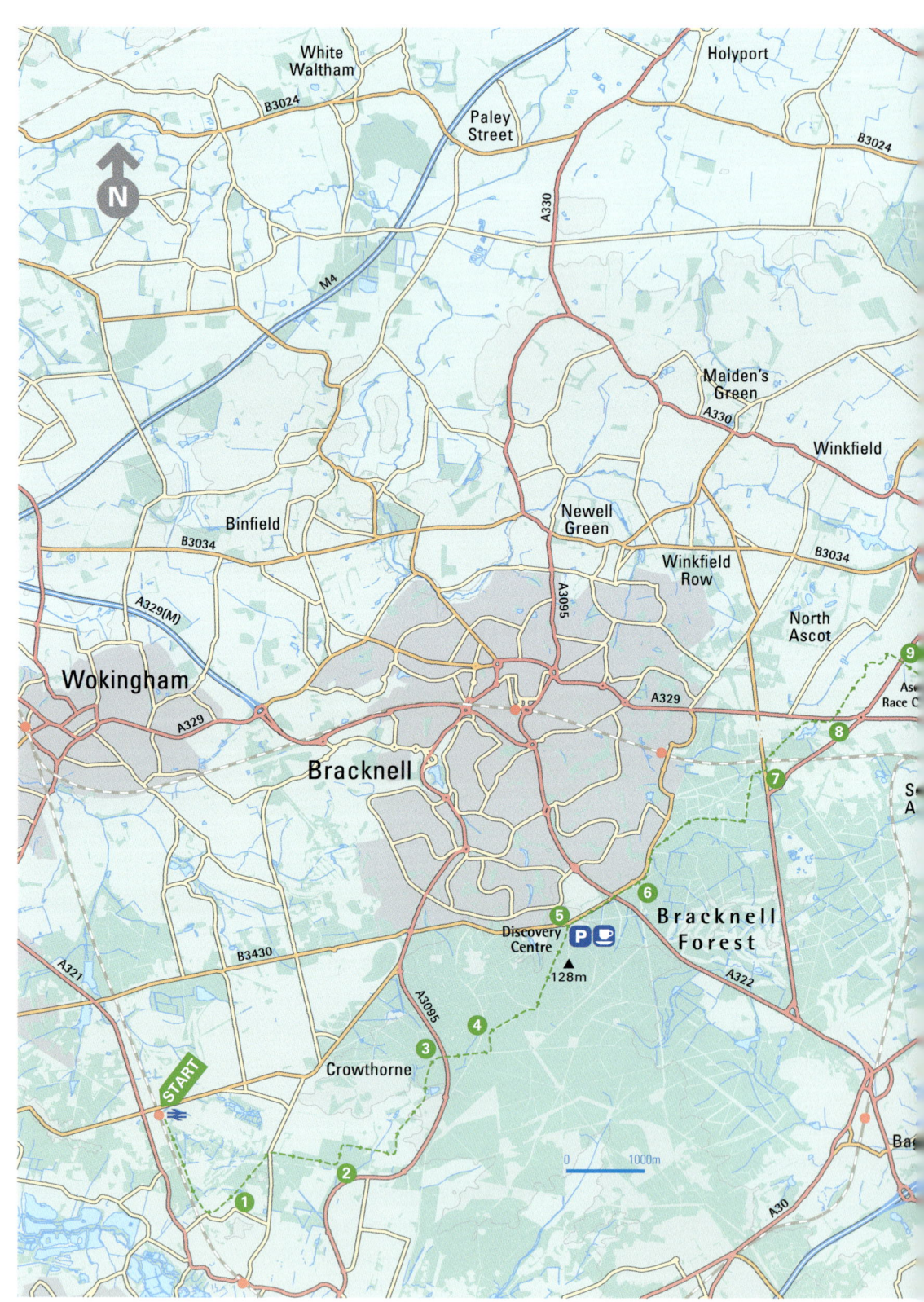

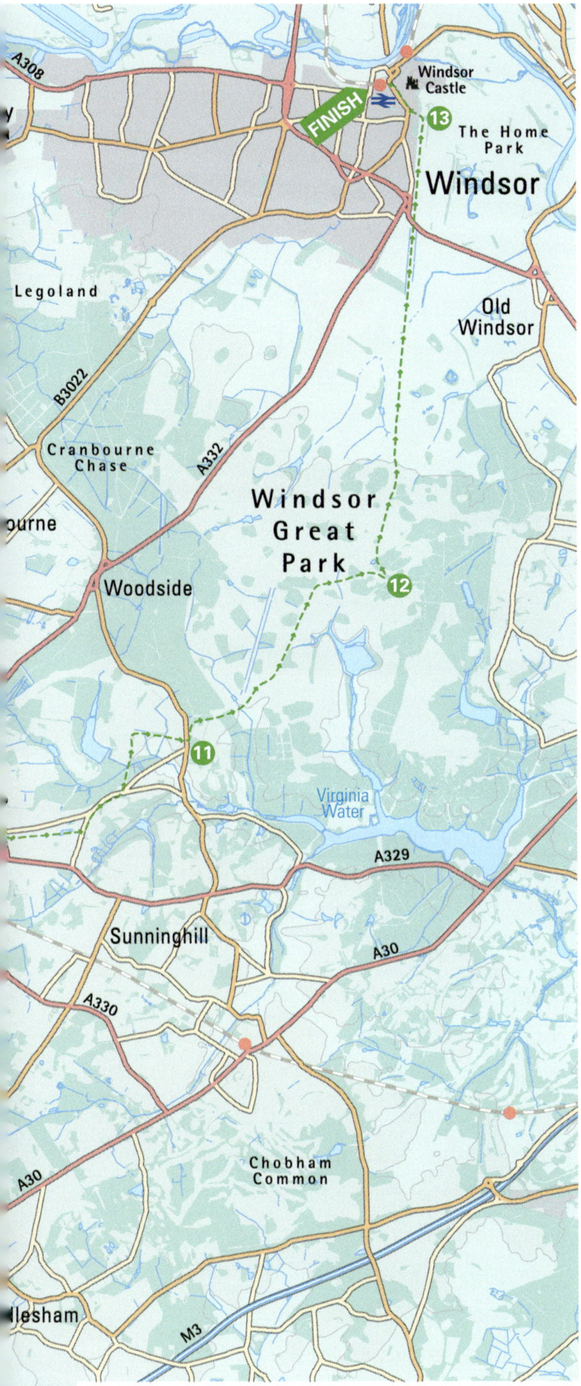

Windsor Castle 17

a 10km run from one end to the other. The payback for all this effort is the truly astonishing view from the Copper Horse statue, atop Snow Hill; Windsor Castle, the largest and oldest inhabited castle on earth, dominates the landscape from over 4km away along the die-straight Long Walk avenue. The final leg of your outing is the gruelling slog / triumphal sprint along the Long Walk, flanked by the 500-strong red deer population.

If the flag is not flying from Windsor Castle's Round Tower, then the Queen is not currently in residence and unfortunately you have had a wasted journey. Leave a message and come back another day.

Route description

This route largely follows the Three Castles Path, which is marked on OS maps but only intermittently waymarked on the ground.

START From the B3348 Duke's Ride outside Crowthorne Station, look for the footpath leading S through houses, opposite Heatherdene Avenue, and follow this. The footpath passes S between the railway and Wellington College, emerging onto Cheviot Road after 1.4km. Turn left onto this and follow it to High Street. Turn left onto High Street and immediately turn off left onto Sandy Lane (a byway).

1 Follow Sandy Lane NE past the houses to where it becomes a bridleway track, continue ahead to reach Sandhurst Road after 1.1km. Cross the road and continue ahead (E) on the bridleway for 900m (ignoring the first footpath on the left) until you see a footpath track turning off left (N). **2** Turn left and take this footpath track, follow it 270m until

17 Windsor Castle

Snow Hill

you see a track leading off on the right. Turn right and follow this track E, after 390m it passes a crossroads and becomes a footpath, after another 320m it reaches a second crossroads. Turn left (N) and follow a footpath track for 1.5km, ignoring any side turns, uphill past Broadmoor Farm and then Broadmoor Hospital, until you reach a crossroads with an E-W byway track (The Devil's Highway). ❸ Turn right (E) onto the byway track and follow it under the A3095. The byway ends but the track continues E, entering Swinley Forest. Continue ahead at the first crossroads reached (370m after the A3095) and then turn left (N) at the second crossroads, (600m from the A3095). Follow the track N for 220m until you see a track leading off NE on the right, turn right to take this. ❹ Follow the track for 630m NE, passing a crossroads, to a T junction. Turn right (E) at the T junction and follow this track just 100m to a crossroads. Turn left (N), this track leads 1km NNE before reaching a T junction with a N–S track, just before the Look Out Discovery Centre (Visitor Centre for Swinley Forest). Turn left to reach the B3430 road (Nine Mile Ride) after 140m. ❺ Cross the road and take the path opposite. Turn right to follow the path NE along the road. It becomes a footpath and crosses the A322 via a footbridge after 560m. Turn right after the footbridge to follow a path NE along the B3430. After 370m and just after a roundabout, cross the road to take the path signposted ('Rambler's Route') on the right. ❻ You pass through a gate into Swinley Park. Turn left (NE) and follow a track 160m to a left turn. Take the left turn and follow the track 1.7km to a crossroads (fourth crossroads reached). Turn left (N) at the crossroads and follow the track N for 600m to a junction of multiple tracks. Take the first track on the right which leads to a car park and the B3017 after 150m. ❼ Turn left (N) onto the B3017 (leaving Swinley Park) and cross the railway bridge. Immediately on the right is a gate signposted 'Englemere Pond', pass through this and follow the path 700m NE (passing the pond) to reach the A329 London Road. Turn right and follow the road 320m E until you see Blythewood Lane (a byway lane) turning off on the left. ❽ Turn left and follow

Windsor Castle

the byway lane for 700m to Burleigh Road (also a byway lane). Turn left and follow Burleigh Road N to a crossroads, turn right at the crossroads (still Burleigh Road) and follow this 400m to where Kennel Ave (another byway lane) leads off on the right. Turn right and follow Kennel Ave 250m to reach the A332 and Ascot Race Course. ❾ Cross the A332 and go through a gate into Ascot Racecourse. Follow the zigzagging waymarked trail across the racecourse (give way to horses!) and Ascot Heath, leaving via a tunnel after 900m. When you exit the tunnel, immediately turn right and ascend steps. Follow this path S, crossing another branch of the racecourse, to reach the junction of New Mile Road and the A330. ❿ Turn left (S) onto the A330 and then immediately turn off left onto a footpath leading E. This reaches Cheapside Road after 850m. Turn left and follow Cheap-

Residents of Windsor Great Park

Swinley Forest

side Road 600m NE to the gated entrance to Sunninghill Park, on the left. Turn left into this entrance and follow the footpath track N. It turns right after 700m and reaches the B383 Sunninghill Road after 1.2km. ⓫ Cross the road and go through the gated entrance to Windsor Great Park. Follow the track (Duke's Lane) which leads straight ahead (N) from the entrance and continue on this for 2.2km to a crossroads. Go ahead at the crossroads to reach a second crossroads after just 50m, where you turn right (E). Follow the track for 700m to a junction of multiple tracks, turn sharply left to take the furthest left track (heading NW). ⓬ Follow the track, which bends N, past a pond to where it becomes a path. Pass through a deer gate and ascend Snow Hill to the Copper Horse statue. Continue ahead (downhill) to join the straight track (The Long Walk) leading towards Windsor Castle. Follow the track 3.7km N to where gates bar the track ahead and you have to turn off left through Cambridge Gate onto Park Street (end of the TCW). ⓭ Follow Park Street 170m to the end, pass St Alban's Street and then turn right onto the B3022. Follow this 270m to the castle walls; pass the Harte and Garter Hotel, then turn off left under an arch to reach Windsor Railway Station.

Trip planning

This route might bother purists as there is a higher proportion of tarmac than in any other route in this book. It's possible to sidestep much of it by running on grass and suchlike, but a fair amount is unavoidable. The experience of the route is absolutely worth it, however.

The logistics of shuttling back to the start are not too onerous. Leaving a car outside Crowthorne Railway Station is no problem (free parking across the road on Heatherdene Avenue, for example). Numerous combinations of bus and train will get you from Windsor back to Crowthorne, all taking about an hour, but the simplest is to just use the trains, changing at Slough and Reading. Driving between the two spots takes about half an hour with no traffic, which is of course a virtual impossibility.

Crossing Ascot Racecourse is entirely legal, as there is public access to Ascot Heath in the centre! On race days

Windsor Castle

(Royal Ascot and suchlike) you can still cross but you may be asked to sign a disclaimer before proceeding. The only easily accessible place to get refreshments (and fill water bladders) along the route is the Look Out Discovery Centre after 9km at ❺, where there is a Coffee Shop (it sells ice lollies!) and other facilities. When you reach Windsor, your cup will runneth over for choice.

Other routes

If you want to chop this route into manageable halves (or bail out halfway), then Ascot Railway Station is the key. From ❽, head further E along the A329 and turn right onto Station Hill to reach the station. Trains from here can get you to either Crowthorne or Windsor in an hour or so.

Swinley Forest and Windsor Great Park are both well worth extensive explorations in their own right; they size up at 1,100 and 2,020 hectares respectively, so you won't struggle to find space to stretch your legs. For Swinley Forest, park at the Look Out Discovery Centre RG12 7QW / **SU 877 662** on the B3430 Nine Mile Ride. The car park closes at 6pm. Watch out for mountain bikers on the trails.

Windsor Great Park, open from dawn to dusk, is served by numerous car parks. For the Home Park (the deer park around the Long Walk), either use one of the car parks along the A332 south of Windsor or park in Windsor and enter on foot from Park Street ⓭.

Virginia Water in Windsor Great Park is a popular spot to run; the 7km circuit of this lake from Virginia Water Pavilion takes in the 'Cascade' waterfall at its outflow, and (improbably) a section of the Roman ruins of Leptis Magna, transported here from Libya in the nineteenth century. Start from Virginia Water car park GU25 4QF / **SU 980 687** on the A30 London Road.

Events

Bracknell parkrun is held weekly at Great Hollands Recreation Ground in Wokingham.

Bracknell Forest Runners hold the Forest 5 in Swinley Forest, a 5-mile off-road route.

F3 Events hold the Royal Windsor 10K River Trail Run, based along the bank of the River Thames and utilising the Thames Path National Trail. They also organise the Royal Windsor Half Marathon River Trail Run, on the same format. This shouldn't be confused with the Windsor Half Marathon, which is held within Windsor Great Park, all on tarmac.

The Three Castles Path

The full Three Castles Path extends from Winchester to Windsor, being 99km / 61 miles in length. The route is mostly easy-gradient (including a stretch along Basingstoke Canal) but there are hilly sections, such as across the chalk downs approaching Winchester. The 'three castles' are Winchester Great Hall (the only surviving part of Winchester Castle), Odiham Castle (a characterful ruin beside Basingstoke Canal) and Windsor Castle. The TCP is worth noting as one possible way to connect the South Downs Way / Clarendon Way (which meet at Winchester) and the Thames Path. The route is marked on OS maps but is not consistently waymarked on the ground; the guidebook published by Heron Maps is helpful.

The 3 Castles Ultramarathon is organised by Ultraviolet and offers the choice of 50km from Winchester to Odiham Castle, or 100km to Windsor Castle.

Greenham Common 18

Greenham Common

18 Greenham Common

Distance		14km (9 miles)	**Ascent**	100m (310ft)
Map		OS Landranger 174 OS Explorer 158		
Navigation	●●●	Some unmarked / unsigned paths, a compass will help		
Terrain	●●●	Muddy and rooty paths and tow paths, gravel tracks. One easy ascent		
Wet feet	●●●	The nature reserve paths can become swampy		
Start / Finish		Thatcham Nature Discovery Centre RG19 3FU / SU 505 670		

A stunning mix of natural landscapes and Cold War history

If (like the author) you're ancient enough to remember the 1980s, the name 'Greenham Common' will conjure up memories. The US Air Force controversially stationed nuclear cruise missiles at the airfield here, making it a centre point both of the peace movement and the Cold War itself. The base closed down in 1993 and the runway was torn up. Amazingly, given its turbulent history, Greenham Common has now returned to nature. The largest area of wild heathland in Berkshire is a peaceful spot to stretch your legs, while taking in a few relics of its former status. The surrounding woodland, meadows and reedbeds on the outskirts of Newbury are equally worth exploring by trail shoe, consisting of a series of nature reserves managed by the Berks, Bucks & Oxon Wildlife Trust (BBOWT) and known collectively as West Berkshire Living Landscape.

18 Greenham Common

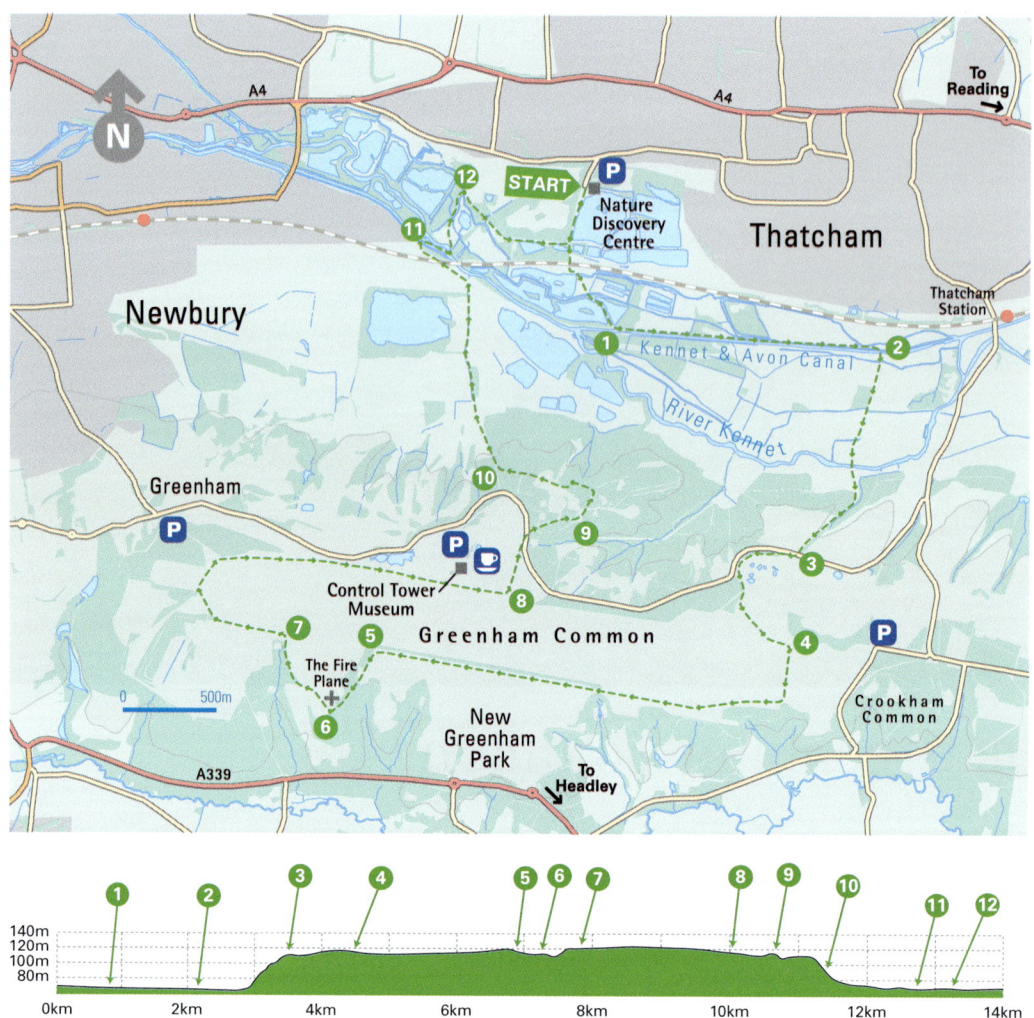

Route description

START From the parking area outside the Nature Discovery Centre, turn left (S) and follow the main track (Muddy Lane), or the paths parallel along the lake shore. After 270m you reach a crossroads, continue ahead on a footpath and cross the railway (careful!). 850m from the start, you reach the canal. ❶ Turn left (E) and follow the tow path footpath for 1.4km to a swing bridge across the canal. ❷ Cross the swing bridge and follow the bridleway track which leads S across the valley. After 600m it crosses the River Kennet and begins to ascend; after another 600m it reaches a road (Burys Bank Road) at the top of the hill. ❸ Cross the road and go through the gate signposted 'Greenham and Crookham Commons'. Turn right to follow the path leading W, parallel with the road. After 400m, the path bends SSE and leaves the road, shortly followed by a fork. Take the left fork (smaller path) and follow it for 300m to where it merges with a bigger path heading SE; follow this path (which circuits around the perimeter of the former runway). ❹ In another 200m the path forks, take the right fork which heads S to cross the former runway. After 300m this reaches a T junction, turn right (W) to follow the main track along the southern perimeter of

Greenham Common

the runway area for 2.1km, passing along the fence of Greenham Business Park. ❺ When you reach the end of the industrial park fence, turn left and follow various paths heading SSW for 400m until you reach the 'Fire Plane' (metal mock-up of a plane). ❻ Turn right at the plane to take the main path leading NW. This passes through trees and reaches the runway perimeter path after 500m. Turn left to follow this. ❼ Follow the runway perimeter path along the fence of the nuclear missile bunkers(!) and then follow it as it bends N and then E at the end of the runway. After 2km you reach the former runway control tower. Continue on the runway perimeter path another 300m (ignoring two more junctions) to a five-way junction beside a flag pole. Turn left onto the second of the two paths leading off left, the smaller path heading NE into the gorse. ❽ Follow the path for 300m until it reaches a road (Burys Bank Road) at a metal post. Cross the road and follow the tarmac track opposite. After 300m the track reaches a car park, with signs for Bowdown Woods Nature Reserve. ❾ Leave the car park by the path at the back, first exit on the left. Follow this path for 170m NE until you see a left turn, take this and follow it through woods and past a large house (on your left). 500m after the junction the path ends at a T junction with a footpath track, turn right (downhill) to follow this. ❿ Follow the footpath track for 2.4km, eventually joining a lane (Hambridge Lane) beside the canal, and passing under the railway. Shortly after this you'll see a footbridge over the canal, turn right to cross this. ⓫ Turn right (SE) and follow the tow path footpath for 170m past Bull's Lock and over a footbridge. Immediately after crossing the footbridge, turn sharp left onto the footpath across the River Kennet and follow this footpath upstream along the river. The footpath veers N away from the river and after 300m reaches a T junction with another footpath. ⓬ Turn right and follow this footpath (becomes a track) 700m to the crossroads which you passed back at the start. Turn left, the car park is 300m N.

Greenham Common Bunkers

The Fire Plane

Kennet and Avon Canal

Trip planning

Thatcham Nature Discovery Centre is on Muddy Lane, signposted off Lower Way. There is a free car park immediately on your left when you enter Muddy Lane, or continue 120m to park beside the Discovery Centre building (limited parking here).

If you just wish to run at Greenham Common, the free car park off Burys Bank Road beside the Control Tower RG19 8DB / SU 499 651 is the obvious place to start from, although it is closed early morning and around

Greenham Common

dusk. There are also free parking areas at Pyle Hill RG19 3BX / SU 484 652 (Burys Bank Road, western end of the Common) and Crookham RG19 8EJ / SU 524 645 (Crookham Hill, eastern end) which never close. The Nature Discovery Centre has a café and this lakeside location is a pleasant place to wind down after your run. The Control Tower is definitely worth investigating afterwards (or even during), with a community café and a free museum about Greenham Common's history, located upstairs in the tower.

Other routes

A run just around the former runway would be about 7km, extendable to c. 10km by following all the perimeter paths.

BBOWT publish a series of 'Wild Walks' which explore the Living Landscape. The first is largely incorporated within this route, the second is a 10km route visiting the River Enborne, further east. The routes can be downloaded from their website, or obtained as leaflets from the Discovery Centre or Control Tower.

The Kennet and Avon Canal's tow path offers a continuous 92km green trail, bridging Southern England from the River Thames to the River Avon. Notes about the K and A are found in *South West Trail Running*.

Events

A 5km parkrun is held at Greenham Common, every Saturday.

The Step Up 4 Good 10K is held by the Greenham Trust and follows a loop linking Greenham Common and Newbury Racecourse. Newbury Athletic Club organise the Roc Newbury 10K, 7km of which is off-road.

Newbury Racecourse is the location of a simultaneous 5K / 10K / Half Marathon event organised by RunThrough, although endlessly looping around a groomed racecourse might not be everyone's ideal of trail running freedom.

Saturn Running have run endurance events such as Runner of Azkaban, 7 hours continually looping around Greenham Common.

Greenham Common and the Cold War

In 1951, this RAF airfield was loaned to the US Air Force. In 1958 a plane carrying a nuclear bomb exploded on the runway; this allegedly released radiation over the local area. Greenham Common became a household name in 1980, when it housed 96 nuclear cruise missiles. A 'Women's Peace Camp' was set up outside in 1981, and remained there for 19 years. Their radical protests (such as encirclements of the base by up to 50,000 women) kept the tabloid newspapers happy with an endless supply of misogynistic reports. The last cruise missiles were removed by 1991, the base finally closed in 1993 and was designated in 1997 as public land.

Various Cold War relics can be seen while running; six bunkers designed to survive a nuclear blast lurk behind rows of barbed wire (the missiles would have been safe while everyone in West Berkshire was vaporised), the Control Tower has reopened as an excellent museum (and café) and the remarkable 'Fire Plane' (used for firefighting practice) is a listed monument! The Women's Peace Camp is memorialised by a Peace Garden near the entrance to Greenham Business Park, off the A339.

Lough Down 19

Lough Down

19 Lough Down

Distance	10km (6.5 miles)	Ascent	275m (870ft)
Map	OS Landranger 174 OS Explorer 159, 170		
Navigation ●●○	Barely deserves the second star, nothing can go wrong		
Terrain ●●●	Rough rooty trails, one very steep ascent		
Wet feet ●●○	Plenty squelchy enough in places		
Start / Finish	Lardon Chase National Trust car park RG8 9AF / SU 582 806		

Steep climbs above Goring Gap

Lough Down, where this route begins, boasts tremendous panoramic views of Goring Gap; this is the valley which opens up before you, with the River Thames squeezing between the towns of Goring and Streatley below. The Berkshire Downs end abruptly here; across the river to the east are the Chiltern Hills. Before the Anglian Glaciation (478,000 to 424,000 years ago), these chalk downs formed an unbroken barrier, redirecting the River Thames north-east. Glaciers dammed the river and a lake formed. Around 425,000 years ago the lake overtopped the downs and the River Thames burst through, gouging out Goring Gap and establishing its modern course to the sea. Running there today, you'll encounter no obvious hint of this epic catastrophe, just a bucolic backdrop of rolling hills and some rather steep gradients. You'll also encounter winding trails following ancient earthworks, beautiful hidden valleys and (if the author's experience is anything to go by), hundreds of scattering game birds, with an uncertain future.

19 Lough Down

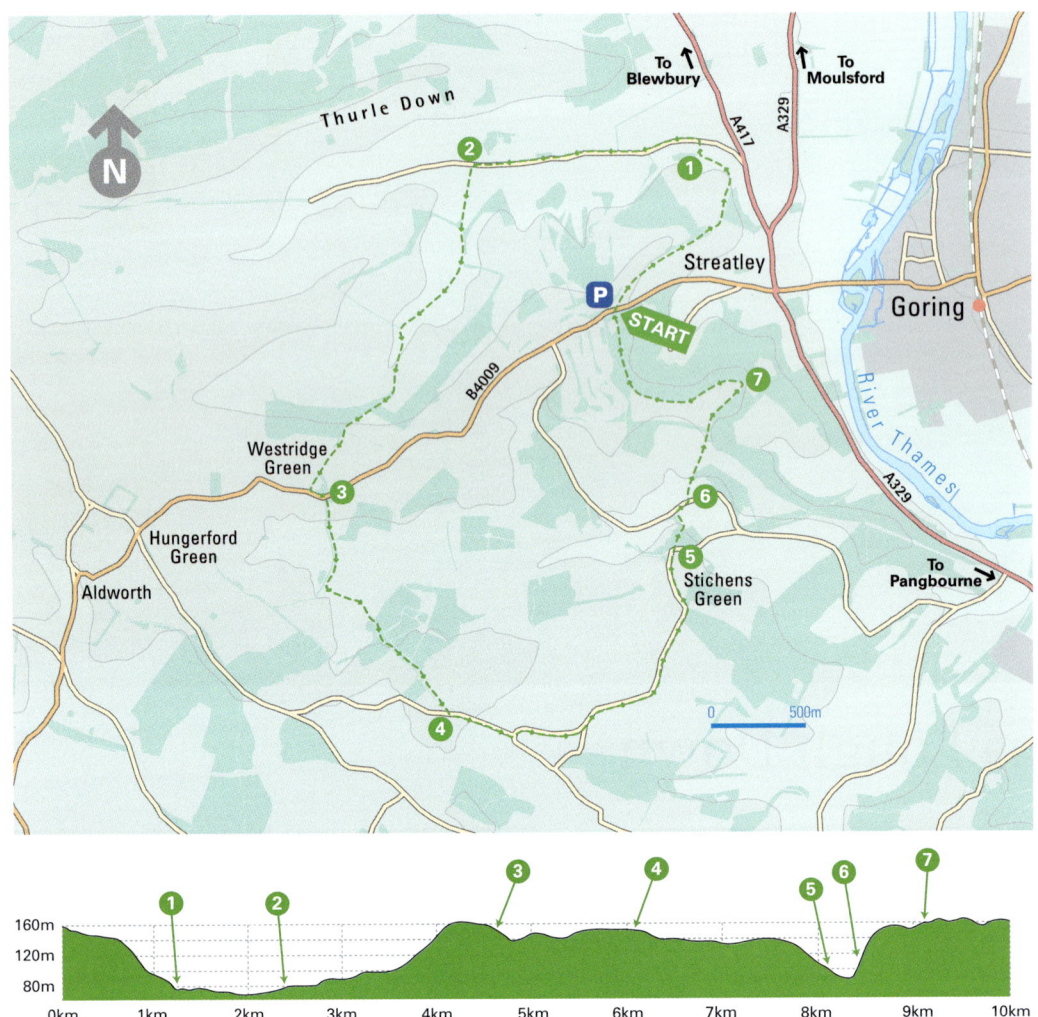

Route description

START Leave the car park by the gate at the rear (downhill) end and follow the path which leads NE along the uphill edge of the field. After 700m you reach a gate, pass through it into another field. Follow the path which leads steeply downhill (NNE) until you reach the downhill edge of the field. Turn left and follow the field boundary W until you reach a gate exiting the field beside a National Trust sign (there are many other gates but they lead into private gardens!). ❶ Pass through the NT gate and head downhill 60m to a lane (Rectory Road). Turn left (W) onto the lane (which is also the Ridgeway National Trail) and follow it for 1.1km to where a footpath track leads uphill on the left, just after passing Thurle Grange. ❷ Turn left (uphill, S, leaving the RNT) onto the footpath track and follow it for 2km until it ends at a road (after 1.3km the track splits at a woodland, the footpath is the left / more uphill track). Turn left onto the road (B4009) and follow it just 90m to where a footpath track leads off on the right. ❸ Turn right onto the footpath track and follow it for 1.5km, ignoring side turns, to where it joins a lane beside a cottage (it becomes a bridleway in the last 200m). Turn left (E) onto the lane. ❹ Follow the lane for 2km; bear left at the first

Lough Down

junction (after 400m) and also at the second junction (after 800m). After 2km the lane begins to descend steeply and just after passing a byway track signposted off on the left, the lane turns right; look for the footpath signposted on the left here, and turn off left to take it. ❺ Follow the footpath downhill through woods and along a field edge (steep) to a lane. Turn right onto the lane and follow it for 100m to where a footpath is signposted off on the left. Turn left onto the footpath. ❻ Ascend steeply along the footpath, reaching a gate entering Common Wood after 350m. Continue on the footpath into the woods until you reach a crossroads of tracks after 300m. ❼ Turn left at the crossroads and follow the track leading W beside open ground. After 700m this bends right (N) and then descends to pass through a gate before ascending again to reach the B4009. The car park is across the road.

Trip planning

The National Trust's Lardon Chase car park is free, located directly uphill from Streatley on the A4009. It's popular and not very big, don't arrive too late. If there is no space here, parking on one of the quiet lanes after ❹ might be possible, but it probably makes more sense just to park in Streatley and climb the steep bridleway beside the youth hostel, joining the route at ❼.

The Village Café in Goring is cheap and un-fancy; rare and valuable qualities in this part of the world. On the author's last visit however, they crossed a red line when they slathered his hotdog with cheese.

Other routes

Lough Down / Lardon Chase (they are effectively different sides of the same hill) is one of several local spots owned by the National Trust; there is also Common Wood (through which the latter part of this route passes) and Holies Hanging, a wooded coombe descending steeply into Streatley. All of these have open access and are ideal for a short run; see the NT website for more

Berkshire Downs

Common Wood

Mutton Copse

Goring Gap

19 Lough Down

Common Wood

info and route suggestions. Still on the National Trust theme, Basildon Park is just 3km south of Streatley; the landscaped estate around this stately home is good for a (far-from-flat) 5km circuit. Enter and park from the A340 south of Streatley, free to NT members.

See Route 26 for notes on running the Thames Path National Trail north of Goring and Streatley. To the south, the TP is a delightful 6km run (along the Goring bank) downstream to Pangbourne, however returning on the Streatley bank isn't practical without excessive road time.

Events

Centurion Running's Chiltern Wonderland 50 (don't be fooled by the name), is a 50-mile ultra-marathon following an epic loop from Goring, via Turville and Watlington (Routes 28 and 27) and returning along Grim's Ditch (Route 26). If that seems a bit tame, their truly demented Autumn 100 is four different 25-mile Chiltern loops out and back from Goring, run consecutively. If that still doesn't do it for you, Challenge Running's biennial Thames Ring 250 is – yes – a 250-mile loop from Goring. Oh, the humanity!

Goring to Avebury 20

The Ridgeway

20 Goring to Avebury

Distance	69km (43 miles)	Ascent	975m (3230ft)
Map	OS Landranger 173, 174 OS Explorer 157, 170		
Navigation	●●○ Almost entirely along the well-signposted Ridgeway National Trail		
Terrain	●●○ Roads, chalk trails, mild gradients, rutted byways (second * is for the ruts!)		
Wet feet	●●○ Add a star in winter, the Ridgeway's ruts fill with water		
Start	Goring and Streatley Railway Station RG8 0ER / SU 602 806		
Finish	Red Lion pub bus stop, Avebury SN8 1RF / SU 102 699		

Run the rolling rutted Ridgeway's remoter reaches

So, who is up for a 70km-ish ultra-run following an ancient trail along remote high ground, across three counties? You are, you just might not know it yet. *Any* motivated runner can aspire to complete this. Either tackle it in shorter sections bit by bit, take it on as a multiday fastpacking adventure, or just accept that you are going to have a very long day out which will inevitably include some walking and / or staggering; you are only human!* The western half of the Ridgeway National Trail was tailor-made for such an exceptional challenge. The navigation is simple, the gradients are mostly gentle and the overall ascent is pretty mild for the distance. Shuttling by public transport is quick and simple. Although the route is genuinely remote, with zero settlements (let alone shops or services) along the trail, roads cross intermittently, meaning that

* *If you really can run 43 miles non-stop, I bow before you.*

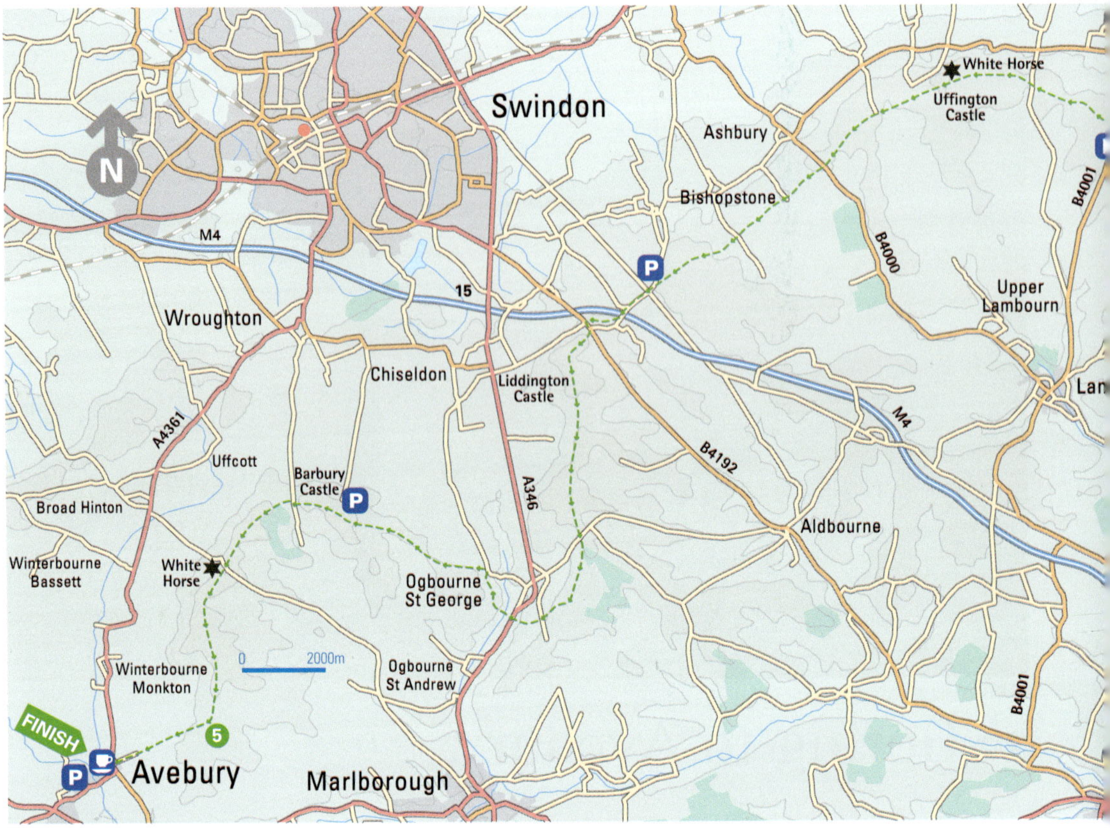

20 Goring to Avebury

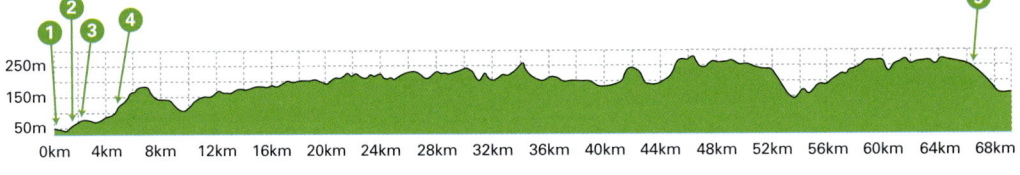

a support team can keep you fuelled up and motivated. There is a tangible goal to aim for; finishing at the centre of Europe's largest stone circle has got to count for something! The biggest physical challenge (beyond the distance) is the trail itself, which is straight but often rutted and uneven, requiring care ... and these ruts fill with water in winter, at which times only the certifiable would attempt this.
You know you want to, and you know you can.

Route description

START From the railway station entrance and car park, turn left (N) and follow Gatehampton Road. After 130m it merges with the B4526, and after another 110m it reaches the junction with B4009 High Street. ❶ Turn left (W) onto High Street and follow it over the railway. Continue ahead through the centre of Goring; after 570m, the Ridgeway National Trail joins from the right from Thames Road, continue ahead and cross the River Thames (via Goring and Streatley Bridge) into Streatley. Continue uphill along High St to reach a crossroads with Wallingford Road and Reading Road, 350m from the bridge. ❷ Turn right (N)

Goring to Avebury 20

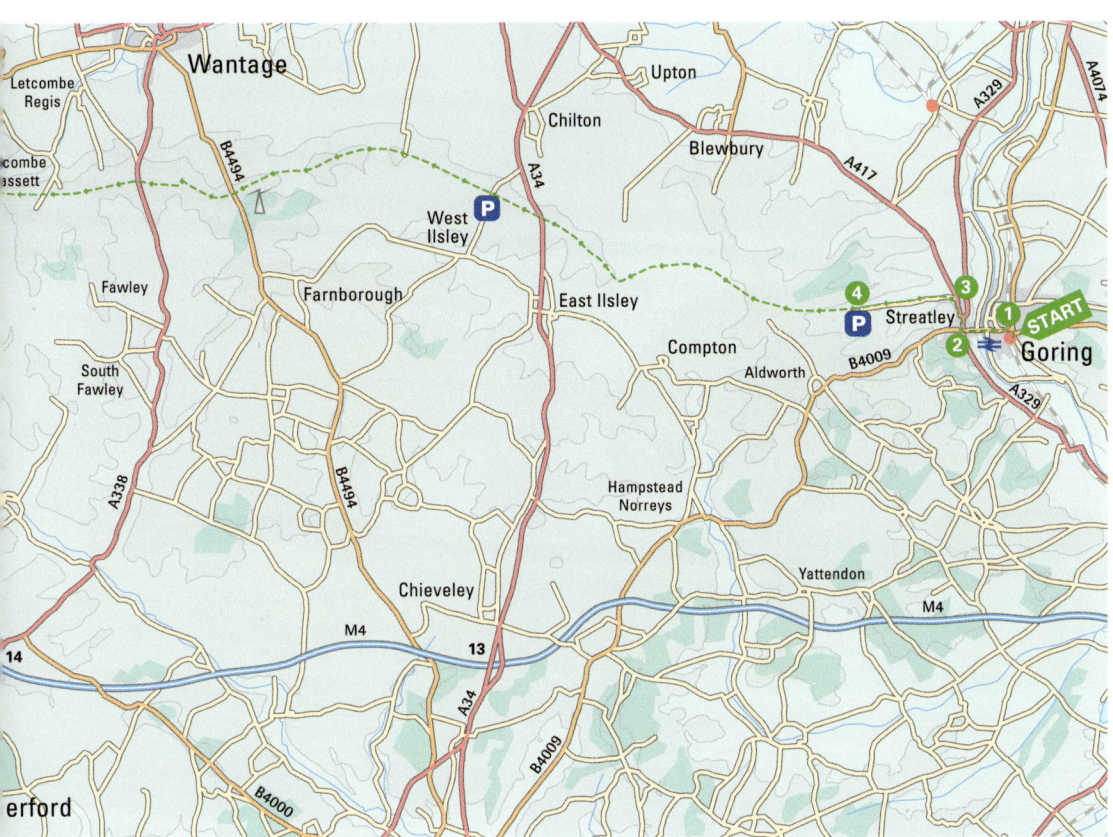

onto A329 Wallingford Road and follow it 300m to where Wantage Road turns off left. Turn left onto Wantage Road and follow it uphill for 400m to where Rectory Road turns off left. ❸ Turn left onto Rectory Road and follow it for 2.4km to where it ends at a parking area. ❹ Continue ahead on the RNT for 62km! The route is extremely well sign-posted. A few recognisable landmarks, measured from the parking area; tunnel under the A34 at 8.6km, Wantage Monument at 16km, Whitehorse Hill and Uffington Castle hillfort at 29.3km, bridge across the M4 at 39km, Barbury Castle hillfort at 54.8km. 7km after Barbury Castle hillfort (61.8km from the parking area), the RNT begins to descend, look out for where a bridleway joins the RNT from the left (with an entrance and sign to Fyfield Down National Nature Reserve) and a byway track turns off on the right. ❺ Turn right here (leaving the RNT) and follow the byway track downhill (WSW) for 2.4km into Avebury village; it becomes a tarmac lane (Green Street) for the last km to the A4361 road. The bus stop is beside the Red Lion pub.

Trip planning
Shuttling from Avebury to Goring by public transport is fairly simple, taking around two hours. The 49 or 42 bus goes to Swindon Bus Station, beside Swindon Railway Station. From here, take a train to Goring and Streatley Railway Station via Reading (for some irritating reason this generally involves changing at Reading, which is actually past Goring). Of course, you need to check transport times beforehand, but the last bus will certainly have left Avebury by 8 pm. For this reason (and also the fact that negotiating public

20 Goring to Avebury

The Ridgeway

transport might be the last thing you want to do after your big run), consider parking at Avebury and shuttling across to the start *before* your run.

If shuttling by driving, it is about 75 minutes between the two points. There is expensive parking beside Goring and Streatley Railway Station, otherwise head north a short distance along the B4009 Wallingford Road and find a space on a residential side street. There is a large National Trust car park SN8 1QT / **SU 099 696** at Avebury (free to members), just off the A4361 and well signposted.

Here are some suggested access points (with parking), with distance from the previous suggested access point, where you might start or finish a selected section, or where a support crew might meet you (and anyone else daft enough to have been dragged along); Bury Lane RG20 7AY / **SU 479 840**, just off the A35 (14.5km from the start); B4001 RG17 8UB / **SU 343 850**, north of Lambourn (14.5km); B4192 SN4 0DR / **SU 232 814**, 70m NE of The Burj restaurant, along lane (13.3km); Barbury Castle car park SN4 0QH / **SU 157 760**, signposted off the B4005, east of Wroughton (16km, 10.5km from the finish).

Give some thought to what food and gear you will need along this journey; there are no shops or cafés after Goring! One difficulty (if unsupported) is finding water; the *Ridgeway* map from Harvey Maps helpfully flags up the (very limited) locations of taps along the trail.

Should you choose to ditch an attempt, dropping off the Ridgeway to the north is usually the shorter option to get you to a village or main road.

Having crossed Berkshire, Oxfordshire and Wiltshire to reach Avebury, it's perhaps a bit perverse to immediately

Middlehill Down

Goring to Avebury

leave this remarkable village and stone circle. If you can somehow factor time and energy into your plans for a wander around, do so! The National Trust Visitor Centre (and café) are a good starting point.

Approaching the Wantage Monument

Other routes

Route 63 in *South West Trail Running* tours the highlights of the incredible prehistoric landscape around Avebury. If you arrive at Avebury and still feel fresh, you may wish to be aware of the 58km / 36-mile Great Stones Way, which leads south from Barbury Castle, past Avebury (yes, you've already done the first bit) and on to Stonehenge and then Old Sarum near Salisbury.

River Thames at Goring

Events

See below.

The Ridgeway National Trail

This prehistoric road follows the high ground for 140km / 87 miles west between Ivinghoe Beacon in Hertfordshire and The Sanctuary at Avebury in Wiltshire. The 71km of the Ridgeway east of the Thames are quite varied in terrain and surface; there are many challenging hilly sections in the wooded Chiltern Hills, while easier parts merge with the lower-lying Icknield Way Trail (see page 170). The Ridgeway crosses the River Thames at Goring Gap and the western half is characterised by long straight trails following rolling, grassy ridgetops with mild ascents and descents; Route 20 has this western half covered; all of it! Routes 19, 20, 22, 26, 27, 29, 30, 31 and 32 all utilise some part of the Ridgeway National Trail.

The Trail Running Association hold the Ridgeway Challenge, covering the entire Ridgeway; this solo event is also the UK Ultra Distance Trail Running Championship. The author once completed this, but don't be too impressed; it took 22 hours. A less extreme variant is the Race to the Stones, clocking in at a mere 100km. This event can be completed in stages, has a 'festival' feel and was voted the UK's 'best endurance event' in 2016. XNRG's Druid's Challenge breaks the Ridgeway up over three days and Marlborough Running Club organises the Ridgeway Relay, a team relay race along the entire Ridgeway. There is also the LDWA's Ridgeway 40 (miles, from Avebury to Goring).

20 Goring to Avebury

Avebury

River Thames from Winter Hill

21 Winter Hill

Distance		15km (9.5 miles) Ascent 125m (410ft)
Map		OS Landranger 175 OS Explorer 172
Navigation	●●●	Mostly on the well-signposted Thames Path National Trail
Terrain	●●●	Mostly mild trails, a short climb at the end
Wet feet	●●●	Plenty of mud along the river banks
Start / Finish		Winter Hill car park SL6 9TU / SU 871 861

Meadows and woodland which inspired 'The Wind in the Willows'

This River Thames-centric run starts from Cookham Dean, where Kenneth Grahame wrote *The Wind in the Willows* in 1908. The story was set in a riverine Arcadia inspired by the surrounding landscape; over a century later, it's still possible to experience a glimpse of this when running early morning through Quarry Wood (Grahame's 'Wild Wood') or along undeveloped stretches of river bank. Albeit, with fewer talking animals.

As with most of the River Thames, it's constantly engaging and much lusher than you might perhaps imagine. Winter Hill is the start point, its flanks shrouded by the beeches of Quarry Wood. Down at river level, the footbridge across the river at Temple Lock (named for the Templar Knights who owned a mill here) gives a good view of Winter Hill before you follow the Thames Path National Trail downstream. You're now several metres into Buckinghamshire, but don't tell anyone. Landmarks along the river include

Winter Hill

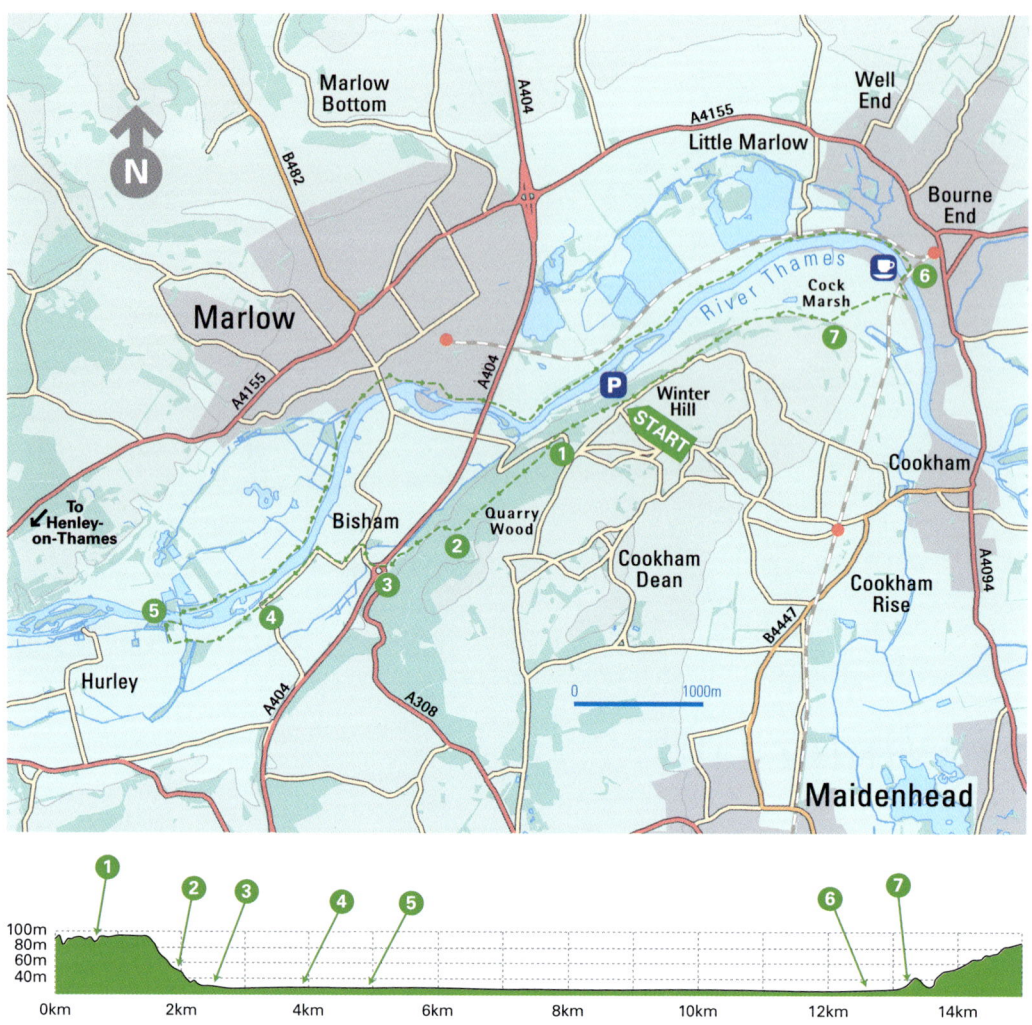

Bisham Abbey (now the National Sports Centre), beautiful Bisham Church, the town of Marlow (look out for the statue of Sir Steve Redgrave) and the extensive meadows approaching Bourne End. At Bourne End, you cross the river back into Berkshire and make your way across the ancient unploughed pasture of Cock Marsh (named for the archaeologist who excavated the burial mounds here) towards Winter Hill.

Route description

START Head SW along the road (Winter Hill Road) from the car park, to the junction with Startins Lane. Turn right onto the footpath on the opposite side of the road, which leads behind a house. Follow the footpath ahead for 600m to reach a road (Quarry Wood Road), bearing right when the footpath forks, halfway. ❶ Cross the road and take the footpath ascending on the other side, beside a 'Quarry Wood' sign. After 50m the footpath merges with a permissive bridleway, continue ahead (SW) through Quarry Wood on the bridleway (following blue posts) for a kilometre to where the bridleway ends at a T junction with a bridleway track leading uphill / downhill. ❷ Turn right onto the bridleway track and descend steeply. After

Winter Hill

200m you reach a 5-way junction, follow the signposted restricted byway, continuing downhill. This ends at a track leading past houses, and you reach a roundabout on the A404 after 600m. ❸ Cross the A404 (carefully!) and follow the path around the roundabout to take Marlow Road, on the far side. Follow Marlow Road for 200m and then turn off left onto Temple Lane. Continue for 1km on Temple Lane, around two sharp corners past the National Sports Centre, to the village of Temple. When the lane bends sharp left in the village (becoming Bradenham Lane), do not follow it, instead continue on the lane straight ahead. ❹ The lane becomes a footpath track leading past mansions(!). After 800m the footpath reaches open fields and there is a footpath leading off on the right. Turn right to take this footpath and follow it to the River Thames. ❺ Turn right (E) and follow the Thames Path National Trail, which you will continue on for 8km. Immediately, you cross Temple Footbridge. After 2.7km, you are signposted through the town of Marlow, passing behind the spired church. After 8km, you reach Bourne End Railway Bridge. ❻ Cross the river by the footbridge beside Bourne End Railway Bridge, still following the TP. Pass under the railway at the far side, following the TP, then turn right (leaving the river and TP) and pass under the railway again through an arch, to reach Cock Marsh. Cross Cock Marsh (open grassland) by the obvious path leading WSW towards Winter Hill. After 500m this crosses a boggy stretch via a raised walkway, to reach the base of Winter Hill. ❼ Turn right (W) to follow the footpath track which leads along the base of the hill. After 400m, a footpath track branches off on the left, leading uphill. Take this track, after 900m it reaches Winter Hill Road. Turn right and follow the road for 500m to the car park.

Bisham Church

Cock Marsh and Winter Hill

Marlow

Trip planning

Parking at the start on Winter Hill Road is free. Starting from Marlow is another possibility, with plenty of (distinctly un-free) parking options.

Marlow, a few minutes' drive from Winter Hill, is the obvious place to head for shops, food and all other needs. However, the Bounty at Bourne End is well worth going out of your way to find. This popular riverside pub can only be accessed on foot, by crossing the footbridge at ❻ after parking in Bourne End. In fact, it's close enough to the end of the route to consider an early finish here. Just stay off the pop, you still have Winter Hill to climb afterwards.

The National Trust manage much of Winter Hill and Cock Marsh.

Winter Hill

Other routes

A worthwhile 3km extension is to continue following the TP as far as Cookham Bridge after crossing the river at ⑥ and to loop back to Cock Marsh via the 'inland' footpath. Downstream of Cookham is 4km of the TP where the stately home of Cliveden looks down upon Cliveden Reach, among the loveliest scenes on the whole river. There isn't a decent alternative return route, so you'd have to run out and back. Separately visiting the National Trust Cliveden Estate and running within the grounds might be more satisfying.

The 11km of the Thames upstream of Temple Lock to Henley-on-Thames are simply stunning, with highlights including the islands of Hurley Lock, the restored mill at Hambleden and Temple Island (start line of the Henley Regatta races). It's around 12km one way on the TP, with the possibility to return on footpaths following the opposite (northern) bank by incorporating some awkward road time. The only spot to cross the river and cut the loop shorter is Hambleden Lock, 4km downstream of Henley. Note that rare free riverside parking can be had at Aston, near Henley RG9 3DH / **SU 787 845**.

The Cookham Bridleway Circuit is signposted locally. This 18km route was marked out with horse riding in mind, but will suit trail runners just as well. Details can be found online.

Events

The Water of Life Marlow to Henley Half Marathon and 10K heads along the TP and overlaps some of this route.

Just upstream, Henley hosts various events such as the Henley Trail Run (5km or 10km), the Henley Half Marathon and 10K (along the TP), and the Temple Trail (a hilly 50km ultra which passes through this route).

The Thames Path National Trail

Routes 21, 23 and 25 incorporate parts of the Thames Path National Trail. This follows Britain's most famous river for 296km / 184 miles downstream from its source in the Cotswolds to the Thames Barrier. The first 40km of the TP is described in *South West Trail Running*. Given that the Thames winds right through the heart of Southern England (Churchill called it, *"the golden thread of our nation's history"*), the potential for engaging and beautiful riverside runs is pretty much endless. Runners might also be tempted by the fact that this National Trail is relatively flat!

Inevitably, various race events utilise the TP for ultra-distance masochism. T184 (T Series Racing) and the Thames Challenge (Ultrarunning Ltd) both tackle the entire National Trail; the former ending and the latter starting at the source. The T184 offers a relay option and the Thames Challenge divides up the 184 miles over four days. Centurion Running's offering is the Thames Path 100, 100 miles from London to Oxford. Go Beyond's Thames Trot Ultra (Oxford to Henley) seems barely worth mentioning, clocking in at a mere 50 miles.

Oxfordshire

Here in the South East's north-west(!), Oxfordshire's lush countryside offers plenty of variation of trail running experiences. The engaging landscaped park at Blenheim Palace, the River Thames' lush meadows and the prehistoric Ridgeway's downlands all feature in this chapter. The Ridgeway stretches along the high ground of the southern part of the county, following the Berkshire Downs (part of the North Wessex Downs Area of Outstanding Natural Beauty) to the west of the Thames, and the Chiltern Hills Area of Outstanding Natural Beauty to the east. All of these routes bear reminders of the past, from stately homes and commemorative columns, to earthen hillforts and mysterious chalk figures.

Newbridge (Route 23)

The Ridgeway

The Uffington White Horse 22

Uffington White Horse

22 The Uffington White Horse

Distance	15km (9 miles)	**Ascent**	225m (770ft)
Map	OS Landranger 174 OS Explorer 170		
Navigation	●●○	Well signposted, care needed on the farmland section	
Terrain	●●○	Chalk tracks, grasslands, agricultural land	
Wet feet	●●○	Depends if the farmer has been ploughing …	
Start / Finish	White Horse Hill car park SN7 7QJ / SU 293 865		

Prehistoric Ridgeway splendour

Here at the South East's north-west extremity(!) is a landscape redolent with our ancient past. Whitehorse Hill, the highest point in Oxfordshire, is surrounded by an array of mysterious monuments. Uffington Castle, the hillfort at the summit, overlooks the incredible Uffington White Horse, etched into the chalk hillside amidst numerous burial mounds. The prehistoric Ridgeway track links to nearby Wayland's Smithy, a huge chambered tomb. From this commanding position on the Berkshire Downs*, these sites gaze down upon the Vale of White Horse, with six counties visible to the horizon.
Running among, around, atop and below this landscape is an almost overwhelming experience.

*This part of Oxfordshire was in Berkshire until 1974, and although the borders have shifted, the hills have not.

The Uffington White Horse

Route description

START Leave the car park at the NE (downhill) end and take the path leading E around the hill towards the White Horse. After 500m this reaches a lane (Dragonhill Road), cross this and continue ahead on the bridleway leading uphill towards the hillfort (Uffington Castle). When you reach the hillfort, follow the bridleway along the earthworks to the trig point and then continue 150m S to a T junction with the Ridgeway National Trail. ❶ Turn left onto this byway and follow it E, ignoring two footpaths and one permissive footpath turning off on the left. After 1.8km, turn left off the RNT onto a footpath (chalk track) on the left and follow this downhill for 700m to the B4507 road. ❷ Cross the road and continue downhill on the footpath opposite. Follow this N across a field, through an orchard, across another field and then 130m NE across another to reach a lane (Fawler Road). ❸ Turn left (downhill) onto the lane and follow it for 400m to a footpath off on the left, signposted for Woolstone. Follow the footpath W along six successive fields to reach a lane (Broad Way) after 1.7km. Turn right and follow the lane just 25m N before turning off left onto a footpath and continuing W. Cross four successive fields to reach another lane (Woolstone Road) after 900m. ❹ Turn left

The Uffington White Horse

The Vale of White Horse

Wayland's Smithy Long Barrow

(SW) onto the lane and follow it through Woolstone village (it becomes Marsh Way), bearing right at the junction just before the White Horse Inn, so you pass the inn on your left. When the lane bends hard right, continue ahead onto the footpath signposted ahead. ❺ The footpath crosses two fields and reaches a byway track (Hardwell Lane) after 400m. Cross the byway and continue on the footpath ahead around two fields, reaching a lane after 750m. ***The author once found the first field blocked by tall maize, in such cases head 575m N along the byway and then follow the footpath on the left across three fields to the lane*** ❻ Cross the lane and follow the bridleway which leads 300m through woods to join another lane. Continue ahead 60m (past a sign for Compton Beauchamp) along the lane. Pass the gates of Compton House (mansion) and take the tarmac drive to the right of the mansion entrance, this is a footpath. ❼ Follow the footpath past the church and uphill. It passes along at least five successive fields before you reach buildings (Odstone Farm) and a bridleway track leads off to the left (SE). ❽ Turn left and take the bridleway track past the farm uphill to the B4507 road. Cross the road and take the byway path leading uphill signposted 'D'arcy Dalton Way' (NOT the parallel chalk farm track). The byway is narrow and merges at the top of the hill with the chalk track, continue ahead on this for 550m to a crossroads with the RNT byway. ❾ Turn left onto the RNT and follow it NE. After 300m, detour on the left to visit Wayland's Smithy Long Barrow. After another 1.6km on the RNT, a crossroads is reached. ❿ Turn left at the crossroads, leaving the RNT. After 350m a tarmac lane (Dragonhill Lane) is reached. Go through the gate across the lane and head N along the field for 250m to reach the car park.

The Uffington White Horse

Trip planning

White Horse Hill car park is free to National Trust and English Heritage members. Non-NT / EH folk wishing to park for free could instead start from the village of Woolstone ④, perhaps parking near the White Horse Inn on Marsh Way SN7 7QL / **SU 293 878**. As they took the trouble to name their pub after the reason you're here, it would be rude not to patronise the establishment after running.

Does someone *very important* live in Compton Beauchamp? Rather unsettlingly, the author was followed right through this village by a slowly-moving black car with blacked out windows ... a window wound down, to reveal a man in shades and ear piece, bodyguard style. Answers on a postcard ...

Other routes

If you don't fancy the lower part of this route (mostly crossing agricultural fields) or want to avoid the steep climb onto the ridge, simply running out and back on the Ridgeway National Trail and around the National Trust's land on Whitehorse Hill is a perfectly pleasant alternative. Remember to turn around at some point, the RNT is 140km long (see page 115)!

A longer (c. 22km) variation on this route (but with an easier gradient) is to start from Lambourn to the south and ascend to and descend from the Ridgeway by any of the various bridleways and byways that cross the Lambourn Downs.

Route 20 passes over Whitehorse Hill, see the description for more detail about the RNT to the east and west. 9km to the west, the RNT reaches Liddington Castle (another hillfort) and then Route 65 in *South West Trail Running*.

Events

The Ridgeway Run is a 5- or 10-mile race from Ashbury and along the Ridgeway, past the monuments.

Prehistoric Uffington

It's easy to visualise all of these prehistoric monuments as part of the same story, but that is probably a mistake; they span three millennia before the birth of Christ! Uffington Castle is youngest, dating from the early Iron Age (8th Century BC), while the White Horse has been carbon dated to 1380 BC in the Bronze Age. Wayland's Smithy long barrow is named after a Saxon god, but actually dates from c. 3590 BC! Around 150 similar chambered tombs survive across southern England, Britain's oldest known architectural form.

The White Horse is a complete mystery. It is 111m long, formed by deep trenches cut into the chalk. It overlooks Dragon Hill, a flat-topped but natural 10m mound. This in turn overlooks the Manger, a remarkable dry valley with rippled sides known as the Giant's Steps, caused by melting permafrost at the end of the last Ice Age. What the horse is for, and how it relates to the surrounding monuments and dramatic landscape, is anyone's guess.

23 Chimney Meadows

Duxford Ford

23 Chimney Meadows

Distance	14km (8.5 miles)	Ascent	25m (80ft)
Map	OS Landranger 164 OS Explorer 180		
Navigation ● ● ●	Well signposted trails, partly along the Thames Path National Trail		
Terrain ● ● ●	Mostly flat clear trails, some rough meadow surfaces and rooty riverside trails		
Wet feet ● ● ●	Riverside trails get muddy, more crucially you are going to wade through two fords!		
Start / Finish	Chimney Meadows Nature Reserve car park OX18 2EH / SP 353 012		

Wading across the Thames

It may seem odd to describe the River Thames as being wild or remote, but it certainly can be; this route, despite looping around largely agricultural land, will hopefully convince you. It explores a landscape only accessible by foot, around Chimney Meadows Nature Reserve. At its heart is uninhabited Shifford Island, created in 1896–7 when the man-made Shifford Lock Cut channel was dug to bypass a loop in the Thames. The lock keeper at Shifford was self-sufficient until the 1950s! The Thames' various channels need to be crossed repeatedly, as well as the Great Brook and River Windrush. Usually there is a bridge, on two occasions there isn't! There is no getting away from it ... you are going to get wet feet on this outing.

23 Chimney Meadows

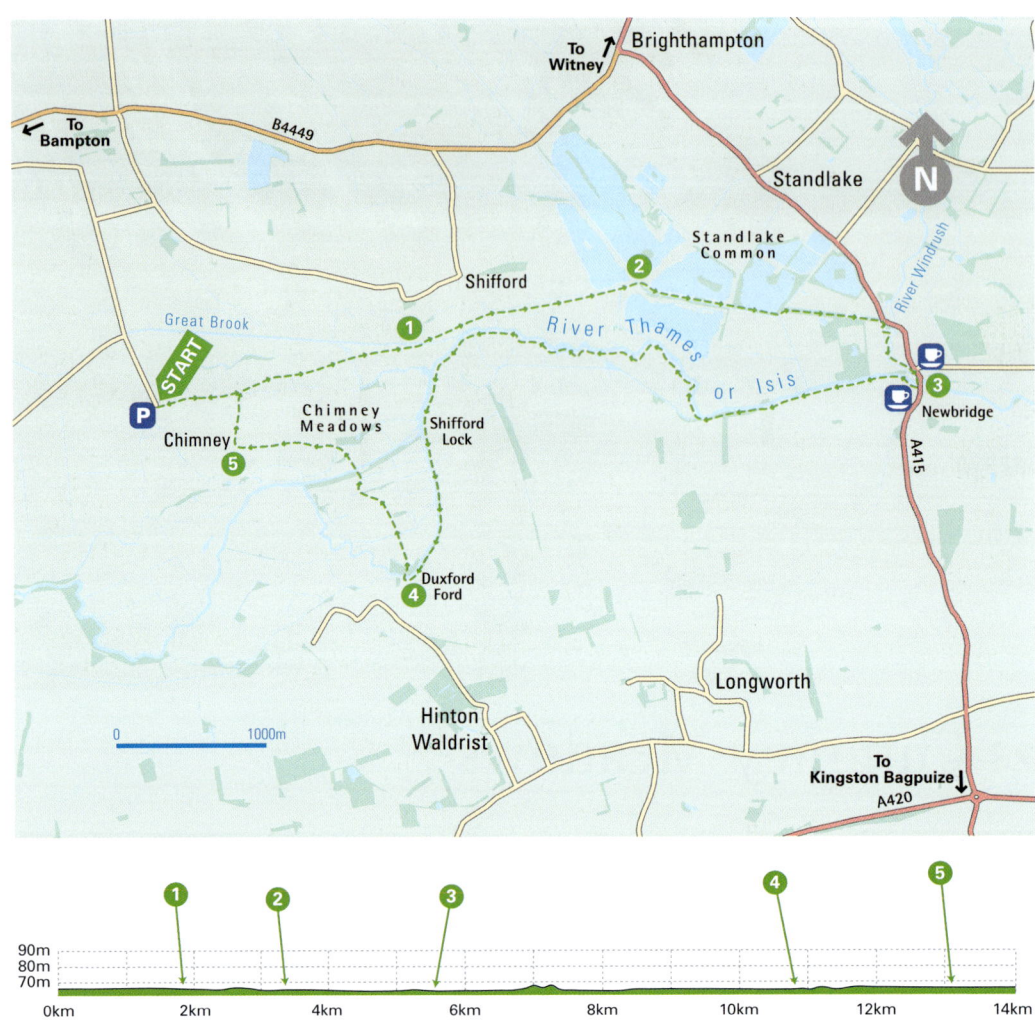

Route description

START From the car park, continue 550m E along the lane to a sharp right bend. Don't go around the bend, instead continue straight ahead by passing through the gate to join the footpath signposted 'Standlake 3 via ford'. Follow the footpath for 1.3km E across three large meadows. The footpath reaches a stream (Great Brook) two-thirds of the way along the N edge of the third meadow. ❶ Cross the stream via the ford and continue following the footpath for another 1.4km E through three more large meadows; the footpath follows the N edge of the third meadow and then enters a tunnel of trees, becoming a byway path. After 100m a footpath leads off on the right. ❷ Turn right onto the footpath and follow it for 1.6km (midway it bends left, then right) until it reaches a road (A415). Don't go onto the road, instead turn right to follow the footpath which leads off S here. This reaches and follows the River Windrush, crossing via a footbridge next to a pillbox, and reaching the road again after 600m. ❸ Turn right onto the road and cross the River Thames via the road bridge (Newbridge). Pass the Maybush Inn and immediately after, turn right (W) onto the Thames Path National Trail footpath. Follow the TP through the pub buildings and upstream

Chimney Meadows 23

Newbridge

along the S shore of the River Thames; after 4.2km the river splits at a weir. The TP crosses a branch of the river via a footbridge here, but don't cross. Continue following the footpath along the riverbank S for 1.1km until it ends at a bridleway, leading S away from the river. ❹ Do not continue ahead away from the river, turn right (N) onto the bridleway, which crosses the river via a ford (Duxford Ford). Cross the ford and continue N on the bridleway track; after 900m it crosses the main channel of the River Thames (Shifford Lock Cut) via a footbridge, it then bends left (W) and after 1.8km reaches the end of a lane. ❺ Follow the lane for 900m back to the car park.

Ford across Great Brook

Trip planning

Chimney Meadows Nature Reserve car park is signposted alongside an unnamed lane which is the continuation of Bull Lane in nearby Aston. There is no charge. Entrance to Chimney Meadows Nature Reserve is free. There are no facilities.

How about those fords? They should normally involve no consequences worse than wet trail shoes; however if the Thames or Great Brook are flowing at a high level, then they may be dangerous or impassable. If Great Brook ❶ looks dodgy, there is no alternative other than to retrace your steps back to the start. If Duxford Ford

Shifford Lock

Chimney Meadows

Chimney Meadows

is too high, backtrack 1.1km along the footpath to the footbridge you previously passed, and cross this; follow the TP for 450m to the bridge across Shifford Lock Cut between ❹ and ❺.

Being out in the sticks, there are no shops or amenities on hand. Two very fine historic pubs are located beside Newbridge ❸ however, the Rose Revived and the Maybush. Oxford, Abingdon and Witney are all only about 10km away.

Other routes

The Thames Path upstream of here to Lechlade is just glorious; 20km following the winding infant river, with only occasional interludes from the outside world when road bridges are reached. Returning via alternative footpaths is possible. The 6km downstream of Newbridge to Bablock Hythe are similar to those in this route (but no fords!), however the TP then leaves the river for a few km before normal service is resumed as far as Oxford, reached 20km from Newbridge.

Chimney Meadows Nature Reserve

Chimney Meadows Nature Reserve is the largest run by Berks, Bucks & Oxon Wildlife Trust, at 308 hectares. It stretches for about four kilometres along the north bank of the Thames to just after Shifford Lock, also including Shifford Island on the opposite bank. The site of a former farm, Chimney Meadows is home to a wide range of species: roe deer hide among the trees, bats roost in pillboxes, wildflowers bloom in the ancient meadows and little egret, little grebe and kingfisher thrive in the wetlands.

Blenheim Palace

Blenheim Palace

24 Blenheim Palace

Distance	9.5km (6 miles)	**Ascent** 175m (540ft)
Map	OS Landranger 164 OS Explorer 180	
Navigation ● ● ●	Stern estate signs deter you from going off-piste	
Terrain ● ● ●	Gravel trails, tarmac, grass. The mildest of mild inclines	
Wet feet ● ● ●	Part of Shakespeare's Way becomes a stream in winter	
Start / Finish	Park Street, Woodstock OX20 1SW / SP 443 167	

Quiet estate trails around Churchill's birthplace

Blenheim Palace is a jaw-droppingly vast Baroque mansion, built 1705–22 for the 1st Duke of Marlborough and named in honour of his military success at the 1704 Battle of Blenheim. It is better known in recent times as the ancestral home of Winston Churchill. This makes for a rather impressive backdrop to this easy but engaging trail run, which takes advantage of the public rights of way crossing the current (12th) Duke of Marlborough's front lawn. The route outlined here explores both the formal landscape of Blenheim Park overlooked by the palace (part of a UNESCO World Heritage Site) and the surrounding estate, which is surprisingly quiet and unvisited.

24 Blenheim Palace

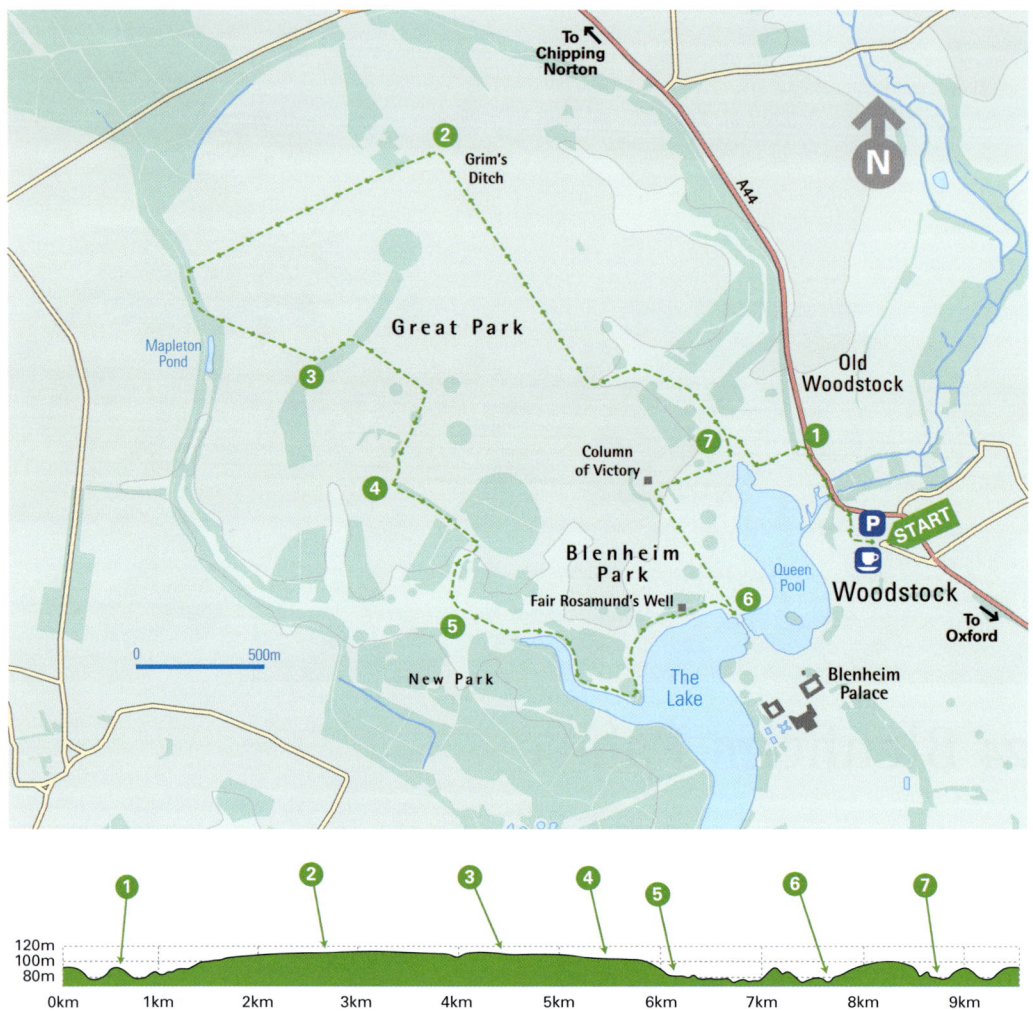

Route description

START Head W along Park Street (ascending house numbers) for 70m, then turn right into Chaucer's Lane. After 60m the lane bends right, continue ahead on the path which descends down steps. At the bottom of the steps you reach the A44 Oxford Street. Turn left and follow the A44 for 300m to where Manor Road turns off on the left. Turn left and follow Manor Road 30m to its end. Pass through the gate at the end of the road into Blenheim Park. ❶ Follow the footpath downhill for 100m to where it reaches a tarmac bridleway track. Turn right onto the bridleway track and follow it for 1.9km uphill, around a right bend (it becomes a footpath track, no visible change though) and dead straight ahead (NW) to the second gate (and cattle grid) it passes through. Don't pass through the gate, instead turn left onto the footpath which crosses here. ❷ Follow the footpath ahead (WSW), passing alongside several fields. After 1.1km the footpath enters woods and crosses a track; turn left here onto the footpath track and follow this downhill. After 180m the footpath bends left away from the track and leaves the woods, crossing fields to reach a T junction with another track after 500m. ❸ Turn left onto this footpath track and follow it for 170m to a

Blenheim Palace

crossroads of tracks. The footpath turns right (signs forbid any other direction) and leaves the tracks. Follow the footpath around the edge of a field (ignoring the footpath which turns off to the left) to Park Farm, where it becomes a tarmac track. This footpath track bends left at the farm, keep following it. ❹ Follow the footpath track for 400m to a 3-way junction. Turn sharp right (downhill) and descend along the footpath track. ❺ When you reach the valley floor, turn left off the footpath track to follow a signposted path downhill along the valley floor. After 230m this path joins a footpath and reaches a lake ('The Lake'). Follow the footpath along the N shore of the lake for 1.3km until you reach the Grand Bridge. ❻ Turn away from the bridge to face the Column of Victory; go through a gate onto the grass and ascend directly towards the column. 50m before the column, a (barely visible) footpath crosses your route. Turn right and descend on the footpath down to the tarmac track along the lake shore (Queen Pool). Pass through the gate onto this tarmac track and head 100m left to a junction beside a ruined house. ❼ Turn right at the junction and follow this bridleway track 170m, back to the footpath you entered the park along. Turn left (uphill) onto this footpath and retrace your route back to Park Street.

Trip planning

This route is described from Park Street, in the town of Woodstock. There is free roadside parking here. Check the signs, some areas are restricted for time of day and suchlike. Failing that, try Union Street car park OX20 1JF / SP 446 168.

Woodstock has various eating opportunities, but the Park Street parking happens to be directly outside the Bear Hotel, which can offer posh or bar food, as suits. It's a 'Macdonald' hotel, but has no relation to the burger chain!

A visit to Blenheim Palace itself could probably occupy a whole separate day. It isn't cheap (especially if you

The Column of Victory

Shakespeare's Way

Great Park

Wychwood Way

Blenheim Palace

have a family), but it's a memorable place to soak up. Highlights include the Palace State Rooms and the Churchill Exhibition, as well as the opportunity to explore the Formal Gardens; check out the Temple of Diana, where Winston proposed to his wife.

Other routes

A number of footpaths make it possible to shorten this route; for example, the footpath which leads off left, about 1.3km after ❶ will lop 2.5km off. An interesting out and back 4km extension is to follow the footpath track across the valley (S) and uphill at ❺, to cross the high park and reach the ornamental waterfall at The Lake's outflow.

The signposted Oxfordshire Way passes through the park, and is part of this route after ❷. Following it W gives the possibility of expanding the loop, turning left (S) onto a bridleway after 3km and following this and a lane 2km until you reach the Wychwood Way, which leads back to the park in another 4.5km.

A map of park trails is downloadable from the Blenheim Palace website, with distances up to the 8km Park Perimeter trail.

The Grand Bridge

Events

The Blenheim 7K loops around the palace and Great Lake, with alternative distances for buggies, wheelchair users and children. The Rotary Blenheim 10K and 5K Run follows a similar route. The British Heart Foundation Blenheim Palace Half Marathon, 10K and Family Fun Run start right in front of the palace and follow trails (often tarmac) around the estate.

Tough Runner UK's Oxfordshire Epic 10K is held in the grounds of nearby Cornbury Park.

The Lake

Blenheim Park

Running the grounds of Blenheim Palace gives you the opportunity to 'read' this artificial landscape and consider what each element was intended to achieve. The park was first designed by Sir John Vanbrugh, architect of the palace. The 41m-high Column of Victory was placed in front of the palace, connected by a line of elm trees. Vanbrugh's Grand Bridge was not loved by all; this vast edifice had 30 rooms(!) and crossed the River Glyme, a tiny stream. When Lancelot 'Capability' Brown (see page 280) was commissioned to re-landscape Blenheim Park in 1764, he remodelled the entire landscape in his typical style; hills were artificially created, clumps of trees positioned and the River Glyme dammed to create a series of snaking lakes and waterfalls, flooding the Grand Bridge to a depth where it didn't look quite so daft.

25 Wittenham Clumps

Round Hill

Distance	7km (4.5 miles)	Ascent	100m (330ft)
Map	OS Landranger 164 OS Explorer 170		
Navigation	•••	Nothing can go wrong	
Terrain	•••	Grassy and stony trails, short steep ascents	
Wet feet	•••	Thames Path can get puddly	
Start / Finish	Bridge End car park OX10 7JP / SU 578 940		

An airy dash around a Thames beauty spot

Their outline is unmistakable; a pair of rounded hills rising over the River Thames, topped by wooded crowns. These are the Wittenham Clumps, also known as the Sinodun Hills and sometimes the Berkshire Bubs or Mother Dunch's Buttocks(!). The western top is Round Hill and the eastern top is Castle Hill, recognisable by its Iron Age hillfort. This popular beauty spot overlooks an idyllic bend in the river and enjoys spectacular views of the surrounding countryside (recently improved by the demolition of Didcot Power Station's cooling towers).

This route takes you from Dorchester through the impressive 'Dyke Hills', a pair of huge earthworks which once enclosed an Iron Age settlement. You cross the river at Day's Lock and Weir, whose claim to fame is having hosted the World Pooh Sticks Championships! The ascent through Little Wittenham Wood (an

25 Wittenham Clumps

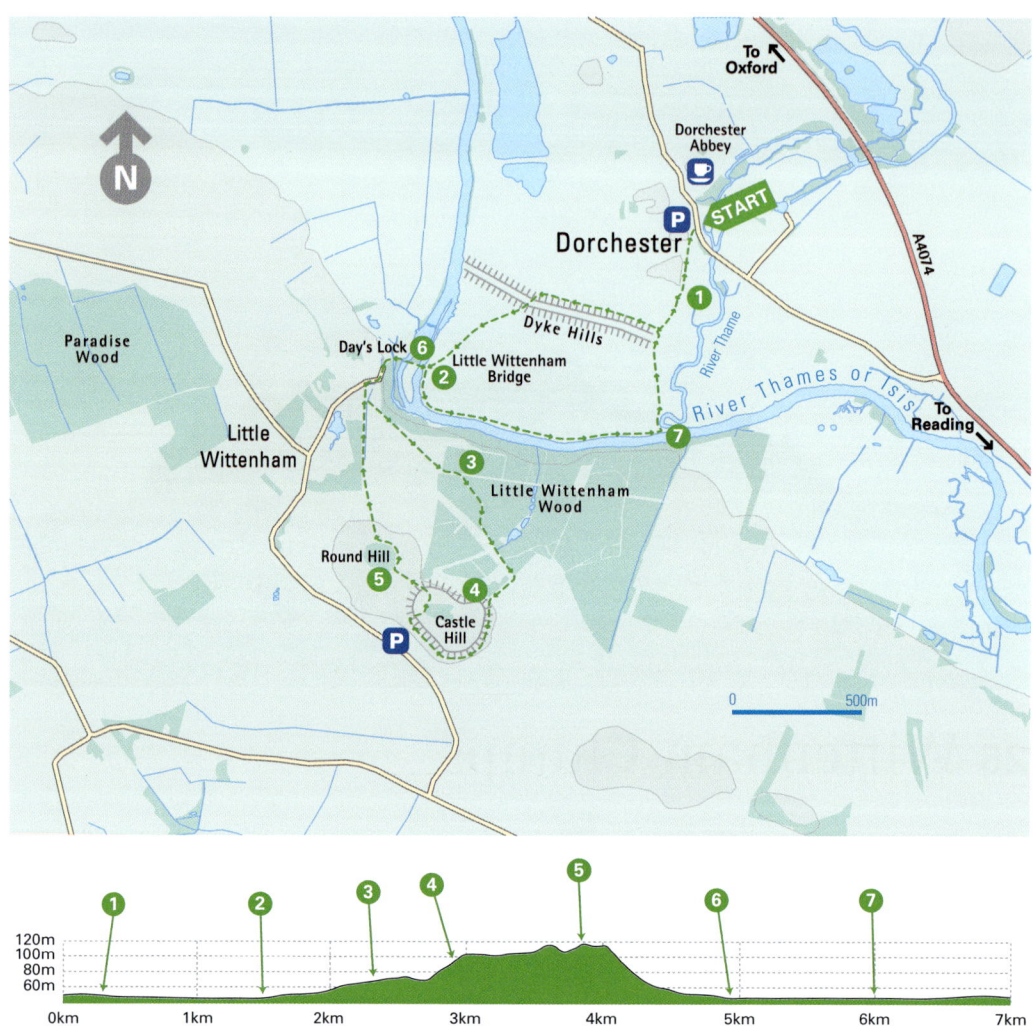

Earth Trust nature reserve) is fairly remorseless, but once you're up on top, the world is your oyster; more specifically, you are free to run around the two Clumps and soak up their 360° panoramas at your leisure, while red kites glide and screech above.

Route description

🏃 **START** ▶ Head S along Bridge End Road from the parking area. After passing the church, you reach a junction; turn right into Watling Lane and immediately turn left into Wittenham Lane. Follow Wittenham Lane to its end. ❶ The lane ends at a gate leading to a footpath. Follow the footpath 200m to reach the Dyke Hills earthworks. The footpath splits, turn right to follow the footpath leading W along the edge of the earthworks. This becomes a bridleway path, keep following it W along the earthworks, across them and then across a field to reach the River Thames at Day's Lock. ❷ Cross the River Thames by the footbridge and then continue ahead on the byway track for 150m to St Peter's Church in Little Wittenham village. Go through the gate across the track from the church, signposted 'Bridleway Shillingford Bridge' and follow

Wittenham Clumps

this bridleway path for 500m SE across a field to the edge of Little Wittenham Wood. ❸ Shortly after the bridleway (now a track) enters the woods, look for a footpath leading off on the right and take this. Follow it for 500m SE across a small valley and then steeply uphill to reach a T junction with a footpath at the edge of the woods. Turn right (uphill) and ascend steeply on the footpath along a field edge to the earthworks of Castle Hill. ❹ Turn left to climb onto the outer earthwork and follow the earthwork clockwise until you reach a T junction with another footpath at the main entrance (gap in the earthwork). Turn right and head to the trees inside the earthwork. Pass around or through the trees following the footpath. Continue on the footpath through the earthworks towards Round Hill to the NW (the other Clump!). ❺ When you reach the trees at the summit, turn right and follow the footpath around them anti-clockwise until you see the footpath leading steeply downhill back towards St Peter's Church (beside the third bench). Descend back to this church, then turn right onto the byway track and follow it to cross the River Thames by the same footbridge as before. ❻ After crossing the footbridge, turn sharp left and pass underneath it to join the Thames Path National Trail. Turn left (downstream) onto the TP footpath and follow this for 1.1km E until you reach a footbridge crossing the River Thame (a much smaller river). ❼ Turn left just before this footbridge to take the footpath which leads inland back towards the Dyke Hills earthwork. After 450m you pass a large pillbox and reach the first footpath you used; retrace your steps along this back into Dorchester.

Castle Hill

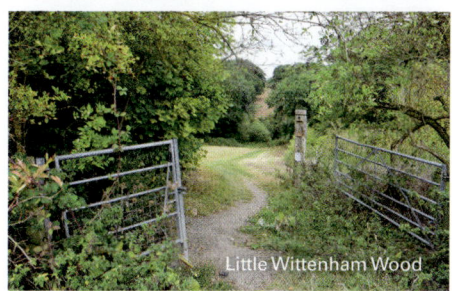
Little Wittenham Wood

Days Lock

Trip planning

The car park is roadside, located beside public toilets. There is no charge. It's found by turning off the High Street onto Bridge End, beside the bridge over the River Thame.

The Earth Trust run Clumps car park OX11 9BG / SU 567 923, which is free and gives you direct access to Wittenham Clumps at ❺. It's found on a quiet lane which leads on from Little Wittenham Road. The Earth Trust Centre in Little Wittenham is a helpful interpretative centre for the nature reserve, and can supply leaflets and maps.

Within Dorchester, there are various shops and eateries. The Tea Room at Dorchester Abbey is highly recommended, for its selection of massively unhealthy and athletically-inadvisable homemade cakes.

25 Wittenham Clumps

Descending the Clumps

Days Lock

Other routes

Extending this route isn't too hard, with the Thames Path National Trail (see page 120) passing through. It really is a delight in this part of the world; it is 29km upstream to Oxford and 20km downstream to Streatley (Routes 19 and 20), all of which is (of course) easy-gradient and steers clear of civilisation.

One simple 8km extension or alternative, is to follow footpaths and roads from St Peter's Church after ❷ across the bend of the river to Clifton Hampden Bridge, then return to the same spot following the TP. A 6km extension is to continue following the TP downstream from ❼ to Shillingford Bridge, then cross the river and return via bridleways to Little Wittenham Wood.

There are many more trails to explore within Little Wittenham Wood. The Earth Trust have a helpful map on their website.

Events

Thames Valley Orienteering Club hold events at the Clumps.

Grim's Ditch

26 Grim's Ditch

Distance		13km (8 miles)	Ascent	200m (660ft)
Map		OS Landranger 175 OS Explorer 171		
Navigation	● ● ●	Most of this route follows straight(ish) trails, including the Ridgeway National Trail		
Terrain	● ● ●	Rough and rooty sections, this is why you came		
Wet feet	● ● ●	After rain, Grim's Ditch becomes … a grim muddy ditch		
Start / Finish		Constitution Hill OX10 8BX / SU 610 877		

Technical trails along a mysterious ancient earthwork

This route is personally resonant for the author. Some years ago, I found myself totally out of my depth, taking on a non-stop race along the whole 139km of the Ridgeway National Trail. Around about the 50km mark, two very memorable things happened. Firstly, the heavens opened and torrential rain soaked us from head to foot. Simultaneously, the trail narrowed to become rough, rooty and tree-strewn, winding downhill towards the River Thames along and above a deep and overgrown culvert and dyke. This, I later learned, was Grim's Ditch. It was a joy to run, drenched shoes and all, and reinvigorated me at just the right moment. You ascend gradually from the River Thames through classic Oxfordshire scenery; rolling downs and large open fields. After passing through Mongewell Woods, you turn downhill and run the Ditch! This appears die-straight and even-surfaced on the map, but is anything but. Whether you wish to commune with your Iron Age forebears through immersing yourself in their landscape, or whether you simply like running great trails … this route should work for you.

26 Grim's Ditch

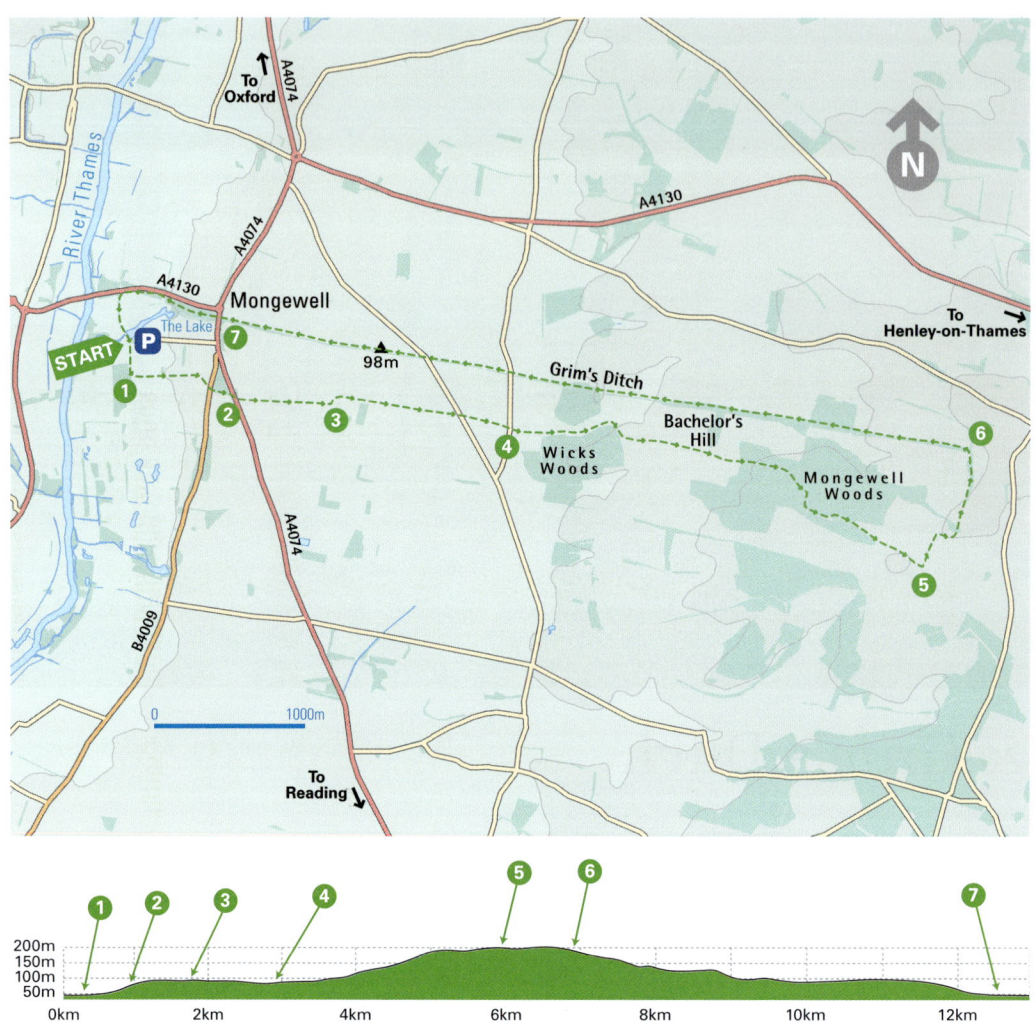

Route description

START From the start point, head S along the bridleway track, following signs for the Ridgeway National Trail. After 250m, a footpath is signposted leading off to the left (E), take this. ❶ Follow the footpath uphill along the edge of two fields. When you reach the house at the top of the second field, either continue on the footpath through their garden, or follow the path which avoids it on the right. Both paths bring you to the B4009, cross this and take the bridleway which is 30m to the S and continues uphill (E). After 150m this reaches the A4074. ❷ Cross this and take the bridleway which is (again) 30m to the S and continues uphill (E). Follow this bridleway 625m across a field to Sheepcote Farm. ❸ Bypass the farm on its left (N) side, following the bridleway which continues E for 700m to reach a lane. Cross the lane and continue ahead (E) on the byway track opposite. After 350m it crosses another lane, beside houses. ❹ Continue E on the byway. After 400m keep left when the byway forks (signs will deter you from taking the 'private' right fork), after 1.5km you enter Mongewell Woods, after 2.7km you emerge from the woods. The byway is now tarmac, look for a crossroads with a footpath 300m after leaving the woods and turn left (N) onto this

Grim's Ditch 26

Approaching Mongewell Woods

Grim's Ditch

footpath. ❺ Follow the footpath along a field edge to a house and then around the house. After passing the house it continues N through a copse, beginning to descend. After 600m the footpath reaches a signpost at a junction, indicating that you have reached the RNT. Turn left (W) to join the RNT. ❻ Follow the RNT 6km back to the start! The route (alternately a footpath and bridleway) is well-signposted, largely straight and retraces the previous crossings of lanes and roads. When you reach the A4074 (the final crossing), note that the RNT is located 25m to the right (N), not through the gate entrance directly across the road. ❼ 700m after the A4074, you reach a T junction with a bridleway path; turn left (S), following the RNT, back to your start point.

Trip planning

The start is reached by heading south from Wallingford on the A4074; directly after passing the roundabout junction with the A4130, the tiny lane Constitution Hill is signposted on the right. Drive 550m to the T junction at the end of the road and park roadside at this quiet spot.

At some points the trails through Grim's Ditch are single-file narrow (narrow for the National Trail, anyway) so be mindful and considerate of other trail users ... you may have to give way!

The very pleasant town of Wallingford is the place to get food and supplies. If you want to avoid crossing the river into the Waitrose-dominated centre, you could do worse than park at the Riverside Park beside Wallingford Bridge and enjoy ice cream beside the paddling pool (recommended for sore feet).

Grim's Ditch

Grim's Ditch

Other routes

For a cherry-picked shorter outing of 7km, start from the lane at ❹ OX10 6PU / **SU 632 872** and of course turn left when you reach it again.

Continuing S along the RNT from ❶ as far as Goring, crossing the Thames and then returning N along the Thames Path National Trail to cross again at Wallingford, makes for a beautiful 21km of riverside trail running, with only a short interlude of tarmac away from the river at Moulsford.

Events

The Wallingford Thames Run is a 5K and 10K race held along the river, passing close to the start of this route. The Chiltern Chase is a well-established 5K / 10K / 15K race based from Ewelme, several kilometres north of this route.

Centurion Running's Chiltern Wonderland 50 is outlined in the notes for Route 19.

Grim's Ditch

Running along the earthwork is fun enough, but what exactly *is* it? The origin and purpose of Grim's Ditch are lost to the mists of time. This section is just one of many surviving Iron Age earthworks with the same name, stretching across southern England from Dorset to Norfolk and Essex. All were built around 300BC, although the name came much later, being Anglo-Saxon. 'Grim' could just mean 'ditch', but is thought to be a name for the pagan god Odin / Woden. Later still, 'Grim' came to be associated with the Devil.

27 Watlington Hill

Distance	17km (10.5 miles)	Ascent	350m (1170ft)
Map	OS Landranger 165, 175 OS Explorer 171		
Navigation ●●●	Trails are well-signposted, however numerous junctions to keep track of		
Terrain ●●●	Chalk, mud, roots, tarmac, several tough ascents		
Wet feet ●●●	Pretty slippery and heavy going in the winter months		
Start / Finish	Watlington Hill National Trust car park OX49 5HS / SU 709 935		

A hilly slice of classic Chiltern scenery

This fantastic run has it all. It's a tour of the patchwork of complementary landscapes which make up the Chiltern Hills: chalk grassland, farmland, ash and beech bluebell woodland, groomed parkland. You start on the summit of 235m Watlington Hill on the Chiltern escarpment, overlooking the Vale of Oxfordshire. You hurtle downhill to said Vale, but then head back into the Chiltern hinterland of seemingly endless quiet trails which wind through valleys and over steep hills, with infrequent human traces. For example, the 107-hectare Warburg Nature Reserve which you pass through is described by the Wildlife Trust as, 'remote'. It isn't (in literal terms), but nonetheless you'll see exactly what they mean. Enjoy the red kites gliding above the valley sides and the Adonis blue butterflies down at ground level. Try to dwell less on the climbs, of which there are many. One final thought: why is there an 85-metre high chalk triangle carved into the face of Watlington Hill? This is the White Mark, created in 1764 for the local squire who felt that Watlington's church needed a 'spire'.

27 Watlington Hill

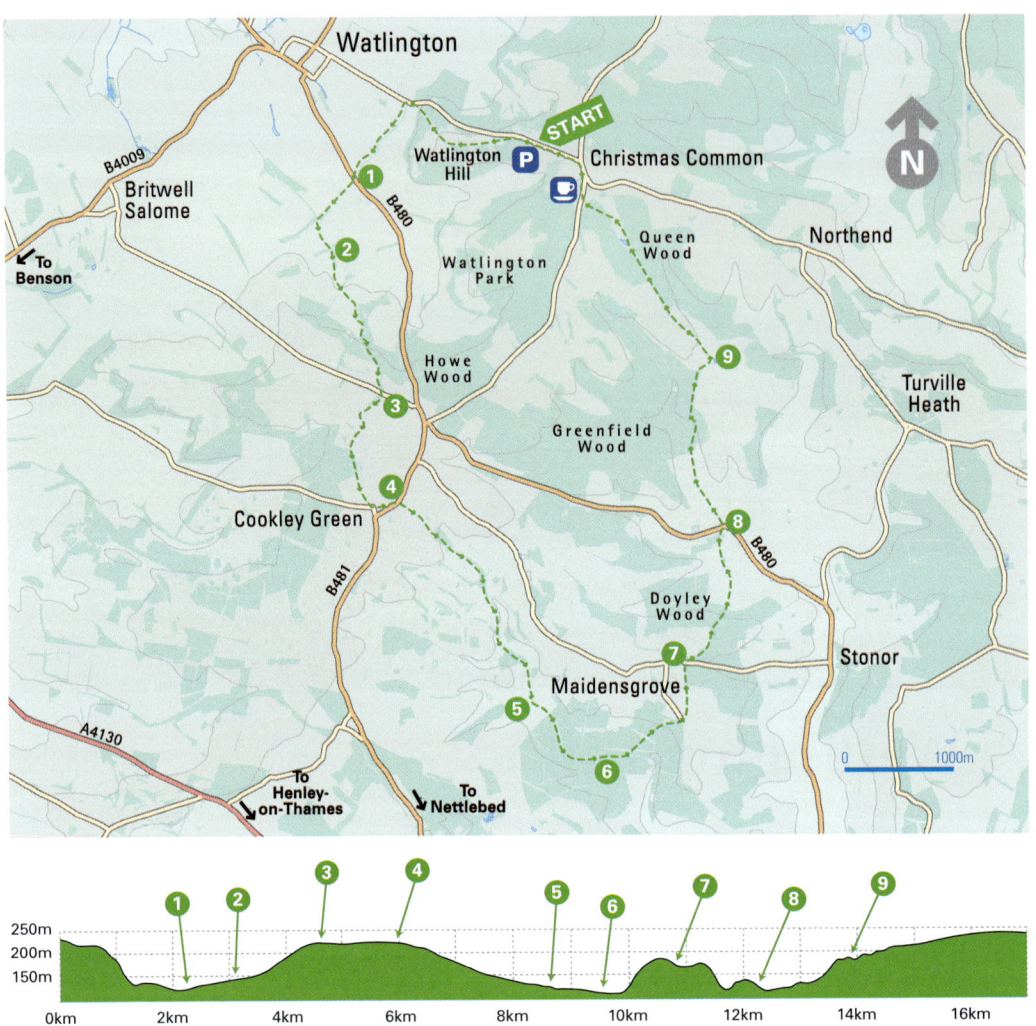

Route description

START Leave the car park by the path beside the National Trust 'Watlington Hill' signboard. Follow the path W through woods and out onto the open hill top. After 700m, the path descends steeply towards the village of Watlington; follow it until you reach a lane (Hill Road) and then immediately turn left onto a byway track signposted 'Ridgeway National Trail'. Follow the byway track SW for 900m to where it reaches a lane (Howe Road). ❶ Cross the lane and continue ahead; instead of taking the tarmac byway track, follow the parallel 'Copas Farms' alternative path along the field to the left. After 500m you reach a crossroads. Turn left (S) and take the bridleway track leading uphill. The bridleway track shortly reaches Dame Alice Farm. ❷ Before you reach the farm buildings, cross over to the path which is parallel on your right, as the main track peters out. Keep following this bridleway track uphill for another 1.5km; it passes through woodland, then becomes tarmac and reaches a lane (Britwell Hill Road). ❸ Cross the lane and take the tarmac footpath track on the opposite side (called Coates Lane). Stay on the footpath track (ignoring

Watlington Hill

any side turns), passing Coates Farm and a water tower. After 1.2km you reach a lane (Church Lane), in the centre of Cookley Green village. Turn left (E) here and run along the village green for 200m to where it ends at the B481 road (Red Lane). Cross the road and take the bridleway track located 30m to the left. ❹ Follow this track downhill. It follows the valley floor, ignore all of the numerous side turns. After 2.4km a five-way junction is reached, at a 'Chiltern Way' signpost; take the left turn signposted as a restricted byway ❺. Follow this byway downhill along the valley floor. After 900m you reach a crossroads with a bridleway, be alert; 200m after this, a footpath crosses the byway. Turn left and take the footpath, through a gate signposted 'Nature Reserve'. ❻ Ascend steeply uphill on the footpath. At the top of the hill, ignore the right turn signposted 'restricted byway' and continue ahead into Lodge Farm. A sign marked 'Oxfordshire Way Bridleway' directs you left (N), follow this bridleway. You cross a field of crops diagonally and then pass through woods to reach a lane (Park Lane). ❼ Cross the lane and take the bridleway opposite, still following the signposted OW. Over the next 1.4km, the bridleway leads downhill through woods, across an open valley and uphill past Pishill Church to reach the B480 road. Turn right onto the road and follow it 60m to a right bend. Turn off left here onto a footpath heading uphill along a valley bottom (still signposted 'Oxfordshire Way'). ❽ Follow the footpath along the valley bottom. After entering woodland, the footpath leaves the valley bottom and ascends steeply. At the top, the footpath leaves the woods and reaches a crossroads with a byway track (Hollandridge Lane) at Hollandridge Farm. Turn left (uphill) onto the byway track. ❾ Follow the byway track for 1.6km to reach a footpath signposted on the left, take this. Follow the footpath for 300m through woodland to reach a lane in the village of Christmas Common. Turn right and follow the lane N past the Fox and Hounds pub, to a junction. Bear left and continue 150m N along the lane to where a lane turns off left, signposted 'Watlington'. The car park is 400m along this lane.

Warburg Nature Reserve

Chilterns Way

Pishill

Watlington Hill

Trip planning

The National Trust car park on Watlington Hill is reached by driving uphill on Hill Road from Watlington. It is free, however at time of writing the NT have made an application to begin charging non-members ...

It is worth being clear that once you start this route, there isn't really any infrastructure until you reach the end; no shops, eateries, public transport. This part of Oxfordshire isn't exactly the Yukon, but you are still largely on your own. Carry enough water and snacks for the distance.

The Fox & Hounds pub is 1km further along Hill Road from the car park, on Christmas Common. 'Walkers, cyclists and dogs are all welcome' and experience has suggested they can just about tolerate serving trail runners, too.

Britwell Hill

Watlington Hill

Other routes

Given the lattice of trails hereabouts, there are no end of permutations to shorten this route, or try something different. One 14km possibility it is to turn off left onto the Chiltern Way bridleway, 1km after ❹, and follow the CW across to Hollandridge Farm ❾.

A good starting point for short route ideas starting from Watlington Hill is the National Trust website, which describes several alternatives.

This route very effectively partners with Route 28, just over the border in Buckinghamshire. Route 28 offers similar Chiltern awesomeness, only with a bit more severity on the hill front. Combining both routes at once makes for a challenging delve into deepest darkest Chilternland (33km). When you reach Hollandridge Farm at ❾, skip to ❹ in Route 28 and follow that route's loop via Turville and back to Hollandridge Farm. Enjoy, it's a fantastic outing!

Events

Watlington Runners organise *'the best fell run in the south'*, namely the Watlington XC 10K. It involves a direct ascent of Watlington Hill from Watlington, among other horrors.

The Maverick Original Oxfordshire Race has distances of 7, 11 and 22km, covering the area of this Route and also Route 28.

The Temple Trail is a hilly 50km ultra which passes through this area, having started at Henley. Centurion Running's Chiltern Wonderland 50 also passes through and lays on the same sort of brutality, see the notes accompanying Route 19.

Buckinghamshire and Hertfordshire

The trail running in these two counties is described together, because geographically they are closely intertwined. The majority of the routes here are focused on the Chiltern Hills, where the best of the trail running (and it really is great) is found; the Chilterns pass from Bucks to Herts and back to Bucks, before passing into Bedfordshire (a little bit of which has been squeezed into this chapter). The steep scarps and muddy trails found beneath the Chilterns' dense beech cover make for endless challenging and entertaining runs. Also included here is some of the easiest and most accessible trail running in the South East; at Forestry England's Wendover Woods and further east among the commuter belt towns of Hertfordshire, where Hatfield Park and Lee Valley Park offer sharply contrasting landscapes within the valley of the River Lea.

Tring Park from the Ridgeway (Route 31)

Cobstone Mill

Climbing to Great Wood

28 Turville

Distance	16km (10 miles)	Ascent	450m (1,480ft)
Map	OS Landranger 165, 175 OS Explorer 171		
Navigation ●●○	Trails are well signposted, but numerous junctions to keep track of		
Terrain ●●●	Chalk, mud, roots, tarmac, multiple gruelling ascents		
Wet feet ●●○	Chalk and rain have very poor synergy		
Start / Finish	School Lane, Turville RG9 6QX / SU 767 911		

Tough Chilterns love

Confession time! This route was an unplanned consequence of researching Route 27, just across the border in Oxfordshire. I enjoyed that route so much that I just kept on running, and scoped out everything you see here on the same hot exhausting day. The good news is that it's a complete gem. All of the gorgeous Chiltern landscape hallmarks described in Route 27 are found here as well, if anything amplified at locations such as beautifully-landscaped Stonor Park and the picture-postcard village of Turville. This route is also amplified in terms of challenge; the hills pack more of a punch than in Route 27. Take this route on as a superb, testing trail run in its own right, or go all out and combine it with Route 27, perhaps better prepared than the author was.

28 Turville

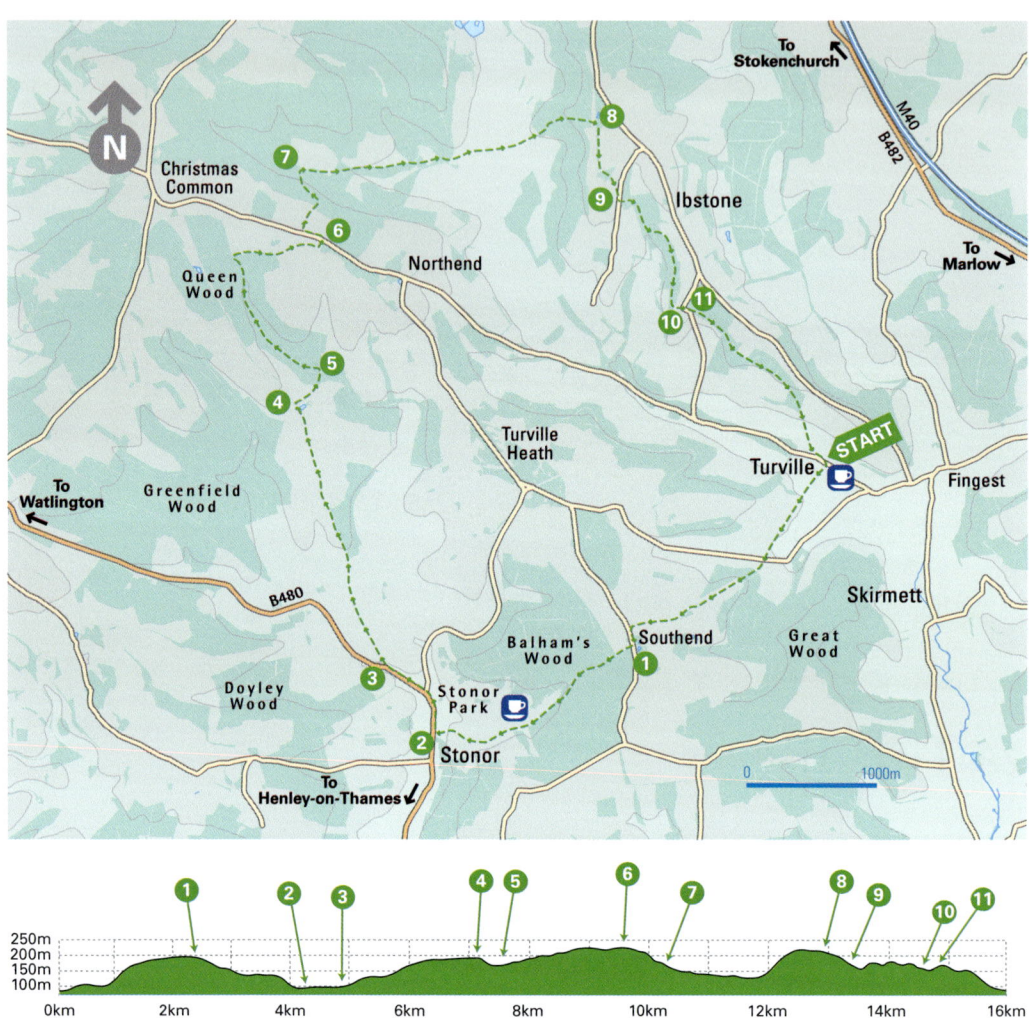

Route description

START From the triangle of grass at the centre of Turville, take School Lane. Follow this 180m to where it ends, and continue ahead (SSW) on the Chiltern Way bridleway. Follow the CW bridleway for 2km, crossing a lane (Dolesden Lane) after 750m, to reach a second lane (Drovers Lane). Turn left (S) onto this lane and follow it for 150m to where a footpath track turns off on the right. Turn right onto this footpath (still the CW). ❶ Follow the footpath track for 1.8km downhill, passing through Stonor Park, to reach a road (B480 Stonor Road). Turn right onto the road. ❷ Follow the road for 700m to where a byway track (Hollandridge Lane) turns off on the right, signposted for 'Christmas Common'. Turn right onto the byway track. ❸ Follow the byway track for 2.2km uphill, until you reach Hollandridge Farm. Just after the buildings is a crossroads with a footpath (CW), turn right onto the footpath. ❹ Follow the footpath for 400m downhill into woods, to a crossroads of tracks. Turn left at the crossroads onto the bridleway heading W (still the CW). ❺ Follow the CW bridleway uphill for 1.2km to reach a footpath signposted on the right (first right turning encountered), turn right (E) to take this footpath (leaving the CW). Follow the footpath

Stonor House

downhill and out of the woods to reach Launder's Farm, where it reaches a T junction with a bridleway track. Turn left onto the bridleway track, which leads to a lane. ❻ Turn left onto the lane and follow it for 160m past houses, to where a footpath track is signposted off on the right. Turn right and follow this footpath track into woods and steeply downhill. 600m after the lane, it reaches a T junction with another footpath. ❼ Turn right (downhill) and follow this footpath E; after 1.2km it merges with the CW and emerges onto open parkland. After another 500m it crosses a crossroads with a bridleway track and then begins to climb steeply into woods. 50m after entering the woods, the footpath reaches a T junction with a bridleway; turn right onto the bridleway (uphill) and keep ascending to reach Ibstone Common at the top. ❽ At the top of the climb, you reach the bridleway path heading N–S along the edge of Ibstone Common. Turn right (S, leaving the CW) and follow the bridleway path along open ground for 300m where it becomes a bridleway track; continue on this for another 200m to reach a lane (Grays Lane). ❾ Turn right (S) onto the lane and follow it 90m until you see two footpaths signposted off on the left. Take the righthand of the two footpaths, which leads steeply downhill through woods. After 500m the footpath reaches a junction; take the righthand of two footpaths, not the one leading uphill. Follow this footpath S for another 800m, where you will see a church (St Nicholas Church). Turn left off the footpath and pass beside the church to reach a track. ❿ Turn left onto the track in front of the church, which immediately meets a lane (Ashfield Barn Road). Turn right onto the lane (downhill) and follow it for just 75m to a right bend, where a footpath track leads off to the left. Turn left to take this footpath track. ⓫ Follow the footpath for 1.6km, ignoring any side turns; it initially follows the side of the valley and then finally descends steeply into Turville, the end.

28 Turville

Trip planning

Parking in Turville is roadside. Given that it is a popular 'pub lunch' destination, arriving early is a good idea at weekends. Be considerate of the residents in this tiny village.

The Bull and Butcher in Turville describe themselves as, 'a quintessentially English pub' and that seems accurate enough. If you intend to eat here at weekends, you have no chance unless you book ahead. There are also several pubs in the neighbouring villages of Fingest and Skirmett.

As with Route 27, note that the local trails are as close as you can get to remote in Buckinghamshire, pack for self-sufficiency. That said, with a bit of a detour off-piste in Stonor Park, you may be able to secure yourself an ice cream ... their Chilterns Pit Stop Café welcomes walkers passing on the Chiltern Way.

If Turville looks vaguely familiar, it's because it has been used as a filming location on multiple occasions; for example, the windmill featured heavily in *Chitty Chitty Bang Bang*.

Other routes

As noted above, nearby Route 27 is similar but with fewer climbs to contend with.

To combine Route 28 with Route 27, follow the instructions given in Route 27, if starting from Watlington Hill. If starting from Turville, run Route 28 until you reach Hollandridge Farm at ❹ and skip to ❾ on Route 27. Nothing can go wrong!

Turville

Events

The Ibstone Circle is a 5km and 10km run based from Ibstone Common, which tours the usually private Wormsley Estate.

Not too far away, the LDWA's Chiltern Marathon Challenge Event starts from Lane End.

See also the event notes accompanying Route 27.

The Chilterns Area of Outstanding Natural Beauty

Routes 26–33 are all within the 840km² Chiltern Hills AONB; this is an exceptional area for trail running adventures. The Chiltern Hills form a 75km-long chalk barrier guarding London from the north-west, stretching from the River Thames in Oxfordshire, across Buckinghamshire and into Hertfordshire and Bedfordshire. The scarp slope of the Chilterns consists of a series of promontory hills reaching out into the Vale of Aylesbury, while the dip slope is complex and extensive, approaching the fringes of London. The Chilterns AONB consists of two-thirds enclosed farmland and 22% woods. The woods primarily consist of beech trees planted in the eighteenth century for furniture production; their dense leaf cover makes for slightly gloomy muddy trails beneath them. When you do emerge onto open grasslands, you are often greeted by red kites, screeching above. The AONB is served by an extraordinary network of well-signposted trails (over 2,000km of footpaths and bridleways), not to mention the Chiltern Way (see page 156), Icknield Way (see page 170) and Ridgeway (see page 115), which between them lace the region together.

Chequers

29 Chequers

Distance	16km (10 miles)	Ascent	375m (1,240ft)
Map	OS Landranger 165 OS Explorer 181		
Navigation	●●●	Excellent signposting (as per usual in the Chilterns), however lots to keep track of …	
Terrain	●●●	Stony, rooty, muddy trails, lots of steep climbs	
Wet feet	●●●	Chiltern mud seems stickier than other varieties	
Start / Finish	Coombe Hill National Trust car park HP17 0TU / SP 851 062		

A demanding yomp around the PM's place

This arduous but engaging route tours the Chilterns around Chequers Court, a Tudor mansion which is the Prime Minister's country residence. The house was gifted to the nation after the First World War; previously it was expected that a PM would own their own country estate! The route starts on 257m Coombe Hill overlooking Chequers, a superb viewpoint where you might just pick out the Cotswold Hills on a clear day. The monument here commemorates the 148 Buckinghamshire soldiers who died in the Boer War; it was restored and rededicated in 2010 after lightning damage. The next stage through gloomy Low Scrubs woods is a sharp contrast; the gnarled beech trees and sunken pathways recall ancient coppicing, as this area was common land for the local people for perhaps a thousand years until the Second World War.

The route crosses the Chequers valley to explore Whiteleaf Hill and Pulpit Hill, opposite. Whiteleaf Hill is incised with the mysterious, chalk 'Whiteleaf Cross' and the trails around Pulpit Hill pass through

29 Chequers

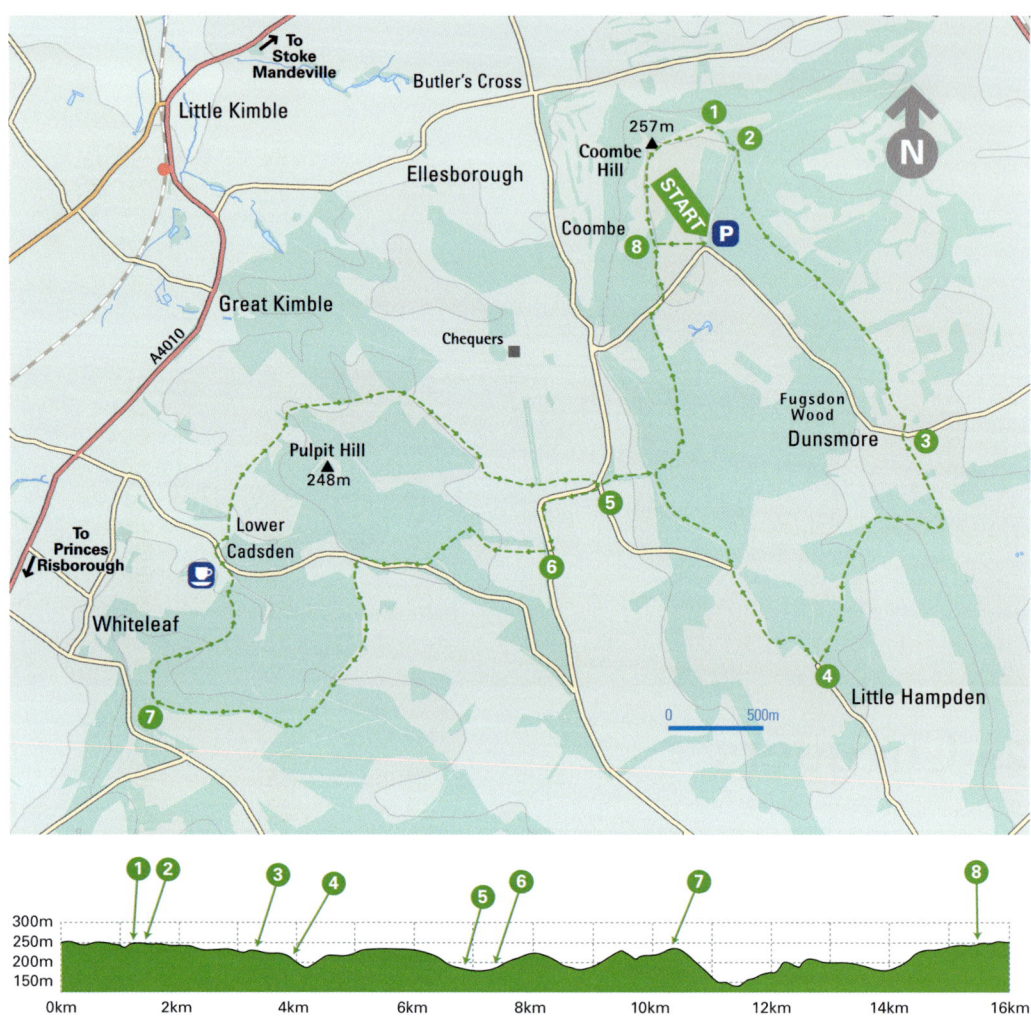

Grangelands and Rifle Butts Nature Reserve, gorgeous chalk grasslands which were previously a rifle range. You then descend from Chequers Knap to pass in front of the mansion (don't deviate unless you wish to be swarmed by armed police). The avenue of beeches that you cross lining the front entrance is Victory Drive, planted for Winston Churchill.

Route description

START Head to the gate located on the left-hand side of the entrance to the car park. Pass through it and take the left-hand footpath, which leads W along the field boundary, to reach a junction with the Ridgeway National Trail footpath after 250m. Turn right (N) onto the RNT footpath and follow it 400m along the hillside to a monument. Continue another 350m along the RNT footpath (now heading E) until a crossroads with a bridleway. ❶ Turn right (uphill) onto the bridleway and follow it just 150m to a junction of multiple trails, in woodland. Take the furthest left trail, a bridleway track heading NE. Follow this for just 75m to where another bridleway track leads off on the right (S), turn right and take this bridleway. ❷ Follow the bridleway track through the woods, leading roughly SE. The bridleway splits and re-joins at various points, however follow trails heading in the same direction and you will be fine. After 1.9km the bridleway merges with the Icknield Way Trail (for the next 7.5km until ❼, follow IWT signs when you see them) and you reach the village of Dunsmore, emerging at a crossroads with a lane. ❸ Cross the lane and continue S following the tarmac bridleway ahead. 400m after the crossroads, look out for where a bridleway turns off sharp right (downhill). Turn right, take this bridleway and follow it downhill steeply. After 400m it reaches and crosses a track at the valley floor and then bends left (SW) and climbs again, emerging at a parking area on a lane. ❹ Turn right (NW) onto the lane and follow it 50m to where a bridleway turns off on the left, signposted 'South Bucks Way'. Follow the bridleway for 1.4km, ignoring side-turns, until you reach a crossroads of tracks with the left turn (downhill) signposted for the RNT. Turn left and follow this downhill to a lane (Missenden Road). ❺ Don't cross the lane, instead cross the tarmac drive to the left (leaving the RNT) and take the bridleway path which leads along the field to the S of the lane. Follow this bridleway around the field and

Grangelands

Low Scrubs

Coombe Hill

then across the lane after 500m, at a sign for the IWT. ❻ Having crossed the lane, ascend steeply following the IWT bridleway and keep following it, ignoring side-turns, for 3km; after 1.1km you reach and cross a lane (Longdown Hill), after 2.2km the IWT bridleway turns right (W), while another bridleway continues ahead. After 3km, the IWT bridleway reaches a crossroads with the RNT, atop Whiteleaf Hill. ❼ Turn right (N) onto the RNT and follow it along footpaths and bridleways 5.4km back to the start; after 1km the village of Lower Cadsden is passed through, after 3km you descend to pass in front of Chequers mansion, after 3.8km you cross a lane (Missenden Road) and head uphill overlapping with your earlier route, after 5km you cross a lane (Lodge Hill). ❽ When you reach the very first junction at which you joined the RNT, turn right (E) to leave the RNT and retrace your steps 250m back to the car park.

Trip planning
Coombe Hill National Trust car park is free, but can get busy if you leave it too late in the morning. An alternative to consider is Whiteleaf Cross car park, outlined below.
For post-run dining, consider booking into the Plough at Cadsden, the pub you ran past at Lower Cadsden. This is the only pub on the entire Ridgeway National Trail and the food is very decent. However, its real

Chequers

fame is due to then-Prime Minister David Cameron's visit in 2015 with President Xi of China. The forgetful PM left his eight-year-old daughter behind when he went home!

The trail across the front drive of Chequers has public access (it's a footpath and indeed the Ridgeway National Trail) but heed the stern warning signs about sticking to the trail and note that there are hidden security cameras monitoring your passage.

Other routes

As this route consists of two loops, it's easy enough to squish it to 8km by skipping from ❺ to just before ❽ by turning around and heading back uphill when you first reach Missenden Lane. To run the other half as a loop, park at Whiteleaf Cross car park HP27 0LH / **SP 823 035** on Peters Lane near Princes Risborough and ascend the hill a short distance to join the route at ❼. After passing in front of Chequers and crossing Missenden Lane, skip to ❺.

One interesting (and slightly more challenging) variation to this route is to pass around the back (N) of Chequers Court by ascending Beacon Hill. Take the footpath which leads left (N) off the Ridgeway 2km after ❼ and 1km before you cross the drive to the house, following it to the village of Ellesborough. From Ellesborough, a footpath heads E to climb Coombe Hill steeply. Near Beacon Hill is Cymbeline's Castle, a motte and bailey castle earthwork.

In addition to the Ridgeway National Trail (see page 115) and Icknield Way Trail (see page 170) which of course form part of this route, the Chiltern Way (see box below) passes close by to the south, and is well worth investigating.

Events

Coombe Hill Fell Race, organised by Tring Running Club, has been going since 1973. The 7km route (with 220m of ascent) starts from the Shoulder of Mutton pub in Wendover.

The Maverick Original Buckinghamshire Event starts from Princes Risborough and traverses the same hills as this route, with 8km, 14km and 22km options.

The Chiltern Way

The Chiltern Way is a 215km / 134-mile loop out and back along the length of the Chiltern Hills, officially starting and finishing at Hemel Hempstead railway station. It was only opened in 2000, but has already been expanded by three extensions; the North Chiltern Trail (43km), the Southern Extension (50km) and the Berkshire Loop (45km). The result is a sprawling network of trails stretching north-east from the River Thames across Berkshire, Oxfordshire, Buckinghamshire, Hertfordshire and Bedfordshire. There is plenty of hard running here, as the route endlessly descends and ascends, determined to take in both the villages below and the hills above. The Chiltern Society have an excellent website and publish a guidebook to their long-distance route, both essential to make sense of it! The CW is marked on OS maps and waymarked on the ground by white disks with green writing. Routes 27, 28 and 33 include parts of the CW.

Challenge Running previously organised the Chiltern Way 100K and 214K. They no longer run this über-tough event, but will still give medals to those loons who complete the distance independently.

Wendover Woods

Viewpoint of Halton Camp and Weston Turnville Reservoir

30 Wendover Woods

Distance	5km (3 miles)	**Ascent**	100m (330ft)
Map	OS Landranger 181 OS Explorer 165		
Navigation	●●●	Simply follow the clear signs, it barely deserves the star	
Terrain	●●●	Firm tracks, gently undulating, one mild ascent	
Wet feet	●●●	Easy to avoid puddles, can be slippery near the hillfort	
Start / Finish	Wendover Woods Forestry England car park HP22 5NQ / SP 888 089		

A safe but beautiful training ground on the roof of Buckinghamshire

Haddington Hill (267m), where this route starts, is the highest point in Buckinghamshire and indeed the entire Chiltern Hills. The road to the car park here climbs Aston Hill so steeply that it gave name to Aston Martin cars! This sounds like the makings of an epic gruelling trail run, but actually this is the easiest Chiltern adventure in this book (and shorter options are available). Here among the beautiful surrounds of Wendover Woods, Forestry England have marked out the perfect beginner's trail run, with easy navigation, a (mostly) wide level surface and just the one challenging ascent. It warrants inclusion here for those who want to test their fitness and navigation in a relatively safe environment before taking on more arduous and less groomed challenges. Plus, it has a Gruffalo!

30 Wendover Woods

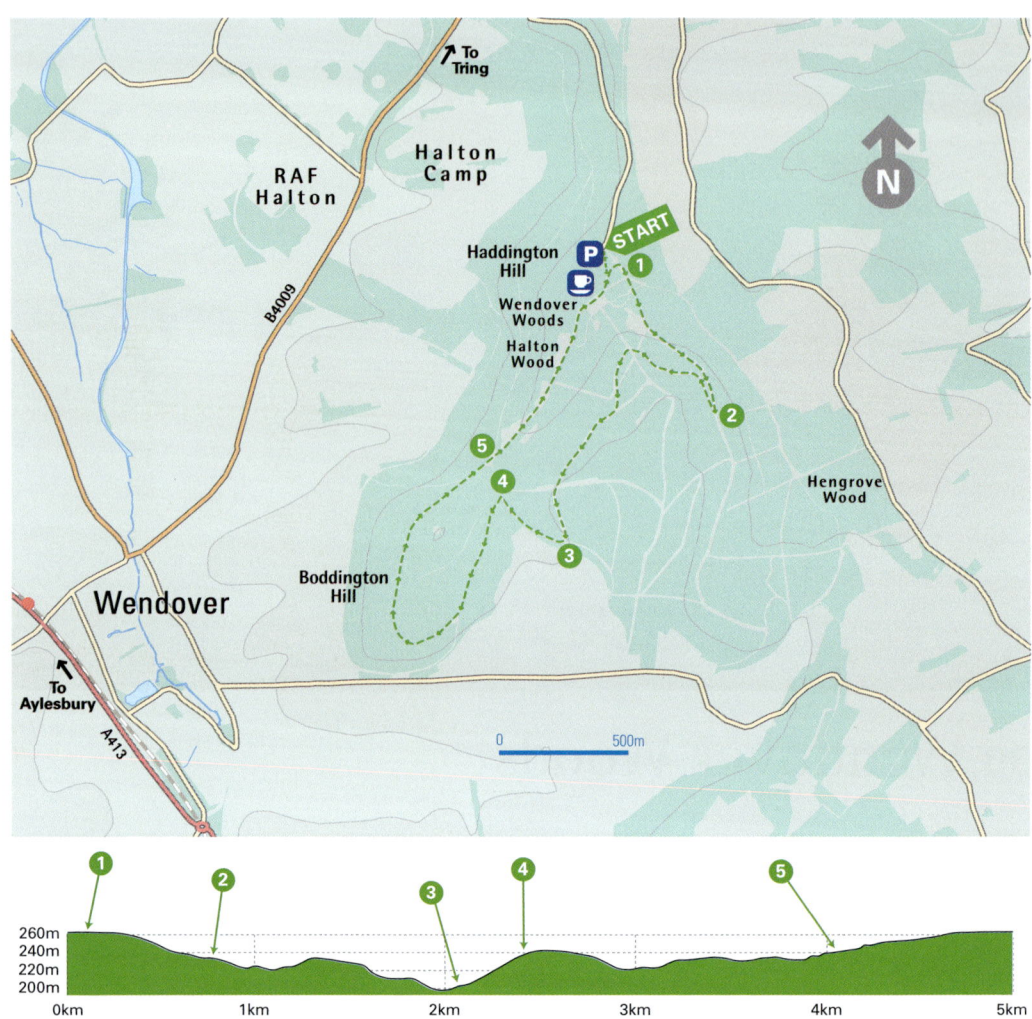

Route description

Wendover Woods' '5km Running Trail' is clearly waymarked, simply follow the dark blue '5km running route' signs; nothing can go wrong! However, the route is outlined here for those who wish to practise following this book's descriptions before venturing onto wilder trails.

START From the car park, pass the ticket payment area and head to the large café and toilets building, passing the wooden Forestry England booth on the left (where you can buy a map). Turn left at the café building, passing the toilets, and follow the building around the corner onto the footpath track that leads SE. ❶ Follow the footpath track SE (downhill), reaching a Gruffalo statue after 200m. Continue ahead on the footpath track, still heading downhill, for another 500m to where a track leads sharply off on the right. ❷ Turn sharp right (leaving the footpath track) onto this track and follow it downhill (NW). After 400m it bends left (S), continue following the track for another 800m (mostly downhill) until it ends at a T junction with a footpath track. ❸ Turn right onto the footpath track and follow it steeply uphill. After 300m, a footpath track leads off on the left, turn left to take this. ❹ Follow the footpath track SSW

Wendover Woods

along the edge of Boddington Hill Fort. After 500m the track splits, take the smaller righthand track (no longer a footpath) and continue contouring around Boddington Hill Fort. The track bends N and is joined by a footpath from the left after another km, continue ahead on the track (now a footpath again). In another 100m it reaches a crossroads beside a sign for Boddington Hill Fort, continue ahead (N). ❺ In the final km from the crossroads, you pass the viewpoint of Weston Turville Reservoir on your left and then the Go Ape adventure complex on your right, before reaching the café and car park.

Trip planning

Wendover Woods is signposted off the B4009, north of Wendover. Follow the road up Aston Hill until you see the entrance, then drive along the (long) entrance road. As with all of Forestry England's most popular sites across the country, parking is monitored by cameras which read your number plate on entry and won't let you leave until you've paid at the booths beside the car park. Queues tend to be annoyingly long for these.

The information hut / booth between the car park and café building can sell you inexpensive maps of the walking and running trails; these may also be available to view or download from Forestry England's website. The café building speaks for itself and there are also play areas and even the Go Ape ropes course to keep friends and family entertained while you are running.

Be mindful of, and considerate for, other folk while you run the trails; some parts for example overlap a cycling route.

Other routes

Wendover Woods' 1km running route is simply an out-and-back from the Go Ape complex, following the final leg of this route in reverse as far as the last crossroads ❺ and back again. The 3km running route starts the same but turns left at the crossroads to join this route at ❹, following it around Boddington Hill Fort.

There is also a 'fitness trail' signposted off this route near ❺ which involves a series of exercises, all aimed at reminding you how long it is since you either did anything active other than running, or even just properly stretched.

Forest inhabitant

The first corner

Wendover Woods cafe and toilets

Wendover Woods

The good news for those who want to explore is that trails criss-cross 325-hectare Wendover Woods, making an almost infinite number of routes possible. The catch is that while the route described here mostly hugs the high ground along the summit ridge of Haddington Hill, anything more adventurous is definitely going to involve some significant descents and ascents! You will also have to be mindful of navigation as keeping track of your position is tricky (take a ball of string?). Most of the trails are wide forestry tracks, but there are narrow paths to discover. Forestry England's 5km Firecrest Trail is one waymarked option, but note that it will be popular with families and other slow-movers.

The Ridgeway National Trail passes the southern edge of Wendover Woods and offers a way to link up with Routes 29 and 31.

Boddington Hill Fort

Signage

Events

Tough Runner UK lay on the Bucks Epic Trail 10K, which explores all corners of Wendover Woods.

Nice Work organise both a Wendover Woods Spring Festival (half marathon and 10km, also with a canicross event*) and a Wendover Woods Autumn Festival (5- and 10-mile races).

Centurion Running's events involve loops around a circuit in the woods; the Wendover Woods 50 refers to miles, while the Wendover Woods Night 50 refers to km, run in the dark.

Runaway Racing organise the Chiltern Ridge 50km Ultra Trail starting and finishing at Aston.

*I had to look this up; it is running being towed by your dog via a harness. It sounds quite inadvisable.

Forestry England trail running

Forestry England were previously the Forestry Commission, until a 2019 rebranding. Their forests are among the best resources available to trail runners, being criss-crossed by unsurfaced access roads and smaller paths which you can explore freely; visitors enjoy open access to all of FE's freehold land.

FE manage over a quarter of a million hectares of forest in England and they estimate that over 85% of people in England live within 30 minutes of their forests. Their website outlines only a handful of selected forests and obtaining location details of their thousands(?) of sites is tricky; scanning your OS map for their symbol (deciduous and coniferous trees, side by side) seems to be the best bet.

FE actively promote trail running. They are currently expanding the number and variety of marked trails within their forests. These marked routes range from 1km to 10km in length, with a healthy number being in the South East; Bedgebury Forest in Kent has an 8km trail, for example. See FE's website for details.

Tring Park lime tree avenue

31 Tring Park

Distance		9.5km (6 miles) Ascent 200m (670ft)
Map		OS Landranger 181 OS Explorer 165
Navigation	● ● ●	Gets a bit fiddly in the woods, map recommended
Terrain	● ● ●	Rough woodland trails, meadows
Wet feet	● ● ●	Chiltern mud is the best mud
Start / Finish		Natural History Museum and Tring Park car park HP23 6AP / SP 924 109

Wondrous woodland trails

What a lovely run! Wide trails through a beautiful landscaped park to warm you up, followed by excellent narrow woodland trails to sharpen your trail running (and navigation) skills.

This was formerly the estate around Tring Park Mansion (the building you see behind while crossing the A41 footbridge), designed by Sir Christopher Wren in 1685 and now a Performing Arts school. The estate was bought by the Rothschild family in 1872. A zoological museum was built as a 21st birthday present(!) for Walter Rothschild who kept zebras and kangaroos in the park. This is now the Natural History Museum, where you start. The A41 rudely sliced through Tring Park in 1975, but once across this, you'll see an avenue of lime trees crossing a meadow teeming with buttercups and butterflies to a steep, wooded hillside. Hidden in the trees are traces of the estate including the Roman temple-style Summer House and the tall obelisk known as Nell Gwyn's Monument, reputedly built to commemorate a visit from Charles II and his

Tring Park

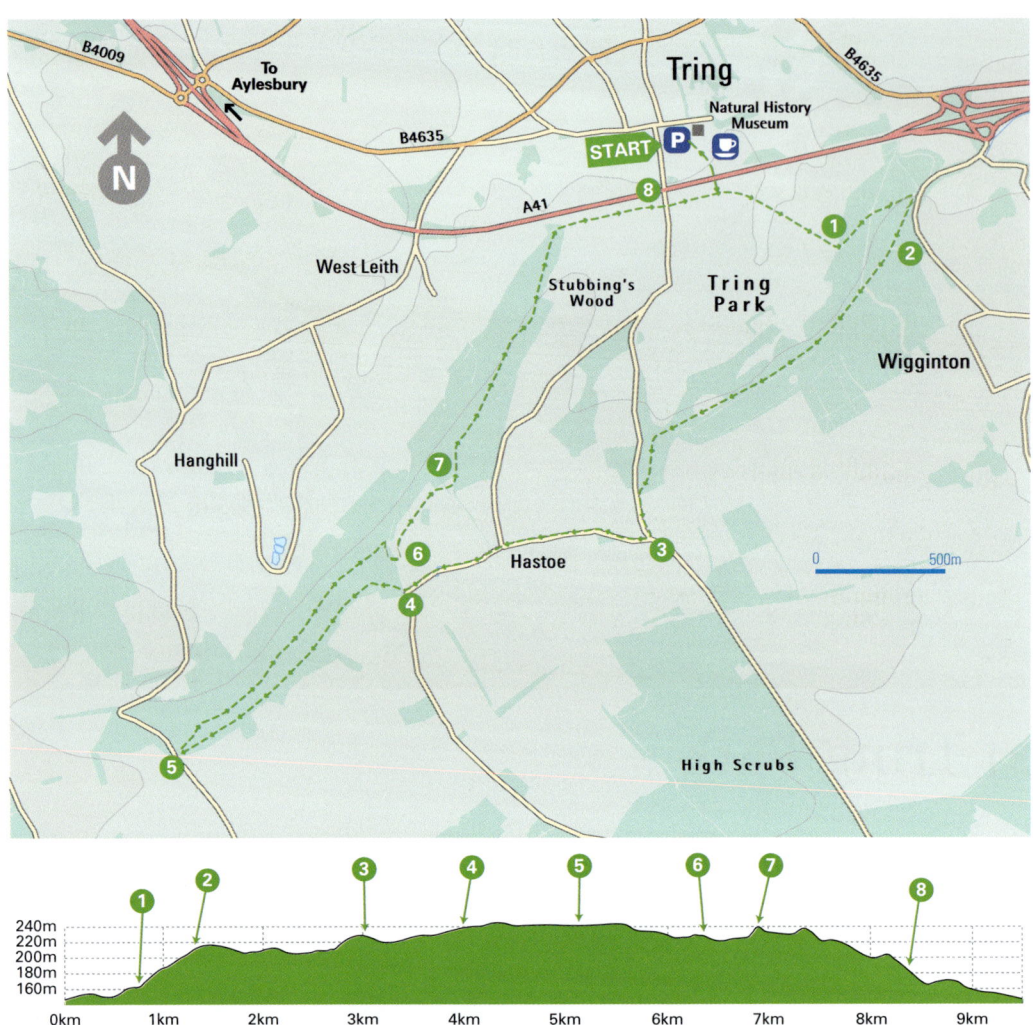

mistress. The wide trail that you follow along the hillside is King Charles Ride. The Woodland Trust manage the remaining 107 hectares of Tring Park; sharpen your dendrological skills by looking out for beech, oak, ash, horse chestnut, scots pine and even redwood trees.

Before you about-turn and head back towards Tring, Hastoe Hill, the highest point in Hertfordshire, is crossed. You won't notice this though, partly because there is no defined summit, but mainly because the trails on the return leg are just brilliant; narrow, flowing, exhilarating and mostly downhill.

Route description

START Find the footpath which leads along the back hedge of the car park and turn right (S) onto it. Follow the footpath a short distance to a footbridge across the A41, cross this. At the other side, take the footpath which crosses the meadow in front of you, leading SE and gradually uphill (not the avenue of lime trees). After 500m this reaches woodland. ❶ Two footpaths lead uphill from the edge of the woodland, take the left-hand one which is a footpath track heading NE. After 200m this reaches a junction at

Tring Park

Pavis Wood

an obelisk; continue straight ahead uphill on the track (not a footpath now) for another 160m to a white 'temple' building (the Summer House). Follow the track around a sharp right-hand bend and uphill for another 200m to a junction where footpaths join from the right and the Ridgeway National Trail (also the Icknield Way Trail) joins from the left. ❷ Follow the RNT bridleway SW through the woods for 1.4km to reach a lane (Marlin Hill). Turn left (S) onto the lane and follow it for 200m to where another lane (Church Lane) turns off on the right, signposted 'Hastoe'. Turn right onto this lane. ❸ Follow the lane W, still following the RNT; after 500m it becomes Gadmore Lane, after another 500m it bends sharp left and the RNT continues straight ahead into woods (Pavis Wood) as a bridleway. ❹ Leave the lane and continue ahead on the RNT bridleway. Follow this for 1.1km SW until a junction where two trails lead off downhill on the right (if you reach a lane, you have slightly overshot the junction). Take the furthest right trail, which is a bridleway leading NE. ❺ Follow this bridleway downhill for 100m to where a permissive footpath is signposted off on the right. Turn right onto the permissive footpath and follow it along the hillside through the woods for 400m to a crossroads with a footpath. Continue straight ahead at the crossroads onto the footpath ahead. After 600m, you reach a T junction with a byway track in a deep ditch. Turn right (uphill) and follow the byway track 100m to where a footpath leads off on the left. Take this left turn, which leads into a meadow. ❻ Follow the footpath around the downhill edge of the meadow; after 400m it enters the woods again and reaches a crossroads with another byway track. Cross the byway track to continue ahead along the hillside on the footpath to reach a crossroads with a third byway track after 50m. ❼ Turn right (downhill) onto the byway track and follow it for 150m to where a permissive footpath is signposted off on the right. Turn right onto this permissive footpath and follow it along the hillside and gradually downhill for 1km, to where it joins another footpath at the bottom of the hill. Continue ahead (E) on the

Tring Park

footpath which leads out of the woods and over a small hill to reach a lane (Hastoe Lane) after another 500m.
❽ Cross the lane and enter Tring Park. Follow the path ahead for 170m to reach the footbridge across the A41. Cross this back to the car park.

Tring Park

Trip planning
The car park is on Hastoe Lane and is easily found; once you reach Tring, follow signs for the Natural History Museum. The car park is free, serving both the NHM and Tring Park. If you find the car park full, head further along Tring Road, there may be roadside parking just after passing under the A41 at ❽ on the route. Otherwise, make use of one of the car parks in the town centre, which inevitably are not free.

Tring Park Obelisk

The Natural History Museum (donated to the public by the Rothschilds in 1892) is an offshoot of the famous Kensington Museum, but much less crowded. It is well worth a visit, especially if seeing a stuffed polar bear works for you as a post-trail running treat. Entry is free (donations invited) but check ahead whether pre-booking is necessary.

The NHM has the Ugly Bug Café on site, otherwise there are various eating options a few streets away in the (very attractive) centre of Tring.

Tring Park is open to the public at all times. Only one small part is occasionally closed for sheep grazing; Oddy Hill, located east of the Summer House and not on this route.

Other routes
The Woodland Trust offer several waymarked routes within Tring Park, from 2.5km to 3.5km in length. A map of these is downloadable from their website.

The Ridgeway National Trail offers a way to connect this route with nearby Ivinghoe Beacon via Tring, see the notes in Route 32. Wendover Woods (Route 30) are just 2km W from ❺ on this route.

The network of canals and feeder reservoirs at Tring lends itself to some pleasant easy-gradient trail runs. For example, a loop of about 12km can be enjoyed by heading N from Drayton Beauchamp village on The Holloway lane until you reach the Grand Union Canal; turn right onto this and follow the tow path footpath E until you reach the junction with the Wendover Arm of the canal. Turn right and follow the footpath along the course of this arm (the last part is disused) back to Drayton Beauchamp.

Events
A weekly 5km parkrun is held in Tring Park; it's one of the hillier parkruns!
XNRG's Humanity Direct Tring Ultra starts in Tring; see Route 32.

Tring Park

The highest points?

Trail runners love hills (well, this one does), so knowing which are highest is an important business. Yet, formulating a list of the highest hills in South East England is a confusing and even controversial affair. The (dauntingly thorough) online database of British and Irish Hills (known as 'DoBIH') suggests that there are around 450 hills hereabouts. However, many of the highest listed 'hills' are either indistinct points in an elevated landscape, or multiple summits on the same area of high ground.

Listed below are the county tops (the highest point in each county, regardless of prominence) and the ten highest 'Marilyns', of the sixteen in the region. A Marilyn is a hill with a prominence of 150 metres (490 feet) or more above the surrounding landscape.

County Tops

1. Berkshire – Walbury Hill 297 metres / 974 feet (Route 16)
2. Surrey – Leith Hill 294 metres / 965 feet (Route 62)
3. Hampshire – Pilot Hill 286 metres / 938 feet
4. West Sussex – Black Down 280 metres / 919 feet (Route 57)
5. Buckinghamshire – Haddington Hill 267 metres / 876 feet (Route 30)
6. Oxfordshire – Whitehorse Hill 261 metres / 856 feet (Route 22)
7. Kent – Betsom's Hill 251 metres / 823 feet
8. East Sussex – Ditchling Beacon 248 metres / 814 feet (Route 53)
9. Greater London – Westerham Heights 245 metres / 804 feet
10. Hertfordshire – Hastoe Hill 245 metres / 803 feet (Route 31)
11. Isle of Wight – St Boniface Down 242 metres / 794 feet (Routes 4 and 5)
12. Essex – Chrishall Common 147 metres / 482 feet

Marilyns

1. Walbury Hill 297 metres / 974 feet in Berkshire (Route 16)
2. Leith Hill 294 metres / 965 feet in Surrey (Route 62)
3. Black Down 280 metres / 919 feet in West Sussex (Route 57)
4. Butser Hill 271 metres / 889 feet in Hampshire (Route 11)
5. Botley Hill 269.6 metres / 885 feet in Surrey
6. Haddington Hill 267 metres / 876 feet in Buckinghamshire (Route 30)
7. Ditchling Beacon 248 metres / 814 feet in East Sussex (Route 53)
8. Crowborough 242 metres / 794 feet in East Sussex
9. St Boniface Down 242 metres / 794 feet on the Isle of Wight (Routes 4 and 5)
10. Chanctonbury Hill 240 metres / 787 feet in West Sussex (Route 55)

31 Tring Park

Tring Park

32 Ivinghoe Beacon

Ivinghoe Beacon

Distance	8km (5 miles)	Ascent	200m (650ft)
Map	OS Landranger 165 OS Explorer 181		
Navigation	●●● Signposted clearly		
Terrain	●●● Chalky trails, grass, steep steps, several steep climbs		
Wet feet	●●● A few sections can get gloopy		
Start / Finish	Ivinghoe Beacon National Trust car park HP4 1NF / SP 963 159		

Sprint, jog or stagger up an ancient landmark

Ivinghoe Beacon is a windswept outlier from the Chiltern Hills, a chalk promontory with grand views all around and far across the Vale of Aylesbury; on a good day you can see Milton Keynes*. Its prominent location has been utilised for millennia; the hill is covered with burial mounds from the Bronze Age, and the summit bears the outline of an Iron Age hillfort. Two ancient routeways pass through here, the Icknield Way and the Ridgeway (was it the prehistoric equivalent of a motorway junction?) and today the summit is the start point for long-distance trails based on both. More recently, the easy proximity to blue skies and fresh air has made it a popular film location. It has featured in no less than four Harry Potter films! There is plenty here for trail runners. A compact network of trails criss-crosses the Beacon, successively descending and ascending the scarpland with scant regard for your feelings. In a short distance,

*On a better day, you can't.

Ivinghoe Beacon

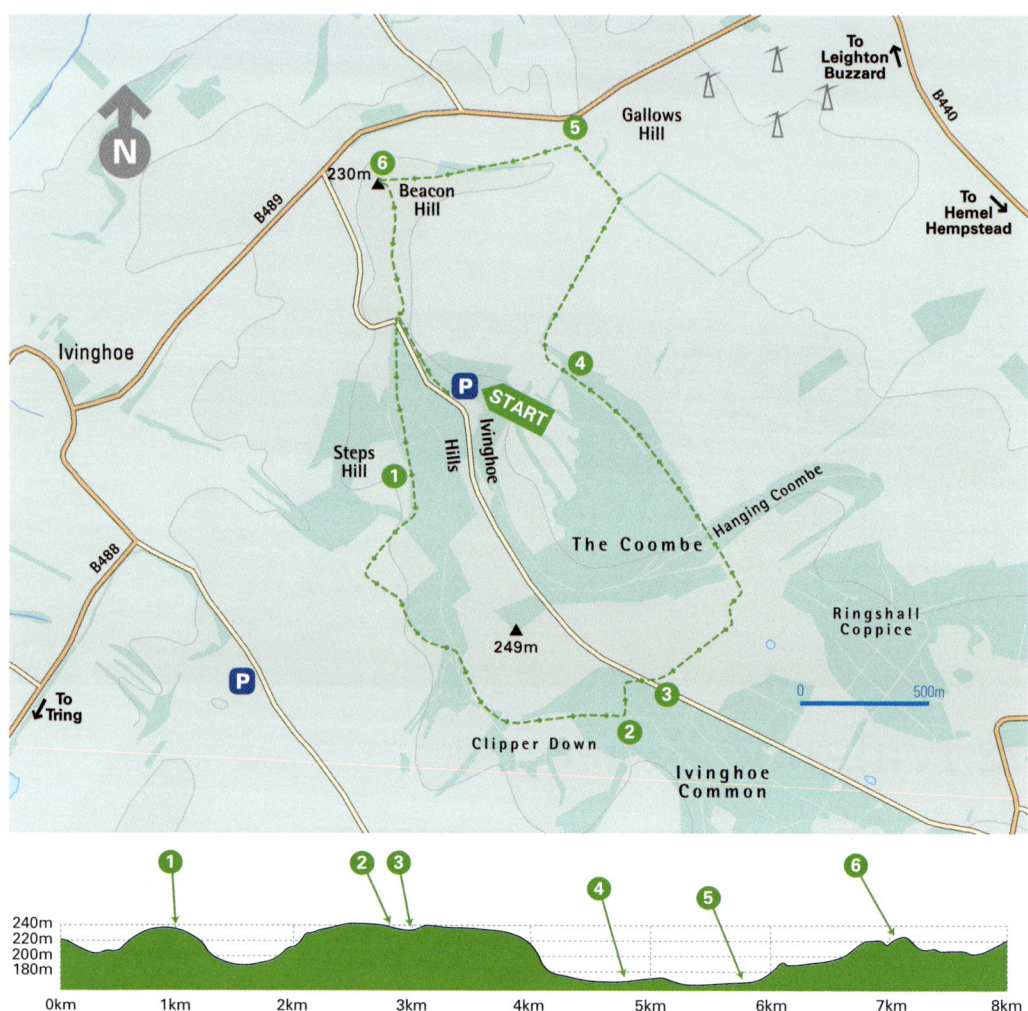

you successively transition through a range of environments: airy ridgetop, beech and ash woods, orchid-strewn chalk grassland, prehistoric earthworks, claustrophobic plantation and open farmland. You won't get bored.

Route description

START Locate the path which leads out of the car park at the N end (Ivinghoe Beacon direction) and take this. After 300m the path forks, turn left (uphill) to reach the road after 30m. Cross the road and take the main track leading uphill (S), it leads along the ridgetop. After 600m you'll see a gate on your right. Go through the gate onto the Ridgeway National Trail footpath, which is parallel. ❶ Follow the RNT downhill until you reach a crossroads of footpaths beside a signpost. Turn left (SE) and follow this footpath for 1.3km along the hillside and into woodland, ignoring two right turns leading downhill. ❷ You reach a crossroads with a footpath, turn left (uphill) and follow this footpath for 300m until you reach the road (Beacon Road). ❸ Cross the road to the track signposted 'Ward's Hurst Farm'. Follow this footpath track to

Ivinghoe Beacon

The Vale of Aylesbury

and through the farm buildings (route is clearly signposted). When you reach the pond, turn left (NW) behind it and follow the footpath into woods and then steeply downhill via steps. After a kilometre, you emerge from the woods and see Ivinghoe Beacon in front of you. ❹ Take the footpath track bearing right, ignore the left-hand footpath which leads uphill. Follow the footpath track through a gate and across a field, heading NE. After 900m, the footpath track bends sharp left (uphill) and ascends steeply. ❺ When you reach the top of the ridge (Gallows Hill) turn left and follow the footpath along the ridge for 750m to the summit of Ivinghoe Beacon. ❻ Follow the footpath leading S for 500m along the ridge to the road. Cross the road and retrace your steps along the path back to the car park.

Ivinghoe Beacon summit

Steps Hill

Trip planning

The car park is free and often comes with a bonus café caravan (apparently that is the thing now), the 'Van Café'. It's reached by a right turn off the B489 (1.5km from the village of Ivinghoe), signposted 'Ashridge'. If the caravan is not there, the Curiositea Rooms (see what they did there?) in Ivinghoe village can offer you afternoon tea; there are also a couple of pubs.

Ivinghoe Beacon

If Ivinghoe Beacon car park does not suit, an alternative is to start from Pitstone Hill car park on Stocks Road LU7 9EN / **SP 955 149**. Cross the road from the car park and ascend along the footpath for 500m to join the route just after ❶.

Ivinghoe Beacon is part of the National Trust's 2,000-hectare Ashridge Estate, which has a visitor centre and café on Monument Drive near Albury HP4 1LX / **SP 971 130**.

Other routes

A satisfying variation which doubles the distance is to start and finish from Tring railway station, approaching on the Ridgeway National Trail until it merges with this route just after ❶. Return the way you came, or for variation via the Grand Union Canal's tow path.

Berkhamsted Common to the south is also part of the Ashridge Estate; there are numerous trails to explore and the NT recommend a few routes on their website.

Events

Tring Running Club's Ridgeway Run covers a hilly 15.5km around the Ashridge Estate.

The LDWA's Chilterns Kanter Challenge Event is based from Pitstone and has 13-, 18- and 26-mile routes. XNRG organise the Humanity Direct Tring Ultra which starts in Tring and ascends Ivinghoe Beacon, and pretty much every other local hill, over its 50km course. Entry is free if you raise money for Humanity Direct. Various ultras along the RNT start at Ivinghoe Beacon's summit.

The Icknield Way

The Icknield Way is an ancient route from Norfolk to Dorset, following chalk hills. It is a contender for Britain's oldest road, certainly dating from the Iron Age (the name possibly refers to Boudicca's Iceni tribe) and possibly from the Neolithic (c. 5,000 years ago!). Its course is recalled by a series of long-distance trails; the Peddars Way National Trail in Norfolk, the Icknield Way Trail, the Ridgeway National Trail (see page 115) and the Wessex Ridgeway (see *South West Trail Running*). How about that for a summer project?

The Icknield Way Trail, not to be confused with the whole Icknield Way, is a series of interconnected trails winding 274km / 170 miles between Thetford in Norfolk and Chinnor in Oxfordshire. It is signposted along its route by a distinctive 'stone axe' design with alternative routes for walkers, cyclists and horse riders. The cyclist's route of the IWT overlaps and interweaves with the Ridgeway National Trail for some distance, often offering a lower level and easier-going alternative. To add further confusion, the walker's route of the IWT is called the Icknield Way Path and finishes at the summit of Ivinghoe Beacon, 177km / 110 miles from Thetford. The IWP skims the northern edge of Hertfordshire and is a good starting point for trail runs north of Stevenage.

Excellent info is available from the IWT website.

Dunstable Downs

Dunstable Downs

33 Dunstable Downs

Distance	14km (9 miles)	Ascent	275m (900ft)
Map	OS Landranger 166 OS Explorer 181, 192, 193		
Navigation ●●○	Clear trails, numerous fairly obvious junctions		
Terrain ●●○	Rutted chalk trails, farmland, numerous mild ascents		
Wet feet ●●○	The farm fields are a bit grim when wet		
Start / Finish	Chilterns Gateway Centre LU6 2GY / TL 008 195		

A classic Chiltern viewpoint and a hidden castle

Dunstable Downs is a dramatic escarpment facing Ivinghoe Beacon (Route 32). It is the last significant summit of the Chiltern Hills (heading north-east), and strictly speaking shouldn't be in this chapter as it is two kilometres outside Hertfordshire, being the county top of Bedfordshire at 243m / 797 feet. Why did we put it in? Because it's a great spot to trail run, and also just because we can.

The route here starts at the architecturally-distinctive Chilterns Gateway Centre, where there are always crowds of Dunstable and Luton folk, picnicking and kite flying. You rapidly leave the hordes behind however, and explore the trails at the foot of Dunstable Downs before crossing farmland to reach the Totternhoe Knolls, an intriguing landscape of overgrown Medieval chalk quarries with the impressive earthworks of a Norman motte and bailey castle at its highest point. Chalk byways (following the Icknield Way Trail) lead back to Five Knolls, the hill at the northern end of Dunstable Downs. The steep hillside

33 Dunstable Downs

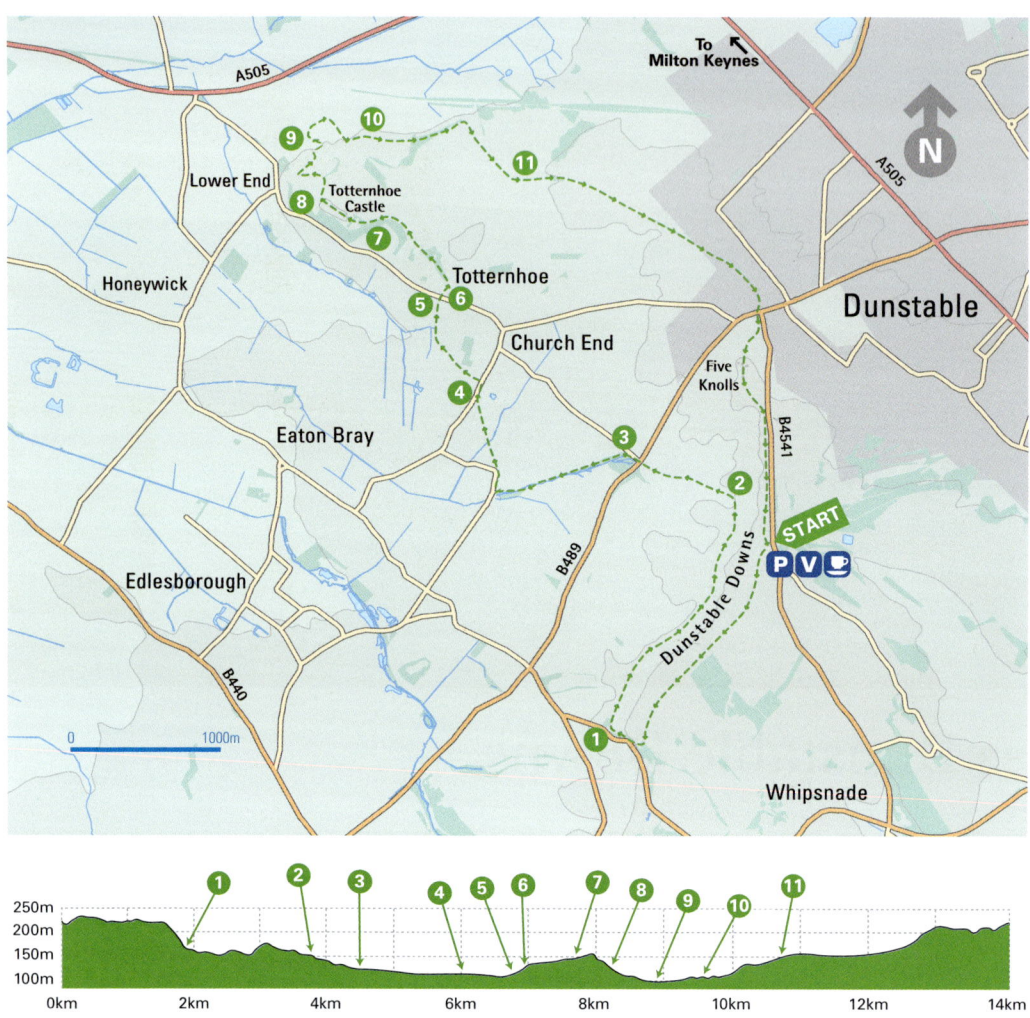

here was the site of Easter 'orange rolling' for two centuries until the 1960s, when it was deemed too dangerous! The knolls are a line of burial mounds (actually seven of them) dating up to 5,000 years old. Enjoy the vista across the Vale of Aylesbury as you run atop Dunstable Downs back to the start, even better if you can synchronise this with sunset!

Route description

START From the visitor centre, head to the metal sculpture on the edge of the hill, and turn left (S) to follow the bridleway path which leads along this. After 1.6km the bridleway path reaches a car park and road. Turn right (downhill) and follow the bridleway path steeply downhill (via steps) to the bottom of the hill. ❶ Turn right at the bottom of the hill, onto the footpath which leads along the base of the hill. Follow this for 1.9km (it splits for a while, either fork is fine) until you see a bridleway path leading off on the left (downhill). ❷ Turn left and follow the bridleway path downhill until it reaches a road (Tring Road). Cross the road and continue straight ahead on the lane (Well Head Road) which leads off directly opposite.

Dunstable Downs

Follow this for just 100m until a bridleway path is signposted on the left; turn off left to take this. ❸ Follow the bridleway path for 900m until it reaches a lane (Doolittle Lane). Turn right onto the lane and follow it for just 120m until it bends left. A footpath is signposted to continue ahead across a field; turn right off the lane to follow this footpath. After 500m the footpath reaches another lane (Church Road). Turn right onto this lane. ❹ Follow the lane just 90m N and then turn off left onto another lane (The Ride). Follow this 100m to its end, where two footpaths are signposted. Take the left-hand footpath which leads NW across two fields (ignore any side turns), and then bends N (uphill) to reach a road (Castle Hill Road). ❺ Cross the road and turn right; just 30m along the road (just before a bus stop), a tarmac byway leads off on the left

Descent from Dunstable Downs

Five Knolls

(uphill). Turn left onto the byway. ❻ Follow the byway uphill. After 300m, a footpath leads off on the left, take this. Follow the footpath ahead, ignoring any side turns (it becomes a bridleway track), until you reach a right turn where there is an entrance gate to a nature reserve on the left. Go through the gate. ❼ Follow the path through the nature reserve, over earthworks to the trig point on top of the castle mound. Then descend just 50m to the N (choice of paths) until you reach a chalk byway track. Join this byway and follow it downhill. ❽ The byway track bends sharp left; 200m after this corner (still heading downhill), look for a footpath leading sharply off on the right and take this. Follow the footpath for 400m around several corners (it becomes a bridleway track) until it reaches a lane (Knolls View). ❾ Turn right onto the lane, and follow it to its end where it continues as a bridleway track. After 150m the bridleway track bends right, keep following it for another 200m to where a byway track leads off on the left (E). Turn left and follow this byway track. ❿ After 200m a footpath leads off through a gate, turn off onto the footpath and follow it for 600m until it ends at a T junction with a footpath. Turn right (uphill) onto the footpath. After 600m the footpath stops climbing and merges with a byway track (Green Lane). ⓫ Follow Green Lane byway (E, then SE) for 1.9km until it ends at a traffic roundabout! Cross the roundabout to the grassy area opposite and ascend steeply following the footpath up Five Knolls. When you reach the Five Knolls (burial mounds), choose any path leading along the scarp to the visitor centre, 1.5km to the S.

Trip planning

The Chilterns Gateway Centre is on Whipsnade Road and is not hard to find; follow signposts for Dunstable Down, then choose one of the large car parks along the road, ideally the one beside the Gateway Centre. Parking is free to National Trust members. The Gateway Centre has a café, shop (they sell kites!) and information displays about the Chiltern Hills. Dunstable is of course a very short distance away, for shops and services.

33 Dunstable Downs

Other routes

The National Trust and Chilterns AONB websites both suggest numerous possible short routes to explore Dunstable Downs.

The Icknield Way Trail (see page 170) and Chiltern Way (see page 156) both form part of this route, running along the top and bottom of Dunstable Downs, respectively. The Chiltern Way loops right around Dunstable and Luton between Studham and Flamstead, an epic 60km mission awaiting the intrepid.

The continuation of the escarpment south from Dunstable Downs is interrupted by the presence of Whipsnade Zoo, which is perched atop the hill and is advertised by the lion tastefully carved into the chalk. However, the hillside is Access Land and there are paths here to explore. The Icknield Way Trail instead heads inland to pass around the zoo, visiting Whipsnade Tree Cathedral after about 1km; this is an enclosure planted in the 1930s as a memorial to fallen soldiers of the First World War. The National Trust have a car park on Bushey Close LU6 2LQ / **TL 009 180**. For a long outing, you could do worse than continue another 7km along the Icknield Way Trail to combine Dunstable Downs and Ivinghoe Beacon.

Events

A weekly parkrun starts from the Gateway Centre. In addition, the National Trust hold one of their free monthly Trust10 Trail Run events here.

Dunstable Road Runners (despite their name) organise the Dunstable Downs Challenge, which offers a choice of the Half Marathon, 20 Mile, Marathon or Hilly Billy 50K events.

Hatfield House 34

Hatfield House

34 Hatfield House

Distance	7km (4.5 miles)	**Ascent**	100m (300ft)
Map	OS Landranger 166 OS Explorer 182		
Navigation	●●●	Mostly on waymarked trails	
Terrain	●●●	Dirt trails, estate tracks, grass, tarmac, small climbs	
Wet feet	●●●	Potential for muddiness in the first half	
Start / Finish	Hatfield Park entrance AL9 5HX / TL 236 085		

A safe introduction to trail running, in a private park

Hatfield House is a glorious Jacobean Mansion dating from 1611, surrounded by Hatfield Park. The River Lea flows through the estate, dammed into lakes. Do you remember your Tudors from school? The Old Palace beside Hatfield House was the childhood home of both Edward VI and Elizabeth I. Elizabeth was confined here under house arrest by her sister Mary I when she ascended to the throne; the 'Queen Elizabeth Oak' on this route is the site where she received the news of her sister's death, uttering the (not exactly grief-stricken) words, *"This is the Lord's doing: it is marvellous in our eyes".*

Including this route is a bit controversial because this is the only route in this book which doesn't have open public access; you have to pay to enter the private grounds. So, why was it included? It's a really pleasant and simple run in beautiful surroundings, with an engaging mix of rough woodland trails and landscaped estate. Finishing at what might be the most attractive house and gardens in Britain isn't

34 Hatfield House

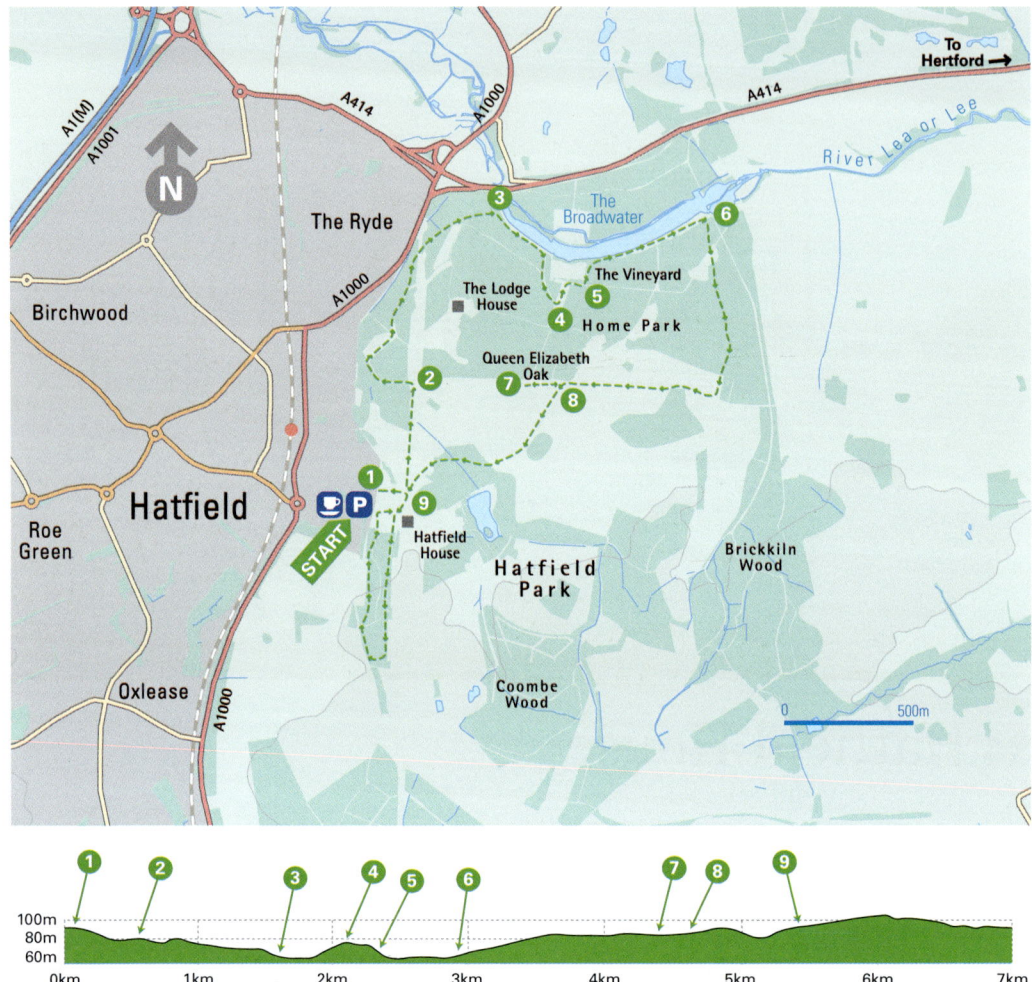

exactly a minus point, either! Regarding the pay-to-access situation, it's not so bad. Hatfield House have a 'pay once, visit all season' policy for the park, so as long as you don't lose your ticket down the front of the dashboard (like, um, the author did) you can keep returning here (with free parking) and trying to improve upon your times! Any runner should enjoy running here, but for Hertfordshire locals wanting a safe and attractive training ground, Hatfield Park is a particular asset.

Route description

Hatfield House's 'Red Walk', which forms the majority of this route, is waymarked; obtain a free 'Woodland Walks' map at the entrance and then simply follow the coloured posts. When faced by a choice of directions, follow the 'red' markers.

START Walk 150m from the car park to the entrance to Hatfield Park (beside shops and a café in the Stable Yard); pay your entrance fee / show your ticket, acquire a 'Woodland Walks' map and pass through the entrance gate. The route properly starts here. ❶ Head from the gate to the main track leading N–S (Hatfield House can be seen directly S) and turn left (N) onto it. Follow the track 430m N to a crossroads

Hatfield House

of tracks and turn left (W) here; henceforth you will see coloured marker posts for the 'Red Walk'. The 'Red Walk' follows well defined trails, some of which are not marked on OS maps. ❷ Follow the coloured posts ahead along a series of tracks for 1.1km through woods to a lake (The Broadwater); the tracks bend N and then NE, ignore any side turns. ❸ When you reach the lake, follow the shore E for 300m until the shore ahead is blocked by a fence. Turn right and follow a path which takes you uphill to a major N–S track. ❹ Turn left (N) onto the track and follow it a short distance to the entrance of a large stone building (The Vineyard). Turn right to follow the track leading E in front of this entrance. After 70m, a path leads off on the left downhill towards the lake. Take this and descend to the lake. ❺ Follow the lakeshore for another 500m E, until you reach a fence and can follow the lake no further. ❻ Turn right (S) and follow the marked track leading uphill into the woods. Follow the coloured posts for 750m S along tracks until you emerge from the woods at a T junction with an E–W track. Turn right (W) and follow this track for 800m until you reach the Queen Elizabeth Oak, marked by signage. ❼ Turn around at the QE Oak and backtrack 150m to where a path is signposted across grass on the right, leading SW. ❽ Turn right and follow this path SE past an ornamental garden. The path veers right (W), downhill into Elephant Dell. Follow the path across grass through the dell and then uphill though trees to the front of Hatfield House. ❾ You can finish here (5.5km) or walk up to the front of the house and pass through the entrance on the right-hand (W) side of the house's front; walk 100m past the house to the Viewing Bay. Then simply run the length of the Woodland Garden (recognisable as being mostly woodland) and return by the parallel paths. Finish when you reach the Sundial Gardens (recognisable as being very ornamental). Wind down by walking through the Sundial Gardens and the (stunning) Old Palace Garden back to the front of Hatfield House.

Home Park

The Old Palace

The Broadwater

Elephant Dell

Woodland gardens

Hatfield House

Trip planning

Hatfield House is signposted from miles around, but stay awake because when you finally get there it's actually quite easy to miss the sudden turning off the A1000 Great North Road into the car park. Parking is free, you pay your entrance fee at the gateway to the park in the Stable Yard (or book and pay online beforehand, recommended). The ticket you need is 'Adult: Garden, Park & Woodland Walks' which is inexpensive (at time of writing!), although of course visiting other parts of the estate (such as Hatfield House itself) will cost you more. Hatfield House have for years operated a very reasonable 'pay once, visit all season' policy, meaning that your ticket is good for all year. Check for up-to-date information; for example, this policy was suspended in 2020 due to Covid-19 restrictions.

The Coach House Kitchen in the Stable Yard can feed you. There are also a number of surrounding shops, selling stuff only of interest to the moderately wealthy (no joke; among other retailers there is a gunsmith, a purveyor of bespoke dog cushions and 'The Jodhpur Company', whatever that is).

Hatfield Park change or modify their waymarked routes from time to time, so changes may occur; however, the 'Woodland Walks' routes mentioned here were newly-established in 2020, and in any case the trails will remain even if the waymarking is re-rerouted. You share these trails with walkers and other visitors to whom you should naturally defer and give way, but (outside bank holidays and suchlike) there is plenty enough space to make congestion unlikely.

Open air events such as concerts sometime happen at Hatfield Park, generally being located in the field near the Queen Elizabeth Oak ❼. It is well worth checking Hatfield House's website before setting off, to check that your way will be clear.

Other routes

The waymarked 'Woodland Walk' trails in Hatfield Park are the Yellow Walk (2.3km), the Blue Walk (3.4km) and the Red Walk (5.2km). The Red Walk combines elements of the Yellow and Blue Walks and is what is described above. There is plenty enough open parkland to vary your route slightly and explore a bit, but naturally don't enter marked-off or barriered areas.

The Lea* Valley Walk passes along the north edge outside Hatfield Park; one possibility for a different outing would be to run from Hatfield railway station to Marshmoor Bridge railway station by following the Lea Valley Walk and then the succession of footpaths, bridleways and byways that lead clockwise around the outside of Hatfield Park; this totals at about 11km.

Events

An annual running event is held within Hatfield Park, with distances of 1km, 5km, 10km and half marathon. Runners participate to raise funds for a charity of their choice.

---

*The river is alternately called both the Lee and the Lea. The versions used here are those adopted by the Ordnance Survey.

Lee Valley

Lee Valley Park

35 Lee Valley

Distance		9km (5.5 miles)	**Ascent**	25m (75ft)
Map		OS Landranger 166 OS Explorer 174		
Navigation	●●●	Obvious paths, but not all signposted or mapped		
Terrain	●●●	A mix of surfaced and dirt trails, no gradient		
Wet feet	●●●	Not a chance		
Start / Finish		Pindar car park, Windmill Lane EN8 9SA / TL 368 023		

Easy trails in a beautiful waterscape

Lee Valley Country Park is a complex waterscape of lakes, rivers and canals sprawling over 400 hectares between Waltham Abbey and Broxbourne, part of the 40km-long Lee Valley Regional Park. Running through the idyllic pastures and lakes, it's hard to believe that the valley has been reclaimed and re-greened from 4,000 hectares of derelict industrial land; for example, the lakes were gravel pits. It is now a haven for aquatic wildlife, especially wildfowl. Kingfishers can be glimpsed flitting colourfully across the water, and the booming call of the bittern may be heard. Vigilant (and lucky) early morning or late evening runners may even spot the elusive otter. Less discreet are the muntjac deer, who wander freely. The trails winding through the waters of Lee Valley Country Park are mostly simple to negotiate, with almost no gradient and plenty of surfaced sections. This route seeks out a few of the more rough-going and out of the way trails, but even so those first dipping their toe into trail running will find nothing to fear here.

Lee Valley

Route description

🚶 **START** Head to the end of the car park where you will find a canal (River Lee Navigation). Turn right onto the tow path footpath and follow it 500m S to a lock. Cross the canal at the lock and continue following the tow path footpath S. After 100m it crosses Powdermill Cut (a water channel) by a path, leaves the canal and reaches a fork. ❶ Take the left path to follow Powdermill Cut. Follow the path along Powdermill Cut 300m to a crossroads. Turn left (N) and cross a footbridge. Follow this path winding between Friday Lake and Hooks Marsh Lake along Hooksmarsh Ditch. After 1km this ends at a T junction with a footpath, turn right (E) onto this. ❷ The footpath crosses a bridge between Seventy Acres Lake and Hooks Marsh Lake and after 400m reaches a metal trellis bridge across Horsemill Stream. Don't cross this, instead turn left onto the path following another winding course, between Seventy Acres Lake and Horsemill Stream. After 1.5km the lake ends and a path leads off left; don't take this, continue another 300m N and take the next path on the left, beside a sculpted bench. ❸ Follow the path W, crossing the canal by a footbridge and after 300m reaching a junction of several paths, at a clearing. You will see a small path

Lee Valley

Lee Valley resident

leading across a footbridge, 50m away across the main paths. Head to this footbridge and cross it. ④ The footbridge crosses the Small River Lea to a path winding N along a raised causeway. After 900m, this path forks, take the left fork which continues following the banks of Ashley Lake. Follow the path as it bends W around the top of Ashley Lake, continue 120m ahead to reach a T junction in front of a railway track. Turn left onto the path, heading S. ⑤ Follow the path alongside the railway for 1km S before reaching a T junction. Turn left (E). After 120m the Small River Lea is crossed by footbridge and a junction is reached, continue ahead across the junction onto the small path which leads into the woods. After 300m (bear right when the path forks) it emerges onto a bigger path, turn left (S) onto this. ⑥ Follow the path for 700m S along a lake (North Metropolitan Pit) to a crossroads. Turn left (E) and follow this footpath 260m to the canal. Turn right onto the tow path footpath and follow it 500m S to the car park.

Hall Marsh

Trip planning

Pinder car park is located at Cheshunt Station Entrance to Lee Valley Park, which is of course close to the railway station. A generally quieter alternative is to park and enter at the Hooks Marsh Entrance on Fishers

Lee Valley Park

Lee Valley

Green Lane EN9 2ED / **TL 377 026** at the opposite side of the park, which would start your run at the metal trellis bridge described after ❷.

A map of the park can downloaded online (Visit Lee Valley website), and is useful for making sense of the water features and the web of trails around them.

Lee Valley Country Park and the River Lee Regional Park (of which it is part) have a huge range of facilities for leisure activities; the Queen Elizabeth Olympic Park is the most notable of these! The Visit Lee Valley website gives more detail on the infrastructure for cycling, boating, white water rafting, sculpture walks and much more. The Lee Valley Nearly Wild Campsite at Broxbourne is a great place to stay and explore these facilities further.

If you can find an excuse for time out during your run, the Bittern Information Point which is passed between ❷ and ❸ is an interesting place to learn more about these rare birds; a tenth of the UK population is here in the park. You might just spot one, from their hide.

Other routes

It is simple to alter or shorten this route; obvious short cuts are available at several points, for example between ❸ and ❺.

Lee Valley Park

The Lee Valley's 40km green corridor into London has a huge range of trails to explore; the simplest to start with is the Lea Valley Walk, which follows riverbanks and tow paths for 80km from Leagrave (near Luton) to Limehouse Basin beside the River Thames, passing Route 44 along the way. Fanning out from the LVW, the options are endless; the dauntingly thorough Visit Lee Valley website supplies detailed route cards for over 30 runs, stretched along the Lee Valley Regional Park.

Nearby Broxbourne Woods has a 17.5km trail around the National Nature Reserve; details and maps can be found online.

River Lee Navigation

Events

Run Fest at Lee Valley (*'race within a flat traffic-free nature-full oasis'*) is an event with 10km and Half Marathon distances, starting from Lee Valley White Water Centre.

Essex

Essex is regarded by some as the last place you might head seeking open spaces and adventures in the wild. Showcased here are numerous good reasons why such folk need to actually visit and challenge their preconceptions! In the west of the county, the ancient Royal Forests at Epping and Hatfield are glorious places to literally lose oneself in the woods. To the south, the Thames Estuary's marshes, combined with the steep overlooking hills, are the site of a great route in the shadow of Hadleigh Castle. A run in Dedham Vale Area of Outstanding Natural Beauty is included in the north, to see the River Stour as Constable did. The hidden trump card of Essex's landscapes is however found to the east; the North Sea coast is the second longest coast of any English county and it can be a hauntingly wild and desolate place, as the two routes described here will impress upon you.

River Crouch Estuary (Route 40)

Centenary Ride

36 Epping Forest

Distance		8.5km (5.5 miles) **Ascent** 100m (330ft)
Map		OS Landranger 167 OS Explorer 174
Navigation	●●●	The official Epping Forest map is useful, a compass might also help
Terrain	●●●	Rooty trails, some off-piste woodland
Wet feet	●●●	Some of the smaller trails can get pretty stodgy
Start / Finish		Pillow Mounds car park IG10 4AE / TQ 412 983

Ancient woodlands, inside the M25

Epping Forest is a remarkable survival, a 12km-long 2,400-hectare woodland which has nestled on a sandy ridge between the valleys of the River Lea and Roding since the last Ice Age ... yet it is inside the M25, flanked by London's suburbs! Known as the 'People's Forest', Epping Forest is the largest open space available to Londoners, and is managed by the City of London Corporation ... however it is located firmly within Essex's borders.

Alarm bells might ring at the proximity to the capital, but do not be put off; the forest is a genuinely wild place where you can quickly lose yourself (figuratively and quite possibly literally) along the loamy trails. This is no bland plantation; the trees have real character. Some 55,000 of the beech, silver birch, hornbeam and oak were pollarded (pruned to make them expand outwards) in their youth, but have since grown

Epping Forest

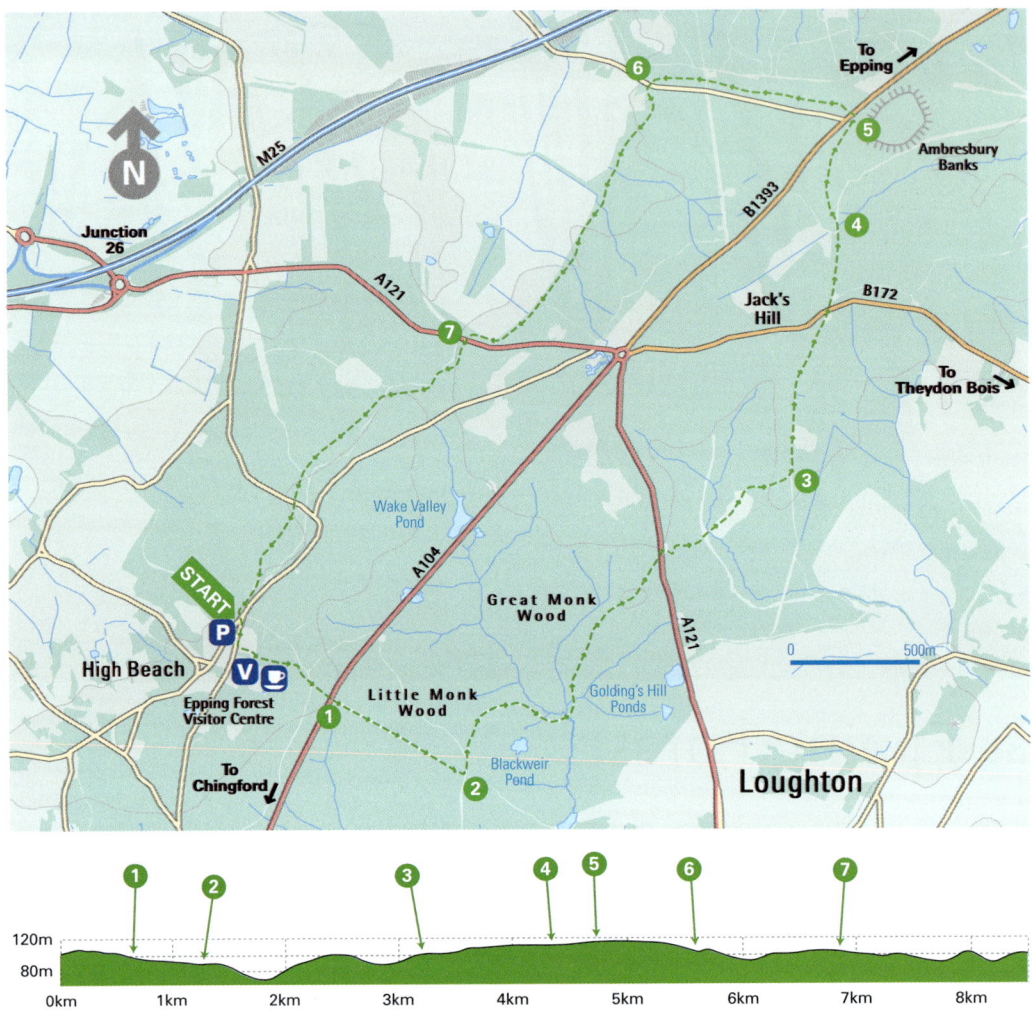

uncut for a century and a half. The result is a forest full of sprawling characterful trees which would not seem out of place in a fairy tale!

This route is offered as just a taster of Epping Forest's 284km+ network of trails. You will, for sure, return here and explore further.

Route description

START From the parking area, head along High Beech Road towards the Visitor Centre building (behind the King's Oak Hotel). At the entrance to the Visitor Centre parking area is a black 'City of London' sign. Don't enter the car park, instead follow rough paths through the woods heading E (away from High Beech Road) along the boundary fence of the Visitor Centre. After 150m you reach the end of the boundary fence, and a N-S path crossing your route. Cross this path and continue following the path leading straight ahead (ESE). You are now following a route (occasionally signposted) called the 'Centenary Walk'. The footpath reaches a road (Epping New Road) after another 150m. ❶ Cross the road and continue

Epping Forest

following the footpath ESE along a treelined corridor. After 600m, a large crossroads is reached. Turn left (N) onto a track known as the 'Green Ride'. ❷ Follow this winding and undulating track for 1.4km, ignoring side turns, to reach a road (A121 Golding's Hill). Cross the road and follow the path ahead NE for 600m to a T junction with a N–S track (known as 'The Ditches Ride'). Turn left (N, uphill) onto the track. ❸ After 700m, the track reaches a road (B172) and parking area (Jack's Hill car park). Cross the road and continue following the track N. After about 150m, you will notice a parallel path on a raised bank, to your left; join this (leaving the 'Centenary Walk' route). ❹ The path follows the raised bank roughly N, winding tightly through the trees, emerging beside a road (B1393 Epping Road) after about 350m. Turn right and follow paths alongside the road a short distance, until you see the earthworks of Ambresbury Banks hillfort on your right. ❺ Cross the road at the junction with Crown Hill Road. Either follow very rough paths through the woods just N of Crown Hill Road, or follow the road itself for 550m to the entrance to the Copped Hall Park Estate (white gates between two gatehouse buildings). Cross the entrance drive and run another 200m alongside the road, and then cross it to join the dirt track heading S. ❻ The dirt track leads to the gates of a house, then continues SSW along the edge of the forest, marked by white posts. After 1.4km, it bends right and reaches a road (A121 Woodridden Hill). Cross the road and take the path leading ahead (this is part of the 'Forest Way' route). ❼ Follow the Forest Way path roughly SW for 1.5km back to the parking area, ignoring any paths leading off on the right (downhill) and crossing a lane (Claypit Hill) after 1km.

Epping Forest trails

The Warren entrance

Green Ride

Trip planning

Pillow Mounds car park is free roadside parking on Manor Road; leave the M25 at Junction 26 (Waltham Abbey Interchange) and follow signs for 'Epping Forest Centre' onto the A121, turning right after 500m beside a car park onto Forest Side Road. After 1km this becomes Claypit Hill Road and you arrive at the car park. If driving from central London, Junction 5 of the M11 deposits you in the vicinity.

Accessing Epping Forest by public transport from London is easy; Loughton and Epping underground stations on the Central Line both deposit you close to the forest, although 3km from this route. Chingford railway station is right on the southern edge, 4.5km away from this route.

Epping Forest Visitor Centre at High Beach is at the start of this route, and calling in to buy a copy of the

Epping Forest

Official Map is recommended; this highly useful map seems impossible to obtain elsewhere (and the visitor centres only accept something archaic called 'cash'). The King's Oak pub is alongside the visitor centre, solving your hunger issue.

There are two other visitor centres; Epping Forest Gateway at Chingford is useful if arriving from the south, and is beside Queen Elizabeth's Hunting Lodge (worth a visit), while the other is in Wanstead Park, far south of the main part of the forest.

Other routes

Truth be told, you'll be doing well to stick on this route and avoid temptation to deviate and improvise! A good starting point for further exploration is to obtain the Official Map (see above), as many of Epping Forest's 284km of trails are not well marked on the standard OS maps. There is open access within the forest, but be sensible where you tread as it is an SSSI and a Special Area of Conservation.

If looking for a bit more guidance, the City of London website outlines nine waymarked routes, for example the Oak Trail which is a 12km loop close to Epping underground station.

The route described here barely touches the southern half of the forest; one introduction to it could be to set out from Chingford railway station and run 4.5km north along the Green Way to the start of this route. The Three Forests Way (see page 192) passes through the centre of the forest, and the Essex Way (see page 208) starts from nearby from Epping railway station.

Events

Run Nation organise the Run London Epping Forest Trail 10K, starting from Chingford and looping around the southern part of the forest.

Orion Harriers' John Clarke Memorial Fell Race is, unsurprisingly, the only full fell race held inside the M25! The requisite ascent is achieved by multiple climbs of Pole Hill.

The People's Forest

The open access that you enjoy while running Epping Forest has deep historical roots. During the twelfth century, Henry II created Waltham Forest (a 'Forest' being a Royal hunting ground). Commoners could not hunt in the Forest, but had rights to graze animals and gather wood ('lopping'). By the nineteenth century, Epping Forest was the only surviving part and was shrinking due to rapacious landowners 'enclosing' parts; literally, fencing them off from commoners.

The Forest was saved by the 1878 Epping Forest Act, which gave control to the City of London Corporation and tasked them to, *'at all times keep Epping Forest unenclosed and unbuilt on as an open space for the recreation and enjoyment of the people'*. Queen Victoria visited in 1882 (the Green Walk was made for her) and declared, *"It gives me the greatest satisfaction to dedicate this beautiful forest to the use and enjoyment of my people for all time"*. Henceforth, it was known as, 'the People's Forest'.

Entrance from Takeley Street

37 Hatfield Forest

Distance	8km (5 miles)	Ascent	50m (125ft)
Map	OS Landranger 167 OS Explorer 183, 195		
Navigation	● ● ●	Clear, wide tracks, although little signage	
Terrain	● ● ●	Level grass and earth	
Wet feet	● ● ●	Muddy bits are dodge-able	
Start / Finish	Hatfield Forest car park CM22 6NF / TL 547 202		

Easy trails around an ancient Royal Forest

Hatfield Forest is (unsurprisingly) a forest, in the sense of being a bunch of trees. However, its name refers to the older meaning of 'forest'; a Royal hunting ground. Hatfield's dates from the eleventh century and is the best preserved anywhere. As it happens, it's also a fine spot for some enjoyable, but not overly taxing, trail running.

This outing starts by visiting the ornamental lake at the heart of Hatfield Forest. The long tree-free corridors which you next run through were planned 'rides' for pursuing, and in more modern times shooting, deer. The 400-hectare woodland around has over 800 ancient ash, hornbeam and oak trees, some believed to be 1,200 years old! Early-bird runners will spot fallow and muntjac deer, among other wildlife. For variation, you head outside more than once. The pond on the forest's western boundary was in 1999 the impact site of a 747 airliner! Korean Air Flight 8509 crashed 55 seconds after take-off from Stansted Airport, killing all

37 Hatfield Forest

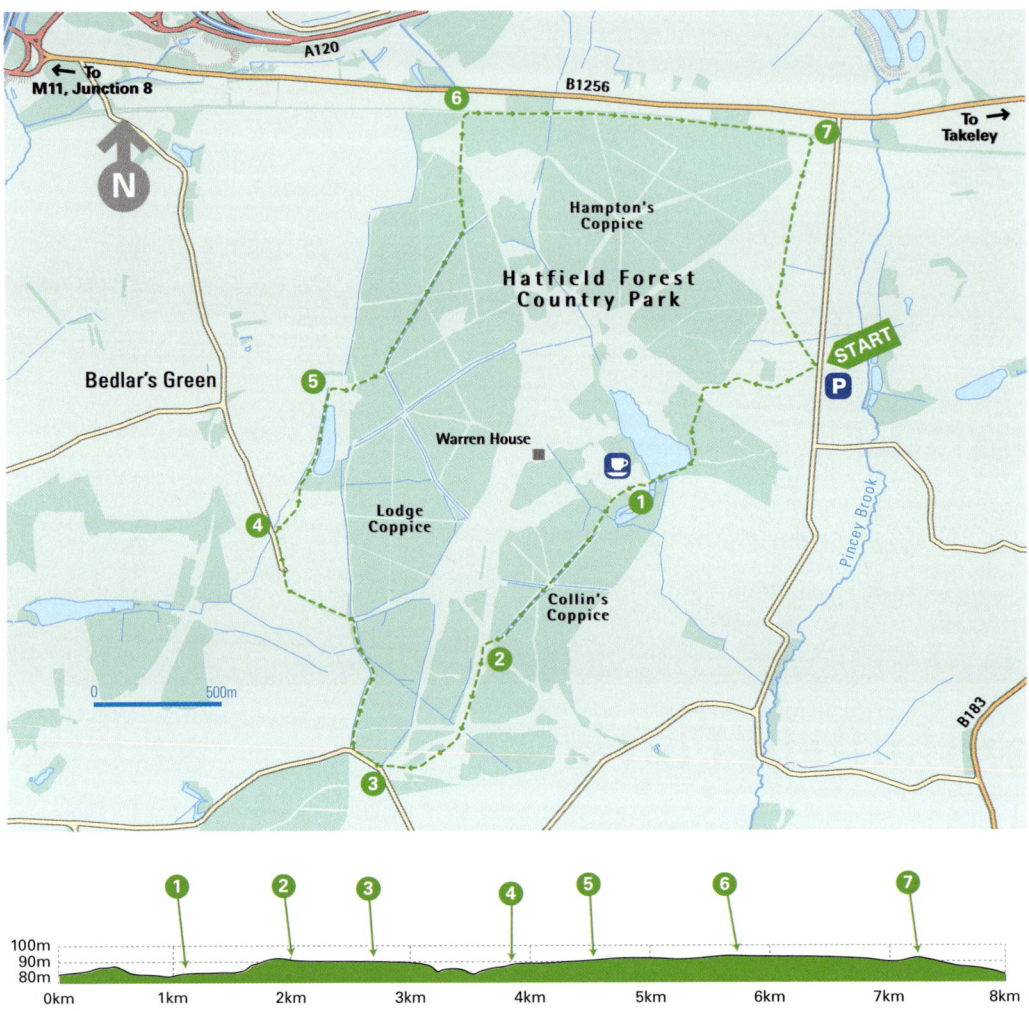

four crew. The track along the northern boundary is a disused railway, which leads you to a final airy run across open ground punctuated by scattered ancient oaks.
Incidentally, Hatfield Forest is nothing at all to do with Hatfield House (Route 34).

Route description

START From the car park, pass through the entrance gate and follow the main track. After 330m, a boardwalk path leads off on the left, follow this. It leads S into woods and reaches a lake. Follow the path along the lake until you reach the causeway / dam across the lake, turn right and cross this to Shell House. ❶ The path continues SW, passing benches along the lake. After passing the SW tip of the lake, you reach a wide straight grassy avenue heading SW. Follow the path along this avenue for 600m until it ends at a larger avenue, leading N–S. Turn left (S) and follow this wider avenue. ❷ After 300m the path along the avenue gradually bends to the right (W), continue to follow the path until you reach the South Gate, beside a lane. ❸ Don't go through the South Gate, instead follow the path NW through the woods,

Hatfield Forest

Hatfield Forest

paralleling the road. After 150m this path ends, turn right (N) onto the footpath leading N along the outside edge of the woods (and of Hatfield Forest). After 500m this veers away from the woods to pass around houses, and after another 300m it becomes a tarmac lane (The Street), with a footpath track leading off to the right. ❹ Turn right to take this footpath (signposted for Marston Farm). Follow it N past a pond to a T junction with another footpath track. Turn right onto this footpath, which leads E back into Hatfield Forest. ❺ After you re-enter Hatfield Forest, follow the avenue through the trees which leads NE, ignoring any side turns. After 850m the track bears left and heads N across a clearing in the woods, to reach the northern boundary of Hatfield Forest, with National Trust signs and a gate. ❻ Go through the gate onto a disused railway (known as Takeley Street). Turn right and follow this E for 1.4km to a sign on the right for 'Flitch Way Country Park'. Go through the gate here (S) and re-enter Hatfield Forest. ❼ Follow paths S across the open ground for 1km back to the car park.

Trip planning

Hatfield Forest has been owned by the National Trust since 1924. Entry is free to all, however non-members will be charged for parking. This route starts from the car park directly outside the main entrance. The car park should always be open but fills quickly, early arrival is a good idea. It's reached by turning off the B1256 Dunmow Road heading west out of Takeley, following National Trust signs. A free and quieter alternative is to

The Lake

Hatfield Forest

start from the South Gate at ❸ where there is a small layby CM22 7UG / **TL 530 186**.

After running, it's well worth visiting the quirky Shell House beside the lake, which was built in the 1750s and decorated with ... yes, shells, by the landowner's daughter. This is close to the National Trust's café so it would be rude not to sample their cuisine.

For any other needs, there is a supermarket in Takeley and the town of Bishop's Stortford is just 5km away.

The NT close Hatfield Forest when very strong winds are forecast. Runners should also be aware that they protect Hatfield Forest (which is an SSSI and a National Nature Reserve) in the winter months by putting diversions around some paths and asking runners to avoid muddy woodland trails, to limit erosion. See their website for updates.

Hatfield Forest

Takeley Street

Other routes

There are of course numerous trails to explore in Hatfield Forest; start with the 'rides' and see where they bring you! The NT website suggests routes to explore different aspects of the forest.

Looking to explore this corner of Essex further? The gently-rolling hills around Saffron Walden (15km north of Hatfield Forest) offer many trail possibilities, mixed with road intervals. A pleasant place to start is the footpaths around the English Heritage property of Audley End.

Events

There are no trail running events currently held within Hatfield Forest, although there have been in the past (including a parkrun). The closest event is the Takeley 10K, which heads out and back along the disused railway.

The LDWA organise the Stansted Stagger Challenge Event, 25.6 miles based from nearby Stansted Mountfitchet. Challenge Events organise the Stort30 Ultra, which involves running 15 miles along the Stort Navigation from Bishop's Stortford, then doing it again in reverse (running in the other direction, not running backwards).

The Three Forests Way

The Three Forests Way is a 94km / 58-mile circular trail linking Hatfield Forest, Epping Forest (Route 36) and Hainault Forest, partly following the Stort Navigation. Gradients are mostly mild, with 939m of ascent along the route. There is no guidebook or 'official' source of information, but the route is marked on OS maps and a gpx route file can be downloaded from the LDWA website.

The LDWA hold the 54-mile Three Forests Way Challenge Event every year, with runners welcome.

Hadleigh Castle 38

Hadleigh Castle

38 Hadleigh Castle

Distance		10km (6.5 miles)	**Ascent**	125m (440ft)
Map		OS Landranger 178 OS Explorer 175		
Navigation	●●●	Fairly simple, a limited range of footpaths to choose from		
Terrain	●●●	Grass, marsh, medieval stonework		
Wet feet	●●●	Hadleigh Marsh lives up to its name, add a star in winter		
Start / Finish		Hadleigh Park car park SS7 2QH / TQ 800 868		

Thames estuary views from up high and down low

I have to be completely honest; back in 2012, when I heard that the London Olympics Mountain Biking event was being held near Southend-on-Sea, I laughed out loud. Having since visited Hadleigh Country Park to trail run (and ride), I realise that the joke is entirely on me.

Hadleigh Country Park occupies 152 hectares of steep hillside descending to undeveloped marshland, with expansive views across a complex landscape of creeks, islands and mudflats leading into the Thames Estuary. On an adjacent summit, the ruins of Hadleigh Castle brood over the tidelands. Built around 1215 and later a favoured residence of King Edward III, it's not hard to grasp the castle's strategic importance in controlling the approaches to London. Down on the marshes, eccentric houseboats provide some colour to break up the bleak surrounds, where only the calls of wading birds (and the occasional passing train) disrupt the silence. So yes, it's well worth running (and riding) here.

38 Hadleigh Castle

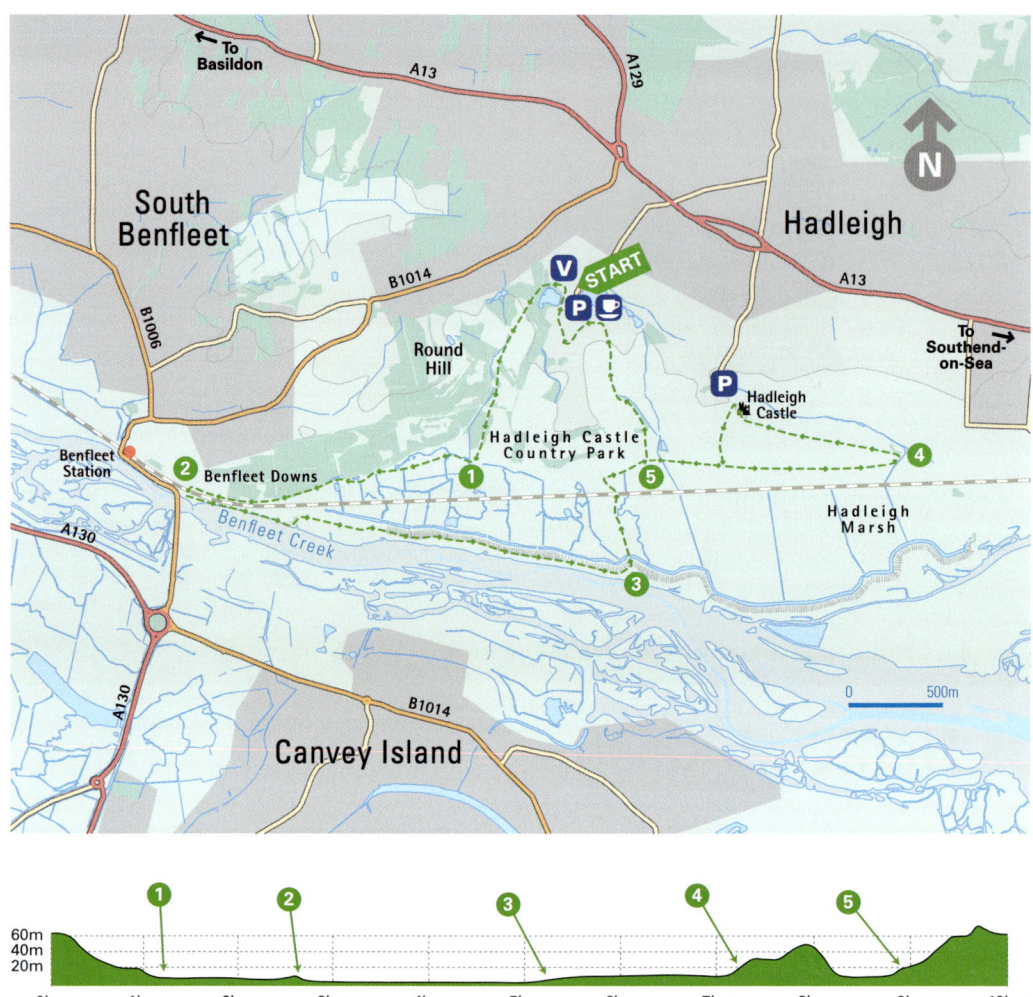

Route description

START A footpath leads N–S along the W side of the car park (opposite side from the café and other buildings). Pass through a gap in the trees to this footpath and turn left (S) onto it. Follow this footpath directly downhill, ignoring any side turns. After 1.2km the footpath ends at a T junction with a bridleway path. ❶ Turn right (W) and follow the bridleway path along Hadleigh Marsh. After 1km it comes close to the railway and splits; take the path nearer the railway, which is a footpath. After another 500m you reach a foot crossing, cross the railway with care (if the crossing is closed, continue another 450m W to cross underneath by road). ❷ Having crossed the railway, turn left (E) and follow the footpath (initially a tarmac road beside a flood barrier) along the estuary (Benfleet Creek), past the moored boats. The footpath is signposted as the 'Thames Estuary Path' and elevates to follow a wide sea wall crossing Hadleigh Marsh. Ignore the left turning after 900m which leads N to a railway crossing, continue to the second left turn which is 2.4km from the flood barrier where the footpath bends left around a side-creek. ❸ Turn off left and follow this path N. Cross the railway and continue ahead to a T junction with a

Hadleigh Castle

Benfleet Creek

bridleway path (same bridleway as earlier). Turn right (E) and follow this bridleway. After 250m the bridleway becomes a footpath, continue ahead along the base of the hill. 1.6km from the T junction the footpath reaches a junction, with the left-hand footpath leading uphill towards Hadleigh Castle; take this left turn.
❹ Ascend to the castle, and deviate from the footpath on the left, to pass through the ruins. Exiting the castle

Hadleigh Park

at the far end, you reach a footpath track. Turn left (downhill) and descend steeply. After 350m you reach a T junction with the footpath running along the base of the hill. Turn right (W) and follow this for 400m (re-treading your earlier route) to where a footpath leads off uphill on the right, entering Hadleigh Park.
❺ Turn right and follow this footpath uphill. After 800m the footpath becomes tarmac and you will see the Park facilities and buildings; before returning to the car park, bear left across grass to visit the highest point (Sandpit Hill).

Trip planning

Hadleigh Country Park is found at the end of Chapel Lane, signposted off the A13 between Southend-on-Sea and South Benfleet. There is a charge for the car park, otherwise access is free. The Hub building beside the car park has a decent café, as well as various facilities related to mountain biking. This is a great place to visit with family and children; nip off to run while they enjoy the play park or the fantastic riding (including a pump track and skills area).

Hadleigh Castle

It's possible to park for free by starting the run from the end of Castle Lane SS7 2AF / **TQ 808 864** near Hadleigh Castle. This fills up quickly and is a narrow lane with no turning spot, so avoid if you don't like long reverses! From the end of the lane, it is 150m down a footpath track to the castle.

Other routes

There are of course numerous alternative paths within the Country Park to explore; a map can be downloaded or obtained at the Hub building. Just don't stray onto the mountain bike paths!

It is possible to extend this route to around 18km by circumnavigating beautiful Two Tree Island, an Essex Wildlife Trust nature reserve (it was formerly a waste dump!). Continue ahead along the sea wall at ❸ until you reach the bridge crossing to the island. Follow the paths around the island before returning back across the bridge, then turn right to follow the footpath along the sea wall 500m to join a lane which crosses the railway. Turn left onto a road (Belton Way) and shortly after, take the tarmac footpath (signposted 'Castle Drive') on the left towards Hadleigh Castle, re-joining the route at ❹. There is a car park SS9 2GB / **TQ 824 853** on the island if you want to explore it in isolation.

The Thames Estuary Path leads 47km / 29 miles along the South Essex Marshes from Tilbury to Leigh-on-Sea, passing through this route at the end. Details and maps available online.

Events

A 5km parkrun is held at Hadleigh Park, every Saturday.

A variety of races are based from and around the Park. Active Training World's Run Hadleigh Park event has options of 5, 10 or 15 miles; the Essex Cross Country 10K Series includes one event at the park and there is also Nice Work's Benfleet 15 (miles), which extends a bit further into the marshlands.

Essex parks

Below are some more suggestions for public spaces within the county where you can stretch your legs freely:

Danbury Country Park, Woodhill Road, Danbury CM3 4AL / **TL 768 047** – landscaped estate and woodlands around Danbury Palace (Danbury Commons is nearby, owned by the National Trust).

Great Notley Country Park, Great Notley CM77 7BN / **TL 734 213** – grassy pathways across open meadows.

Hylands Park and House, Chelmsford CM2 8FS / **TL 680 047** – large privately-owned landscaped park with open access.

Marsh Farm Country Park, Marsh Farm Road, South Woodham Ferrers CM3 5WP / **TQ 810 957** – marshland beside the River Crouch Estuary.

Thorndon Country Park, Brentwood CM13 3RZ / **TQ 607 915** – extensive woodland trails.

Weald Country Park, Weald Road, Brentwood CM14 5QX / **TQ 568 941** – large area of rolling landscaped parkland with grasslands and meadows.

The Broomway

Wakering Stairs

39 The Broomway

Distance	14km (8.5 miles)	Ascent	25m (60ft)
Map	OS Landranger 178 OS Explorer 176		
Navigation ●●●	Forgetting your compass could prove fatal		
Terrain ●●○	Firm sand, some squidgy mud		
Wet Feet ●●●	You are running in the actual North Sea		
Start / Finish	Victoria Drive, Great Wakering SS3 0AT / TQ 953 868		

Britain's deadliest path, also a wonderful trail run

The Broomway is an ancient route across Maplin Sands *in the North Sea*. Only accessible at low tide, the Broomway is the only way for the public to access Foulness Island, which is owned by the Ministry of Defence and used for weapons testing. This legal byway (marked on OS maps) is simply unmarked sand. The risks are numerous: rising tide, fog, quicksand mud, getting lost, incoming ordnance. For these reasons the path has claimed many lives over the centuries and gained the reputation of being 'Britain's deadliest path'. Why might you wish to run here? With appropriate care, traversing the Broomway is an incredible experience and a reminder that Britain (and yes, even Essex) can offer truly wild adventure for those willing to seek it out. The author ran here barefoot, at dawn. Despite careful navigation, it was impossible to shake the sense of being utterly lost in this vast empty liminal space between land, sea and sky. After eventually returning to the mainland, I lingered on the shore for a good while, trying to coax life back into numb but battered feet … and reluctant to leave.

39 The Broomway

Route description

START At the end of Victoria Drive, there is a wire fence with a gate in it; if the gate is open (see 'Trip planning' below), pass through and cross the drive behind to the footpath. Follow the footpath ahead. After 950m the footpath reaches the sea wall. Ascend onto this, turn left and follow the footpath 900m to Wakering Stairs (slipway into the sea). ❶ Follow the slipway until it peters out and reaches sand. Continue out to about 400m from the shore, then take a bearing of 058°. ❷ Follow this bearing for 1.4km, this should bring you to the 'Maypole', a post with crossbars stuck in the sand for navigation. ❸ Take a bearing of 050° and follow it. After 2.8km you'll reach the seaward end of a track leading onto Foulness Island, marked by a post with a triangle on top. ❹ Follow the track 350m to the shore of Foulness Island at Asplins Head; this is muddy, you may wish to stay offshore instead. ❺ Return the same way you came (reverse the bearings across the sand: 230° for 2.8km and then 238° for 1.4km).

The Broomway

Foulness Island

Trip planning

This route presents challenges and risks unlike any other trail run, however with appropriate thought and planning it can be a safe and enjoyable experience.

Most importantly, your run must be timed to coincide with the tide being **out**; three hours either side of Low Water, based on Southend-on-Sea. Tides can be unpredictable and may come in earlier or later than forecast, so do not push this envelope. Southend-on-Sea tide times can be obtained online.

A compass is absolutely essential, and you need to be confident to follow a bearing across open ground, even if fog rolls in and you lose visibility (this happened to the author!). A phone app which gives your precise position on the map (such as Viewranger) might also be a good idea. Carry a mobile phone (in a waterproof bag) and in an emergency, dial 999 and speak to the Coastguard.

The Maypole

Once you are offshore, there is no route marked. The Broomway's surface is firm damp sand, however there is a band of soft mud along the shore. Trainers will get soaked, consider leaving them at Wakering Stairs and running barefoot.

The Broomway is almost always closed on weekdays. It is usually open at weekends, check by calling the Range

Asplins Head

The Broomway

Control Office 01702 383211 during weekday working hours. You will know on arrival if it is closed; the access gates at the start will be locked and red flags will be flying if the firing ranges are active (really not a good time to run). You are not allowed to deviate from the Broomway's course; the sand flats are a Site of Special Scientific Interest and there may also be unexploded ordnance lying around.

The MOD's information leaflet *MOD Shoeburyness – Public Access, a guide for recreational visitors* is obtainable online and is a recommended read.

Other routes

It is also possible to access Wakering Stairs via the 1.5km road from Landwick Gate SS3 0DH / **TQ 959 875**.

A longer run is possible on the Broomway. It continues nearly 4.5km beyond Asplins Head, changing after 1km at Rugwood Head from a byway to a bridleway (of course there is still no visible trail). The Broomway terminates at Fisherman's Head, where another slipway leads ashore. A runner could return to Asplins Head via the footpath leading along the sea wall.

There are many kilometres of legal footpath around the coast and interior of this highly secret island, and exploring them is appealing. You will of course be constantly mindful of the need to return to the Broomway in time to beat the tide.

Start point

Broomway selfie

The Broomway

The Broomway has existed since at least 1419, when it is first mentioned in records. It is however likely to be much older (the Romans left traces on Foulness Island, for example), possibly following an ancient land route which was subsequently inundated by the sea. The name refers to the 'brooms' formerly used to mark out the route for islanders; bundles of twigs wired to poles stuck in the sand. No trace of these markers exists today. The Broomway has fallen out of use since Havengore Creek was bridged in 1922, but before that it was the main way of accessing Foulness Island. It still sees occasional use by military traffic too heavy for the bridge; this apparently accesses the island at Fisherman's Head, the only maintained slipway. Is the Broomway *really* Britain's deadliest path? The short answer is, yes. sixty-six of the bodies buried in Foulness churchyard lost their lives along the route, with the total death toll estimated to be over a hundred. Take your compass and double-check the tide times.

Dengie Flat

40 The Dengie Peninsula

Distance		28km (17.5 miles) **Ascent** 25m (80ft)
Map		OS Landranger 168 OS Explorer 176
Navigation	●●●	The ability to follow a large wall is a prerequisite
Terrain	●●●	The trail is flat but uneven and rutted
Wet feet	●●●	You run high and dry above the sea and marsh
Start		Belvedere Road, Burnham-on-Crouch CM0 8AJ / TQ 954 955
Finish		Waterside Road, Bradwell Waterside CM0 7QX / TL 996 078

The lonely sea and the sky

The remotest, loneliest and wildest trail run in this book is right here in Essex. The Dengie Peninsula is an area of reclaimed land separated from vast salt marshes by the sea wall along which you run. For the first two-thirds of this long outing beneath big skies, the only landmarks are distant farm buildings and the intermittent Second World War pillbox (the inexplicably massive one was a 'minefield control tower'). The only company you are likely to have is sea birds and the wind. Once you leave the River Crouch Estuary behind, you might not even see the sea for a good while as the marshes extend far offshore. Agoraphobics may wish to give this route a miss!

Eventually you reach The Chapel of St Peter-on-the-Wall, one of the oldest surviving churches in Britain (built c. 660AD!). You can finish here at 22km, or continue 8km into the River Blackwater Estuary past the

40 The Dengie Peninsula

The Dengie Peninsula

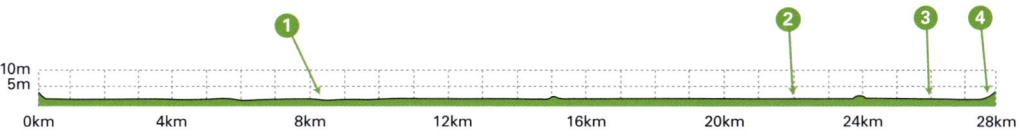

looming bulk of Bradwell Nuclear Power Station. The advantage of this latter extension is the ability to use public transport to shuttle back to the start.

Route description

 **START** Ascend onto the sea wall at the end of Belvedere Road in Burnham-on-Crouch. Turn left (E). Follow the wall, ignoring all paths you see that lead inland from the wall, for 28km! After 8.3km the sea wall becomes concrete. ❶ The concrete continues until the 11km mark; sections of beach are runnable alongside, as a possible alternative. After 22km you reach St Peter's Chapel. ❷ At 26km you pass Bradwell Nuclear Power Station (decommissioned). ❸ At 28km the sea wall reaches Waterside Road in Bradwell Waterside. ❹ The End.

St Peter on the Wall

Shell Bank beach

Trip planning

Buses are timetabled to run between Bradwell Waterside and Burnham-on-Crouch every couple of hours or so, all days except Sunday, taking about 45 minutes. However, this is the Essex and Suffolk DaRT service, which stands for 'Demand Responsive Transport'. You need to call a couple of hours ahead and book, otherwise the bus won't run.

Crouch Estuary pillbox

Plenty of on-street parking spaces are available near the start in Burnham-on-Crouch, for example along High Street (B1021). There is limited public parking in Bradwell Waterside, but you should be able to deposit a car in a side street or outside one of the pubs, with their permission.

If you finish your run after 22km at St Peter's Chapel, you'll need a vehicle there to pick you up. The (free) parking area is 800m along the track leading inland, CM0 7PN / **TM 024 078**.

Aborting this run before St Peter's Chapel is problematic. A glance at the OS map will reveal that although a number of tracks (few of which are Rights of Way) lead inland to join roads, you are still looking at an 8km+ trek before you reach any settlements, unless someone can come by car and meet you part way. In other words, it might be just as easy to continue to the chapel.

40 The Dengie Peninsula

Other routes

As explained above, shortening this route before St Peter's Chapel doesn't really work.

Diehards who need to go further could make this into a loop by continuing along the River Blackwater to St Lawrence or Mayland before heading south to Burnham-on-Crouch via footpaths and road, an extension of 15–22km.

St Peter's Chapel is the finish point of St Peter's Way, a 72km / 45-mile trail from Chipping Ongar. A detailed guide can be downloaded online.

Events

If you wish to stretch running along sea walls to its illogical conclusion, then enter the Salt Marsh Ultra. This is held in October and leads 52.4 miles around the Dengie Peninsula from Woodham Ferrers to Maldon (in 2020 it was reduced to 38 miles to make it Covid-safe). Incidentally, they describe the Burnham-on-Crouch to St Peter's Chapel section thusly; *'as hostile and remote as it is unique and noteworthy.'* The Saltmarsh Half Marathon runs concurrently, ending at Burnham-on-Crouch.

The St Peter's Way Ultra follows the long-distance trail for 45 miles to its finish point at St Peter's Chapel.

The Smugglers Trail is a 9.3- or 5-mile trail race held at Burnham-on-Crouch in March, partly along the coast.

St Peter on the Wall

Crouch Estuary

The Dengie Marshes

The Dengie Marshes (pronounced 'dengy') span over a dozen kilometres between the Crouch and Blackwater estuaries, and extend 2–3km offshore from the sea wall. They are an internationally important habitat for the salt-tolerant plants that stabilise the mud flats from erosion, and for the enormous populations of sea birds which roost here in the winter months. When the tide is high, you will see tens of thousands of wading birds pecking along the shoreline at once, or taking to the air to form breathtaking formations known as murmurations. North of St Peter's Chapel where the sea comes closer (protected by a line of sunken Thames barges) is Bradwell Shell Bank, comprised of millions of cockle and oyster shells. The Dengie Marsh landscape and habitat is protected by a whole panoply of environmental designations: SSSI, NNR, SPA, NCR, GCR, RAMSAR and no doubt some other acronyms too. Regardless, it should be obvious to the runner plodding along with all of this spread before them, that this is a unique and precious place.

Dedham Vale

River Stour near Dedham

41 Dedham Vale

Distance		12km (9.5 miles)	**Ascent**	75m (260ft)
Map		OS Landranger 168 OS Explorer 184, 196		
Navigation	●●●	Well signposted, follows Essex Way for half of route		
Terrain	●●●	Mild ascents and descents, muddy and grassy trails		
Wet feet	●●●	Mildly muddy farmland and seasonally soggy riverbanks		
Start / Finish		Mill Lane car park, Dedham CO7 6DH / TM 057 334		

Constable Country

This lovely run combines parts of the Essex Way and Stour Valley Path as they converge along the Essex / Suffolk border within the Dedham Vale Area of Outstanding Natural Beauty. The AONB covers just 90km^2; a peaceful stretch of the River Stour valley comprised of water meadows and gently rolling farmland. It's pleasant enough for its own sake, but achieved iconic status in the nineteenth-century oil paintings of John Constable, who grew up here. Even the most culturally-bereft trail runner will recognise *The Hay Wain*? Constable's landscapes of lush vegetation, slow-moving water and big skies filled with dramatic clouds were romanticised, with no rural poverty or squalor depicted! Nonetheless you will find them recognisable along this route, most literally around Flatford Mill, subject of numerous Constable paintings. Top tip – run early on a frosty morning.

41 Dedham Vale

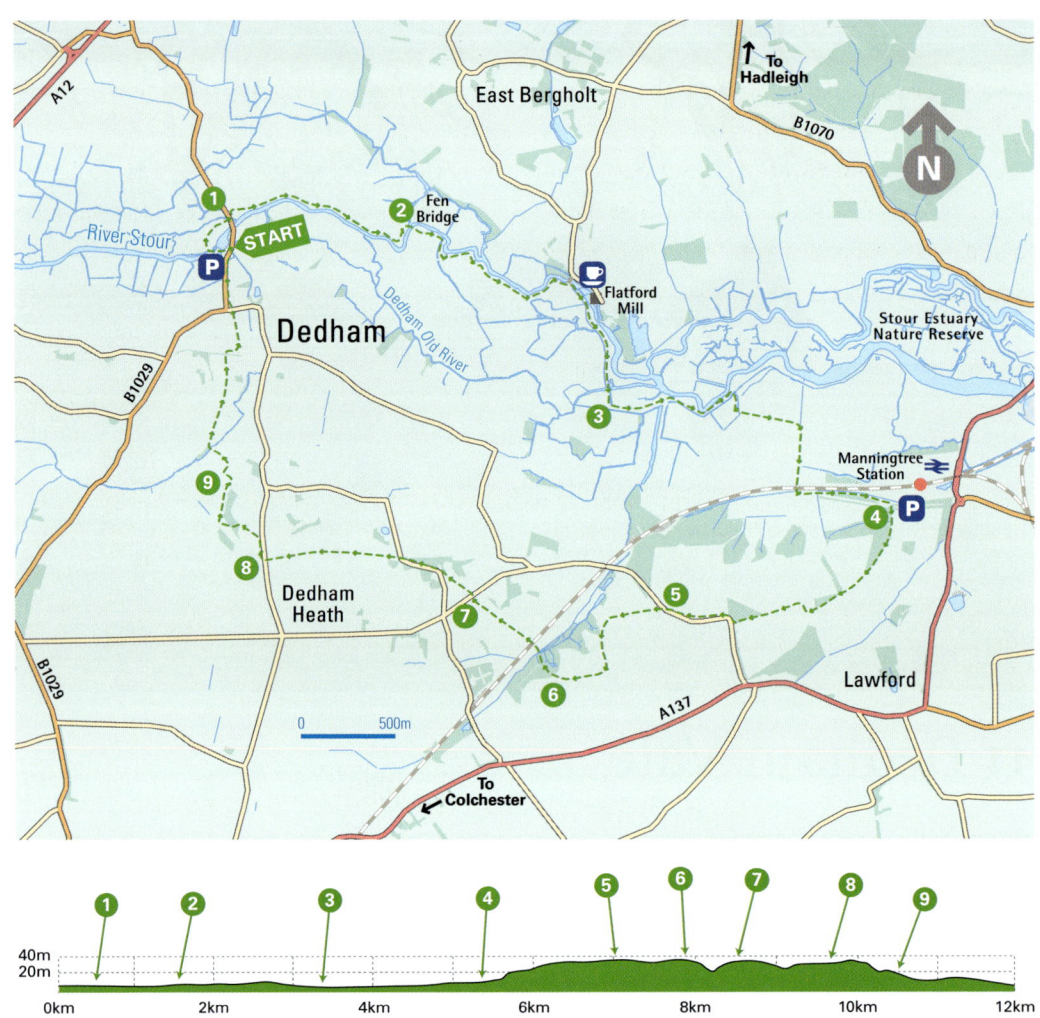

Route description

***In 2020, Fen Bridge at ❷ was closed for repair or replacement. Until this crossing is reopened (check the National Trust or Dedham Vale AONB websites for updates) start this route by following the footpath along the S bank of the River Stour from the start car park, as far as Fen Bridge.

START From the car park, head N (downhill) along the B1029 Dedham Road to the river. Just after passing a large mill building on your left, look for a footpath sign on the left and take this footpath. Follow the footpath past the mill building, across the River Stour and then around the mill pool back to the B1029 Dedham Road. Cross the road and follow it left across the second (smaller) river channel to a footpath sign. Go through the gate to follow this footpath E along the river. ❶ Follow the riverbank (the footpath splits, stay with the footpath beside the river) until you reach Fen Bridge after a kilometre. ❷ Cross this footbridge and follow the footpath along the S bank of the river for another 1.1km to reach a footbridge to Flatford village. Do not cross the bridge, continue on the footpath along the riverbank for 750m, ignoring any side turns, until you reach a T junction with a footpath. ❸ Turn left (E) to follow the footpath along a

Dedham Vale

causeway beside the river. After 700m a footpath leads off on the right, take this. The footpath leads along a track under the railway and then follows the railway E to Manningtree Railway Station. As you pass the railway station car park, look for a footpath leading off the track to the right (uphill), signposted for Lawford. Take this footpath. ❹ Ascend along the footpath. After 750m, St Mary's Church is passed and you reach the end of a lane (Church Hill). Cross the lane and take the footpath directly ahead, leading around a field. This is signposted as the Essex Way, which you'll follow all the way back to Dedham. The footpath leads along a track for 400m to Dedham Road. Turn right and follow this lane (it becomes Mill Hill) 400m to a bridleway track leading off on the left. ❺ Turn off left and follow this bridleway track for 600m past farm buildings to a crossroads of paths and tracks. Turn right (W) following the track and continue ahead following this bridleway. ❻ After 250m, a footpath turns off to the right (downhill) between wooden farm buildings. Turn right and follow this downhill, across a small bridge to a railway crossing. Cross with care and continue ahead on the footpath, uphill to reach a lane (Long Road E). ❼ Cross the lane and continue on the footpath another 170m to reach another lane (East Lane). Turn right along the lane and follow it 200m downhill to where it bends right, with a footpath signposted off to the left, beside gates. Take the footpath and follow it uphill and ahead for 700m, to where it reaches a short lane (Anchor Lane) leading to another lane. ❽ Turn right (N) onto the lane (Castle Hill) and follow it just 120m before taking the footpath on the left. This footpath leads 250m to another lane (Cooper's Lane); turn right onto this and follow it for 230m to a footpath signposted on the left between houses. ❾ Follow the footpath across a footbridge and then turn right (N). Continue ahead on the footpath (through playing fields) to reach the High Street in Dedham after 800m. Cross High Street and continue N along the B1029 Mill Lane to reach the car park.

Essex Way

River Stour near Manningtree

Flatford

Trip planning

Mill Lane car park is in Dedham, naturally on Mill Lane (the B1029). It will cost you. There is also the Riverside car park nearby ... you know where to find it. Dedham is an attractive little town with all amenities. One option is to start your run from Manningtree Railway Station CO11 2LE / **TM 094 321** at ❹, but given the expensive commuter parking there, this only really makes sense if arriving by train.

If you want to delve more deeply into the Constable connections, you really should pay a visit to Flatford

41 Dedham Vale

after running; this tiny hamlet is managed by the National Trust who have opened up various buildings linked to the Constable family (who owned Flatford Mill). The NT perform their first and foremost public duty admirably; that of laying on a decent Tea Room.

Dedham Mill

Other routes

Numerous alternative local routes can be downloaded from the National Trust and Dedham Vale AONB websites. The routes are generally pitched at OAP ramblers, but just *do them faster*.

Essex Way

Events

The Witchfinder Trail is a 5km road and trail race around Manningtree, recalling infamous seventeenth-century local Matthew Hopkins, the self-styled 'Witchfinder General'.

Noah's Challenge is a 12-mile race held at Cattawade (near Manningtree) and hosted by Mid-Essex Casuals; it starts at the Ark pub, then visits a series of animal-named pubs ... they stop the timer to allow you to drink at each pub.

Fen Bridge

The Essex Way and the Stour Valley Path

The **Essex Way** stretches 132km / 82 miles across the county from Epping (Route 36) passing through Dedham Vale on the way to its terminus at Harwich. It's waymarked by signs bearing an insignia of two red poppies. The Essex Way Relay divides the route into ten stages with the race ethos being *'low-key, friendly and cooperative'*. There is also (of course there is) the Essex Way Ultra, with distances of 50km and 100km.

The **Stour Valley Path** snakes 97km / 60-miles from Newmarket to Cattawade, near Manningtree. Most of the route is in Suffolk, the last 26km passing through Dedham Vale AONB (and this route). The Stour Valley Path 100km Ultra Run (SVP100) covers the entire Stour Valley Path, as the name rather implies. A 50km race (SVP50) runs concurrently, starting from Sudbury.

Detailed guides for both routes can be found online, plus both are marked on OS maps.

Kent

Kent's name possibly derives from ancient Celtic, meaning 'corner'. Tucked away here in Britain's bottom-right corner are some fantastic trail running experiences; those who have only previously passed through on the M20, headed for Calais, should next time stop and linger. Kent is often called 'The Garden of England' on account of its orchards and oast houses, but the cliché doesn't do justice to the county's diverse range of natural landscapes. The Kent Downs Area of Outstanding Natural Beauty encompasses the parallel North Downs and Greensand Ridge, which cross the county from corner to corner. Where the North Downs meet the English Channel, the result is the iconic White Cliffs of Dover. These cliffs (the South Foreland Heritage Coast) make for superb trail running, but there is more to the Kent coast; the fenlands which face the North Sea are offered here as an alternative. Finally, the hills of the High Weald AONB extend into the county, showcased here by a route along the beautiful Eden Valley.

Crundale Downs (Route 45)

Dover Patrol Monument on Bockell Hill

42 The White Cliffs of Dover

St Margaret's Bay

42 The White Cliffs of Dover

Distance		18km (11 miles)	Ascent	600m (1950ft)
Map		OS Landranger 179 OS Explorer 138		
Navigation	●●●	All on obvious and well-signposted trails		
Terrain	●●●	Chalk paths, grass, field boundaries, tarmac, several steep climbs		
Wet feet	●●●	The inland section can be muddy and the long grass damp		
Start / Finish		St Margaret's Bay car park CT15 6DX / TR 368 444		

There'll be bluebirds over …

What a fantastic, gorgeous, challenging trail run this is! With France clearly visible just 34km away* across the Dover Strait, this gleaming 110m chalk wall has for millennia been the first and last sight of Britain, and also Britain's first line of defence. Vera Lynn's Second World War hit *(There'll Be Bluebirds Over) The White Cliffs of Dover* captures the significance of the place, but disappointingly (it was written by an American) there are no bluebirds here or anywhere in this country.

This route starts from St Margaret's Bay, start point for the Cross-Channel Swim, if that is your sort of thing. Ascending onto the undulating clifftop you'll encounter lush chalk grassland where you should keep an eye out for rare flora and fauna: peregrine falcon, spider orchids, Adonis blue and chalk hill blue butterflies. A population of Exmoor ponies wander freely, clearing scrub and invasive plants. South Foreland Lighthouse is the first landmark, followed by the National Trust's White Cliffs Visitor Centre, perched

*Expect your mobile phone to keep skipping forwards an hour, confusing your tracking app.

42 The White Cliffs of Dover

above the frenetic Port of Dover. The route offers a stunning view of Dover Castle, the 'key to England', before about-turning short of entering Dover. The inland leg takes you through meadows and farmland, with Second World War pillboxes punctuating the landscape. The final section ascends the cliffs *again* (hopefully you saved something in your legs) and leads along the lower and quieter stretch of cliffs from Kingsdown back to St Margaret's. The obelisk you pass is the Dover Patrol Monument, commemorating the First World War sailors who battled German U-boats to keep the English Channel open.

Route description

START From the beach car park, take the road leading uphill (Bay Hill). After 150m it bends sharp right, instead turn off left onto St Margaret's Road. Follow St Margaret's Road for 50m until it forks; take the left fork, which is Beach Road. After 330m, Beach Road ends at a crossroads of tracks; turn left onto

The White Cliffs of Dover

the footpath track which leads uphill towards the coast, signposted 'Saxon Shore Way'. ❶ Follow this footpath track for 120m until it reaches the cliffs. Turn right (S) and follow the footpath along the coast for 4km to the White Cliffs of Dover Visitor Centre; after 900m the footpath diverts inland around private houses and then turns back onto the clifftop at South Foreland Lighthouse. After 3km you have the choice of running around Langdon Hole (deep valley) or descending in and climbing out. ❷ Either pass through the Visitor Centre car park or follow one of the adjacent paths on the left, until you reach a road (Upper Road). Follow the footpath around the bend in the road and then steeply downhill (via steps) still following the coast, towards Dover. After 150m, take the small footpath signposted on the right (if you reach the A2 Jubilee Way road, you have overshot by 90m). ❸ Follow the footpath uphill (N). After 600m you reach Upper Road and cross the A2 Jubilee Way via a bridge, then you turn off right onto the footpath again. After 900m you pass through Broadlees Farm and the footpath ends at ends at a road (A258). Turn right and follow the A258 for 500m to a roundabout. ❹ Cross the roundabout, and follow the A258 Deal Road for 160m (be careful where the pavement runs out), to where a footpath leads through the hedge on the right. Turn right onto this footpath and follow it for 180m along a field edge to where it bends left into another field and passes between pill boxes. ❺ Follow the footpath ahead for 2.7km, passing through five fields; eventually the footpath becomes a track which leads to a road (Dover Road). ❻ Turn right onto Dover Road and follow it for 120m to a T junction. Turn right onto another road (High Street). Cross this and follow it for 120m until you reach the junction with Kingsdown Road. Turn left and follow Kingsdown Road; after 500m it becomes a tarmac track (signposted as National Cycle Network 1). Continue ahead following this track, eventually it merges into Oldstairs Road. Follow Oldstairs Road ahead, it descends to reach the sea 3.7km from the start of Kingsdown Road. ❼ On reaching the sea, turn right off Oldstairs Road onto the footpath leading up the cliffs, signposted 'Saxon Shore Way'. Follow this footpath along the cliffs for 3.6km to where the footpath joins Bay Hill road. Follow the road downhill to your start point.

Dover harbour

Pillbox near Bere Farm

Hope Point

Dover Castle

The White Cliffs of Dover

South Foreland Lighthouse

Trip planning

St Margaret's Bay car park is pay and display. It is found 1.5km south-east of St Margaret's at Cliffe, it's simply the parking area along the beach front. Free roadside parking can of course be sought inland at St Margaret's at Cliffe, starting the route at ❻. Other possible start points are Kingsdown ❼ or the rather busy National Trust's White Cliffs Visitor Centre CT16 1HJ / **TR 333 421** at ❷. Be careful approaching the visitor centre, as cars frequently wind up in the ferry terminal by mistake! You are looking for Upper Road which winds uphill from the port. Parking is free for National Trust members.

The White Cliffs Visitor Centre has a café and information displays about the area. The National Trust also arrange tours of Fan Bay Deep Shelter (a complex of Second World War tunnels bored into the cliffs) and South Foreland Lighthouse, in which the highlight is the splendid Mrs Knott's Tea Room! While we are covering tourism and culture, it is impossible to ignore enormous, looming Dover Castle. A visit (pretty expensive unless you are an English Heritage member) will take at least a good few hours, there is masses to see.

The White Cliffs maintain their whiteness because they are eroding at a rate of around 30cm a year, with occasional major collapses. Steer clear of the edge and use common sense to avoid becoming a casualty of Newtonian physics.

The inland section

The White Cliffs of Dover

Other routes

The way to shorten this route (to 12km) is simple and obvious; when you reach the High Street in St Margaret's at Cliffe at ❻, just stay on it for 1.5km back to the start, cutting the loop into two. The other half of the loop, via Kingsdown, is about 10km.

The White Cliffs on the far side of Dover are outlined in Route 44.

The Saxon Shore Way north of this route is flat, passing the towns of Kingsdown, Walmer and Deal on the way towards Pegwell Bay and Ramsgate. However, it often follows attractive coastal heath and the Henrician castles at Walmer and Deal add interest. The White Cliffs Country Trails are a series of linked trails (marked on OS maps) between Dover and Sandwich, some of which overlap with this route. They total about 45km and can be used as the basis of longer or alternative routes.

Events

Endurance Life organise one of their Coastal Trail Series (CTS) Events on the White Cliffs, with a full range of distances available.

The LDWA's White Cliffs Challenge starts from St Margaret's at Cliffe and has 18- and 30-mile options, to be completed in 8 and 12 hours respectively.

The Ragnar White Cliffs is a 170-mile team relay from Sittingbourne via Dover to Brighton. It's billed as a 'bonding' experience, although after two sleep-deprived days squeezed into a van, you might just as likely want to kill your team.

See also the events listed in Route 44.

The Kent Downs Area of Outstanding Natural Beauty

The Kent Downs AONB protects 878km² of chalk downs and greensand hills which arc across the county from the Surrey border to the White Cliffs of Dover. It is a direct continuation from the Surrey Hills AONB (see page 301) and the two AONBs share similar geology, as well as the parallel North Downs Way (see page 232) and Greensand Way (see page 312) long-distance trails. Despite all this, the Kent Downs are notably distinctive and different. Given that this is the 'Garden of England', nearly two-thirds of the AONB is comprised of farmland, especially orchards and hop gardens. These rural areas have their own distinctive buildings made of flint, ragstone and chalk, as well of course as the ubiquitous oast houses. A fifth of the AONB is woodland, most of which is 'ancient', the definition of which is (apparently) having been present since at least AD 1600. Routes 42, 44, 45, 46 and 47 are all within the AONB.

42 The White Cliffs of Dover

Langdon Hole

43 The Reculver Towers

Reculver Towers

Distance	12km (8 miles)	Ascent	50m (140ft)
Map	OS Landranger 179 OS Explorer 150		
Navigation •••	Well-signposted trails, but some run unmarked across farmland		
Terrain •••	Grass, dirt, concrete, tarmac, the mildest of mild ascents		
Wet feet •••	The trails on agricultural land can get pretty muddy		
Start / Finish	Reculver Towers car park CT6 6SS / TR 224 692		

Big skies, wide horizons and lush fenland

Twin imposing towers overlook the sea at Reculver, all that remains of twelfth-century St Mary's Church. This was the site of an Anglo-Saxon monastery built within the huge Roman fort of *Regulbium*, but the sea has claimed all bar a few walls. The towers have been preserved as a navigation marker and they form the only landmark on this run through a strange waterworld of marsh and fenland.

This route leads inland through Chislet Marshes and Wade Marsh, reclaimed land latticed with drainage channels and rivers. This was once the Wantsum Channel, a seaway separating the Isle of Thanet from Britain's mainland. As you run beneath big skies, you will notice the lushness of this landscape; meadows flourish, wild plants grow tall and insects buzz along the waterways. Between Whitfield Sewer (which is nicer than it sounds) and the River Wantsum, dozens of mounds (some several hundred metres long) offer variation in these flatlands; they are traces of medieval salt works, formed by waste sludge dumped

43 The Reculver Towers

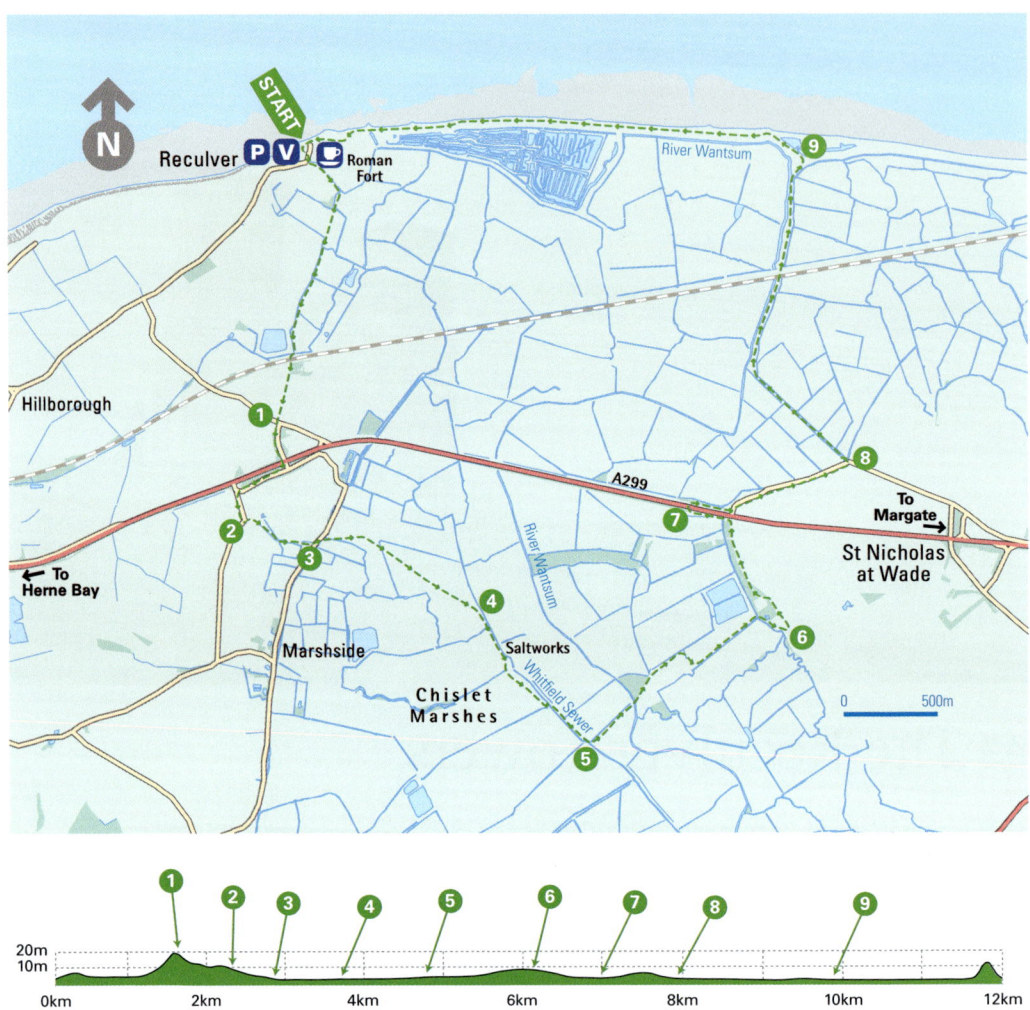

in what was then a tidal waterway. The final part of your run is along the seafront, where a slightly grim concrete walkway separates the lagoons on your left (frequented by brent geese in winter) from the shingle beach and open sea on your right. During the Second World War, the towers' unmistakeable landmark made this coast the ideal spot to test Barnes Wallis' bouncing bomb.

Route description

START From the car park, cross Reculver Lane to the Café Reculver and take the footpath track which leads off left beside it. This is signposted 'Saxon Shore Way', you are following this waymarked route until ❷. Follow the footpath track for 250m alongside a caravan park to where it ends at a gate. Take the footpath which leads off on the right from the gate and follow this through several fields, crossing a footbridge and passing underneath a railway embankment after 1km. The footpath becomes a track and ascends to reach a lane (Brook Lane). ❶ Turn left onto the lane and then immediately turn off right (S) onto another lane (North Stream Lane). Follow the lane 300m, crossing a bridge over the A299 Thanet Way to

The Reculver Towers

reach a T junction. Turn right and follow this lane (still North Stream Lane) along the A299 for 300m. Take the left bend onto Reynolds Farm Road (the alternative is turning onto the A299!) and follow this for 150m to a sharp right bend. ❷ At the sharp right bend, there is a footpath sign pointing four ways. Take the footpath leading off on the left along a house drive (to Reynolds Farm), leaving the Saxon Shore Way. Head 60m along the drive, turn right off the drive before the pond to follow a footpath between two drainage channels and then past houses. After 350m this ends at a lane (North Stream Lane). ❸ Turn left onto the lane and follow it just 50m before taking the footpath leading off on the right, crossing a drainage channel. Continue ahead on the footpath for 900m, crossing several drainage channels, to reach Whitfield Sewer, a much bigger channel. ❹ Turn right and follow Whitfield Sewer SE. Trails lead along both sides of Whitfield Sewer and several bridges cross it, choose the trail which is less overgrown (usually the far side), bearing in mind that you need to be on the far side after 1km (the third bridge encountered is your last chance to cross). ❺ After following Whitfield Sewer for 1km, take the first left turn you will have encountered, onto a footpath track heading NE. This crosses the River Wantsum and after 310m becomes Snake Drove bridleway (also known as Belle Isle Road). Continue along the bridleway lane for 1km to a house. ❻ Directly after the house, turn left onto the bridleway following the edge of woodland (part of the Wantsum Way). After 600m, the bridleway reaches the A299 (Thanet Way). Turn left onto Court Road and follow this for 220m to a bridge across the A299. ❼ Cross the A299 and follow this lane (Chambers Wall) for 900m to a junction surrounded by houses. ❽ Turn sharp left across Wade Marsh Stream onto the footpath track which points NW towards the Reculver Towers. After 700m this turns N to follow the River Wantsum (do not cross this), after 1.3km it crosses a railway and after 1.9km it reaches the sea wall. ❾ Turn left and follow the sea wall footpath (or adjacent track) for 2.7km back to the start.

Approaching Whitfield Sewer

Chislet Marshes

Trip planning

There are two pay and display car parks alongside one another in Reculver, located at the end of Reculver Lane; Reculver Towers car park and Reculver Country Park car park. They are alongside a children's play area and a visitor centre building which hosts a 'Coastal Classroom' and the HatHats coffee shop. The coffee and crepes served here are tempting, but many may prefer to cross the road to dine at Café Reculver, an egg-and-chips-with-a-mug-of-tea sort of place. Also across the road is the King Ethelbert Inn, one of the few buildings surviving from the village of Reculver.

River Wantsum

The Reculver Towers

After heavy rainfall or during exceptional tides, the marshes can flood (they are barely above sea level); at such times the route here will obviously be impassable and dangerous. If in doubt, Google 'Flood Warning Information Service – Chislet Marshes and Wade Marsh' for an update.

Other routes

Directly to the west of the start is 26-hectare Reculver Country Park, a great spot for a short airing of your legs (it's just 2km from end to end). The park occupies the nearest thing to a hill hereabouts, giving great views of the marshes and sea.

The Wantsum Walk is around 40km long (no one quite agrees), from Herne Bay out to Birchington. From Reculver it winds inland (signposted by a sailing ship symbol), sometimes overlapping this route. Following it from Reculver to where it returns to the sea front just before Birchington and then back would be a decent longer alternative (c. 19km) to this route, albeit with more road time.

An intriguing possibility for longer ventures is the Stour Valley Walk (no relation to the Stour Valley Path featuring in Route 41), which connects Reculver with Pegwell Bay to the east, and the North Downs Way at the Wye Downs (Route 45).

Events

A Junior parkrun is held at Reculver Country Park every Sunday morning; this 2km event is run on grass, open to 4 to 14-year olds.

Sporting Events UK run the Smugglers 10K which follows the seafront from Birchington to Reculver, *'Possibly the only race started in Kent with a cannon firing.'*

Saxons, Normans and Vikings Marathons (that really is what they are called) organise various masochistic events based from Reculver, all involving repeated laps around a circuit route. The Moonlight Challenge is an eight-hour endurance event held at night. The Kent 50 Mile Endurance Run and the Viking 100 Endurance Run speak for themselves.

The England Coast Path

How about a trail run around England? When completed, the England Coast Path will be the world's longest coastal trail at 4,500km. In 2009 the Marine and Coastal Access Act opened up the Right of Coastal Access to pretty much all parts other than private houses and MOD land, making the ECP possible. This amazing project was scheduled to be completed by Natural England in 2020, but is (perhaps unsurprisingly) taking longer.

In the South East, the ECP is linking up the existing coastal trails; the Isle of Wight Coastal Path (see page 44), the Solent Way (see page 58) and the Saxon Shore Way (see page 254). The signage along these trails is being upgraded and new trails created to link them all up. The overwhelming majority of the ECP will follow existing rights of way; in Essex for example, footpaths already follow most of the sea walls along this county's epic mileage of shoreline. In 2020, the only section of the ECP in the South East deemed to be fully completed was the 106km from Camber in East Sussex to Ramsgate in Kent.

44 Folkestone Warren

Eagle's Nest Cliffs

Distance	8km (5 miles)	Ascent	375m (1,230ft)
Map	OS Landranger 179 OS Explorer 138		
Navigation	●●●	Narrow paths hemmed in by undergrowth, you can't get lost (probably)	
Terrain	●●●	Roots, rocks, steps, one epic ascent	
Wet feet	●●●	Chalk + humid jungle = slippery bits, be careful	
Start / Finish	Pavilion car park CT19 6AT / TR 239 365		

Welcome to the jungle

You will find Folkestone Warren (or just 'The Warren') squeezed into a narrow packet of land between Kent's classic white cliffs and the sea. This overgrown jungly micro-wilderness was once a popular place for leisure and recreation. Successive major landslips rewilded the landscape and although the area is designated as 'East Cliff and Warren Country Park', there is no development here other than the railway (even this was buried by a 1915 landslip). The trails in here are narrow, uneven and winding, just how you like them!
A somewhat intense zigzagging climb out of The Warren leads you to the top of the cliffs, where, liberated above the tree canopy, the views are tremendous and just a tad vertigo-inducing. The England Coast Path follows the cliff rim back; the Battle of Britain Memorial is an engaging and sober interlude.

Folkestone Warren

Route description

START From the parking area, follow the road (or adjacent clifftop) uphill for 700m to where a footpath lane leads off uphill on the right. Take this and follow it steeply uphill. When the lane bends right near a Martello Tower, instead continue straight ahead and uphill on the footpath. After 225m it crosses a tarmac track (Swiss Way) via a bridge; descend on the steps to the tarmac track and follow it to the right (NE) into Little Switzerland Camping and Caravan Site. Continue ahead through the campsite to the reception building, 100m from the bridge. Just past the building is the start of a footpath (slightly obscured by bushes and tents). ❶ Take the footpath and follow it downhill through dense woodland. Ignore any side paths. After 750m the footpath reaches a T junction beside the railway. ❷ Turn left and follow this footpath ahead (E) for 1.9km until it reaches the top of the cliffs; after 900m ignore the footpath on the left leading up the cliffs, after another 600m your footpath steeply ascends the cliffs. ❸ At the top of the cliffs, immediately turn left (W) onto the footpath following the cliff top; be careful, at first it is narrow and close to the edge. Follow the coast footpath (alternately signposted England Coast Path or Saxon

Folkestone Warren 44

The Warren

Shore Way) for 2.6km, passing the Battle of Britain Memorial after 2km. ❹ When the coast footpath turns sharp right (inland), turn off left onto the footpath leading steeply downhill. After 500m you cross a bridge to reach the footpath you originally ascended on, follow this downhill to your start point.

Trip planning

Parking as suggested is beside the Pavilion Restaurant on Wear Bay Road and is pay and display; cheaper options can be scouted out nearby. The Pavilion Restaurant serves seafood, but for a refuel more in keeping with this run, drive up to the Clifftop Café on Old Dover Road (alongside the England Coast Path) and enjoy the views while dining; you will have passed this while running. The café has a useful parking area CT18 7HT / TR 254 384 and could be an alternative start point for your run, between ❸ and ❹. The Battle of Britain Memorial also has a café.

The author prefers this run early morning or late evening, when the sun is low on the horizon and the Battle of Britain Memorial site is deserted.

The big climb

The Warren

Folkestone Warren

Other routes

The left turn after ❷ leads up the cliffs and emerges at the Clifftop Café, reducing the distance by 2km.

Following the final section of the North Downs Way along the cliffs from Folkestone to Dover is a great airy run of about 16km, with an easy shuttle service supplied by the railway. After the section of coast in this route, you pass above Samphire Hoe Country Park, a possible destination for a separate short 2–3km run; this 30-hectare nature reserve is actually artificial, constructed from Channel Tunnel waste. Samphire Hoe has a car park accessed by a tunnel from the A20.

West of Folkestone, the Saxon Shore Way diverts inland along the Royal Military Canal (see page 250).

England Coast Path

The Warren

Events

Saxons, Normans and Vikings Marathons (I'm struggling to visualise the process whereby they decided upon that company name) organise the epic Saxon Shore Seaside Series, based from Samphire Hoe Country Park. For ten successive days, there are concurrent events ranging from 10km to Ultra distance, each with a random weird name such as 'Bobble Hobble Challenge' and 'Roald Dahl Challenge'. They also hold races here at other times of the year, including the Halloween 100 Mile.

The Battle of Britain Memorial

At the centre of the Memorial, a lone young pilot sits gazing out to sea, his rank and nationality obscured. Behind him are replica Spitfire and Hurricane fighter planes and a Memorial Wall listing the almost 3,000 pilots (half of whom lost their lives) who fought against the German Luftwaffe in the summer of 1940, around a quote from Churchill's famous speech:

"Never in the field of human conflict was so much owed by so many to so few."

Worth breaking your stride, to stop, reflect and pay your respects.

The Battle of Britain memorial

The Devil's Kneading Trough

45 The Wye Downs

Distance	11km (7 miles)	Ascent	200m (650ft)
Map	OS Landranger 189 OS Explorer 137		
Navigation ●●●	Plenty of junctions to keep track of, partly follows the North Downs Way		
Terrain ●●●	Mild ascents on stony tracks and grassy fields		
Wet feet ●●●	Some muddy stretches, in times of wetness – especially the farmland		
Start / Finish	Wye Nature Reserve car park TN25 5PP / TR 079 453		

Quiet spaces, secluded downland and mild trails

The Wye Downs are a lovely enclave within the (already fairly lovely) Kent Downs Area of Outstanding Natural Beauty. This route starts at the Devil's Kneading Trough, a popular beauty spot. This steep-sided dry valley has glorious views across the village of Wye, the River Stour and the Kentish Weald (140m below) and is a National Nature Reserve supporting rare spider orchids. You don't have to venture far before you pretty much have the Wye Downs to yourself. This route ventures into the quiet valleys and woodland secluded behind the main scarp, with long gradual ascents and descents which go easy on your lungs! The route finally returns to the main scarp of the Wye Downs above the Wye Crown; this huge crown shape was cut into the chalk in 1902 to mark the coronation of King Edward VII.

45 The Wye Downs

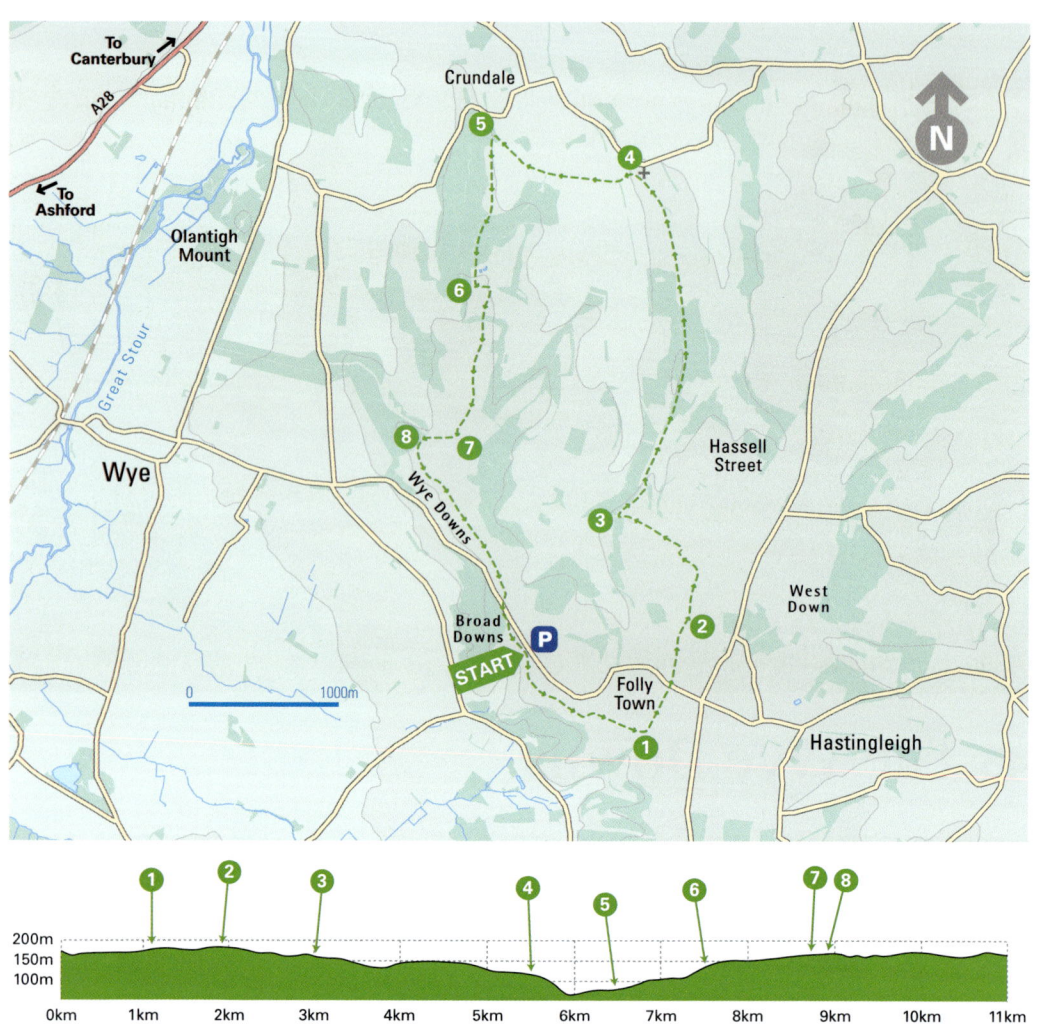

Route description

START From the car park, cross the lane (Coldharbour Lane) and the field behind, to reach the footpath leading along the rim of the hill (North Downs Way). Turn left (S) and follow this footpath for 1.1km until it becomes a gravel track leading into farm buildings. When you reach the farm buildings (Cold Blow Farm), turn left (N) off the NDW and follow the lane out of the farm. ❶ Follow the lane N, going ahead at a crossroads with a lane (Coldharbour Lane). 600m from the farm, a byway track turns off on the right, take this. Follow the byway for 150m to where it bends right, and a footpath crosses the byway; turn off left onto this footpath. ❷ Follow the footpath for 250m across a field of crops to a track. Turn left onto the track and follow it for 250m to where it becomes a byway track, continue ahead for 500m. When the byway track begins to descend downhill and pass through woods, look for a footpath on the right and take it. ❸ Follow the footpath N along the rim of the hillside. After 800m you cross a track, continue N on the byway track (just to the left) that leads ahead. The byway ascends for a short distance, then descends to a church (St Mary) after 1.9km. Opposite the church, on your left, a footpath leads downhill; take this

The Wye Downs

Wye Downs trail

footpath. ❹ Descend on the footpath to the bottom corner of the field. Follow the byway track which leads W out of the field. After 900m, just before entering woods, a footpath crosses the byway; turn left (S) onto this footpath. ❺ Follow the footpath along the uphill edge of a field. After 500m the footpath enters woods and becomes a track, continue ahead (uphill). After 500m, you emerge from the woods, at the top of the hill, at a junction of multiple paths. Turn left (E) onto the byway track. ❻ Follow the byway track 110m to farm buildings (Marriage Farm). Just before the buildings, a footpath track turns off on the right, take this footpath and follow it S for 1km to where it ends at a lane. ❼ Turn right onto the lane and follow it for 160m to where the lane meets woods and the NDW footpath is signposted off on the left. Turn left onto the footpath. ❽ Follow the NDW for 1.7km back to the start. After 200m you turn left to pass the Wye Crown viewpoint, otherwise the footpath simply follows the rim of the hillside.

Above the Wye Crown

Trip planning
Wye Nature Reserve car park is alongside Coldharbour Lane and is free. It's not too large, if you find it full then perhaps consider starting from Wye, see below.
The Wye Coffee Shop and Kitchen welcomes folk

Footpath near the start

The Wye Downs

returning from exploring the Downs, and claims that its homemade cakes are, *'to die for.'* The author has conducted preliminary testing of this claim, and plans to return for further thorough testing. Wye also has a supermarket and indeed a surprising array of other shops.

Other routes

The easiest way to shorten this route (to about 5km) is to ignore the footpath at ❸ and instead continue downhill on the byway to Coombe Manor, before ascending back to the start via the lane leading ahead.

Above the Wye Crown

If this route strikes you as all too mild and comfortable, then spice it up a bit by starting and finishing in Wye, 140m below the main scarp. Park up on Upper Bridge Street and head SE along Cherry Garden Lane and the footpaths that continue beyond it to reach the bottom of the Devil's Kneading Trough. Ascend this steep valley (you did ask for this) to the start and follow the route to ❼. From ❼ continue 250m on the lane past the first NDW footpath which turns off on the left and take the second NDW footpath turning, also on the left; follow this downhill into Wye. This makes for a 14km outing.

Crundale Downs

The NDW south of here continues to follow the high ground and maintains interest, however there is still plenty of ascent and descent to contend with before Folkestone is reached after about 22km (Route 44).

Events

Wye is the finish point of Centurion Running's savage NDW100; see page 232.

The Wye Crown

46 Maidstone to Hollingbourne

Above Detling

Distance	12km (7.5 miles)	**Ascent**	400m (1330ft)
Map	OS Landranger 188 OS Explorer 148		
Navigation	●●●	Mostly following the North Downs Way	
Terrain	●●●	Narrow rooty trails, numerous steep ascents	
Wet feet	●●●	A few mud patches and puddles to dodge	
Start	Bearsted Railway Station ME14 4DN / TQ 798 561		
Finish	Hollingbourne Railway Station ME17 1TX / TQ 834 550		

Steps, views, steps, views, steps, views …

This short sharp segment of the North Downs Way is one of the National Trail's highlights. Trail runners can expect something of a rollercoaster ride. Maidstone is quickly escaped (the M20 keeps it at bay) and after a deceptively mild approach to the base of the North Downs, you ascend steeply via narrow steps. Then you descend. Then you ascend … and so forth. The compensation for your travails is the views; green fields and wild flowers in the foreground, and expansive vistas of the Weald in the background, including Leeds Castle (which turns out not to be in Yorkshire). Each little valley you descend into (and ascend out of) offers new views and perspectives, to keep you motivated. Eventually, you make a final descent into the village of Hollingbourne, where a train will have you back in Maidstone in four minutes flat.

46 Maidstone to Hollingbourne

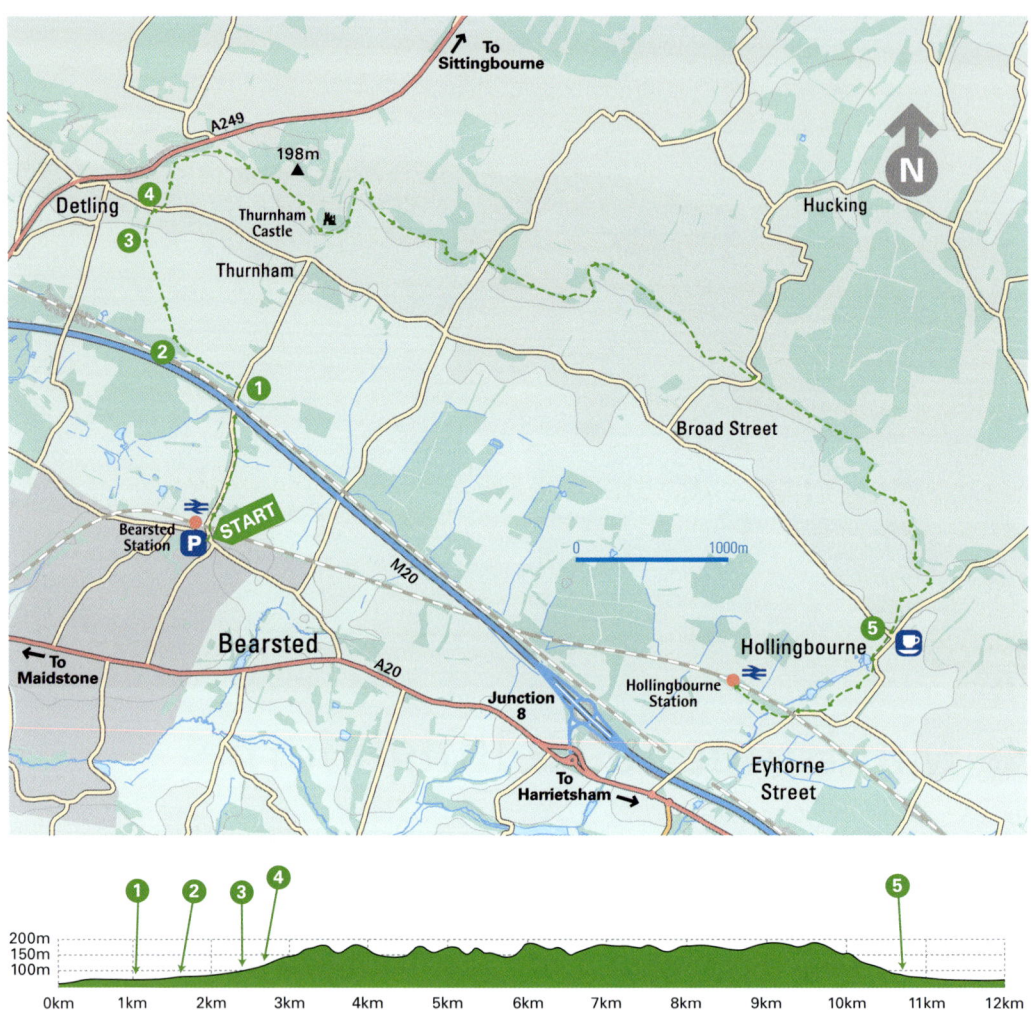

The route passes beneath the earthworks of twelfth-century Thurnham Castle, and (if your knees can bear any more) a short steep muddy detour ascends to the ruins of the castle's flint walls.

Route description

START Turn left (E) out of the railway station car park onto Ware Street. Head 120m along Ware Street to a junction with a lane (Thurnham Lane). Turn left onto this lane and follow it for 1km under the railway and then under the M20 motorway and a second railway. ❶ After passing under, look for a gate into a field on the left, with a metal kissing gate beside it. Turn left off the lane by passing through the kissing gate. Follow the footpath along the field boundary for 500m to where the path turns right into a small woodland. ❷ Follow the footpath for 80m to the far side of the woods, then continue straight ahead across a field to its N corner, passing close to an electricity pylon. The footpath crosses a stile just to the right of the field corner, then immediately crosses a second stile and continues NNW towards the village of Detling. ❸ When you reach a crossroads of footpaths, take the footpath which follows the field boundary N (not

Maidstone to Hollingbourne

the path leading into Detling) and brings you past houses to a lane (signposted 'Pilgrim's Way'). Turn right onto the lane and follow it for 70m to where a footpath turns off on the left, signposted 'North Downs Way'. ❹ Turn left to take the footpath and follow it steeply uphill. Continue following NDW signs for 8.1km, ignoring any side turns. The NDW footpath follows the rim of the hillside, but repeatedly dips and climbs steeply. After 1.4km it briefly joins a lane (Castle Hill) and there is the option for a short detour uphill (off the NDW) to explore Thurnham Castle. After 3.1km the NDW crosses a second lane (Coldblow Lane) and after 5.3km it crosses a third lane (Broad Street Hill). Eventually the NDW descends and emerges at a crossroads of lanes beside the Dirty Habit pub, in the village of Hollingbourne. ❺ Pass the Dirty Habit on your left, heading downhill along Upper Street. After 900m you pass under the railway. Immediately after, a lane leads off on the right, signposted for the railway station. Turn right onto this, the railway station is 430m along it.

Above Hollingbourne

Trip planning

Bearsted Railway Station, on Ware Street, is easily reached by bus (or, of course, train) from the centre of Maidstone. There is pay parking in front of the railway station and also further along Ware Street opposite the junction with Thurnham Lane. Parking is easier and cheaper in Hollingbourne, so you may wish to drive there and take the train before running; this has the added benefit of reducing the platform wait time, if you plan ahead. Trains run hourly between the two stations, taking about four minutes.

Along the NDW

The commuterville of Maidstone naturally has innumerable shops and services, however it would be rude to ignore the presence of the pub located in Hollingbourne just before the end of this route; called The Dirty Habit, no less. They serve food, but at the very least find time for a drink before running for the train.

Hollingbourne

Other routes

If you are averse to trains (I just this moment Googled this, it's called siderodromophobia), it's not too difficult to modify this route into a loop of around 15km. Starting from Hollingbourne (where you can park on the street), you could either just run 5.6km NW along the Pilgrim's Way (a tarmac lane) until you reach ❹; or take the Pilgrim's Way lane but turn left off it after 3km onto Water Lane, then take the footpath on the right after 270m which leads (becoming a bridleway track) to Thurnham Lane, which you follow 100m to the left before turning off right onto a footpath to Detling, which joins the route at ❸.

46 Maidstone to Hollingbourne

The 4km of the NDW to the east, between Hollingbourne and Harrietsham, is one of the easiest parts of the National Trail, following the Pilgrim's Way with little ascent and sometimes surfaced. Harrietsham Railway Station offers an easy return. The following 10km to Charing Railway Station are attractive and a bit more challenging, but tarmacked at first.

The 16km of the NDW north and west of Detling lead to Medway Bridge between Chatham and Rochester. The route follows the high ground and passes interesting spots like Kit's Coty House and Little Kit's Coty House Neolithic tombs. However, returning by train isn't very practical. Do *not* try to cross the busy A249 from Detling, as older maps might suggest; after repeated fatalities, a footbridge was erected in 2002 (named Jade's Crossing after the final victim) and the NDW was rerouted across this.

Events

Hit the Trail Running organise the Lenham Cross Winter Marathon, which traverses the section of the NDW covered in this route in both directions. They note, '*This is a tough course with almost zero chance of a marathon PB!*'.

Riding and Running's Maidstone Riverside 10km and 10m heads out and back from town along the River Medway for either of the two distances, as suits. The 'm' stands for miles, not metres.

The North Downs Way National Trail

The North Downs Way – yet another of the South East's trail running jewels – was inspired by the Pilgrim's Way, a medieval route of religious pilgrimage heading east, beneath the chalk ridge of the North Downs, to Canterbury Cathedral. Traces of the Pilgrim's Way are now often submerged by tarmac (Route 64 is a notable exception) and instead the NDW follows the high ground, where possible. It totals 246km / 153 miles from Farnham in Surrey to Dover in Kent, splitting at Broughton Lees and reuniting at Dover. The southern route is 201km / 125 miles to Dover, the northern route is 211km / 131 miles. The NDW follows roads for 19% of its course.

Compared to the South Downs Way which faces it across the Weald, the NDW threads a course through a far more developed landscape, for example almost touching the M25 at times. Nevertheless, runners following the NDW will be impressed by how effectively the route manages to preserve a sense of peace and open space; there is also notably more variation of scenery than along the SDW. Runners also won't fail to notice the climbs; the southern route totals 3,700m of ascent, with the hilliest stretch being between Guildford and Reigate and some tough sections in the Kent Downs AONB. The final leg along the coast, following epic cliffs, is also a highlight. Routes 44, 45, 46, 61, 63 and 64 all incorporate parts of the NDW. Trail runners will have noticed that there appears to be a law saying that all long-distance trails have to have crazy ultramarathons organised along them, and naturally the NDW is no exception. Centurion Running's NDW100 goes continuously from Farnham to Ashford and yes, that number refers to miles. Their NDW50 is 'only' Farnham to Knockout Pound. XNRG's Pilgrim's Challenge is a bit saner. This is a one- or two-day event, 33 miles from Farnham to Reigate ... with the option of heading back again the following day. The author just entered a single day of this great event, in my defence the ground was covered with snow and it was minus 6 °C in the morning.

Knole Park 47

Knole Park residents

47 Knole Park

Distance	13km (8 miles)	Ascent	325m (1,050ft)
Map	OS Landranger 188 OS Explorer 147		
Navigation	●●●	Simple, using the Greensand Way and mostly just following trails ahead	
Terrain	●●●	Root-strewn sandy trails, numerous small climbs, some tarmac	
Wet feet	●●●	Add a star in winter, when you might constantly wade through mud.	
Start / Finish	Sevenoaks Leisure Centre TN13 1HW / TQ 532 547		

Tame deer and rooty trails

Unless you already live in Sevenoaks, you may be surprised to learn that in the town centre, you can pass through a nondescript gate straight into a vast medieval deer park, like some kind of trail running Narnia! Knole Park is nearly 400 hectares of woodland and heathland around Knole House, a truly massive* Jacobean mansion. Around 350 fallow and sika deer wander the grounds, seemingly unfazed by human presence. Numerous great trails lead through the park and further along the lofty Greensand Ridge. The outward leg of this route follows the always-superb Greensand Way, with rooty and uneven technical trails requiring care and balance, while views of the Weald try to distract you. After reaching the moated medieval manor house of Ightham Mote, the return journey is equally classy, negotiating sunken holloways and wild common land before passing through Knole Park once more. Then, as jarringly as when you departed, you are teleported back into the centre of Sevenoaks ...

*It ranks somewhere in the top five largest residences in the country, apparently.

47 Knole Park

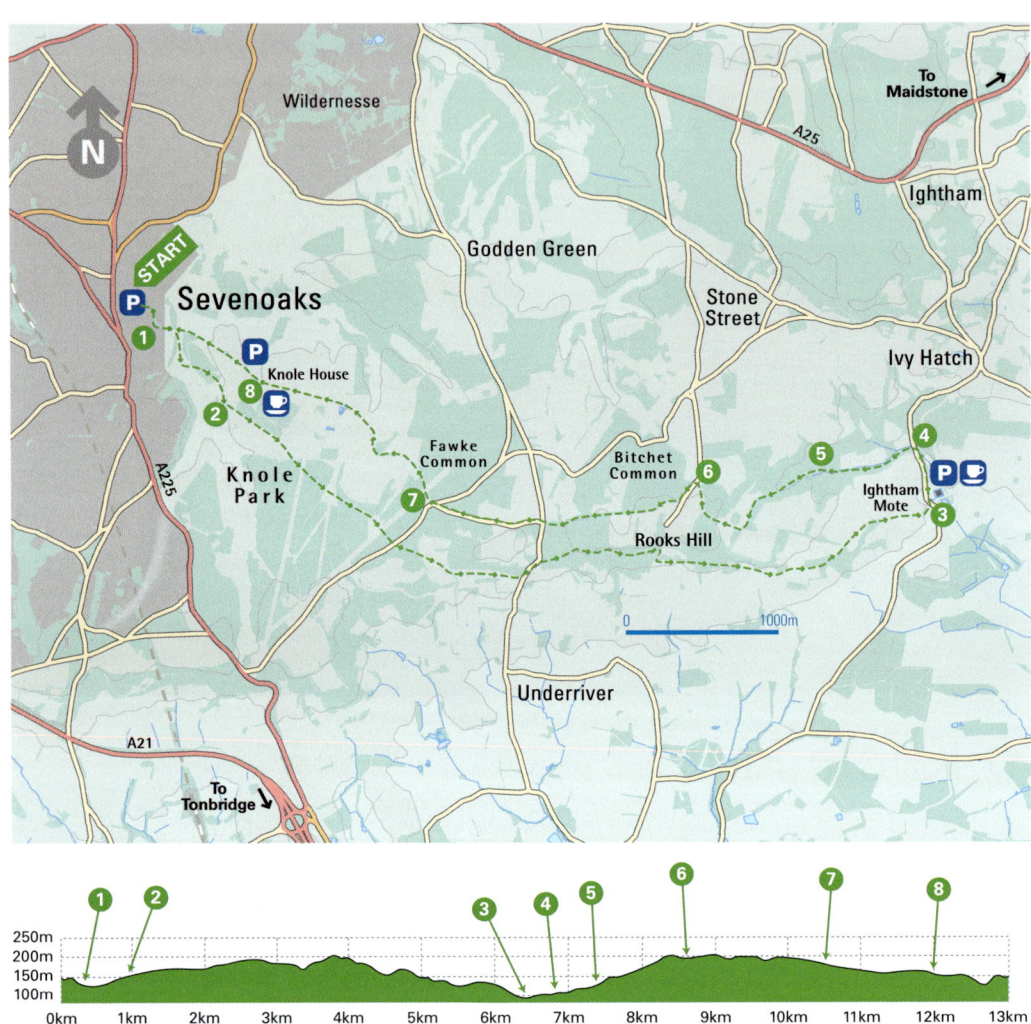

Route description

START Pass by the leisure centre on the right-hand (S) side. You will see a wooden gateway with 'Buckhurst Lane Play Area' inscribed above it. Pass through and turn right to follow a tarmac path S for 75m to a T junction with a tarmac footpath. Turn left (downhill) onto this footpath and follow it 250m to a gate in a deer fence. ❶ Pass through the gate into Knole Park. You will see a treeless valley floor in front of you, leading N–S. Turn right (S) and run along the valley floor for 240m until you reach a lane (Knole Lane). Turn left onto the lane and then immediately turn off right on the footpath leading into the woods. This is the Greensand Way. Follow the GS footpath uphill to reach the wall around Knole House after 400m. ❷ Follow the signposted GS footpath ahead E for 5.8km; it first passes along the S wall of Knole House, after 1.5km it passes through a deer gate and crosses a lane (St Julian Road), after 2km there is a sharp left turn (don't continue ahead, downhill), after 2.3km it follows a lane (Carter's Hill) uphill for 100m, after 3.3km it follows a lane (Rook's Hill) downhill for 100m, after 4.7km it becomes a bridleway track and descends to reach a lane (Mote Road). ❸ Turn left (uphill) and follow the lane for 400m (passing Ightham

Knole Park

Mote manor house) to a bridleway sign on the left. Turn left onto the bridleway track. ❹ Follow the bridleway track uphill for 600m to a right turn, where a permissive footpath is signposted on the left. Take the permissive footpath. ❺ Follow the permissive footpath uphill for 500m to a T junction with a bridleway path. Turn right (W) onto the bridleway path. Follow the bridleway path 500m until it ends at a lane. ❻ Turn left onto the lane and follow it (or the parallel path across the road) for 170m to where a bridleway path is signposted off on the right. Turn right and take this bridleway path. Follow it W for 1km, ignoring side turns, until it reaches a lane (Carter's Hill) at a junction. Cross this lane and continue ahead on the lane opposite (Fawke Wood Road). After 700m it ends at a T junction with another lane (St Julian Road) and the gates of Knole Park. ❼ Go through the deer gate into Knole Park. Follow the footpath tarmac track ahead for 900m until the footpath is signposted on the left, leaving the tarmac track. Follow signs for the footpath through a golf course to reach Knole House after 700m. ❽ Follow the footpath past Knole House and then the car park to ascend the low hill in front of Knole House (Echo Mount). Continue ahead (downhill) through trees until you see the deer gate you first entered the park through. Pass through this and head uphill back to the leisure centre.

Trip planning

The suggested start point is Suffolk Way car park, located on Buckhurst Avenue and directly in front of Sevenoaks Leisure Centre. There are two more car parks directly alongside if this doesn't suit, all are pay and display. Sevenoaks High Street is less than 200m away. Knole Park and House are partly managed by the National Trust, and partly privately owned. This has no bearing on your visit as public access is ensured by the many public footpaths leading across the park. National Trust members may want to start from the car park in front of Knole House TN13 1HX / **TQ 538 543**,

Bitchet Common

Knole Park

Knole Park

Greensand Way through Knole Park

Rooks Hill

Knole Park

Knole House

signposted from the High Street and free to members of course. However, it is arguably less faff (e.g. you don't need to adhere to opening times) to park outside and make your own way into the park, unless of course you want to visit Knole House or make use of their Brewhouse Café.

Another possibility is to combine your run with a visit to Ightham Mote where the National Trust have a café and a car park on Mote Road TN15 0NS / TQ 583 534. This would mean starting from ❸.

The deer at Knole Park are exceptionally unafraid of humans and may well approach you, possibly because far too many idiots have shared their picnics with them. Keep your distance, obviously. In October the rut takes place, where the bucks (fallow deer) and stags (sika deer) try to establish their supremacy via loud grunting and macho territorial battles, definitely keep your distance! The summit of Echo Mount is the most prized territory, consider detouring around it.

Other routes

This is an out-and-back route with the two legs always under 1km apart; if you want a shorter run it's easy on the outward leg to simply take a left turn at any point and shortly after connect with the return leg.

Knole Park can by itself occupy an afternoon of exploring, just checking out the network of footpaths; you will not want for company, local runners are always present (as well as the deer). The National Trust publish a series of c. 5km routes around Knole Park, see their website.

For more information on the Greensand Way, see page 312. The GS connects with the Wealdway about 5km east of Ightham Mote, see page 258. To the west of Sevenoaks, the GS passes by the National Trust properties of Chartwell (Winston Churchill's home in later life) and Toys Hill, both great areas to explore by trail shoe. The NT website suggests some routes.

Knole Park

Events

The Knole Run, organised by Sevenoaks School, is a major schools cross-country event in the park, with distances from 5km to 9.4km. For adults, Sevenoaks AC run the Sevenoaks 7, seven miles around Knole Park. Nearby, PB Race Events organise the Shoreham Woods 10K.

For something a bit lengthier, the LDWA have a Challenge Event called the Sevenoaks Circular; 30-, 20- and 15-mile loops on the Greensand Ridge and the North Downs.

Know your deer

Encountering deer is a commonplace experience for trail runners; the UK wild population is estimated at around two million and they hang out in exactly the sorts of places where we like to run! Usually deer become aware of you before you see them and the experience is harmless to all parties. However, be mindful when rounding blind corners on confined trails; the author guiltily admits that he has more than once startled deer into jumping crazily high fences. There are six species of these beautiful and retiring creatures in the UK, all found in the South East. Red and roe deer are our only indigenous species, while fallow deer have been with us since the Norman Conquest. Sika, muntjac and Chinese water deer are Asiatic species which escaped, or were released, from private parks during the nineteenth and twentieth centuries.

Red – large (over a metre tall at shoulders), rust-red (brown in winter), no spots on adults, short tails, widely branched antlers with multiple points. Encountered sparsely across the South East, but common in the New Forest.

Roe – medium (about 70cm tall at shoulders), rust-red (grey in winter), no spots, white patch on bum, no tail, small antlers with up to three points. Commonly encountered across all of England.

Fallow – medium / large (about 90cm tall at shoulders), variety of colours ranging from white through tan and brown to black, often have black inverted horseshoe pattern on bums and black stripe on tails (which are long), only species with palmate antlers (i.e. like the palm of a hand). Encountered across all of Southern England.

Sika – medium / large (stags about 90cm, hinds about 65cm tall at shoulders), red-brown with white spots (dark grey in winter), white patches on bums, short tails, widely spaced antlers. Mostly encountered south of the Thames, especially the New Forest and Ashdown Forest (Route 52).

Muntjac – small (about 50cm tall at shoulder) and stocky, russet brown (grey in winter), flat tails, small straight antlers, males have striped faces. Encountered across all of South East (especially Lee Valley, Route 35).

Chinese water deer – small (about 50cm tall at shoulder), russet brown (grey in winter), short tails, no antlers but males have 'tusks'. As they originally escaped from Whipsnade Zoo, you are most likely to encounter them around Route 33!

The British Deer Society website is an excellent source of further information about these species and their behaviour.

Knole Park

Knole Park

48 The Eden Valley

Near Edenbridge

48 The Eden Valley

Distance	23km (14.5 miles)	Ascent	200m (670ft)
Map	OS Landranger 187, 188 OS Explorer 147		
Navigation ●●●	Following a waymarked route		
Terrain ●●●	Meadows, field boundaries, earthen / gravel / concrete trails, mild gradients		
Wet feet ●●●	Farmland sections extremely muddy in winter, add a star		
Start / Finish	Edenbridge Railway Station TN8 6HR / TQ 440 474		
Finish	Tonbridge Railway Station TN1 1TX / TQ 587 460		

Welcome to the Weald

The Eden Valley Walk* is a 24km / 15-mile waymarked trail, shamelessly utilised here as a superb trail running tour of what the Weald landscape is all about. The EVW follows the Rivers Eden and Medway through the High Weald Area of Outstanding Natural Beauty, winding in and out of both the Low and High Weald. Hence, you experience a stunning mix of undulating farmland (the clay-based Low Weald) and woodland-patchworked hills (the sandstone-based High Weald). Add to this, the complex waterworld of rivers, lakes and flood relief channels on the latter part of the route, and this all makes for a pretty engaging challenge. Oh yes, there are also four castles along the way; Hever Castle, Chiddingstone Castle, Penshurst Place and Tonbridge Castle, although admittedly you only see two of them close up.

*Let's all agree to ignore the 'Walk' bit.

48 The Eden Valley

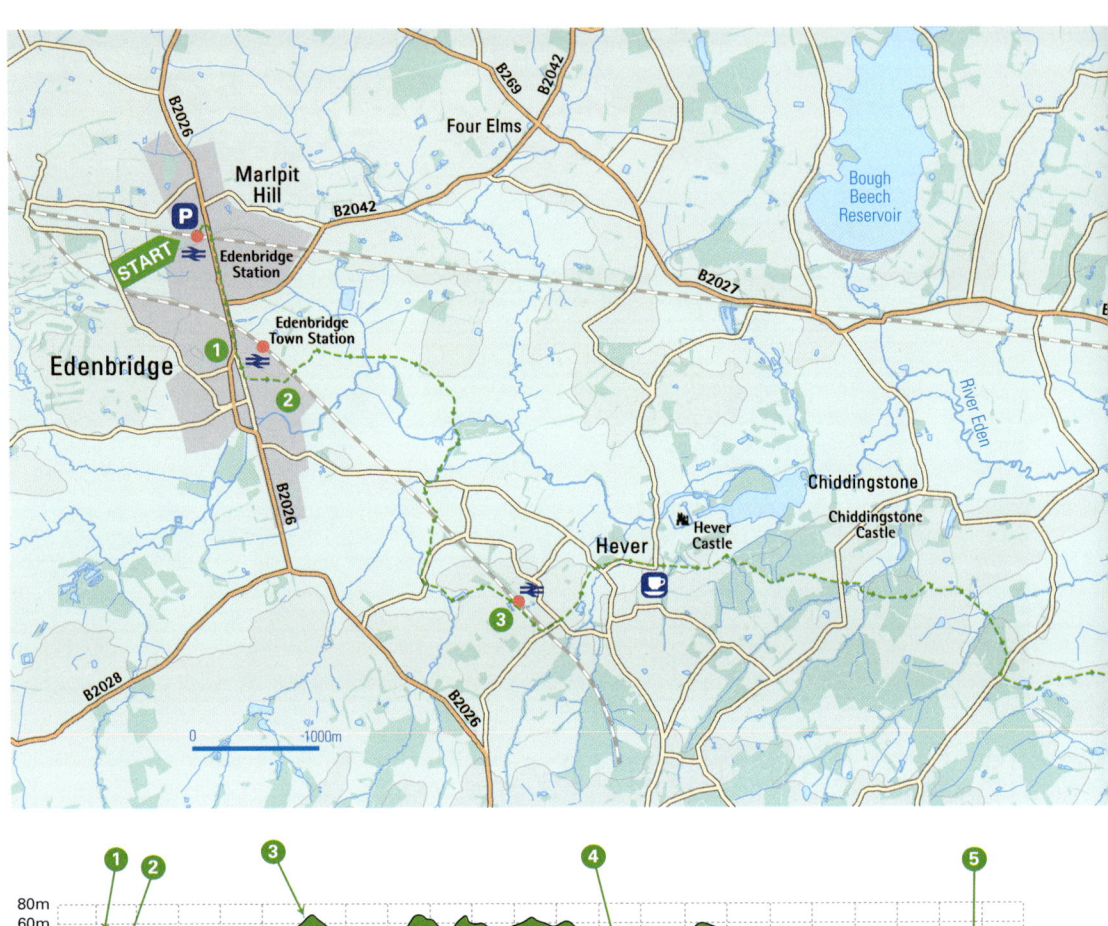

The scenery is simply wonderful, the shuttle is quick and easy, the trails are quiet, varied and engaging. There is no downside.

Route description

START From the car park area N of Edenbridge Railway Station (NOT Edenbridge Town Railway Station) head along Albion Way to the B2026 Main Road / Station Road. Turn right (downhill) and follow this S for 500m, passing beneath two railway bridges. ❶ When the B2026 bends right, instead take the left turning signposted 'town centre'. Follow High Street S for 250m to where Croft Road turns off left (opposite post office). Turn left and follow this winding road E, continuing into Frantfields and Forge Croft. 300m from High Street, you will see a tarmac footpath track signposted uphill on the left between houses (Numbers 7 and 9 Forge Croft). Take this, this is the Eden Valley Walk. ❷ Follow the EVW for 19.8km to Tonbridge Castle! It is well signposted by disks showing either a yellow symbol of castle and tree combined, or a simple yellow arrow. Outlined below is a brief summary with some waymarks to note, measured from the start; from Forge Croft (1.8km), the EVW crosses the railway and follows footpaths across open

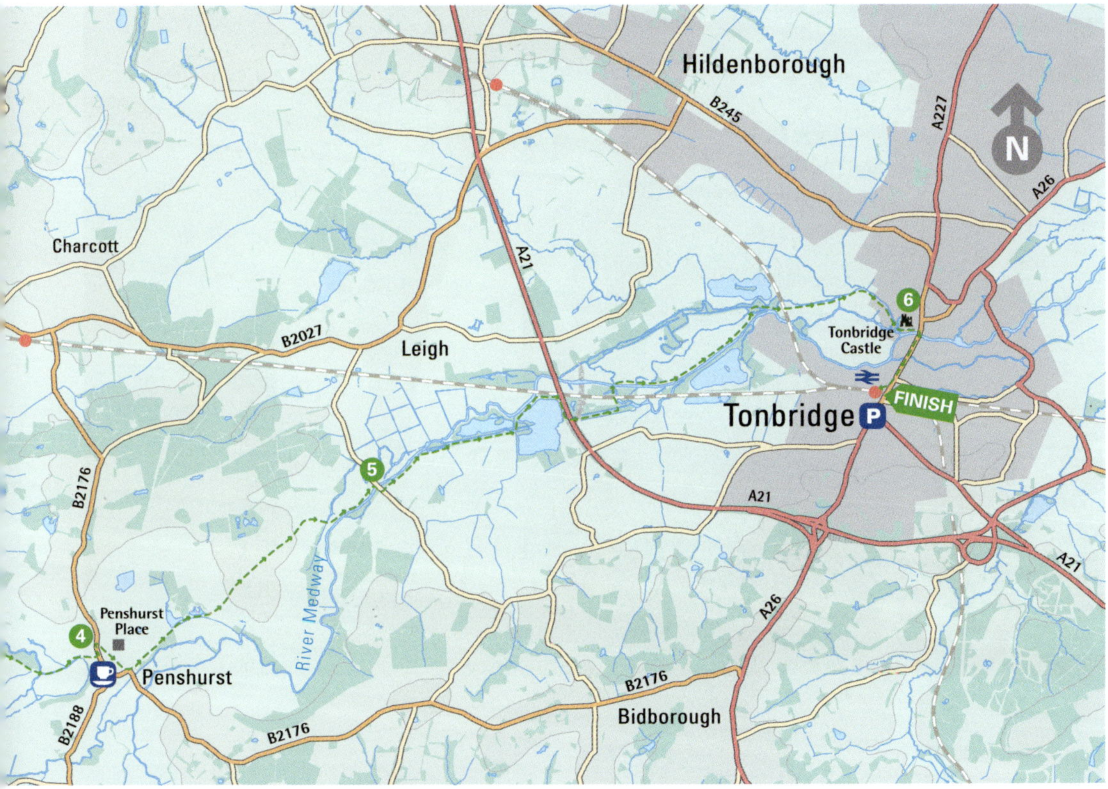

The Eden Valley 48

countryside, crossing the River Eden and passing under the railway to reach Hever Station (6.2km). ③ The EVW follows lanes and footpaths into Hever village, passing the King Henry VIII church and Hever Church. Hever Castle and then Chiddingstone Castle (both not seen) are passed via a series of wooded footpath and bridleway tracks across undulating ground, before descending to cross the River Eden and reaching Penshurst Place (huge mansion, 13.5km). ④ The EVW leads via footpaths and byway tracks through the grounds of Penshurst Place and then steeply (for the EVW) over a hill before descending to the River Medway and crossing this at Ensfield Bridge (16.4km). ⑤ The EDW now remains waterside, mostly following byways along the banks of the River Medway and its associated channels and lakes, all the way to Tonbridge Castle (21.9km), which is the end of the EVW. ⑥ After passing Tonbridge Castle, you reach the bridge over the River Medway on Tonbridge High Street. Cross the bridge and head S for 600m to Tonbridge Railway Station.

Tonbridge Castle

Haysden Lake

48 The Eden Valley

Entering Tonbridge

Trip planning

The first thing to get right in planning this mini-expedition is to leave your car at Edenbridge Railway Station, not Edenbridge *Town* Railway Station! The two stations are on completely different railway lines. There is of course paid parking at both Edenbridge Railway Station and Tonbridge Railway Station, and the train journey between them is just over half an hour (just under half an hour by car). Check times before heading out, as the time gap between train departures is erratic.

You are venturing into the Kent wilderness, so carry sufficient water and food for the duration. Seriously, the route passes only one place that could feed and water you; the King Henry VIII pub, early on in Hever. There is however the Leicester Arms Hotel in Penshurst (about halfway) if you go a short distance off-piste.

Hever

Moor Wood

Other routes

Completists will wish to know that the EVW starts proper at Cernes Farm TN8 5RA / TQ 425 445, an extra 3km SW of Edenbridge, near Starborough Castle. However, if you wish to start here, you'll need to shuttle by car (or run out and back from Edenbridge?) as public transport can't get you here.

The Eden Valley 48

Penshurst Place

If you wish to divide up the route, Penshurst is roughly halfway, and is served by the number 231 bus which can deliver you to either Edenbridge or Penshurst Railway Station, if heading for Tonbridge. Turn right (S) when you reach the road in front of Penshurst Place ④ to reach the village centre.

Eden Valley Walk signage

The EVW links up with a number of long-distance trails. The 47km / 29-mile Medway Valley Walk is effectively a continuation of the EVW, following the river bank downstream from Tonbridge to Rochester Castle (via Allington Castle) beside the Medway Estuary. The Vanguard Way (see page 258) passes by Cernes Farm (the EVW's official start) and the Wealdway (see page 258) briefly overlaps with the EVW on the last leg to Tonbridge Castle.

Events
The Gatliff Marathon is a LDWA Challenge Event, starting and finishing at Edenbridge with distances of 25km or 50km around the surrounding hills.
Runaway Racing's Eden Valley Ultra Trail sketches out an epic 50km loop east of Edenbridge, largely avoiding the EVW route.
Hit the Trail Running's Three Castles 30 is 30 miles from Tonbridge to Rochester Castle, along the route of the Medway Valley Walk.

48 The Eden Valley

Chiddingstone

The High Weald Area of Outstanding Natural Beauty

The 1,450km² High Weald AONB spans Surrey, West Sussex, East Sussex and Kent. If you've read up on the geology of the Weald (see page 48) you'll know that the High Weald is formed of the oldest rocks in the South East. This hard sandstone manifests itself as steep-sided ridges defined by river erosion, usually with flanks covered with trees and often with villages perched on top. A quarter of the AONB is woodland, over half of which is defined as ancient. In between the woods is a patchwork of farm fields stitched together by sunken lanes; this is a surviving Medieval landscape (*Weald* is Anglo-Saxon and means wilderness or forest). Routes 48, 50 and 52 are all within the AONB, but in truth these excellent routes are just an introduction to the trail running potential of this intriguing region; for further explorations, perhaps start with St Leonards Forest in West Sussex or Dallington Forest in East Sussex. The High Weald AONB publish a downloadable guide to the High Weald Landscape Trail, a 145km / 90-mile route across the AONB. There are also the Sussex Border Path (see page 288), Vanguard Way and Wealdway (see page 258) to consider.

East Sussex

East Sussex's most famous landmarks are Beachy Head and the Seven Sisters, where the high ridge of the South Downs is cut spectacularly short by the English Channel. The South Downs National Park extends along the south-east rim of the county, reaching a high point at Ditchling Beacon. East Sussex trail running isn't just about chalk hills, however. More than half of East Sussex is within the High Weald Area of Outstanding Natural Beauty; Ashdown Forest is the most prominent part of this patchwork landscape of farmland, sandstone ridges and woodlands, but there is also superb running to be had where the High Weald meets the sea at Hastings. Further east along the coast, the bleak shingle ridges of Rye Harbour offer an entirely different experience.

South Downs Way approaching Ditchling Beacon (Route 53)

Martello Tower

Camber Castle

49 Camber Castle

Distance	9.5km (6 miles)	**Ascent**	25m (80ft)
Map	OS Landranger 198 OS Explorer 124		
Navigation	●●●	Some unmarked trails, mostly simple route finding	
Terrain	●●●	Concrete tracks, shingly trails, grass, little gradient	
Wet feet	●●●	A short section can become a quagmire in the wet	
Start / Finish	Rye Harbour car park TN31 7TX / TQ 941 189		

Easy trails exploring a shingle wilderness

Camber Castle was built for Henry VIII as part of a chain of impressive coastal defences. It is still largely intact, but now sits forlorn in the midst of a field, nearly 2km from the sea. Five centuries of ceaseless wave motion has laid down successive ridges of shingle between the castle and the English Channel (also stranding a Napoleonic Martello tower 1km inland), and this strange landscape is now Rye Harbour Nature Reserve. For the purposes of trail running, this 475-hectare reserve offers the chance to pace along stony trails weaving through pebble banks, brackish lagoons and grassy marshland. There is almost no gradient, but the trails are often rough underfoot and the wind is omnipresent. The author was struck by the sheer loneliness of this place, away from the seafront. This was perhaps a mistaken impression, as the reserve is home to at least 4,500 species of plant and animal, from the kale and campion clinging to the shingle, to the terns and oystercatcher fishing in the lagoons. Bittern may be heard making their distinctive 'booming'

Camber Castle

sound, but you are unlikely to actually see them; they hide in the reedbeds and there are less than a hundred males in the country. The final part of the route is a marked contrast, running on softer grasslands around the castle, which are actually 'grazing marsh'.

Route description

This route partly follows a numbered trail around the Nature Reserve, the numbers are included in this description as, ①.

START From the car park, follow the concrete footpath track along the River Rother. After 1km, the track splits at a pillbox ①. Take the right-hand permissive track which parallels the beach. After 700m, a shingly footpath turns off right / inland ②, take this. ① After 400m and after passing between lake hides, the path splits ③, take the left-hand permissive path. Follow this for 600m to a T junction with a larger footpath track. ② Turn left and follow the footpath track 1.5km SW past two successive sets of buildings to a crossroads ⑦. ③ Turn right and follow the footpath track NW along the end of a lake (Long Pit).

Camber Castle

Continue on the footpath track 350m past the lake to a junction of footpaths beside a gate marked, 'No parking turning space' and 'Camber Cottage' ❽. ❹ Cross the stile beside the gate and follow this footpath 400m NNE past Camber Cottage and along a field to a T-junction with a footpath track ❾. Turn right and follow this footpath track 300m to the end of a lake (Castle Water) ❿. ❺ Turn left off the footpath onto a permissive path which follows the W edge of the lake. After 750m (shortly after passing an RAF Memorial), turn left ⓫ away from the lake, and follow a permissive path to Camber Castle. ❻ Explore around the outside of the castle, then follow the permissive path which leads N. After 450m a stream is crossed ⓬, keep following the permissive path which now bears NE along Castle Water to reach a gate ⓭ marked 'Wildlife Sanctuary Area'. Go through the smaller gate beside this and follow this permissive path 250m to a T junction ⓮ behind industrial buildings. ❼ Turn right (SE) and follow this permissive path for 700m until it emerges onto Harbour Road. Turn right and follow the road for 1km back to the start.

Harbour entrance

Trip planning

The car park is pay and display, located at the end of Harbour Road, next to a Napoleonic Martello Tower and a caravan site.

Sussex Wildlife Trust have managed the reserve since 2011, and run an information cabin on the tarmac road that forms the very first part of this route. Access to the reserve is free. It is possible to download a useful map from their website, or purchase a paper copy beforehand from Rye Heritage and Information Centre in Rye. Camber Castle is locked and can only be explored via a monthly guided tour, booked with English Heritage. However, you can peer in through the front entrance and get a pretty good impression of its elaborate layout.

Rye Harbour

Pillbox

Other routes

There are two waymarked trails around Rye Harbour Nature Reserve, both starting from the car park; the Short Trail (3.5km, follow 1, 2, 3, 4) and the Long Trail (9km, follow 1, 2, then 5-15) which overlaps with this route to a fair degree.

If you've had enough of running shingly trails, nearby Camber Sands (just across the River Rother, park in

Rye Harbour Nature Reserve

49 Camber Castle

Rye Harbour Nature Reserve

Camber) is a glorious golden expanse to sprint across. If on the other hand you can't get enough of shingle ridges, then the nearby headland of Dungeness has more than you might ever dream of. Footpaths span out from the car park beside Dungeness Lighthouse TN29 9ND / **TR 088 169**; despite the nuclear power station and military firing range, many folk rave about this bleak and otherworldly place.

Events
Nice Work's Rye Ancient Trails 30K & 15K explore the Low Weald countryside inland from Rye, starting and finishing on Rye High Street.

> **The Royal Military Canal**
>
> Looking for a flat 45km waterside run? A footpath (part of the Saxon Shore Way, see page 254) runs along the entire length of the Royal Military Canal, which arcs inland between Hastings and Folkestone, passing Rye en route. It's exactly what it sounds like; a canal built by the army (1805–9) to defend England against Napoleonic invasion, along the edge of Romney Marsh. The north bank is higher ground, the south bank is flat marshland. Today the canal is disused, but a haven for wildlife. Along its course are numerous pillboxes and concrete 'listening ears'; these are acoustic 'mirrors' which were used to detect incoming aircraft before the invention of radar.

50 Hastings Country Park

Fire Hills

Distance	9.5km (6 miles)	Ascent	400m (1,300ft)
Map	OS Landranger 199 OS Explorer 124		
Navigation ●●●	A large number of paths and junctions		
Terrain ●●●	Numerous steep ascents and descents, lots of steps		
Wet feet ●●●	Plenty of confined muddy paths		
Start / Finish	Hastings Country Park Visitor Centre car park TN35 4AD / TQ 860 116		

Superb rugged trails with tough coastal climbs

Some of the best rugged trail running in the South East is hidden in this small (345 hectare) country park outside Hastings. The sandstone of the High Weald meets the sea rather ungraciously, with a frontage of crumbling 100m cliffs. Three steep-sided and overgrown 'glens' have incised down into the cliffs, meaning that the trails along this coast are anything but flat! Expect some demanding climbs and precarious descents, negotiating eroded paths and rough stairs. The full title of this place is Hasting Country Park *Nature Reserve*, a useful reminder that great trail running isn't just about the physical aspect. The glens that you zigzag through literally drip with mosses and liverworts, and if you manage to glance up from the stiff climbs, you'll notice the heather and pink thrift in the foreground, and France in the background!

50 Hastings Country Park

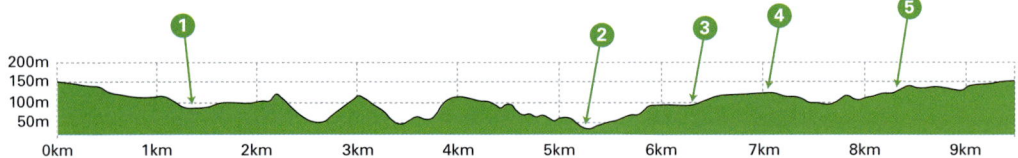

Route description

START From the visitor centre building, pass downhill through the car park. At the end, two wide paths lead downhill; take the left-hand path, heading SE. Stay on this path and ignore side turns. It descends along a field edge, becoming a footpath and enters woodland before reaching the eastern boundary of Hastings Country Park after 1.1km. Turn right (S, towards the coast) and follow the footpath along the edge of Fairlight village for 150m to the coast footpath. ❶ Turn right (W) and follow the coast footpath (signposted as the Saxon Shore Way) for 3.8km to Ecclesbourne Glen. After 1km you descend into and climb out of Warren Glen (deep ravine) and directly after, you repeat the grind with Fairlight Glen. Approaching Ecclesbourne Glen, signs warn of path closure due to landslips and offer diversions; ignore these as the coast path is open as far as the bottom of the Glen (2020). Descend into Ecclesbourne Glen, cross the stream at the bottom and take the footpath leading up the valley on your right. ❷ Follow the footpath along the stream up Ecclesbourne Glen. After 500m you reach a crossroads of trails beside the stream, turn right onto the footpath heading E (still heading up the valley). Follow this for 700m uphill.

Hastings Country Park

Just after passing Ecclesbourne Reservoir, a footpath leads up steps on the right, signposted for Fairlight Glen. Turn right onto this. ❸ After 330m the footpath reaches Barn Pond. Turn left here (signposted 'upper Fairlight Glen') and follow the path for 400m along two fields to a T junction with a footpath. Turn right onto the footpath and descend into Fairlight Glen. ❹ Ignore footpaths leading down Fairlight Glen (towards the sea) and bear left to follow the footpath around the rim of the glen. 200m after crossing the Dripping Well stream, a footpath leads uphill on the left, take this. After 260m the footpath begins to descend into Warren Glen. When you reach a crossroads, turn left and follow the footpath leading up the rim of Warren Glen. After 500m, at the head of the valley, a crossroads of footpaths is reached. Turn right (E). ❺ Follow the footpath to a quarry. A path turns off left and ascends direct through the quarry to reach the car park, alternatively stay on the footpath until you reach Coastguard Cottages (with a mast and radar), then turn left and follow the track uphill to the car park.

Fairlight Glen

Trip planning

The car park is pay and display, located at the end of Lower Coastguard Lane, a right turn off Fairlight Road if coming from Hastings. The car park is beside the Hastings Country Park Visitor Centre, however if this is full you will have passed a bigger car park further back along the lane. A short walk behind the visitor centre on Coastguard Lane (not the lane you drove in on) is the rather pleasant Coastguards Tearoom, who humoured the author hogging a table for an afternoon, while working on this book.

View from the Visitor Centre

Warren Glen

Other routes

The coast path / Saxon Shore Way further west, across Ecclesbourne Glen onto the hillfort of East Hill and downhill into Hastings, has been closed for some years due to ongoing landslips.
The Saxon Shore Way to the east passes through the village of Fairlight Cove and then diverts inland, following the Royal Military Canal (see page 250).

50 Hastings Country Park

Fire Hills

The 1066 Country Walk joins up footpaths passing north of Hastings for 50km / 31 miles from Pevensey (where Duke William of Normandy landed) via Battle Abbey (the site where Duke William was promoted to King William) and onwards to Rye. The route is marked on OS maps.

Events

The 1066 100 Ultramarathon is *102* miles from Westminster Abbey to Battle Abbey, recreating the march of King Harold's army to the Battle of Hastings. Harold took three days, but for some sadistic reason the organisers have a cut-off of 30 hours. Presumably they also jab an arrow into your eye, upon completion.

The Saxon Shore Way

The Saxon Shore Way is the long-distance trail spanning 262km / 163 miles of the coast (with 3,311m of ascent) from Hastings in East Sussex to Gravesend in Kent. Routes 42, 43, 44, 49 and 50 follow parts of the SSW, which is now of course subsumed into the England Coast Path (see page 220). The route is a bit quirky as it follows the Roman course of the coast, not the modern coast. This means for example, diversions inland at the Royal Military Canal (see page 250) and the Isle of Thanet. The name is a reference to the Saxon Shore Forts, massive forts built by the Romans in the latter days of their occupation of Britain to guard against Saxon invaders (traces of one can be seen in Route 43). The SSW is waymarked with a red Viking helmet.

51 Seven Sisters and Beachy Head

Beachy Head Lighthouse

Distance	10km (6 miles)	**Ascent**	700m (2,330ft)
Map	OS Landranger 199 OS Explorer OL25		
Navigation	●●○	Simple, following the South Downs Way along the coast path	
Terrain	●●●	Easy trails, repeated steep climbs and descents	
Wet feet	●○○	Little to worry about	
Start	Seven Sisters Country Park Visitor Centre, Exceat BN25 4AD / TV 519 995		
Finish	Beachy Head car park BN20 7YA / TV 590 959		

Stunning views and steep climbs atop iconic white cliffs

A decade ago, the author attempted his first ultramarathon, right here. I hadn't visited the area before and I was blown away by the endlessly undulating white cliffs, dazzling in the morning sunshine. When I rounded a corner and looked down upon the Cuckmere River meandering across the valley towards the sea, I actually gasped. To cut to the chase, this scenery is just incredible*.

This is one of Britain's most recognisable landscapes, and makes for exceptional (and exceptionally challenging) trail running. After approaching the sea along and above the wonderful Cuckmere valley, you are faced by the severest coastal profile imaginable! The Seven Sisters are successive steep hills, each separated by a dry valley from the next summit. Having somehow overcome this crazy geography to reach Birling Gap, several further climbs remain; to Belle Tout Lighthouse and finally to 162m Beachy Head, Britain's

* *Admittedly, a few hours later, ascending Beachy Head for a third time, the novelty had worn off somewhat.*

51 Seven Sisters and Beachy Head

tallest chalk sea cliff. Stand triumphant atop 100-million-year-old Cretaceous chalk (kept pristinely clean by regular rockfalls), gazing down on Beachy Head Lighthouse and the wheeling kittiwakes and fulmars. It's quite the experience.

Route description

START From the visitor centre, cross the A259 (East Dean Road) and head to the bus stop opposite. Behind the bus stop, go through the furthest left gate with a signpost behind for the South Downs Way. Follow the footpath up and along the hillside (Combe Bottom). After 750m the footpath begins to descend, reaching the valley floor after 1.3km. ❶ Don't join the permissive tracks on the valley floor, follow SDW signs along a footpath for 200m S. This footpath then ascends a second hillside (Haven Brow), reaching clifftops after 1km. ❷ Turn left (E) and follow the footpath along the coast. After 3km (and descending into / climbing out of seven valleys!) the footpath leads down a track beside houses to Birling Gap (hotel, car park, beach). ❸ Cross the car park entrance and follow the SDW uphill. Belle Tout Lighthouse is

Seven Sisters and Beachy Head

reached after 1km, the footpath passes this on the inland side. It is another 3km (and three more valleys) to Beachy Head car park.

Trip planning

There is plenty of (pay and display) parking at both ends of this route. Seven Sisters Country Park has two car parks; Forest and Riverside, which are self-explanatory. There are interesting displays about the park's history, geology and wildlife at the visitor centre, which is nearest to the Forest car park.

At Beachy Head, there is a large car park beside the Countryside and Visitor Centre and there are other parking areas back along Beachy Head Road.

It is easy to shuttle back to the start using public transport … on Sundays, when the 13X bus runs hourly between the start and finish. For the rest of the week, you need to catch the 12X, which bypasses Beachy Head; from Beachy Head either descend into Eastbourne following the SDW (see below) or follow the other branch of the SDW 3km north to the bus stop where it crosses the A259.

This is a very popular tourist spot, so if you want to enjoy the scenery without crowds, an early start (or late evening jaunt) is highly recommended.

The cliffs are receding at a rate of 30–40cm a year *on average*. More usually, much larger sections peel away without warning; there are two or three major falls each year. Keep your distance from the edge, no matter how Instagram-able the selfie prospects are.

The Saltmarsh Café, behind the Seven Sisters Country Park Visitor Centre, is one feed option, but fills or even books up quickly. The National Trust run a café and shop at Birling Gap; but it's an open debate as to whether a cream tea is a good idea when you still have a few hundred metres of climb left. Your best bet for a full stomach is probably the rather bland Beachy Head pub at the finish.

The Seven Sisters

Cuckmere River

Seaford Head and the Seven Sisters

Belle Tout Lighthouse

Flagstaff Brow

51 Seven Sisters and Beachy Head

Other routes

Finishing this route after the Seven Sisters at Birling Gap will make for a six-kilometre run.

Extending the route can be done in a number of ways. Starting from Seaford and following the coast path and Vanguard Way will add 6km and despite the urban beginning, rewards you with the famous view of the Seven Sisters from Seaford Head Nature Reserve. At the other end of the route, it's only 2km steeply downhill from Beachy Head into Eastbourne, following the SDW / Wealdway. Your thighs may not thank you for this.

The 13X bus service (Sundays only) stops at all of the locations above, allowing for flexibility in your plans. The 12X service (all week) also offers options.

The route can be extended easily into a pretty challenging 28km loop, all following the SDW. This is because the SDW splits inland at Alfriston, with one branch reaching Beachy Head via the Seven Sisters (followed by the route described here), while the other branch approaches Beachy Head from the north after a steep ascent of Windover Hill (beside the Wilmington Long Man, an ancient chalk figure). Probably the best way to tackle this loop is anti-clockwise, starting at Beachy Head itself (or, for a free option, the parking area 2km inland on the B2103 Warren Hill Road BN20 7TZ / TV 587 978) and heading inland to Alfriston first, before following the other branch of the SDW downstream along the banks of the Cuckmere River to reach Seven Sisters Country Park.

Events

Beachy Head Marathon, Half and 10km (formerly known as the Seven Sisters Marathon) are among the biggest off-road events in the country. All distances start and finish way down at the bottom of the hill in Eastbourne.

Endurance Life's Coastal Trail Series Sussex event is also massive (in terms of entry numbers) and has a choice of distances from 10km to Ultra. This was the author's first Ultra event, as noted above. My favourite part was running through cheering crowds after 26.2 miles ... only to reach a sign, a few metres before the finish line, diverting 'Ultra' entrants off for another eight miles. Cruel.

The Wealdway and the Vanguard Way

Both of these long-distance trails meet the English Channel at Route 51, having crossed the North Downs, Weald and South Downs from the Thames valley. Their routes run roughly parallel and at Ashdown Forest (Route 52) they criss-cross one another. Both are marked on OS maps.

The **Wealdway** (134km / 83 miles) spans from Gravesend to Beachy Head and Eastbourne, briefly merging with the Eden Valley Walk (Route 48). The exceptionally motivated will notice that it nearly forms a loop with the Saxon Shore Way (see page 254) ... anyone for a 400+km trail run?

The **Vanguard Way** (106km / 66 miles) makes the crossing from Croydon (this isn't entirely random; it starts where the Wandle Trail to the River Thames ends) to Cuckmere Haven and then Newhaven. It has been utilised on occasion as part of a London to Paris run!

Gills Lap

52 Ashdown Forest

Distance		15km (9 miles)	Ascent	325m (1,070ft)
Map		OS Landranger 187 188 OS Explorer 135		
Navigation	●●●	Multiple unmarked paths, Ashdown Forest Official Map recommended		
Terrain	●●○	Sandy heath, rutted muddy tracks, mild hills		
Wet feet	●●●	A few swampy sections to hop and skip through		
Start / Finish		Ashdown Forest Centre car park RH18 5JP / TQ 432 323		

The Hundred Acre Wood

Ashdown Forest may look vaguely familiar; it is the real life Hundred Acre Wood, where Winnie-the-Pooh and his friends resided. Author A.A. Milne owned a house on the fringes of the forest, and was inspired to write the stories based on walks with his son Christopher Robin. E.H. Shepard's classic illustrations were also drawn in the wood. So, come run in Winnie-the-Pooh's footsteps ... or Eeyore's, if you're feeling a bit down. Ashdown Forest is a 2,500 hectare / 25km² expanse of common land, the largest area with open public access in South East England. Happily, for your trail running needs, it is also a rather pleasant place! Numerous sandy trails lead across hillsides covered by heathland and beech and oak woods, with expansive views. The modern forest consists of three connected parts, giving a 'squished-triangle' appearance on the map. The route described here is a circuit sampling all three sections and should be more than enough to tempt you back for further and future explorations.

Ashdown Forest

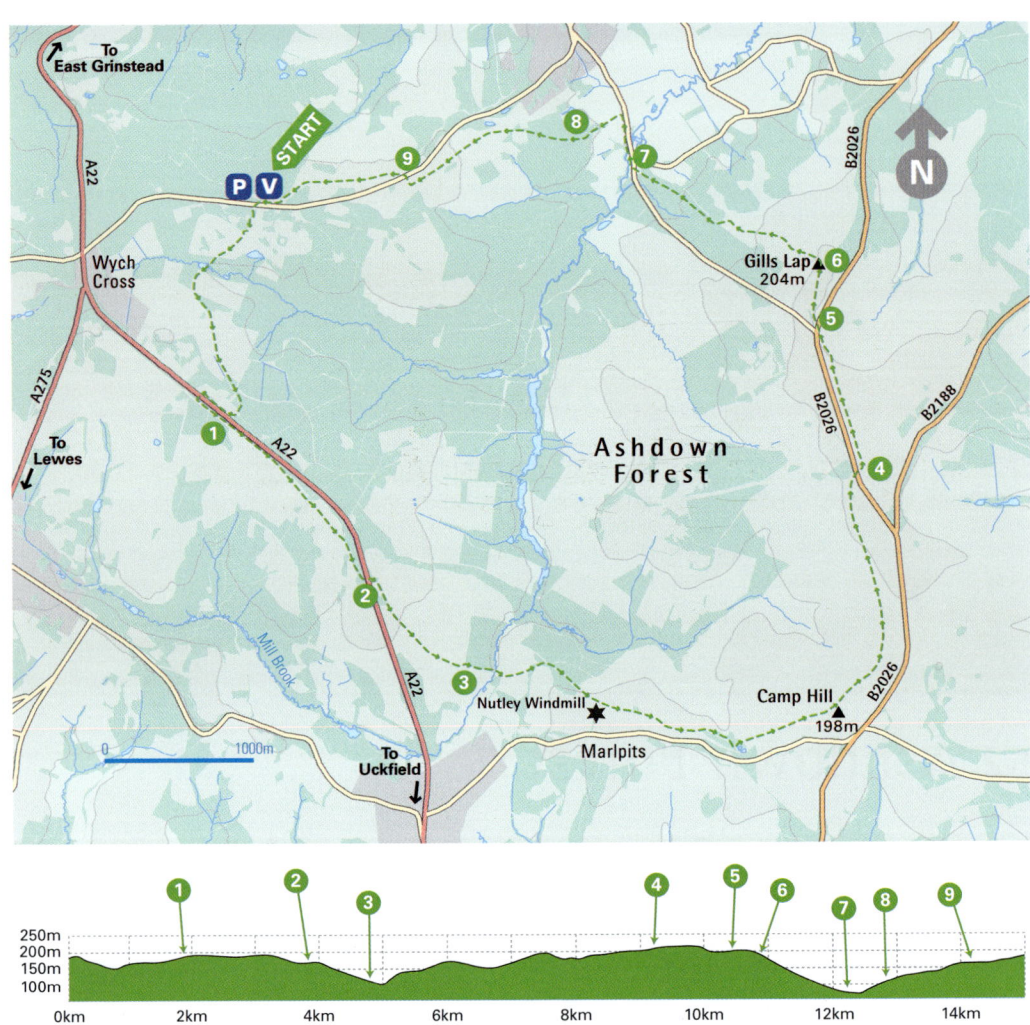

Route description

START From the car park, pass among the Forest Centre buildings until you reach the footpath track on the far (E) side. Turn left to follow this to the road (Colemans Hatch Road). Cross the road and follow it 40m to the right to find a footpath beside a house (almost hidden!) leading S. Follow the footpath downhill through the grounds of Ashdown Park Hotel. Remain on the footpath for 1.7km as it crosses a stream at the bottom of the hill and then ascends through fields to reach a road (A22). ❶ Cross the road and turn right (NW) to follow it for 200m to a car park. Pass through the car park to the NW–SE track at the back. Turn left (SE) and follow this boggy track for 1.6km, bearing left at a fork after 1.4km, to Millbrook East car park on the A22 road. ❷ Cross the road and turn right at the back of the car park to take the path leading SSE. Follow this downhill, ignoring one left turn and then two right forks. After 750m you reach a crossroads of paths, turn left and head just 30m to another junction; turn right onto the heavily eroded / rutted path leading downhill. ❸ You will be following this path ahead for 4.4km, although it winds about and there are numerous side-turns to ignore. The path descends to the valley floor, crosses a stream and then

Ashdown Forest

climbs into woodland. Continue uphill through the woods (when you reach a crossroads, Nutley Windmill is an optional 60m diversion to the right), then ascend on open heath to Friend's Clump ('clumps' are enclosures of trees at prominent points). The path leads E along the high ground, passing Ellison Pond and reaching Camp Hill Clump after another 1km, where it merges with the Wealdway long-distance trail. The path bends NE and then N before reaching the B2026 road (High Road) where a tarmac drive signposted 'Private Road to Old Lodge' joins it. ❹ Cross the B2026 and follow the path leading ahead (NE). After 65m a crossroads is reached, turn left (off the Wealdway) to follow the path leading NNW. Ignore all side turns and continue ahead for 1km to reach the B2026 again, cross this to reach Gills Lap car park. ❺ Take the path out of

Millbrook

Camp Hill Clump

the car park leading N along the high ground to Gills Lap Clump, reached after 400m. At the Clump, look for a small path turning off left (steeply downhill) and take this. ❻ Continue ahead (downhill). At the junctions you reach, and when faced by a choice, always take the option leading downhill. After 1.4km you emerge from woods at a lane. Turn left and follow the lane 30m to a ford and junction with a larger lane (Kidd's Hill). Turn right (N) onto this lane. ❼ Follow the lane 350m uphill to where a track leads off on the left, with a sign permitting access to horses, but not trail bikes. Turn off left onto this track. After 200m it merges with a track joining from the right (N), 30m after this a path turns off right (W / uphill) into the woods: turn right to take this path. ❽ Follow the path uphill, after 500m it emerges from the woods and passes a cricket ground to reach a tarmac lane (Sandy Lane). Cross the lane and locate the path leading W (not the nearby path which leads NW past a bowling green), follow this. It emerges onto a wide track, follow this SW (uphill). At the second crossroads you reach, after 600m, turn right to reach a road (Coleman's Hatch Road) after 75m. Cross the road to reach a car park (Ridge car park or Lintons car park, they are adjacent). ❾ Find the path which leads out of the back of the car park and turn left (W) to follow it along the hillside. After 800m you reach the open grassy area beside the Forest Centre car park.

Trip planning

Parking at the Ashdown Forest Centre is free. There are numerous other free roadside parking areas dotted along the roads around the forest; you are never further than 1km from one on this route. These are helpful if (giving a totally hypothetical example) you trip and twist your ankle *again* and have to hobble to a place where your wife can come and pick you up *again*.

Near the Visitor Centre

Ashdown Forest

The Ashdown Forest Centre is three reconstructed barns. The Information Barn is open seven days a week in summer, volunteer staff allowing, and is well worth patronising to view their displays about the local ecology and history.

It's highly recommended to get hold of a copy of the Ashdown Forest Official Map before running; it shows more detail of the complex local trails than the OS maps. It can be bought for a small fee from the Information Barn or downloaded from their website.

For food and supplies, you will need to head outside the forest to Crowborough or Forest Row.

Other routes

You can run freely within the forest's common land; the official map will help you to keep track of which of the innumerable trails you are currently lost on. Maps outlining a series of routes exploring the forest can be bought from the Ashdown Forest Centre or downloaded (for a small charge) from the official Ashdown Forest website. The longest is a 23km circuit linking up the 'clumps', although you may be more tempted by the Pooh Walks, which seek out iconic locations such as *The Heffalump Trap* and *Eeyore's Sad and Gloomy Place*.

The Wealdway and Vanguard Way long-distance trails intersect in Ashdown Forest; see page 258.

Events

RunBelievable's Winnie-the-Pooh Weekend includes a 6-hour endurance event around a 5-mile loop. Fancy Dress is encouraged!

Trail Running Sussex organise the Weald Challenge, a concurrent half marathon and 50km Ultra which starts from Chiddingly (some distance south of Ashdown Forest) and visits it via the Wealdway and Vanguard Way.

Ashdown Forest

Ashdown Forest is a forest in the historic sense; a Royal hunting ground dating from after the Norman Conquest. Nevertheless, 40% of it is oak and birch woodland, not to mention the distinctive 'clumps', nineteenth-century hilltop enclosures of Scots pine. The remainder is open heathland, which looks natural enough but is actually a man-made environment resulting from centuries of overgrazing, preventing woodland from spreading. Domestic animals still graze on the common land, but they are joined by a population of thousands of deer; mostly fallow, but also roe, muntjac and sika.

The forest spans the highest part of the High Weald AONB (see page 244), reaching 223m. As Ashdown Forest is at the centre of the eroded Weald Anticline (see page 48), its Cretaceous sandstone is the oldest rock in South East England; the landscape you see stretching to the north (to the North Downs) and south (to the South Downs) gets progressively younger.

Ditchling Beacon

South Downs Way approaching the finish

53 Ditchling Beacon

Distance	9km (5.5 miles)	**Ascent**	225m (740ft)
Map	OS Landranger 198, OS Explorer OL11		
Navigation	●●●	Obvious and simple-to-follow bridleways	
Terrain	●●●	Wide and narrow chalk trails, some long ascents	
Wet feet	●●●	Well draining trails, however chalk is slippery in the wet	
Start / Finish	Jack and Jill car park BN6 9PG / TQ 302 133		

A moderate loop around East Sussex's loftiest trails

A chance to run the high ground and gaze down upon the world far below … without too much uphill grind. This popular circuit is a great taster of the South Downs, taking you via mild(-ish) inclines around quiet hills and valleys behind the main ridge to the summit of Ditchling Beacon. The highest point in East Sussex, the Beacon is 248m high and strikingly rears over 200m above the plain below. Its prominence has been utilised as a hillfort in the Iron Age, and as part of a chain of fire beacons to warn of invasion (the clue is in the name). On the final downhill(-ish) leg along the ridge, you can revel in 360° views, stretching along the South Downs, out over the English Channel and far north into the Weald.

While soaking up the distant views, don't lose focus on what is directly underfoot; you are running through precious chalk grasslands. This habitat is gradually being restored to past glory by the National Trust and Sussex Wildlife Trust, through sheep grazing. This removes encroaching hawthorn and allows

53 Ditchling Beacon

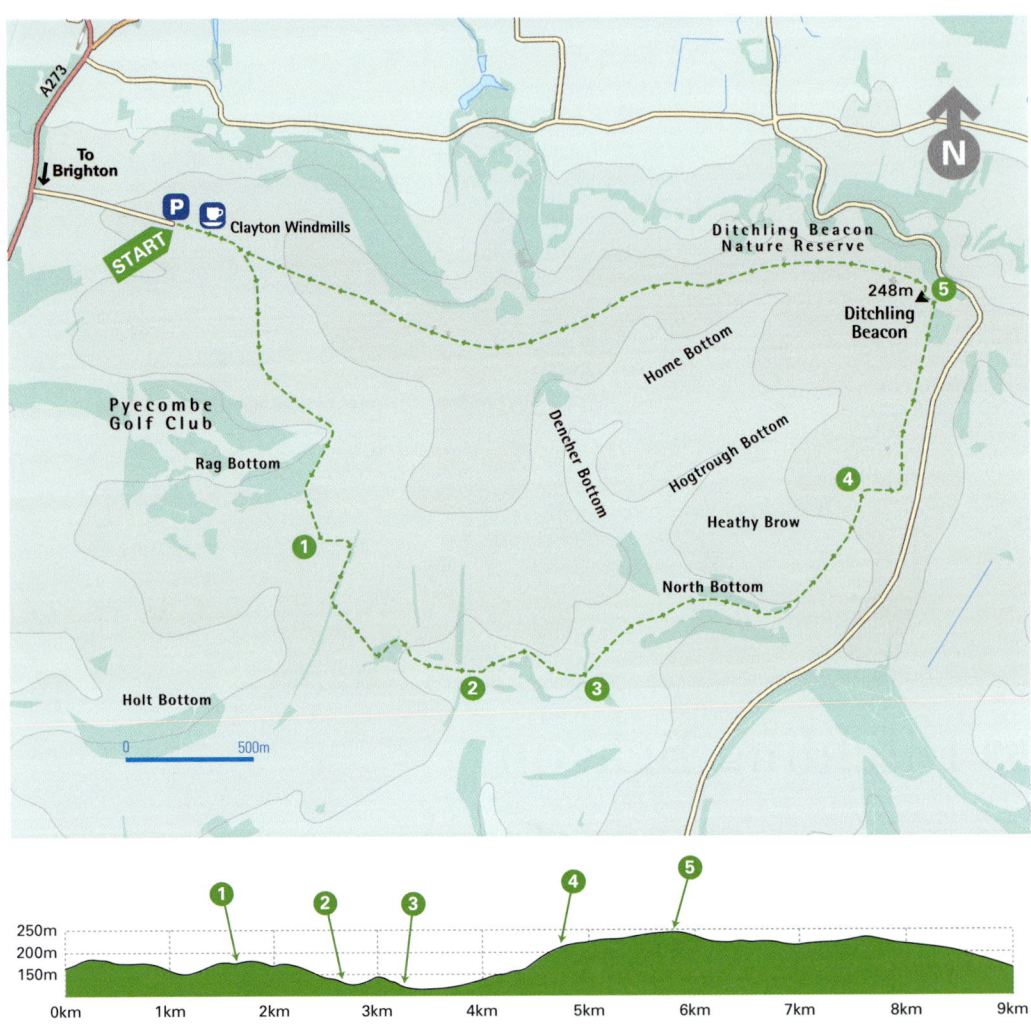

more diverse grasses to grow, along with wild herbs such as marjoram and thyme, and a range of rare orchids in mid-summer. You may spot the lovely chalk hill blue butterfly fluttering by; this is blue and lives on chalk hills.

Route description

START Follow the bridleway uphill (E) from the car park, past the windmills. After 250m there is a junction, take the bridleway leading off to the right (SE) signposted 'Devil's Dyke'. Follow this ahead through New Barn Farm and across a crossroads of bridleways to reach a T junction after 1.3km. ❶ Turn left (E) and follow this bridleway ahead around successive corners, continuing ahead at a crossroads of bridleways after 500m. When you descend towards Lower Standean Farm, look for a gate on the left just before the farm. ❷ Go through this gate and follow this permissive bridleway uphill and around the farm buildings. After 500m the previous bridleway is re-joined, turn left onto it (up North Bottom valley) and follow this. ❸ Keep following the bridleway uphill along the valley floor. Note that the bridleway is

Ditchling Beacon

Ditchling Beacon

located across the wire fence from the main track, and when the valley splits into two forks after 500m, the bridleway leads up the right-hand (E) valley. When you have climbed out of North Bottom valley and the ground begins to level off, look for a bridleway leading off on the right. ❹ Take this, it leads after 150m to a field boundary where it turns left (N, uphill). Ascend along this bridleway for 750m to a gate leading into Ditchling Beacon Nature Reserve. Take paths leading left to find the summit trig point. ❺ Head 40m N from the trig point to find the main South Downs Way bridleway. Turn left and follow this for 3km W along the ridge top, back to your start point.

Trip planning

Jack and Jill car park is at the end of Mill Lane, follow the signage for 'Jack and Jill' from the A273 Clayton Hill Road. The car park is free. Jack and Jill, incidentally, are the two amazing, restored nineteenth-century windmills beside the car park. Jill is open to the public (free of charge) and well worth a nose around.

An alternative start point is the popular Ditchling Beacon National Trust car park BN6 8XD / TQ 333 129 (free to members), which is just off Ditchling Road. Head uphill from the car park to the summit and pick up the route from ❺.

South Downs Way near Ditchling Beacon

The vibrant city of Brighton and Hove sprawls along the coast directly south of Ditchling Beacon and a visit to the centre is always engaging (outrageous parking charges notwithstanding). However, the village of Ditchling, just north of the Beacon, is a quieter spot

Ditchling Beacon

from which to rest and fuel up. The corner newsagents are memorably friendly and the Green Welly Café do a breakfast fry-up (served inside something posh called a 'ciabatta', for some reason). There is also a splendid tiny counter selling tea and homemade cake within the Jill windmill.

Firle Beacon from Ditchling Beacon

Other routes

If you turn off right at the crossroads of bridleways 1.8km after ❶, you can visit the Chattri Memorial. This 2.5km out-and-back detour is an opportunity to pay your respects to the 62,000 'Indian soldiers who gave their lives for their King-Emperor in the Great War,' as the memorial puts it.

Ascending Ditchling Beacon direct from the north side will involve the kind of grinding misery which this route is specifically designed to avoid! However, if you really must (note that nearby Route 54 offers plenty of said masochism), either start from the village of Ditchling or use the car park on Underhill Lane at BN6 8XD / TQ 325 137. Footpaths lead directly from the car park to the summit, joining the route at ❺.

There are numerous ways to approach Ditchling Beacon from the Brighton direction. For example, ascending the bridleway north from the car park on Braypool Lane off the A27 at BN1 8YU / TQ 301 094 (passing the Chattri Memorial) will bring you onto this route between ❶ and ❷, making for a 5km longer outing. The South Downs ridge extends 7km east of Ditchling Beacon to the town of Lewes, with precisely the same scenery and network of excellent trails all the way. Note that halfway, the South Downs Way uncharacteristically drops off the ridge to the south (bypassing Lewes), which can catch out those following it as part of a longer outing (author included, more than once).

Events

Maverick Race's East Sussex event ascends Ditchling Beacon from the University of Sussex in Brighton, with 5km / 15km / 23km options.

The Brighton Trailblazer Run is a 10km race around hills to the south-east of this route, starting from Woodingdean.

Sussex Trail Events' Hilly Half Marathon pretty much explains itself. They hold the Downland Challenge alongside this, a 30-mile ultra.

Ultra Challenge's London 2 Brighton Challenge is 100km (tackled wholly or in sections), passing through the Ditchling vicinity before descending to the coast.

There is also the Mid-Sussex Marathon Weekend, a medley of races from a mile to a marathon in length, held in various locations north of Ditchling (e.g. Hayward's Heath).

West Sussex

West Sussex is the UK's sunniest county, according to the Met Office! This sun shines on a county blessed with the lion's share of the South Downs National Park. The defined chalk ridge of the South Downs naturally forms the basis of several routes in this section, but there is more variation to the national park than might be imagined; Petworth Park is a remarkable engineered landscape where you can run among lakes and woods arranged according to eighteenth-century taste, while Black Down (the 'county top') is part of the Greensand Ridge and hence characterised by sandstone heathland. While much of West Sussex's coast is developed, the shores of Chichester Harbour (designated as an Area of Outstanding Natural Beauty) remain bleakly wild and a run around secretive Thorney Island is a must-do.

Beacon Hill (Route 59)

Devil's Dyke

54 Devil's Dyke

Fulking Hill

Distance	9.5km (6 miles)	Ascent	475m (1,560ft)
Map	OS Landranger 198 OS Explorer OL11		
Navigation	•••	Numerous minor trails to keep track of; map recommended	
Terrain	•••	Chalk tracks, rough rooty trails, steep ascents	
Wet feet	•••	Lower trails become slick and slippery after rain	
Start / Finish		Devil's Dyke Viewpoint car park BN45 7AB / TQ 258 110	

A testing trail traversing tough topography

Dreaming of a leisurely stride atop the undulating South Downs ridge, idly soaking up the stunning views? Sorry, but this is not that route*. This route hates you and you might just hate it back. Steep ascents and descents, sketchy narrow paths, tricky navigation and did we mention the steep ascents? This route even includes a Fulking Hill. If your interest is already piqued, then read this introduction no further. Normal non-masochists will need a bit more persuading however, so ... what is the upside?

All the classic beauty of the South Downs is of course here, with the scarp plunging 150m to the Weald plain and views on the southern side reaching the Isle of Wight. Wild flowers and butterflies pepper the grasslands, while the deer roam the woods clinging to the slopes. The standout however is the Devil's Dyke, where you finish (with, yes, a brutal ascent). This is a curving dry valley, the longest and deepest in

*Nearby Route 53 could well be, though.

54 Devil's Dyke

the country, formed by a short-lived river as the last Ice Age receded. This aberrant landscape really confuses the senses; Iron Age folk acknowledged its power by building a hillfort atop it, while the Victorians attempted to tame it with a (now long gone) cable car and funicular railway! It's a fair reward for your exertions; running early morning along this remarkable feature, you feel like the star at the centrepiece of a vast empty auditorium.

Route description

START Leave the car park by the footpath which heads SW along the ridge top. After 500m this reaches a junction with numerous bridleways. Take the bridleway which continues atop the hill leading W, this is the South Downs Way. ❶ Follow the SDW for 2.3km over three successive hills (Fulking, Perching and Edburton) before descending to a dip in the ridge where numerous trails converge. ❷ Turn right to take the bridleway path which steeply descends leading NE (not the track which descends but leads ahead). After just 60m, a footpath leads off on the left; take this and follow it steeply downhill. After 300m, the

Devil's Dyke

tree line is reached; look for a small permissive footpath leading off on the right and take this. ❸ Follow the permissive footpath E along the hillside, crossing a bridleway after 400m and passing through a field to join a footpath after another 400m. Turn right onto the footpath and continue E. The footpath begins to climb uphill, instead turn off left and keep contouring along the hillside E (this is a permissive footpath) to reach a wide track (Bostal Track) leading uphill. ❹ Cross the track and take the footpath which leads off it and continues to contour E along the hillside. After 250m this reaches a T junction with another footpath, turn right (uphill) and follow this steeply up to reach the Bostal Track again. Continue steeply uphill (SE) on the footpath which leads alongside the track, separated from it by a fence. ❺ At the top of the hill you reach the SDW bridleway again, turn left (E) and follow it for 700m over Fulking Hill to the first junction you reached on your run. ❻ Take the bridleway on the left leading steeply downhill, heading NNE. After 700m this enters woodland and levels out; look for a permissive footpath on the right. ❼ Turn right onto the permissive footpath and follow it around the hillside. After 200m it crosses a footpath leading uphill, after another 500m it reaches a T junction with another footpath leading uphill. Turn left (downhill) and descend a short way to reach a bridleway. ❽ Turn right (E) onto the bridleway and follow it just 200m uphill until you see a permissive footpath on the left. Turn off left to take this and follow it 500m around the hillside until it emerges from the woods at the Devil's Dyke (wide dry valley). ❾ Cross the Devil's Dyke and turn right onto the bridleway leading uphill along its eastern edge, alternatively, follow the path up the bottom of Devil's Dyke (very steep towards the end). Both routes reach a lane at the top, turn right and follow the lane back to the car park.

Permissive footpath

Ascent onto the ridge

Paraglider

Trip planning

This trip is notably awkward / challenging for navigation; although the paths are defined and mapped, they are often unsignposted and unkempt. A map (or mapping app) will help.

Devil's Dyke Viewpoint isn't too hard to find; follow Devil's Dyke Road uphill from the A27. It does get busy in the summer. National Trust members park for free, everyone else ...

Devil's Dyke

Devil's Dyke

The Devil's Dyke pub is beside the car park. The author hasn't eaten here, but notes that it has hundreds of one-star *Tripadvisor* reviews with headings like, *'Satan is alive and cooking at the Devil's Dyke pub!'* Take your chances, or perhaps try the (better-rated) pubs downhill in the villages of Poynings or Fulking. There is also Bob's Café in Poynings. The nearest shops are in Hove, a short drive south.

Other routes

Needless to say, it is entirely possible (and sensible) to enjoy this spot with a mild run out along the ridge and back, following the South Downs Way and adjacent paths, such as the permissive footpath over the summit of Edburton Hill. It's not really worth extending far beyond the section included here, as the SDW becomes surfaced.

Various loops are possible from Shoreham, each gradually ascending bridleways and byways for 4km+; one footpath ascends direct from Fishersgate Railway Station in Shoreham.

Incidentally; the permissive footpath which continues eastwards along the base of the ridge from ❹ exists only on OS maps; the author has tried and failed to locate it!

Events

Various longer races pass through here, along the SDW; see page 294.

The South Downs National Park

Routes 11, 12, 14, 51, 53, 54, 55, 56, 57 and 59 are all within the 1627km² South Downs National Park. This is Britain's youngest national park, designated in 2010. The South Downs are hills extending 140km across the South East from Winchester in Hampshire to Eastbourne in East Sussex. They are formed from Late Cretaceous Chalk (see page 48) in a distinctive ridge with a steep scarp slope to the north, and a gradual dip slope south towards the English Channel. Rudyard Kipling described them as, *"Our blunt, bow-headed whale-backed Downs"*. Humans have lived on the downs for at least six millennia. The downs were denuded of trees around 3,000 years ago, and generations of rabbits and grazing sheep created the marvellous chalk grasslands which today form a haven for bees, butterflies and wildflowers (and, incidentally, a wonderful springy trail-running surface). However, intensive farming and urban encroachments have reduced the grasslands by 80% since the Second World War. It was this relentless threat which spurred the creation of a national park. Chalk grasslands form just 4% of the SDNP, but work is underway to restore large areas.

Surprisingly, 23% of the SDNP is not in the South Downs! Parts of the geologically very different western Weald were incorporated, in particular to protect rare lowland heath. Hence, the highest point in the SDNP is not chalk Butser Hill (Route 11), but greensand Black Down (Route 57).

55 Cissbury Ring and Chanctonbury Ring

Cissbury Ring

Distance	18km (11 miles)	**Ascent**	475m (1,560ft)
Map	OS Landranger 198 OS Explorer OL10		
Navigation	●●●	Trails all clearly signposted throughout	
Terrain	●●●	Chalk tracks, rooty paths, mostly gradual ascents but some toughies	
Wet feet	●●●	Plenty of mud-jumping in the winter	
Start / Finish	Chanctonbury car park BN44 3DR / TQ 145 124		

A superb circuit of imposing hillforts

This is a relatively tough run in terms of ascent and distance, but there is plenty enough here to keep you engaged and motivated. The early big climb over the South Downs ridge may test your faith, but you'll know it was worth it when you top out from the woods and see the empty downland that you have earned access to. Cissbury Ring hillfort is a monster, the second largest in Britain. Its imposing earthworks dominate the landscape around with views far out to sea; our Iron Age ancestors knew how to pick a spot! Actually, they built on top of a more ancient site; a Neolithic flint mine, note the strange pits around the southern half of the hillfort. Leaving Cissbury, you head back across the hinterland to the South Downs ridge, to visit Cissbury Ring's next-door neighbour ... Chanctonbury Ring hillfort. Smaller

55 Cissbury Ring and Chanctonbury Ring

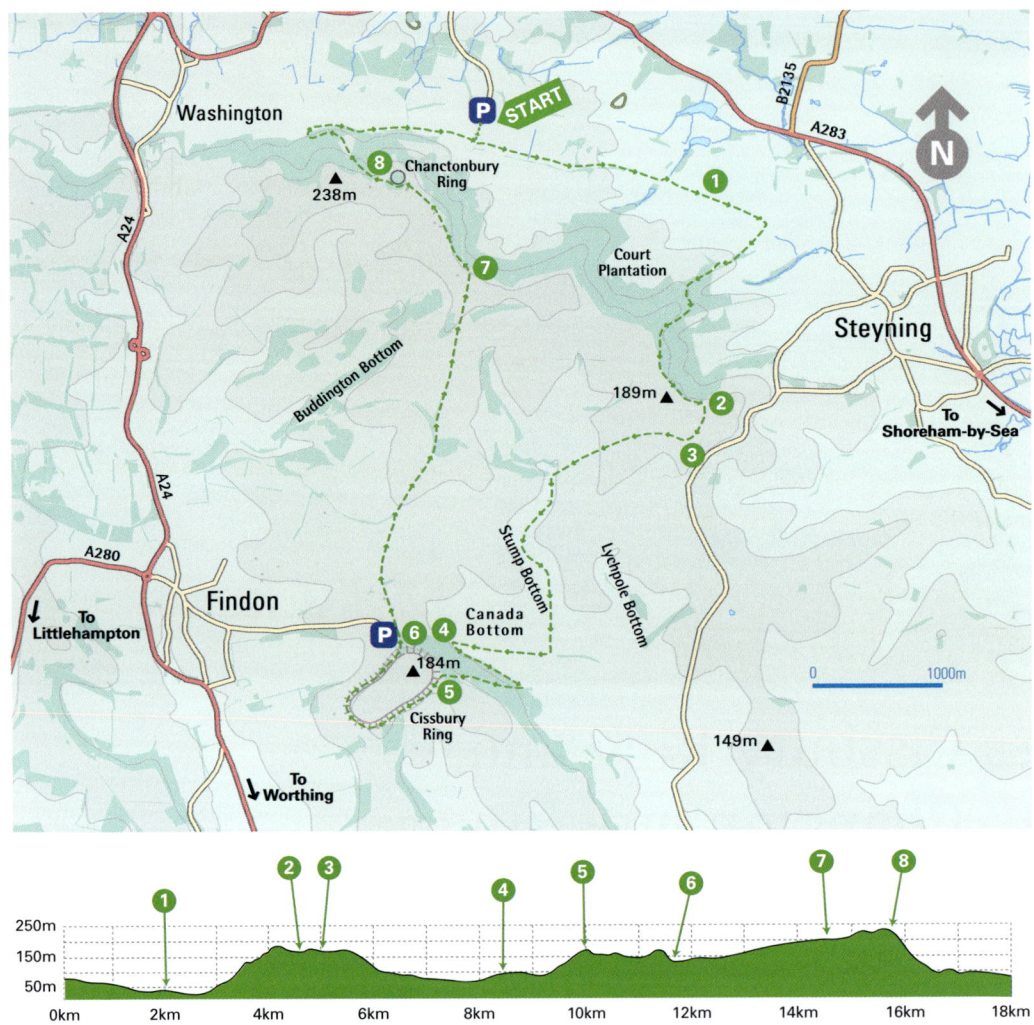

and more mysterious than Cissbury, Chanctonbury is dramatically located atop the scarp side of the ridge. This route's finale sees you descend 150m from the scarp, at a gradient where the distinction between running and freefall becomes blurred!

Route description

START Turn left (uphill) out of the car park and follow the lane 120m to where it becomes unsurfaced. Turn left onto the footpath track which heads E through Great Barn Farm. Keep following signs for the footpath, ignoring any turn-offs. After 1.6km the footpath joins a lane (Mouse Lane), turn right onto this (E) and follow it for 250m before leaving the lane on the right to follow the footpath which parallels the lane. **1** After 500m a bridleway leads right (uphill), turn right and follow this bridleway along the field boundary into the woods. After 800m a fork is reached, take the left-hand bridleway. This ascends to the edge of the ridge and follows it to a junction with a bridleway where you turn right (uphill). **2** Follow this bridleway over the top of the hill for 250m to a five-way junction. Take the byway leading ahead (W) and

Cissbury Ring and Chanctonbury Ring

downhill (this is the Monarch's Way). ❸ After 1.2km the byway reaches the bottom of the valley and a six-way junction, take the furthest left option which is a bridleway path heading S. This winds along Stump Bottom valley, reaching a T junction with a byway after 1.5km. Turn right (uphill, W) and follow the byway 700m to where it ends at a gate. ❹ Take the bridleway on the left leading back SE along the edge of the woods. After 700m take the bridleway on right (National Trust signpost for 'Cissbury Ring') and ascend this steeply to the earthworks of Cissbury Ring hillfort. ❺ Turn left and follow the top of the earthworks for 1.2km until you see a footpath on your left leading steeply downhill (N) to a parking area. Take this and descend to the parking area. ❻ Continue ahead (N) following a bridleway track, ignoring any turn-offs. After 1km this becomes a byway, keep going ahead (uphill). After another 800m a bridleway branches off to the left at a small wood, ignore this and stay on the byway. Another 1.2km of climbing and the byway reaches the top of the hill and a crossroads with a bridleway (the South Downs Way). ❼ Turn left onto the SDW bridleway and follow it along the ridge. After 1km you reach Chanctonbury Ring hillfort, ascend onto the earthworks (you know the drill) and follow them in either direction to the far side. You will see a gate on the right-hand (N) side of the ridge, 100m ahead. Descend to this gate and go through it. ❽ Descend steeply on the bridleway through woods until you reach the edge of the woods, where you meet a junction with another bridleway. Turn right onto this and follow it for 1.5km E along the edge of the woods, back to your start point.

Stump Bottom

Chanctonbury Ring

Descending from Chanctonbury Ring

Trip planning

Chanctonbury car park is near the end of Chanctonbury Ring road, accessed from the A283 Steyning Road. It is free to use.

Another possible start point is the small parking area near Cissbury Ring BN14 0SQ / **TQ 139 085** at ❻, perhaps more convenient if coming from Worthing and the coast.

This route keeps you well clear of conurbation (or anything built since the Iron Age, anyway) but Steyning

Cissbury Ring and Chanctonbury Ring

is not too far away. There are numerous shops and eateries to choose from, but the White Horse on Sheep Pen Lane gets a mention for refuelling the author effectively during a bikepacking trip.

You will notice winding trails alongside the main bridleway during the ascent after ❶. These are a network of locally-created mountain bike trails, keep clear of them.

Other routes

The easy way to shorten this route is to follow the SDW for 2km between ❸ and ❼. This would make for a tough 10km, or if starting from the Cissbury Ring car park at ❻, a milder-inclined 12km.

For easier-gradient routes, you might consider footpaths along both banks of the River Adur as it cuts through the South Downs at Steyning. The Downs Link (see page 306) also passes close by.

Events

A daunting array of trail races utilise this area, and the hillforts in particular. Suffice to say, none of them are flat. Take your pick from (deep breath): Henfield Jogger's Hangover 5 Fun Run (up Cissbury Ring on New Year's Day), Raw Running's Grand National 10km Trail Run, Nice Work's Downland Devil 9, Steyning AC's Steyning Stinger Marathon / Half Marathon, and the Rotary Club's Three Forts Marathon* (27.2 miles!) / Half Marathon. That isn't including the ultra-distance routes which pass along the SDW (see page 294).

Sussex Trail Events organise the Dark Star River Marathon close by, following both banks of the River Adur.

Cissbury Ring

Which way?

*The third hillfort is Devil's Dyke (Route 54).

Iron Age hillforts in the South East

As the author noted in *South West Trail Running*, he has a thing about hillforts; partly on account of the story they tell in the landscape and partly because the ramparts are simply cool to run around. There are about 4,100 across Britain, with most prominent high ground in the South East hosting one; there are at least 25 for example in East and West Sussex, mostly along the South Downs ridge. Some hillforts also make use of the coast, for example East Hill near Hastings (Route 50).

Despite the 'fort' label, there are no definitive answers as to what they were even for. Cissbury was probably as much a communal gathering place as a military site. On the other hand, excavations at Chanctonbury (after the 1987 Great Storm destroyed the tree cover) found no evidence of settlement but instead found offerings, indicating that it was used for sacred rituals.

Petworth Park

Petworth Park

56 Petworth Park

Distance	7.5km (5 miles)	Ascent	150m (490ft)
Map	OS Landranger 197 OS Explorer OL8		
Navigation	•••	No signposting, but obvious tracks in an open landscape	
Terrain	•••	Grassy paths, stony tracks, mild ascents	
Wet feet	•••	Minimal muddiness	
Start / Finish	Petworth Park National Trust car park GU28 9LR / SU 966 238		

Pleasant perambulations around Capability's landscape

Wild places take many forms! Petworth Park gives all the impressions of being a natural landscape, with sweeping hills covered by pasture and scattered woodlands, where deer roam freely, ranged around a serpentine lane. Perhaps the most obvious hint that all is not as it seems is the absolutely enormous baroque mansion nestled at the front of this scene. This is in fact an entirely artificial and manufactured version of nature, the finest surviving example of over 250 landscapes designed by architect Lancelot 'Capability' Brown during the eighteenth century.

What does Petworth Park offer the trail runner? Most basically, free access to a vast open space in which to stretch one's legs; 283 hectares, surrounded by a 23km deer park wall! Artificial or not, this is a beautiful place; from the ancient trees (one oak is 940 years old) to the vast panorama of Black Down and the South Downs. The largest herd of fallow deer in Britain (c. 700 of them) also make for inspiring spectators!

277

Petworth Park

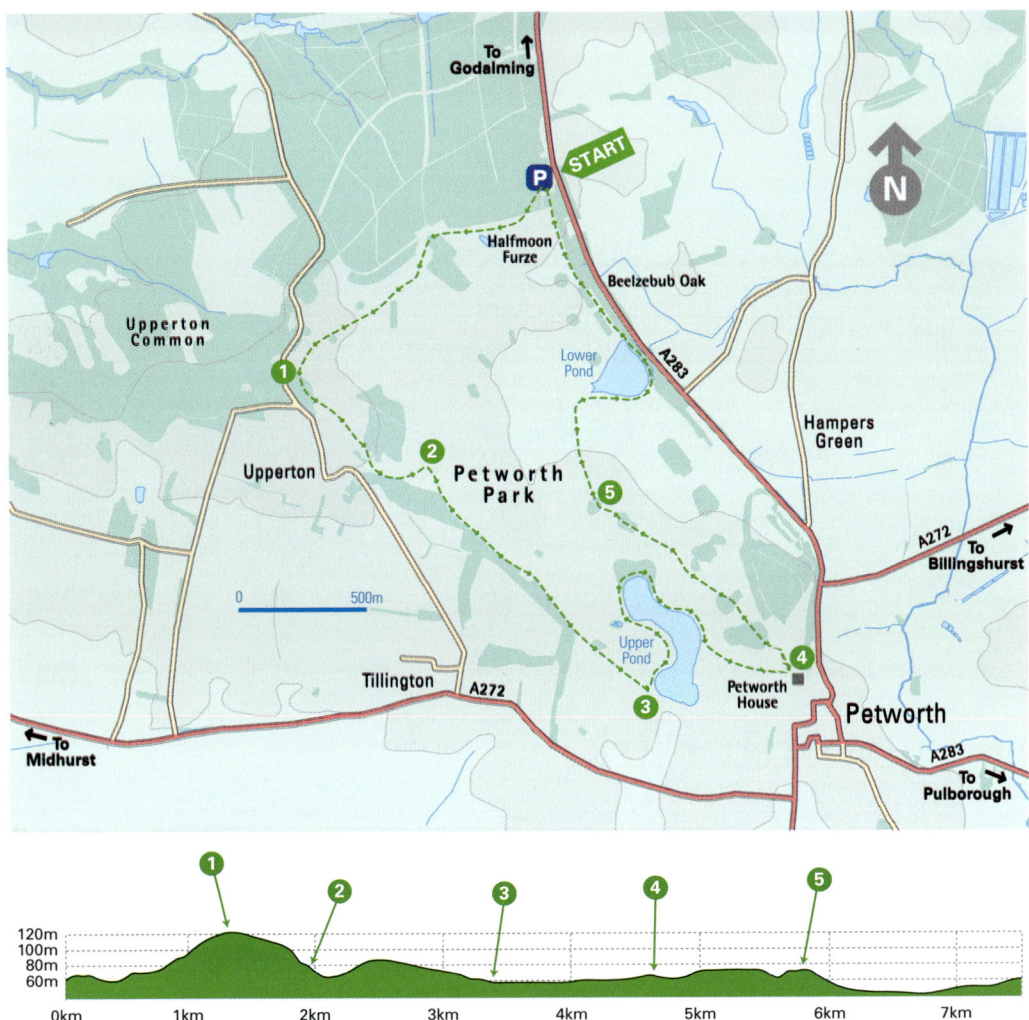

Fundamentally though (and this is where the author goes off on one), Petworth Park is an opportunity to immerse yourself in a remarkable landscape, experience and enjoy it and perhaps begin to understand it better. This is what great trail running is about, so much more than Strava times.

Route description

START From the car park, take a path leading out of the woods (S) into the open park and then turn right (W) onto the path following the S boundary of the woods. After 500m you reach the Lodge (brick gatehouse). Take the track leading S from the gatehouse. After 180m a path bears off to the right (SW), take this and follow it uphill, bearing right at junctions, to a tower. ❶ Continue on the path, which now bears SE paralleling the park boundary. After 750m it descends and joins a track leading SE along the park boundary, turn right onto this. ❷ Follow the track for 1.3km until it reaches a lake (Upper Pond). ❸ Turn left at the lake to follow the W shore (lake on your right), passing through a gate at the N end, to continue around. After passing the boathouse building, head directly to the front of Petworth House.

Petworth Park

Petworth Park

Optional: NT members can pass through the gate at the left (N) end of Petworth House for a short run around the Pleasure Grounds ❹ From Petworth House, head NW to ascend the closest hill. Follow the top of this hill NW for 800m until the ridge abruptly ends. ❺ Descend direct to the small lake you see to the N (Lower Pond). Pass around the shore of this on the E side (lake on your left) until you reach the park boundary. Turn left to follow the boundary 900m back to the start.

Trip planning

The car park is found beside the A283 London Road, 800m north of Petworth. It's free to National Trust members. Admission to Petworth Park is free. It is open from 8 am to 8 pm in summer, closing at 6 pm in winter. There is another useful park entrance on the A272 Tillington Road just west of Petworth, with limited free parking; New Lodge West GU28 0QY / **SU 967 216**. This is 400m from Upper Pond ❸.

It is also possible to access the park on foot from Petworth, via the Cowyard Tunnel which is signposted off the A272 London Road in the centre of Petworth and surfaces in front of Petworth House at ❹.

There is often a trailer serving food in the car park. Failing that, of course the National Trust have a café at

Park inhabitants

Petworth House

Petworth Park

Petworth House and Petworth has plenty of appealing cafés and pubs.

A visit to Petworth House itself is recommended, free to National Trust members. You'll have already noticed that it is somewhat impressive; it was built in its current baroque form in 1688, inspired by the Palace of Versailles near Paris. The interior is predictably grand; it was surrendered to the NT in 1947 along with a job lot of paintings which happens to be the finest collection of art in their possession. Perhaps change out of your sweaty trail gear first.

Other routes

There are of course plenty of ways to vary your route within Petworth Park; simply pick a trail and see where it takes you! The National Trust website suggests routes which focus on different aspects of the park's wildlife and history.

Petworth Park

Outside the park, there are plenty of intriguing-looking trails with which to extend your route or offer an alternative; such as the footpath which leaves the A283 500m north of the car park to Lurgashall (and eventually Black Down, Route 57) or the footpaths around Upperton Common to the west (no access direct from the park).

The Serpent Trail (see page 284) passes along the west boundary of the park, connecting Haslemere and Petersfield.

The Monument

Events

Although various races have been based at Petworth Park in the past, none are currently operative.

Lancelot 'Capability' Brown

Brown is singlehandedly responsible for transforming much of the English landscape. Petworth Park is one of over 250 estates designed and engineered by 'Capability'; this moniker was a marketing slogan, advertising the potential of landscapes for 'improvement'. Trail runners can immerse themselves in his aesthetic vision at Appuldurcombe House (Route 4), the Highclere Estate (Route 15), Blenheim Palace (Route 24), Hatfield Forest (Route 37) and Gatton Park (Route 64).

Brown's work at Petworth during the 1750s and 60s highlights his signature touches; lakes created to give the impression of a meandering river, scattered trees around open pasture, screens of woodland to obscure boundaries, 'ha-has' (hidden ditches to keep deer and sheep at bay) and fake Greek / Roman temples to make the landowner appear wise and learned. At Petworth the road was moved to create a naturalistic scene; in other projects, whole villages were demolished for ruining the illusion of a pastoral Arcadia!

Black Down 57

57 Black Down

Distance	5.5km (3.5 miles)	Ascent	150m (525ft)
Map	OS Landranger 186 OS Explorer OL33		
Navigation	●●●	Plenty of route choice, but it all heads the same way ...	
Terrain	●●●	Sandy trails. One steep, rough descent and ascent	
Wet feet	●●●	Well-draining trails, extra star for the steep bit after rain	
Start / Finish		National Trust car park, Tennyson's Lane GU27 3BJ / SU 920 309	

Epic vistas from the Temple of the Winds

Black Down (which also goes by the name Blackdown) is a bit of an anomaly. The highest point (280m) in the South Downs National Park (and West Sussex), it's not really part of the South Downs as it is sandstone, not chalk. It belongs (geologically) to the Greensand Ridge which continues into Surrey ... however it is a 'Marilyn', meaning that it stands isolated from Surrey's other summits. For the purposes of trail running, it's just glorious. The summit is a rough plateau, covered in purple heather and pine trees. Easy runs can be enjoyed on the sandy and gritty trails, with minimal grind from the car park. The hill is however flanked by steep trails offering fast descents or grinding ascents, so it's simple enough to crank up the difficulty! You won't be the first to run here; 8,000-year-old flints have been found on the heath, and the central trail is called Pen-y-Bos, an ancient Celtic name. All trails converge on the Temple of the Winds, a startling viewpoint where the trees part to reveal the verdant Weald extending to the South

Black Down

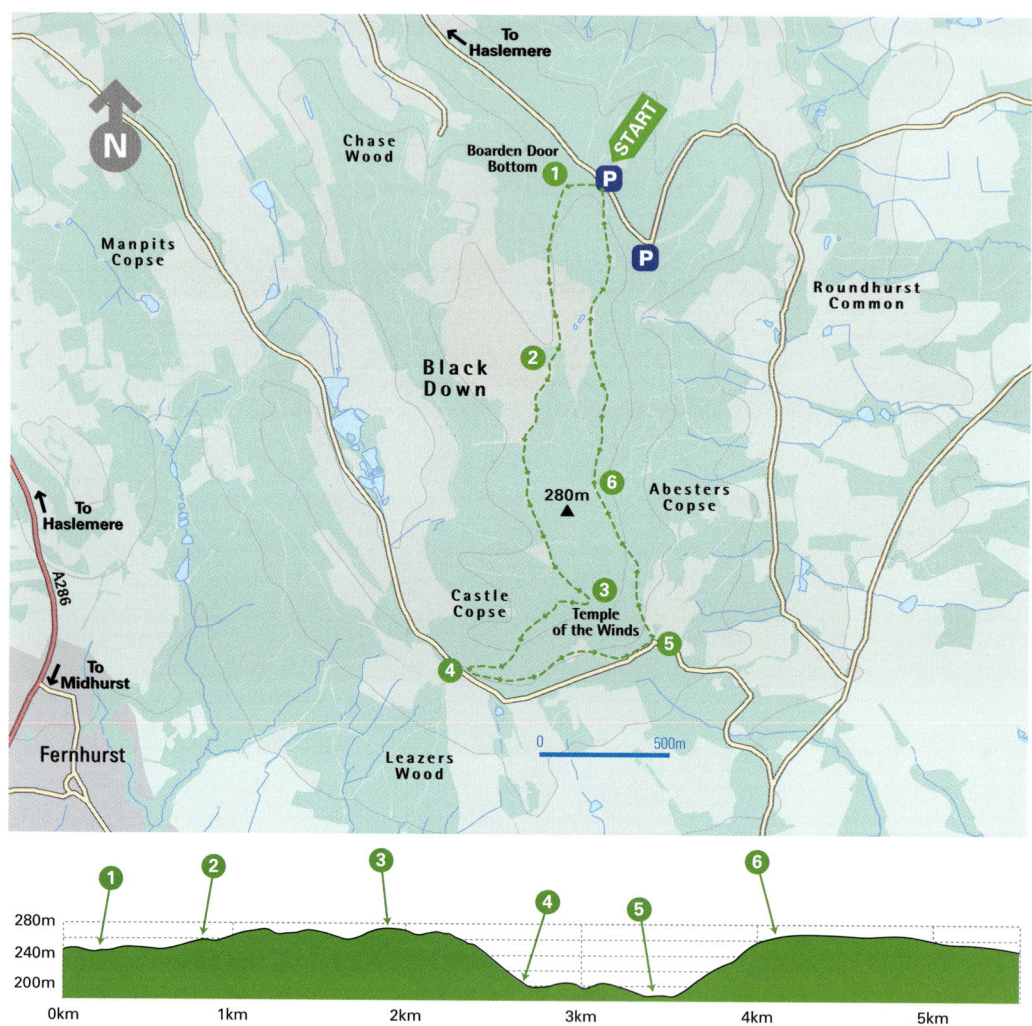

Downs (the 'real' South Downs!). A curved stone seat (have you earned a rest yet?) commemorates the Hunter family, who donated Black Down to the National Trust in 1944. Others who have enjoyed this view include nineteenth-century poet Alfred Lord Tennyson, who owned the hill for a time. In those pre-Strava times, his Personal Best was not recorded.

Route description

START Take the path leading W from the middle of the back boundary of the car park. After 150m this reaches a T junction with a N–S path (Pen-y-Bos Track), turn left to follow this path S. ❶ Follow the obvious track leading S along the W rim of the hilltop; after 600m it merges with a larger track (bear right onto this), after another 100m it reaches a 5-way (at least) junction where you need to take the left-most track (bears S). ❷ Continue following the track roughly S, ignoring any tracks leading off. After 1km the track veers SE away from the rim of the hill, becomes a bridleway (no visible change) and ends at a viewpoint with a bench (the Temple of the Winds). ❸ Turn right to follow paths W along the edge

Black Down

South Downs from Temple of the Winds

of the hill. After 200m you reach a junction with an obvious path leading steeply downhill, turn left to take this (bridleway on OS maps does not exist where marked, this path is the bridleway). Descend to reach a lane (Fernden Lane) after 400m. ❹ Turn left onto the footpath signposted just before the lane and follow this E into the woods. After 400m the footpath emerges beside a cottage, pass in front of the cottage and follow the tarmac drive down to the lane. Follow the lane. ❺ After 200m turn left onto the bridleway clearly signposted, leading uphill. Ascend steeply along this to regain the hilltop after 600m. ❻ Follow the bridleway track N along the E side of the hill, ignoring any side turns. After 1km the bridleway bears off to the right (downhill), however continue N on the track ahead. Follow this track for another 300m to the car park.

Pen-y-Bos Track

Trip planning

The car park is the first encountered along Tennyson's Lane, coming out of Haslemere. It's run by the National Trust and is free. There is a second (smaller) NT car park 300m further along Tennyson's Lane GU27 3BG / **SU 922 306**.

Haslemere is the nearest civilisation, just minutes down the road; see 'Trip planning' in Route 60.

Black Down

Black Down

Other routes

Black Down can be ascended from Haslemere. Follow the footpath leading S from 41 Petworth Road (B2131), opposite a house called 'The Old Manse'. Cross Hill Road and descend on a byway track to Stedlands Farm. From here, turn left to follow signs along a bridleway for the Sussex Border Path. Out and back, this adds about 8km to the route described.

If you don't fancy the big descent and ascent between ❸ and ❻ in this route (I put it in there feeling sadistic), then simply head N along the hill top from The Temple of the Winds ❸ to reach ❻ after 500m.

On the other hand, if you feel this route needs more climbs, then knock yourself out! For starters, follow the Sussex Border Path bridleway NW from the five-way junction at ❷, hang a left at the first crossroads and follow this bridleway S until you reach a choice of two bridleways re-ascending the hill.

Trails criss-cross the plateau atop Black Down, all of which is Access Land, so explore at your leisure.

The Serpent Trail (see below) and Sussex Border Path (see page 288) both pass across Black Down.

Black Down

Events

The RUAlive Trail Run is 5km or 10km over Black Down from the grounds of Camelsdale School, to raise funds for the school. Fernhurst Recreation Trust organise the Blackdown Hill Challenge, ascending 5 miles from Fernhurst Recreation Ground to the top.

The Serpent Trail

The 108km / 67-mile Serpent Trail starts at Haslemere and is so-named because of its snaking route to Petersfield, but also possibly because it tours the South Downs National Park's beautiful lowland heathlands, the habitat of snakes and lizards. Its start links with the Greensand Way (see page 312). The final third runs parallel to the South Downs Way (see page 294) and its end at Petersfield intersects with the Hangers Way (see page 86). Along the way it crosses Black Down (Route 57, above) and passes Petworth Park (Route 56).

The National Park publish an outstanding free guidebook online, with OS mapping.

Freedom Racing present the Serpent Trail Races along these sandy trails, with concurrent distances of 100km, 50km, half marathon and 10km.

Near Prinsted Point

58 Thorney Island

Distance	12km (7.5 miles)	Ascent	25m (80ft)
Map	OS Landranger 197 OS Explorer OL8		
Navigation ●●●	Keep the sea on your right, or was it the left?		
Terrain ●●●	Trails are flat but technically varied: pebbles, sand, grass, stones		
Wet feet ●●●	The paths are narrow enough to make mud and puddles unavoidable		
Start / Finish	Prinsted Lane parking area PO10 8HS / SU 765 050		

The forbidden island

Run along empty windswept beaches and shores, hidden in plain sight in the centre of Chichester Harbour. Most likely, your only company will be the birds (geese, oystercatchers, lapwings and maybe even osprey) and the common seals which haul out on the mudflats. Strictly speaking, Thorney Island (so-named because of the profusion of hawthorn bushes) hasn't been an island since land reclamation in the 1870s effectively changed it into a peninsula. Yet, it remains a place of solitude and wildness because the Ministry of Defence have controlled access since the RAF arrived in the 1930s. The RAF left in 1976, the island then briefly made the headlines when Vietnamese refugees (the 'Boat People') were housed there and now it is the site of the Baker Barracks. The lack of intensive farming and inobtrusive military presence means that nature is in the ascendancy.

58 Thorney Island

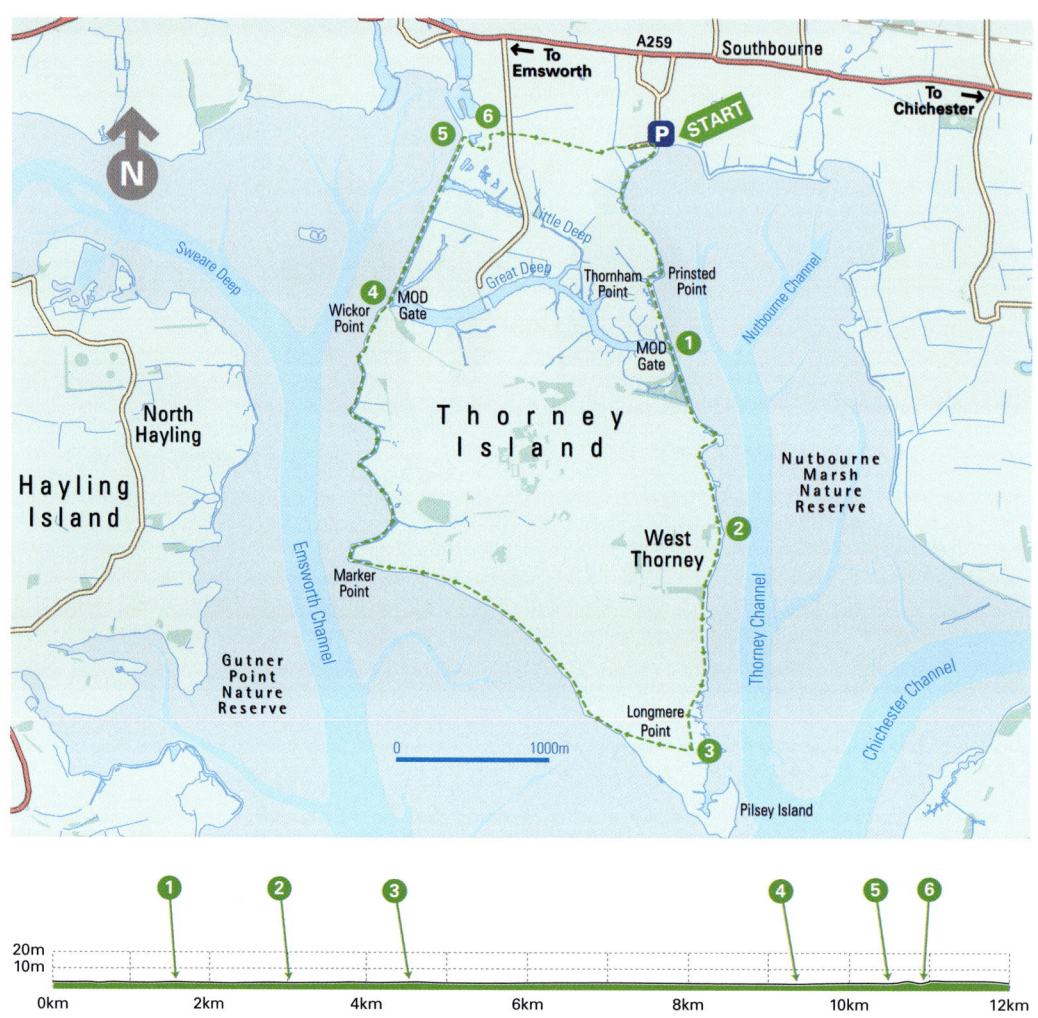

The coastal footpath is initially narrow and muddy before you reach the MOD checkpoint at the Great Deep, a tidal channel cutting the island off from the mainland. You pass the twelfth-century Church of St Nicholas, serving the tiny village of West Thorney. At Longmere Point you glimpse Pilsey Island (an RSPB reserve), where the first egrets to return to the UK nested in the 1970s. Longmere to Marker Point traverses a gorgeous beach. Then, grassy trails (and the second checkpoint) lead to a final, long straight along a sea wall back to the mainland. In short, there is plenty enough to keep your mind on your surroundings, and off your burning thighs.

Route description

START From the parking area, take the footpath leading S along the shore. Follow this narrow footpath through a marina and further S along the shore. When you reach the MOD gate, press the buzzer for permission to go through. ❶ 3km from the start you reach the church at West Thorney ❷. The footpath diverts with an option to take a 'high water' route a short distance inshore, when the coastal

Thorney Island

path is flooded. Follow the footpath to Longmere Point (southern tip of the island, where the coast footpath turns NW). ❸ Follow the footpath NW from Longmere Point, it is now wider with stretches of sand and pebbles. 9km from the start, you reach the second MOD gate. ❹ Again press the buzzer to get through. Follow the narrow footpath atop the seawall for 1.2km to a T junction in front of some raised holiday homes. ❺ Turn sharp right onto the footpath and follow this for 200m until you see a footpath leading up steps on the left. Take this and follow it alongside the holiday homes for 120m until you see a footpath leading off on the right. Take this footpath. ❻ Follow the footpath across a field to a road (Thorney Road). Cross the road and continue ahead following the footpath (becomes a tarmac track) for 1km back to the car park.

Flooded section

Longmere Point

Trip planning

Prinsted Lane car park is free but small and fills quickly. Carry some form of clear identification. The checkpoints are unmanned; you press a buzzer and, in the author's experience, someone at the other end of the CCTV network wordlessly unlocks the gate. People are however sometimes asked via intercom to show ID.

Check the tide times for Chichester Harbour before running. Occasionally, at very high tides, parts of the route submerge. Given that short cuts across the island are not possible (the Army have guns), if you encounter any blockage you will have to return the way you came. The Traveller's Joy pub in Prinsted can feed you, otherwise nearby Emsworth is the place to head for eateries.

Stanbury Point

MOD entrance

Other routes

A similar trail running experience can be enjoyed around the Chidham peninsula, just to the east. If starting from Chidham (Cobnor Farm Amenity Car Park PO18 8TD / SU 793 034) this measures about 9km, or it is 11km starting from the same spot as this route (just turn left from the car park at the end of Prinsted Lane). With both routes taken together, you have yourself a fine coastal Half Marathon (and a bit). The Solent Way leads W from Emsworth (see page 58).

Thorney Island

Approaching Marker Point

Events

UK Running Events ran the first Chichester Harbour Race in 2020, basically a 12.9km or 15km run around Thorney Island. The author isn't sure how 500 runners squeezed onto the island's narrow trails, but it happened. They organise similar events around Chichester Harbour; one along the sands of Wittering Beach and one around the Chidham peninsula.

The Sussex Border Path

The Sussex Border Path leads 222km / 138 miles from Thorney Island to Rye, roughly following the inland border of West and East Sussex combined, with a 53km / 33-mile offshoot 'Mid Sussex Link' for those who also feel the need to divide the two counties. The SBP website has a description of the route with OS mapping and the route is shown on OS paper maps. You've already completed the first part as it starts by going around Thorney Island; along the way the SBP intersects with the South Downs Way at Route 59, passes Black Down (Route 57), and finishes near Camber Castle (Route 49).

Feeling hyperactive? Sussex Trail Events have set up a challenge to run all 222km of the SBP, with the current FKT (Fastest Known Time) being a daunting three days, seven hours and 38 minutes.

Bignor Hill

59 Petersfield to Amberley

Distance	39km (24 miles)	Ascent	925m (3,030ft)
Map	OS Landranger 197 OS Explorer OL33, OL8, OL10		
Navigation	•••	A few footpaths to navigate, then follows the well-signposted South Downs Way	
Terrain	•••	Mostly on chalky rutted trails, numerous grinding ascents	
Wet feet	•••	Add a star for winter, when the chalk turns to goo	
Start	Petersfield Railway Station GU32 3EF / SU 743 235		
Finish	Amberley Railway Station BN18 9LR / TQ 026 118		

On top of the world, following an endless snaking ridge

How does this sound, for a challenge? A point-to-point (near-) marathon, running along the spine of the landscape, high above the surrounding villages, with minimal intrusion from the outside world. This is the brilliant South Downs Way National Trail doing what it does best. The route starts out with a slightly scrappy escape from Petersfield (necessary for the rail shuttle back afterwards), but the run along the Hangers Way is pleasant enough, creeping up on the South Downs via a hidden valley. There is a lot of ascent to be chalked up along the top of the ridge, but just keep the views in mind and think of each descent to follow. Final thought; carry some extra clothing for the journey back. The author didn't and nearly froze, waiting for a delayed train in January.

59 Petersfield to Amberley

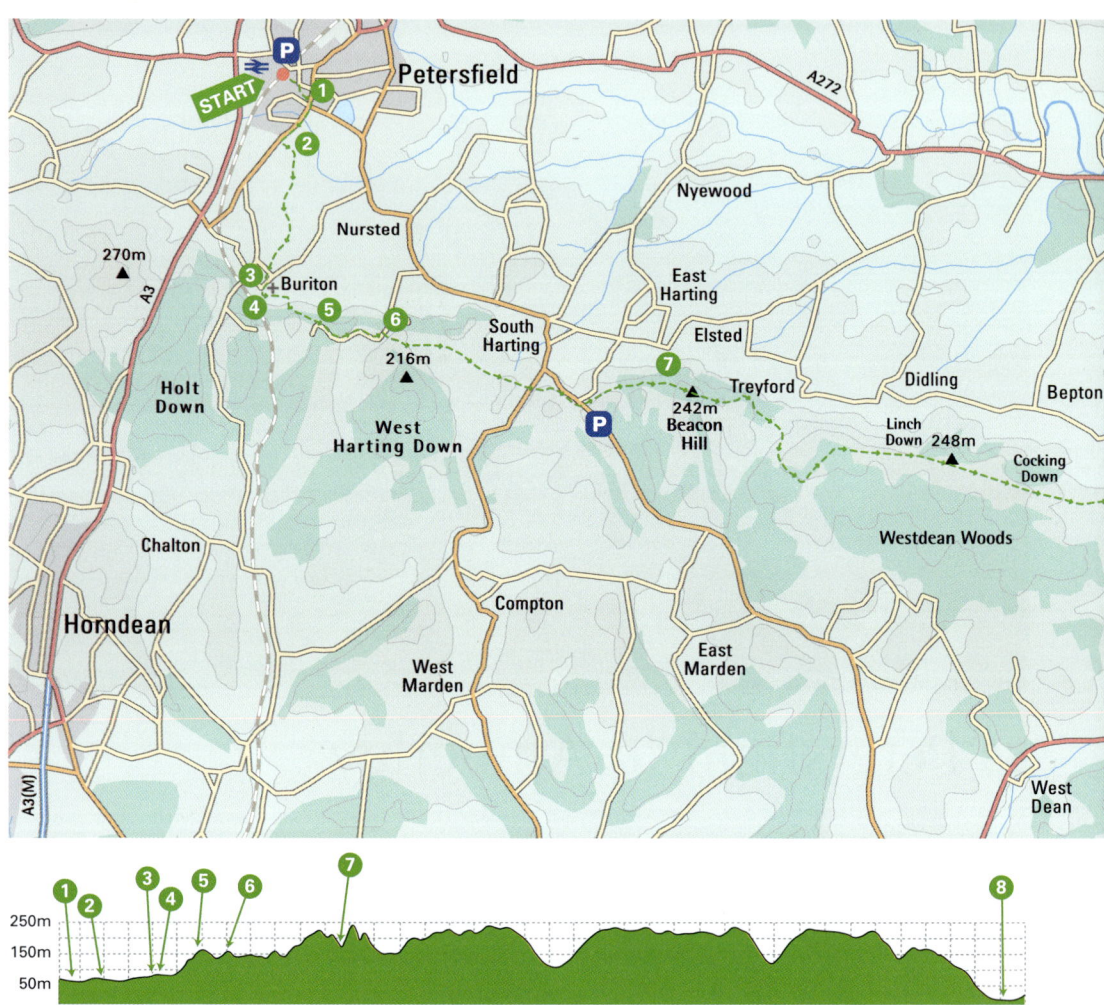

Route description

START Leaving Petersfield Railway Station, turn right (E) onto Station Road and follow it for just 50m before turning off right onto Charles Street (beside Tesco Express). Just 70m down Charles Street, take the left turn onto Lavant Street and follow this 170m to its end. Turn right onto Chapel Street and follow it 110m to its end. Turn left onto Swan Street. After 60m you reach The Square, cross this open space and take St Peter's Road which leads out of the far corner. Follow this to its end. Turn right (S) onto Dragon Street (B2070). ❶ Keep on Dragon Street for 900m, crossing a roundabout. When you approach a second roundabout, look out for the lane leading off on the left, directly after a bus stop. Turn left onto this footpath lane. Follow it ahead for 300m, passing through a caravan park, until it ends at a gate into a field. ❷ Cross the field, heading S along the footpath. The footpath is occasionally signposted as the Hangers Way, stay on it heading S through another two fields downhill to cross a stream, and then along a valley. 2.2km from the caravan park, the footpath ends at a T junction with a tarmac footpath; this is Buriton village. ❸ Turn right (W) onto the footpath and follow it a short distance to Bones Lane. Turn left onto

290

Petersfield to Amberley

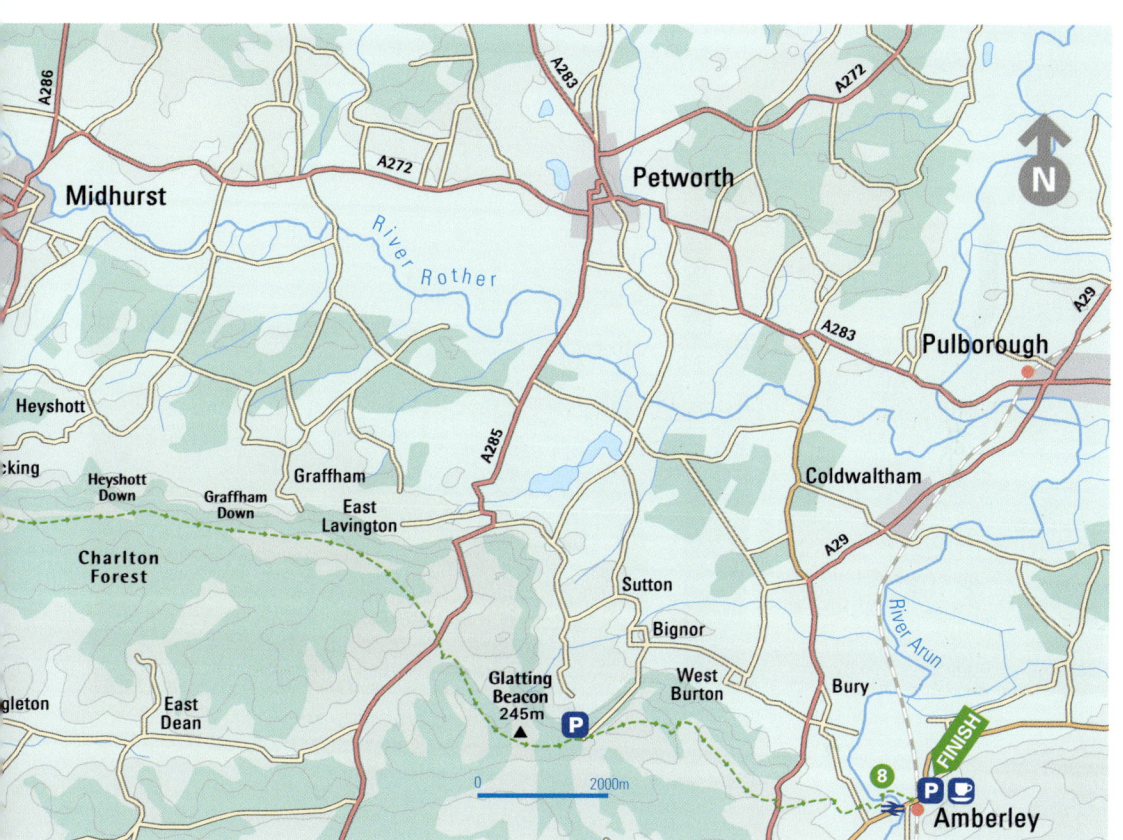

Bones Lane and follow it downhill to a T junction with North Lane. Turn right onto North Lane and you will shortly reach a church (St Mary the Virgin). ❹ Pass through the church car park and take the footpath leading out of the back. The footpath forks behind the church; take the left fork, which leads E (right fork leads uphill). After 600m the footpath ends at a T junction with a byway track (Milky Way). Turn right onto the byway and follow this steeply uphill. ❺ At the top of the incline, the byway merges with a lane; this is now the South Downs Way. Turn left onto the lane and follow it 1.1km to a sharp left at Sunwood Farm; turn right here, off the lane onto a byway track. ❻ Henceforth, the SDW signage is obvious and following it is simple; just look for the acorn! The only deviation from the SDW comes 5km after Sunwood Farm, where the SDW reaches a 5-way wooden sign at the bottom of a valley (Bramshott Bottom). ❼ Instead of turning right as signposted for the SDW, ascend the steep bridleway straight ahead to the summit of Beacon Hill, and then continue ahead to descend steeply on the far side and re-join the SDW. Measured from Sunwood Farm, after 13.6km the SDW descends to a valley floor to cross the A286 road, after 22km it does the same again to cross the A285 road, and after 29.3km it crosses the A29 road. ❽ After the SDW descends to cross the River Arun by a footbridge, it follows the river bank for 180m before turning off left (N). Do not turn off, instead continue following the footpath atop the flood dyke, along the river into Amberley village. When you reach the B2139, turn left onto it and pass under the railway, then immediately turn right (uphill) into the railway station car park.

Petersfield to Amberley

Cocking Down

Trip planning

The logistics of getting back to the start are pretty simple; from Amberley Railway Station it takes about 80 minutes to get back to Petersfield, changing trains at Ford and Havant. If worried about the wait at the end, park at Amberley and make the train journey before running. There are of course car parks at both stations, as well as opportunities for free parking on side streets.

If you are using cars to shuttle, it's a 45-minute drive between the start and finish, although in this instance it might make sense to start outside the centre of Petersfield, e.g. leaving a car parked off Dragon Street after ❶.

Should you bail out part way through this adventure, getting back to the start is awkward as you're quite a distance from anywhere! Your best bet is probably the Number 1 bus service which runs between Petersfield and Pulborough, about 5km north of the SDW. Check times and services beforehand, if you suspect that you might need to rely on this.

If you have time to fuel up before taking the train back to the start, by happy coincidence there are two decent places to eat, right beside Amberley Railway Station; choose from the Riverside Tea Rooms and the Bridge Inn.

Other routes

Quite clearly, there is no end of possible routes sampling parts of the ridge. Recommended shorter routes include:

5–8km loops from the National Trust Harting Down car park on the B2141 PO18 9JY / **SU 791 180**. Follow the SDW E from the car park and return by turning right at Bramshott Bottom or after crossing Beacon Hill.

Petersfield to Amberley

Beacon Hill

Exploration of the extensive forest around Graffham Down, starting from St Giles Church at the end of Graffham Street in Graffham GU28 0NL / **SU 929 167**.

The 12km loop around Glatting Beacon, starting from Bignor Hill car park RH20 1PR / **SU 973 129** (follow the steep lane uphill from Bignor). Follow the SDW 5km W, after crossing the A285 and ascending a hill, turn right onto a byway, follow this to cross the A285 again and then follow bridleways to Glatting Beacon, turning right at junctions.

The Serpent Trail (see page 284) and Hangers Way (see page 86) both end at Petersfield.

Events

The Harting Trail Race is a 10-mile run organised by Liss Runners, ascending Harting Down from Chalton. Southern Multisports organise the Glatting Beacon 5 (miles). Amberley is the start point of Maverick Race's 8km / 15km / 23km Original West Sussex event, exploring the downs to the east. Sussex Trail Events have the Arun River Marathon, out and back along the river; a flatter alternative! Sussex Trail Events' Mouth 2 Mouth Marathon is a 28-mile affair which starts and finishes at the sea (mouths of the Arun and Adur Rivers) and passes through Amberley along the SDW.

Harting Downs

Buriton

Petersfield to Amberley

The South Downs Way National Trail

Decades ago, the author ignorantly dismissed the South East as a wasteland of suburbia and traffic intersections. The first realisation of the extent of the region's wild beauty came when mountain biking the length of the South Downs Way. Although nowadays the author is fully aware of how wrong about the South East he was (which is rather the point of this book), the SDW remains a personal favourite of the region.

The South Downs Way near Winchester

For 160km / 100 miles from Winchester in Hampshire to Beachy Head and Eastbourne in East Sussex, the SDW hugs the high ground, passing through maybe two villages in the entire distance! Along with the dense network of trails either side (usually super-steep on the northern scarp side, milder on the southern dip slopes), the SDW is an almost inexhaustible resource for trail runners. The routes in this book utilising the SDW are chosen to showcase different highlights along its course. To summarise the SDW; it starts meanderingly in Hampshire, linking up elevated points such as Old Winchester Hill (Route 12) and Butser Hill (Route 11). The downs then coalesce into a sharply-defined chalk ridge stretching to the horizon, giving a 'top of the world' sensation. The eastern half of the SDW is intersected by the tidal rivers incising the ridge, forcing long ascents from sea level to regain elevation. The whole SDW clocks in at 3800m of ascent before the ridge finally terminates at the epic cliffs of Beachy Head (Route 51).

The author has completed the SDW numerous times by mountain bike (including one grim non-stop effort), but next hopes to run it! This trail is ripe for multi-day fastpacking adventures; villages are accessible (off the ridge) for supplies, there is plenty of space for discreet bivvying (B&Bs also available) and the whole thing can be easily shuttled by rail. Why not do it before me? The *South Downs Way* map from Harvey Maps is recommended, showing the location of water taps (essential).

Centurion Running organise the South Downs Way 100 along the whole route. People pay to do it! There is also a separate 50-mile event. XNRG break up the SDW over three days for their Devil's Challenge. Ultra Challenge's South Coast Challenge covers 100km (with 2-day, 50km and 25km options) from Arundel to Eastbourne. The Race to the King is 53.6 miles (over one or two days) from Arundel to Winchester. The South Downs Relay mercifully breaks the SDW down into 18 chunks.

Surrey

Surrey is commonly regarded as the 'Stockbroker Belt', where London's high-earning commuters reside in leafy villages, their detached houses hidden behind high gates. This caricature has some truth to it, but neglects to consider *why* they chose this county. Surrey is simply beautiful, and a joy to run ... as evidenced by the vibrant trail-running community and numerous events held here. Surrey has the highest proportion of woodland cover in England (22%, double the national average) and is crossed by the steepest section of the North Downs and the loftiest hills of the Greensand Ridge. The infrastructure of trails is exceptional. Apart from the superb long-distance trails, most notably the North Downs Way National Trail and the Greensand Way, Surrey has 3,482km of footpaths, bridleways and byways to pace along. That works out at about seven pairs of trail running shoes.

View from Leith Hill Tower (Route 62)

Devil's Punch Bowl

60 The Devil's Punch Bowl

Devil's Punch Bowl

Distance		16km / 26km (10 miles / 16.5 miles)	Ascent	400m / 575m (1300ft / 1850ft)
Map		OS Landranger 186 OS Explorer OL33		
Navigation	● ● ●	Excellent waymarking on the Greensand Way, care needed thereafter		
Terrain	● ● ●	Sandy / stony / rooty trails, grassy fields, several steep sections		
Wet feet	● ● ●	Plenty of mud to weave around, damp grass		
Start		Haslemere Railway Station GU27 2PD / SU 898 329		
Finish		Witley Railway Station GU8 5TB / SU 948 379 or		
		Haslemere Railway Station GU27 2PD / SU 898 329		

Explore quintessential Surrey landscapes

The Devil's Punch Bowl is an impressive natural amphitheatre below the plateau summit of 272m Gibbet Hill. It was formed when the Devil gouged out a fistful of earth to fling at Thor, God of Thunder. If you don't buy this Christian-pagan mash-up legend, perhaps consider the less colourful theory that the Punch Bowl was created when an upper sandstone layer was eroded away by water, revealing the clay layer below. It's hard to believe that until the opening of Hindhead Tunnel in 2011, the A3 passed right through this beauty spot, where cattle and wild ponies roam across gloriously multi-coloured heathland, backed by far-ranging views. Actually ... while the Devil's Punch Bowl is the highlight of this long run, it's not quite the point of it. The point is to explore some very fine countryside, both wild and tamed, showcasing classic Surrey landscapes.

The Devil's Punch Bowl

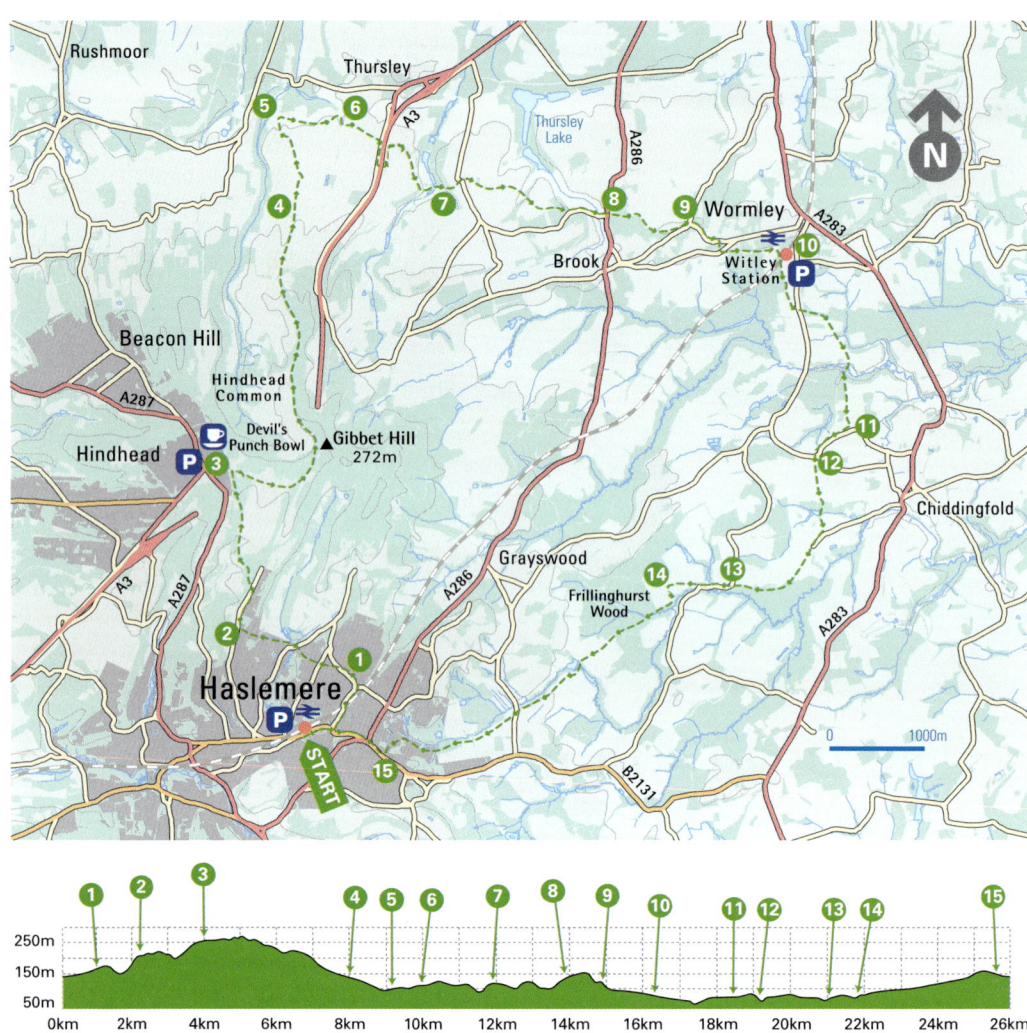

The first part follows the always-excellent Greensand Way through the Punch Bowl's heathlands and then along a series of attractive farms, horse pastures, copses and leafy hamlets (with enough Grade II-listed five-bedroom cottages, and accompanying Range Rovers, to make you feel like a failure in life). Reaching Wormley, you have the option of an easy train shuttle back to the start. If you decide to run back to Haslemere, it's simply more of the same gorgeous Surrey countryside; not a hardship.

Route description

Part I – Haslemere Railway Station to Witley Railway Station

START From Haslemere Railway Station, follow Lower Street uphill (NE) for 250m to the junction with Tanners Lane. Turn left onto Tanners Lane and follow this for 550m, turning left to cross the railway, to St Bartholomew's Church. Pass the church, turning left to join High Lane. ❶ Follow High Lane. After 170m, a footpath leads off on the left (squeezed beside a private drive), signposted 'GW'. Take this footpath. From here to Wormley Railway Station, the route follows the Greensand Way and is waymarked

The Devil's Punch Bowl

throughout, either as 'Greensand Way' or 'GW' with a Tower symbol. The footpath crosses a road (Weydown Road) and then descends to reach a lane (Bunch Lane). Turn left onto the lane and follow it for 75m before turning off right onto a byway track (Stoatley Hollow). This ascends steeply to a lane (Farnham Lane). ❷ Turn right onto the lane and follow it 400m to a footpath on the left, take this footpath. Follow it for 1.5km across heathland to emerge at a road (London Road) opposite Hindhead Common and Devil's Punchbowl car park. ❸ Don't cross the road, instead turn sharp right and follow the GS signage along a bridleway and then onto a byway leading around the Devil's Punchbowl valley. After 4km the byway ends at a lane (Highfield Lane). ❹ Continue ahead on the lane for 300m until it turns right, take the footpath leading off on the left. The footpath leads for 800m across fields and along a farm track to Smallbrook Farm, where you turn right onto another footpath. ❺ Follow this footpath 700m to a lane (The Street). Turn right onto the lane and follow it 90m to where it turns right, take the bridleway track which leads off left. ❻ Follow the bridleway for 1.8km; it joins a lane to cross under the A3 and then descends to a valley beside ponds. ❼ Just after crossing the

Frillinghurst Wood
Photo: Andy Levick

Thursley church

Haslemere

stream between the ponds, turn left off the bridleway onto a footpath. Follow the footpath 1.5km, crossing a lane (French Lane) until it reaches a second lane (Bowlhead Green Road) via a narrow gate. Turn left onto the lane and follow it 500m to a road (A286 Haslemere Road). ❽ Cross the road and continue ahead (uphill) on the bridleway opposite. After 300m a footpath leads off on the right, take this and follow it along the edge of woods for 600m to reach a lane (Church Lane). Turn left onto the lane. After 90m turn sharply right onto a lane (Bannacle Hill Road) leading downhill. ❾ Follow the lane downhill for 300m, to a footpath on the right. Take this footpath, which leads steeply downhill to a lane (Brook Road). Cross the lane and take the footpath track opposite. After 600m it reaches a crossroads with another footpath track. Turn right (leaving the GW) to reach Witley Railway Station. Cross the tracks via the footbridge. ❿

Part II – Witley Railway Station to Haslemere Railway Station

Leaving the railway station building, turn right (SW) and follow the car park alongside the railway track for 130m to the end, where a footpath leads off left (S). Follow the footpath, crossing a lane (Combe Lane) after 500m, for 2.1km to where it reaches a road (Woodside Road) in Chiddingfold village. ⓫ Turn right and follow the road (use the raised pavement on the opposite side) for 600m to a T junction with another road (Ridgley

The Devil's Punch Bowl

Road). Cross the road and take the footpath opposite, across a stile. ⓬ Follow the footpath S for 900m to a lane (Mill Lane). Turn right and follow the lane (which becomes a bridleway track) for 1.2km, when it ends at another lane (West End Lane). ⓭ Turn left (W) onto the lane and follow it 400m to a left bend. Leave the lane and continue ahead at the bend onto a tarmac bridleway track. Follow the bridleway through farm buildings (Frillinghurst Farm) and then take the footpath which leads off on the left, directly after. ⓮ Follow this footpath ahead for 3.7km back to Haslemere; after 1.7 km the footpath passes to the left (E) of a pond, after 2.6km it crosses a lane (Holdfast Lane). Finally, the footpath bends left and reaches Petworth Road in Haslemere, via Collards Lane. ⓯ Turn right onto Petworth Road, follow it into Lower Street to reach the railway station.

Trip planning

This route starts and finishes at Haslemere Railway Station, where there is a paying car park. On weekdays this will be full of commuters' cars, at the weekends it is much quieter. Parking for free on a side street (e.g. Longdene Road) is straightforward at weekends.

This run is divided into two parts because Witley Railway Station makes it easy to shuttle back to Haslemere, if so desired, once you've completed the Greensand Way section. Trains leave every half hour or less, taking just six minutes.

Haslemere is a lovely town, full of appealing cafés and restaurants ... but Metro Pizza and Burgers is right outside the railway station and is pleasingly downmarket. Another possibility after running is a drive up to the National Trust car park at Hindhead Common on London Road GU26 6AB / **SU 890 357** (overlooking the Devil's Punch Bowl), where there is a café.

Other routes

The Devil's Punch Bowl is a great place to base yourself for short trail runs. Start explorations from the National Trust car park (see above) with 'safe' runs around the perimeter; start from ❸, when you reach Highfield Lane at ❹ turn left onto a byway, return up the first bridleway encountered on the left (8km). The Punch Bowl's steep-sided interior is latticed with some fantastic rugged trails. Go see and explore, but remember that every exhilarating descent earns you a brutal ascent. The author hesitates to describe any particular route because whatever I write, you'll almost certainly be off-piste and lost within minutes! The ROAM 639 Trail is however recommended, a tough 6.39 mile (10.28km) route in memory of Richard Overall, a local man who died of muscular dystrophy. Details and a gpx file can be downloaded from the ROAM 639 website, and there is an information board beside the car park. The wooded area east of Gibbet Hill's summit is large and much less visited, also well worth exploring.

The Greensand Way between Wormley and Shamley Green (Route 62) continues to be a delight, 11km of undulating and often wooded trail with little outside intrusion.

The 108km Serpent Trail starts at Haslemere; see page 284.

Just north of this route are Thursley, Hankley and Frensham Commons, 1,900 hectares of interlinked open heathland with excellent access (via rights of way and also Access Land). Hankley Common (owned by the MOD) is famous as the filming location of James Bond's *Skyfall* mansion, supposedly set in the Scottish Highlands. Set out from the car park at GU8 6LL / **SU 890 410** off Woolfords Lane and explore away.

The Devil's Punch Bowl

Approaching Wormley

Events

Various short distance trail races explore the Punch Bowl area: The Devil Run offers 5, 10 and 15km options; Haslemere Border AC host several races annually, including the Gibbet Hill 10K and the Punch Bowl 10K; and Holy Cross Hospital hold a 3.5-mile Boxing Day Fun Run.

The Punchbowl Marathon is one of the LDWA's Challenge Events, with 20- and 30-mile routes starting and finishing at Witley. They also organise the 50-mile Surrey Tops (which you have 20 hours to complete), also starting in Witley.

The Surrey Hills Challenge Ultra starts at Haslemere (see page 312), as does the Serpent Trail Race (see page 284).

The Surrey Hills Area of Outstanding Natural Beauty

All of this chapter's routes except Route 65 are within the Surrey Hills Area of Outstanding Natural Beauty. Britain's second AONB (the first was the Quantock Hills in Somerset) is 422 km^2, comprising a quarter of Surrey. The AONB shares borders with the South Downs National Park (see page 272) and the Kent Downs AONB (see page 215). As the name rather implies, there are hills; the North Downs and the Greensand Ridge, both crossing the county east to west. Chalk and sandstone hills, of which a quarter is Access Land, covered by woodland (40%) and heath and common (18%), with a vast array of trails to explore ... what's not to love?

60 The Devil's Punch Bowl

Near Sandyhills

61 St Martha's Hill

Descending from St Martha's Hill

Distance	10km (6 miles)	Ascent	275m (925ft)
Map	OS Landranger 186 OS Explorer 145		
Navigation	● ● ●	Simple route finding, partly along the North Downs Way	
Terrain	● ● ●	Sandy trails, agricultural land, rooty and chalky trails	
Wet feet	● ● ●	Sticky mud along the fields	
Start / Finish	Newlands Corner car park GU4 8SE / TQ 043 492		

Mild sand and chalk trails around a lofty church

St Martha's Hill near Guildford has the underwhelming status of being the 18th highest hill in Surrey. However, the author had read that you could see eight counties from the top and it seemed worth checking out. We ran up to the 175m summit in darkness, on a pre-dawn mission ... as it happens, it was a dank morning and the sun never even broke through. Yet, as we shivered beside the church which tops the hill, the grey light gradually revealed the bucolic Tillingbourne Valley below, with views across the forests of Blackheath to Black Down in West Sussex and far beyond. Could we see eight counties? I have no idea, but I have kept going back there.

This route samples a medley of the area's varied trails. Newlands Corner is a popular beauty spot on the North Downs ridge, the car park giving access to a 100-hectare nature reserve of chalk downland. There are apparently about 130 ancient yews in the woods, I've never been able to keep count while running.

61 St Martha's Hill

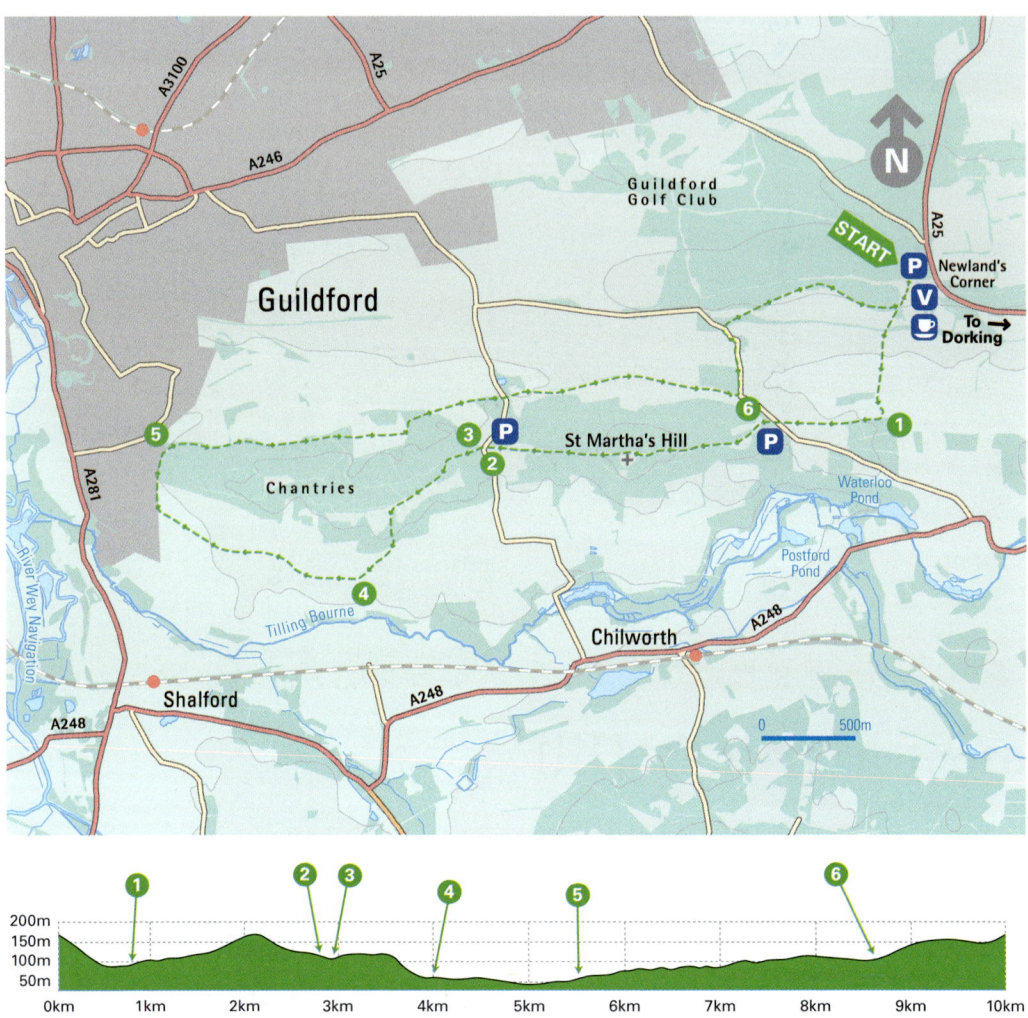

You cross to St Martha's Hill; this is part of the Greensand Ridge and you will curse at the loose sandy inclines! St Martha's Church (also known as St Martha-on-the-Hill) sits atop the hill, attractive in itself but also impressive for its lack of road access. It is Victorian, but there has been a church here on the Pilgrim's Way since Saxon times. You then descend to the surrounding farmland and follow undulating paths and trackways around the base of the hill. On that first dank run here, we were delighted to find the Newlands Corner café hatch was opening for business just as we returned; sausage sarnies all round!

Route description

START Cross the car park from the visitor centre and take the path leading downhill. After 150m this path crosses a footpath, continue downhill to join a footpath descending steeply to the edge of agricultural fields. Follow the footpath S across the fields past a cottage to reach a crossroads with a bridleway. Turn right onto the bridleway. ❶ Follow the bridleway (signposted Pilgrim's Way) W for 600m to reach a road (Guildford Lane) and car park. Cross the road and continue on the bridleway uphill. After 400m the

St Martha's Hill

St Martha's Hill from Albury Downs
Photo: Andy Levick

North Downs Way joins (from the right) and the path uphill becomes a footpath, continue uphill to reach St Martha's Church at the summit. Pass around the church and descend on the NDW (footpath, then bridleway) for 800m to reach a lane (Halfpenny Lane). ❷ Turn left onto the lane and follow it 30m before turning right onto the NDW bridleway. Instead of following the NDW, immediately turn off left onto a footpath leading into Chantry Wood (beside a Woodland Trust info sign). ❸ Follow the footpath through the woods, bearing left at forks until the footpath reaches and leads along the edge of the woods. 275m after passing a picnic area, look for a footpath post pointing left (downhill) and take this route. Descend steeply S to a field, continue on the footpath across this. At the bottom of the field, the footpath joins a footpath track leading E-W, turn right (W) onto this. ❹ Follow this footpath track (it soon becomes a path), ignoring turn-offs, until it reaches a road (Clifford Manor Road) and housing after 1.1km. Turn right onto the road and follow it uphill for just 30m before it bends left; leave the road and continue uphill on the footpath ahead. After 350m you reach a crossroads with the NDW. Turn right (E) onto the NDW bridleway. ❺ Follow the NDW for 1.25km to where a bridleway turns off on the left. Take this and follow it 500m to a lane (Halfpenny Lane). Cross the lane and continue E on the bridleway for another 1.2km to reach a lane (Guildford Lane) and a junction with the NDW. The NDW turns off left (uphill) just before the lane, join this footpath. ❻ Ascend on the NDW footpath beside the lane, crossing it after 400m. Continue along the NDW, contouring the edge of the Albury Downs, to reach Newlands Corner after 1.2km.

St Martha's Church

St Martha's Hill

Trip planning

Newlands Corner is on Drove Road, located by following the A25 east out of Guildford. The car park charges, nevertheless this is a very busy spot at weekends. A visitor centre highlights the local nature and alongside this, food is served from a hatch, with outdoor seating. If chips in a tray does not meet your culinary threshold, then there is a café / restaurant just over the road, the Plucky Pheasant.

Alternative start points are the free car parks on Halfpenny Lane GU4 8PZ / **TQ 021 484** and Guildford Lane GU5 9BQ / **TQ 034 485**. These would start your run at ❷ and just after ❶, respectively.

Other routes

It is simple to shorten this route to about 6km by turning right onto Halfpenny Lane at ❷ and following it for 200m to where the bridleway crosses between ❺ and ❻. Turn right onto this.

The 18km of the NDW west of St Martha's Hill to the National Trail's end (or beginning) at Farnham is unspectacular; after passing through Guildford it, unusually, follows the low ground (the ridge top has been claimed by the A31). However, it's a worthwhile outing with the possibility of shuttling back by train in about half an hour.

The Downs Link (see below) begins at St Martha's Hill, offering a direct (59km) trail to the sea! More sensibly, it is a useful way to extend this route by 6–10km by looping into Blackheath Common and Blackheath Forest and back. If you want to visit the sandy trails around these as a separate outing, the car park on Blackheath Lane GU4 8RB / **TQ 035 462** is a good start point.

Events

The Fitstuff G3 Series is a series of trail races (with various distances from 5 to 15km) held around Newlands Corner and St Martha's Hill, covering similar ground to this route.

Freedom Racing's North Downs Ridge 50K starts at Shalford (below St Martha's Hill), passing along the NDW to Denbies Wine Estate (Route 63) and back again.

The Downs Link

The Downs Link is a 59km / 37mile trail connecting St Martha's Hill with Shoreham-by-Sea via disused railway routes. As the name implies, it connects the North and South Downs, although the start is actually a couple of kilometres south of the North Downs. These 'Sustrans'-type trails following the former rail network are often tediously tarmacked, but the Downs Link is a surprisingly undeveloped green trail, offering decent (if flattish) trail runs and one notable climb around a tunnel. This may change, however; reports in 2020 suggested that sections were going to be 'upgraded'.

Those planning über-long runs and fastpacking adventures will note how it connects the North Downs Way, South Downs Way and Greensand Way. Is there a crazy race along its whole length? Of course there is. Sussex Trail Events hold the Downs Link Ultra, which is at least run in the downhill direction.

Leith Hill Tower

62 The Hurtwood and Leith Hill

Distance		19km (12 miles) Ascent 600m (1,970ft)
Map		OS Landranger 186, 187 OS Explorer 145, 146
Navigation	●●●	Mostly along the signposted Greensand Way
Terrain	●●●	Woodland trails, numerous ascents and descents
Wet feet	●●●	'Mucho' mud in the monsoon months
Start		Red Lion Inn, Shamley Green GU5 0UA / TQ 032 436
Finish		Holmwood Railway Station RH5 4RA / TQ 174 437

Greensand glory

Is it acceptable for a guidebook author to display favouritism? If you don't think so, *then look away now*. If you do think it's okay, then keep reading; *this is my favourite trail run in this book*.

This route largely follows the Greensand Way as it winds through the Hurtwood, traversing the Greensand Ridge*. The Hurtwood (also known as the Hurt Wood) is 800 hectares of common land named either for the abundant 'ground hurts' (blueberries) or from the Anglo-Saxon *ceart*, meaning a rough common. The Greensand Ridge is the sandstone escarpment squeezed between the North Downs and the Weald. For most of the route, you pace along constantly engaging rooty and rutted trails beneath woodland cover (from Scots pines to giant redwoods). Winterfold, Reynards, Pitch and Holmbury Hills loom successively higher,

---

* These hills are also commonly called 'The Surrey Hills', but that term has been avoided here because of the confusion it might cause regarding all the other hills in Surrey!

The Hurtwood and Leith Hill

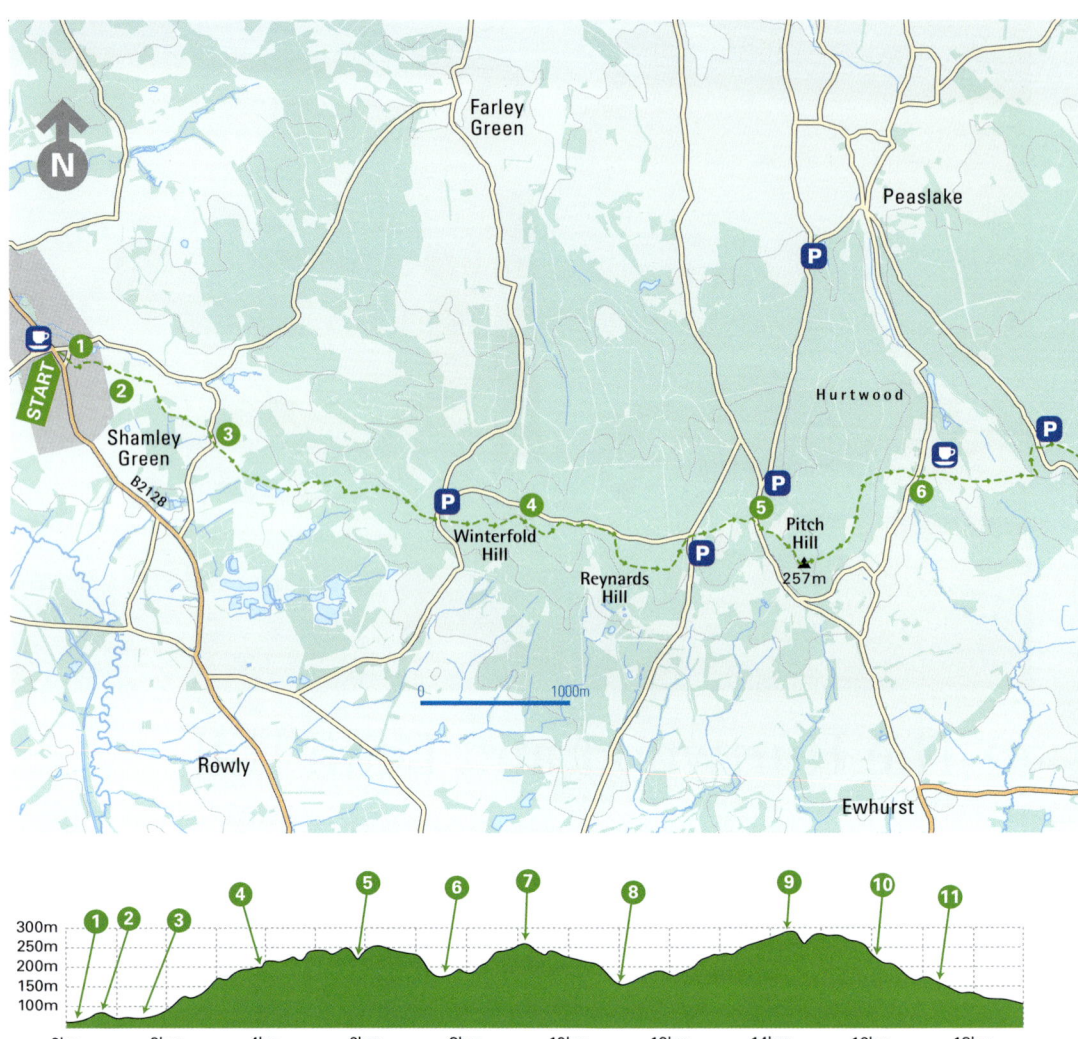

their summits marked by clearings where suddenly the entire Weald opens up below, stretching away to the South Downs. The hillfort atop Holmbury Hill is a particularly phenomenal viewpoint. The final and highest summit comes after leaving the Hurtwood; a slog up 294m Leith Hill, generally regarded as the 'true' highest point in South East England*. The only thing taller within 75km is The Shard in London, which incidentally can be seen from the top of Leith Hill Tower (built in 1765), which incidentally is higher than The Shard! Is there a downside? Well, shuttling this west-to-east traverse is a bit of pain in the bum using local transport. But the hassle really is worth it.

Route description

START From the bus stop outside the Red Lion Inn, head to the junction of the B2128 Guildford Road and Woodhill Lane. Cross Woodhill Lane and head SE across the village green behind, to cross Woodhill Lane again. Continue ahead to locate and follow the footpath leading between the houses.

*Walbury Hill (Route 16) is 3m higher, but is on the fringes of the South East.

62 The Hurtwood and Leith Hill

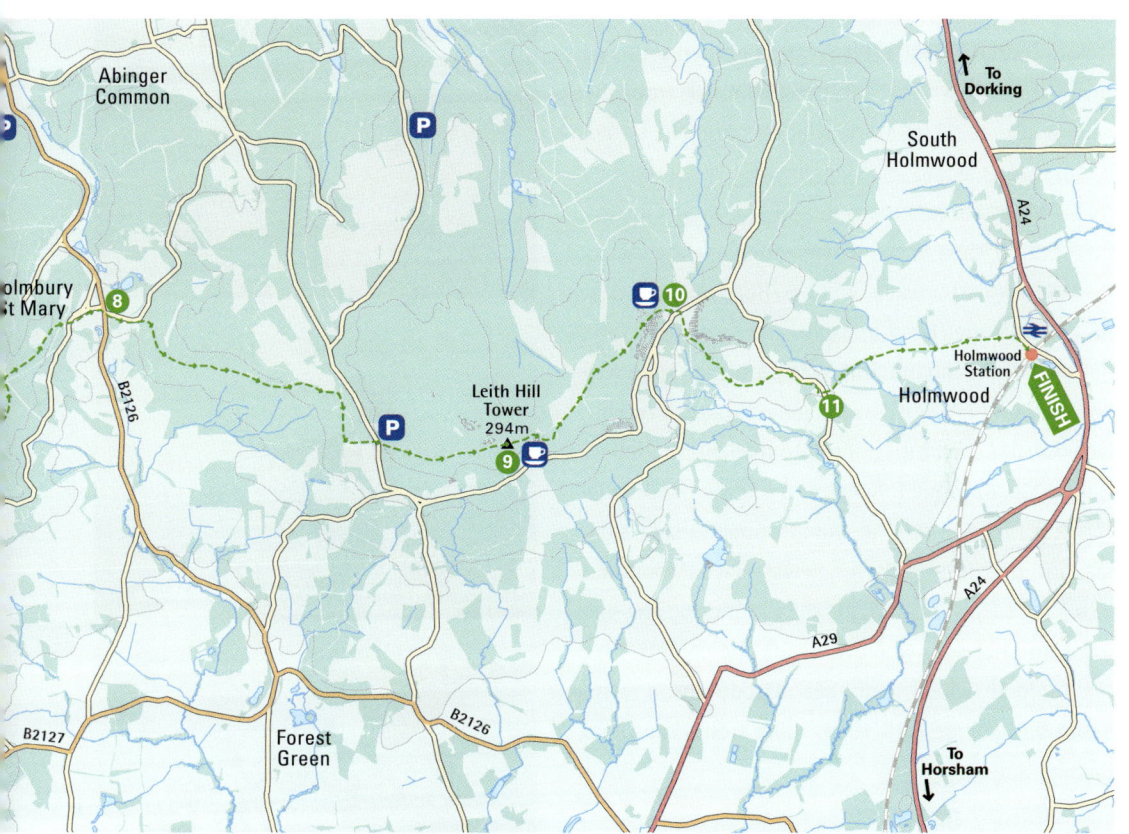

❶ Follow this narrow footpath for 350m uphill to where it merges with two other footpaths and widens; the footpath track joining from the right is the Greensand Way. **❷** For the next 13.8km you are following the well-signposted GW along a series of footpaths and bridleways; summarised in this route description are the key features. The GW follows tracks through farmland, crossing a lane (Stroud Lane) after 1.1km. **❸** The GW ascends through woodland, crossing a second lane (Alderbrook Lane) after 1.5km at Hurtwood car park 6 (Winterfold – Radar Site), to reach Winterfold Hill. After another 600m the GW passes Hurtwood car park 5 (Winterfold Donkins), shortly followed by a curved wooden shelter at a viewpoint. **❹** The GW leads along the scarp of Reynards Hill for 2km, crossing Barhatch Road, briefly ascending to Ewhurst Windmill and then descending to cross another road (Pitch Hill) at Hurtwood car park 3 (Pitch Hill). **❺** The following 1.6km consists of a short steep ascent to the summit viewpoint of Pitch Hill, followed by a long descent, passing through the grounds of Duke of Kent School, to reach Ewhurst Road at the bottom. **❻** After crossing Ewhurst Road, the next 3.5km involves crossing the valley floor and ascending steeply into woodland again. Halfway up the ascent, Radnor Road is crossed at Hurtwood car park 1 (Holmbury Hill) and then the hillfort at the summit of Holmbury Hill is reached, marked by a circular stone plinth. **❼** The GW bears N along the ramparts, and then descends to reach Pitland Street, which leads downhill to Horsham Road. **❽** The following 3.3km is the gradual ascent of Leith Hill; turn right onto Horsham Road and follow it just 40m before turning off left onto Pasture Wood Road. After 300m, the road bends left and the GW leads off right on a bridleway. This

309

The Hurtwood and Leith Hill

crosses Leith Hill Road after 2.1km, and then Leith Hill Tower is reached after another 900m. ❾ From the tower, take the bridleway which continues ahead, leading downhill to reach a junction of numerous tracks after 210m. Turn right (SE) onto the byway track which leads uphill, leaving the GW. The byway then descends to reach Abinger Road after 1.4km. ❿ Cross Abinger Road and take the footpath to the right of the Plough Inn. Follow the footpath for 900m downhill through woods and along a track to reach a lane (Anstie Lane). Turn right onto the lane and follow it for 400m downhill to where a bridleway track bears off left, marked by a 'no through road' sign. ⓫ Turn off left onto the bridleway track (Moorhurst Lane) and follow this straight ahead, ignoring any side turns, for 1.3km to where it bends sharply left. Take the footpath which continues directly ahead, after 150m this emerges at a road, 100m from Holmwood Railway Station.

Ascending Leith Hill

Holmbury Hill fort

Ewhurst Windmill

Trip planning

Shuttling this route by car, it takes about 25 minutes to drive between the start and end. Roadside parking is no problem. Shuttling by public transport is a bit of a faff. The easiest way back from the finish is a train from Holmwood Railway Station to Dorking, followed by a number 32 bus to Shalford and a number 53 bus to Shamley Green. This takes about one hour 40 minutes, but do some planning and check times before you set out.

Jogging or staggering up the 78 steps to the summit of 313m Leith Hill Tower is recommended. Carry your National Trust membership card for free entry, otherwise you pay. The tower also has a welcome café hatch serving drinks and snacks.

There are numerous pubs to check out in the nearby villages; the Plough Inn is actually on the route at ❿, near the end. For light bites, the author recommends finding an excuse to patronise Peaslake Village Stores on Peaslake Lane. They serve hot or cold snacks and drinks, and have long been tolerant of the stinky outdoorsy folk who converge here at weekends.

Winterfold Hill bench

The Hurtwood and Leith Hill

The area is popular with a range of different users; notably mountain bikers, walkers and horse riders. The author has even encountered fully-costumed LARPers (Google it) on the trails! There is a tradition of respecting each other's activities and harmoniously sharing this wonderful place; don't do anything to spoil this.

Reynards Hill

Pitch Hill

Other routes

Where to even start? It's no exaggeration to say that you could fill a decent-sized guidebook with recommended local trail runs; there are over 100km of footpaths and bridleways in the Hurtwood alone.

This route spans the whole range of hills as a 'whistle-stop highlights tour', but you will certainly want to return and delve deeper into the woods around individual summits ... and you really should. Access is made simple by around twenty free car parks dotted across the region, helpfully labelled with clues as to where they give access to, e.g. 'Hurtwood car park 1 (Holmbury Hill)'.

Hurtwood car park 2 (Walking Bottom) on Walking Bottom Lane GU5 9QW / TQ 083 445 and Hurtwood car park 14 (Youth Hostel) on Radnor Lane RH5 6NW / TQ 103 449 are recommended as low-altitude spots from which to ascend Pitch Hill and Holmbury Hill, respectively; summitting each hill following the obvious bridleways will be at least a 5km loop. Leith Hill can be ascended from Surrey County Council's Broadmoor car park on Sheephouse Lane RH5 6JS / TQ 132 454. This again gives a 5km+ run via Leith Hill Tower, but you are recommended to also seek out and incorporate the nearby and rather lovely Tillingbourne Waterfall into your route. Yes, Surrey has waterfalls.

The Greensand Way descends north from Leith Hill after ❾ via a long byway leading to just south of Ranmore Common (Route 63), and is the obvious way to connect the North Downs and Greensand Ridge.

Events

Maverick Race's Original Surrey event has distances of 6, 12 and 22km and loops into the Hurtwood from Chilworth to the north.

A couple of hilly half marathons happen hereabouts. The Surrey Slog Half Marathon ascends Holmbury Hill from Duke of Kent School, while Trionium's Leith Hill Half Marathon ascends to the tower from Dorking. The latter event is usually held alongside the UK Wife Carrying Race .... just don't ask.

Freedom Racing's Hurtwood 50K Trail Ultra starts from Dorking, chugs along the GW following most of this route ... and then chugs back again, the same way.

The Founder's Challenge is a LDWA Challenge Event which visits sites associated with the founders of the organisation (e.g. Pitch Hill). It starts from Guildford and has 19- or 30-mile options. Their 50-mile Surrey Tops starts from Witley but also visits the Greensand Ridge.

62 The Hurtwood and Leith Hill

View from Winterfold Hill

The Greensand Way

The Greensand Way is an absolute gem. Less known than the South East's National Trails like the South Downs Way and Ridgeway, nevertheless many walkers regard it as the best route in the region and for sure it offers some stunning trail running, often along rugged sandstone scarps with epic views. It leads 174km / 108 miles from Haslemere in Surrey to Hamstreet in Kent, with about 3,000 metres of ascent. It follows the Greensand Ridge, which parallels the North Downs, often closely. Routes 47, 60 and 62 make use of the GW as it traverses the Surrey Hills and Chart Hills. Beyond Borough Green, the GW is lower in elevation but still offers fine views of the Weald, and beyond Great Chart (near Ashford) the hills peter out into agricultural land.

The route is shown on OS maps and marked by disks, which in Surrey have an image of Leith Hill Tower and in Kent an oast-house. There is no guidebook in print, but Surrey and Kent County Councils provide excellent information and detailed maps online.

In 2020, new FKTs (Fastest Known Times) were repeatedly set, the record standing at 24 hours, 44 minutes and 25 seconds at time of going to print. Mere mortals might pass on trying to beat this and instead settle for attempting The Surrey Hills Challenge Ultra (the author, just about, completed this), clocking in at 61km one-way along the GW from Haslemere to Dorking, with a concurrent marathon joining the route at Witley.

63 Box Hill

Box Hill

Distance		16km (10 miles)	Ascent	525m (1,720ft)
Map		OS Landranger 187 OS Explorer 146		
Navigation	●●●	Well signposted, but endless junctions		
Terrain	●●●	Chalk, roots, grass, tarmac. Several savage inclines		
Wet feet	●●●	A few paths become mud baths in winter		
Start / Finish		Box Hill National Trust car park KT20 7LB / TQ 178 513		

Gruelling climbs and quiet valleys around an iconic beauty spot

Picnicking at Box Hill, while taking in the famous panoramic view of the North Downs, Weald and Surrey Hills; this has for centuries been a classic day trip for Surrey folk. We trail runners don't do passive picnicking, however! This painfully hilly route aggressively attacks the Box Hill landscape as an enemy to be defeated ... be careful what you wish for though, it might just defeat you.

Right from Salomon's Memorial viewpoint (Leopold Salomon donated Box Hill to the National Trust in 1914), you descend 275 steps to the famous stepping stones across the River Mole. These stones have been here since 1946, the earlier stones having been removed to deter a Nazi invasion! The far side of the 'Mole Gap' is quiet grassland, woodland and farmland, a surprisingly contrast after the crowds at Box Hill. You pass Ranmore Common's woods, then ascend and descend around the estates surrounding two mansions; Polesdon Lacey (Edwardian, National Trust) and Norbury Park (Georgian). After re-crossing the Mole Gap,

63 Box Hill

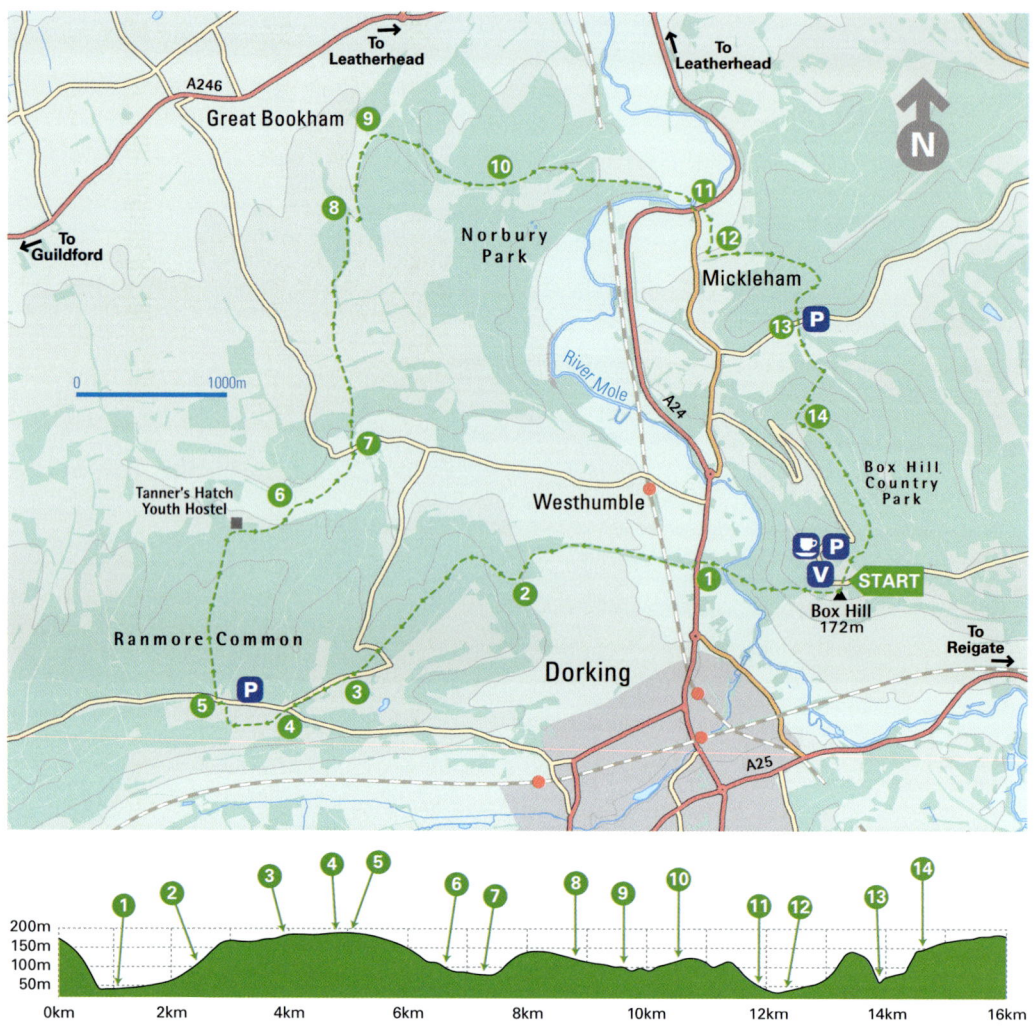

there are (naturally) more savage inclines to negotiate. One reward for your troubles is visiting Broadwood's Folly, a quirky flint tower built for piano manufacturer Thomas Broadwood after the Battle of Waterloo.

Route description

START From the car park, head SE and across a lane (Zig Zag Road) to reach the Salomon's Memorial Hill viewpoint, beside a trig point. Turn right (W) onto the North Downs Way footpath. Follow the NDW steeply downhill to the stepping stones over the River Mole, and cross them. Continue ahead to reach the A24 road. ❶ Turn left and head 50m S, then cross carefully. Continue along the NDW footpath track for 1.2km uphill, passing two crossroads with other footpaths. After the NDW enters woods and begins to climb steeply, look for a crossroads with a bridleway track and turn right (uphill) onto this, leaving the NDW.

❷ Climb steeply uphill on the bridleway track. After 500m the gradient eases and you reach a junction of multiple paths. Continue ahead and when you reach a fork, take the right fork to continue on the bridleway. Follow this bridleway path through woods along the hill top, crossing a lane (Ranmore Common Road)

Box Hill

after 800m. After 1km you reach the same lane again. ❸ Turn right and re-join the NDW alongside the lane for 500m, passing a church. When the lane reaches a junction with a bigger road (Ranmore Road), continue ahead by crossing the road, to follow the NDW through a gate onto open common. ❹ After 400m the NDW enters woods and a footpath leads off the NDW on the right, take this and follow it back to the road. Cross the road and head to the left (W) of the houses opposite, where tracks lead into the woods. ❺ Take the footpath track signposted 'Youth Hostel', leading N. Follow the footpath track downhill. After 1.1km it merges with a bridleway and you reach Tanner's Hatch Youth Hostel. Continue on the bridleway past the YH, leaving the woods. ❻ When the bridleway track reaches the valley floor after 500m, take the bridleway path on the right and follow this down the valley to Bagden Farm. Pass the farm to reach a T junction with a bridleway track, turn left onto this to reach a lane (Chapel Lane) after 200m. ❼ Cross the lane and take the bridleway path leading uphill (N). Climb steeply through woodland, ignoring footpaths leading off. At the top, continue along the bridleway which then descends and reaches a T junction with a bridleway track after 1.3km. ❽ Turn sharp right to follow this bridleway for 90m before

River Mole stepping stones

North Downs Way near Westhumble

turning off sharp left onto another bridleway track, leading along the edge of woods. After 600m this bridleway reaches farm buildings; look for a footpath leading uphill on the right, and take this. ❾ After 300m the footpath crosses a bridleway track, continue ahead on the same path which is now a bridleway. Follow this bridleway ahead through mixed woods and farmland, ignoring any paths or tracks leading off. ❿ After 700m you reach the wall of Norbury Park House (private estate) and the bridleway becomes tarmac. Follow the bridleway along this boundary; after 260m it turns right, off the tarmac track. After 300m a short out-and-back detour to a viewpoint is offered, then the bridleway descends steeply along a track to reach the River Mole after 800m. ⓫ Cross the bridge and then the A24 road. Turn left and follow the A24 for 60m to where a bridleway leads off right. Turn right to take this and continue straight ahead (S) for 300m through the village of Mickleham; the bridleway becomes a footpath and reaches a T junction with a bridleway track, beside the church. ⓬ Turn left (E) and follow the bridleway uphill into woods. After 400m turn right off the bridleway onto a footpath. Climb steeply uphill following the footpath, which bends sharp right at the top of the hill and then descends steeply to a lane (Headley Lane). ⓭ Cross the lane and follow the bridleway track leading up the valley (Juniper Bottom). After 400m a very steep path,

Box Hill

with steps, leads uphill on the right; take this, enjoy! When the gradient eases, follow the path ahead along the hillside until you reach a small tower (Broadwood's Folly). ⑭ Turn left at the tower to take the track leading uphill (SE). Keep on this, ignoring any turn-offs, after 1.3km it reaches the Box Hill viewpoint.

Broadwood's Folly

Trip planning
Box Hill receives around 850,000 visitors a year, so early morning or evening runs are recommended, both for trail tranquillity and parking. A quieter start point is Denbies Hillside National Trust car park at ❹, across Mole Gap on Ranmore Common Road (RH5 6SR / TQ 141 503). Both car parks are free to National Trust members. A quieter start again is the small but free Whitehill car park off Headley Road at ⑬, RH5 6DF / TQ 180 525.

Box Hill

The National Trust café at Box Hill served the author the worst chilli he has ever tasted, but maybe they were just having a bad day.

This route passes the relatively remote Tanner's Hatch Youth Hostel after ❺, making an overnight outing a possibility. Camping is permitted at the hostel.

Mickleham Downs

Other routes
There are numerous trails to explore around the National Trust's Box Hill estate, see their website for a map and route ideas. Likewise across the Mole Gap, at the Polesdon Lacey estate.

The 5km of the North Downs Way heading east from Salomon's Memorial to connect with Route 64 are varied but engaging, descending past old quarries and industrial remains with some tarmac time. The 12km of the NDW leading west from Ranmore Common ❹ to Newlands Corner (Route 61) are lovely, following the scarp through woodland with no major gradient and little interruption from the outside world. Incidentally, the section of the NDW bypassed at ❷ in the route described here is just a tarmac road.

Events
Work off a New Year's Eve hangover by entering Trionium's Knacker Cracker, claimed to be Britain's toughest 10km and apparently 58% uphill. Yikes.

Salomon (the outdoor company, not the family who donated Box Hill) hold a Trail Running Festival at Box Hill every year, with timed runs from 5km to 50km, as well as talks and workshops.

Polesdon Lacey hold a Trust10 (10km) race on their estate.

Box Hill

Bagden Farm

The Bacchus Marathon, Half Marathon and 10km is held at Denbies Wine Estate (just across the Mole Gap from Box Hill) and covers a route including the NDW to the west.

The Surrey Hills Challenge is also based from the wine estate, with 1, 5, 10km and half marathon events starting, and longer events finishing, here. Canary Trail Events run a series of marathons and ultramarathons based out of Mickleham (on this route), including the Raven series and the Copthorne events. Their 'Unique Selling Proposition' is that entrants have to carry a canary. No, we have no clue either.

The LDWA's Winter Tanners Challenge Event has 20- and 30-mile routes starting and finishing at Leatherhead.

National Trust trail running

Finding yourself running on National Trust land is a statistical inevitability, as they own vast tracts of the South East; e.g. 6,000 hectares of the South Downs National Park. The NT have been working to encourage trail running on their land and properties, with many such places now having waymarked trails and / or recommended routes. Within the South East, only two properties currently host organised runs; Poledon Lacey in Surrey has a monthly 10km 'Trust10' race and Osterley Park in London is the base for a weekly 5km parkrun. The NT also partners with England Athletics' RunTogether scheme to organise group and guided runs. Their website has further details.

63 Box Hill

Box Hill steps

64 Reigate Hill

Colley Hill

Distance	10km (6.5 miles)	Ascent	275m (900ft)
Map	OS Landranger 187 OS Explorer 146		
Navigation ●●●	Partly along the NDW		
Terrain ●●●	Chalky trails, rooty trails, unevenly cambered awkwardness		
Wet feet ●●●	Plenty of mud in the wetter months		
Start / Finish	Reigate Hill and Gatton Park National Trust car park RH2 0HX / TQ 262 523		

10km on the Pilgrim's Way

Some routes design themselves! Squeezed between Reigate and the (barely noticeable) M25, parallel trails run along the foot and the scarp of the North Downs, making for an excellent circuit. This configuration is not random. The prehistoric routeway which followed the Downs across the South East had a choice of trails, both atop and contouring below the scarp, for different seasons. The North Downs Way generally follows the upper trail. The lower trail has been called the Pilgrim's Way for centuries but is now often hidden beneath tarmac roads ... yet it is wonderfully preserved here, for your leg-abusing pleasure.

The first (lower) half of the route is more challenging, with splendidly rough and rugged trails along the hillside. Look out for Reigate hearthstone mine, an old quarry; hearthstones were used to clean doorsteps! The return journey on the 'high road' is easier, following more evenly-surfaced trails. There is plenty to keep you motivated. The views from Colley Hill and the Inglis Memorial (built in 1909 as a drinking fountain for

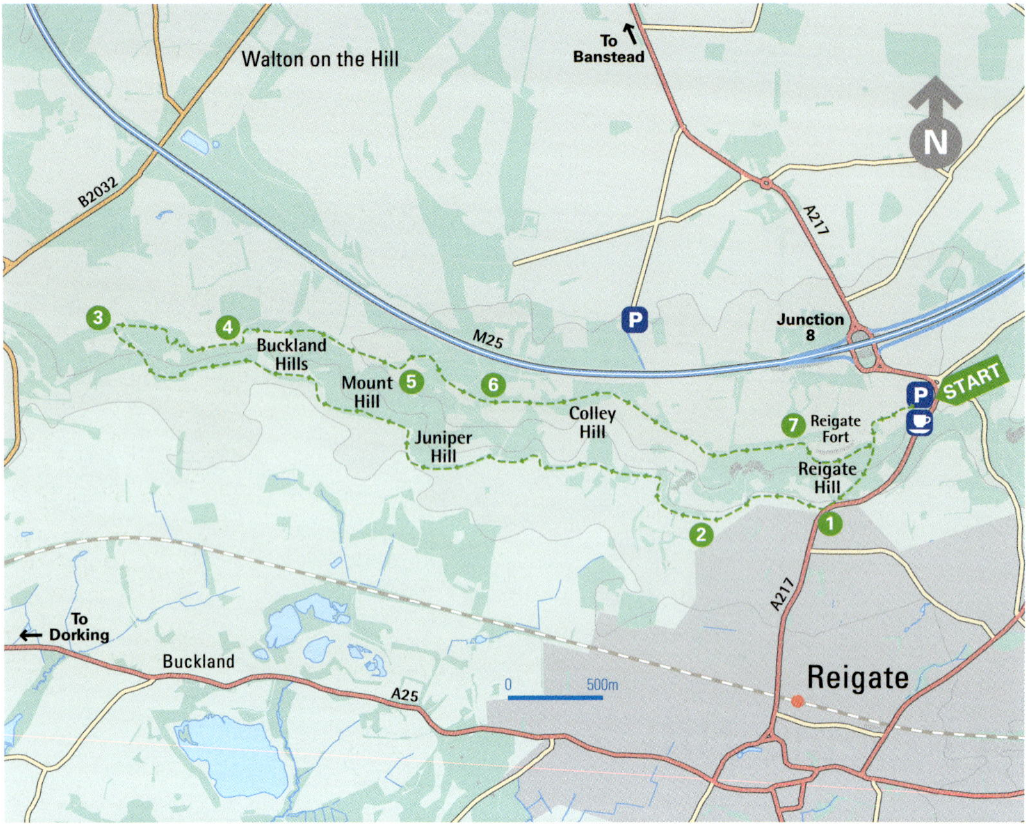

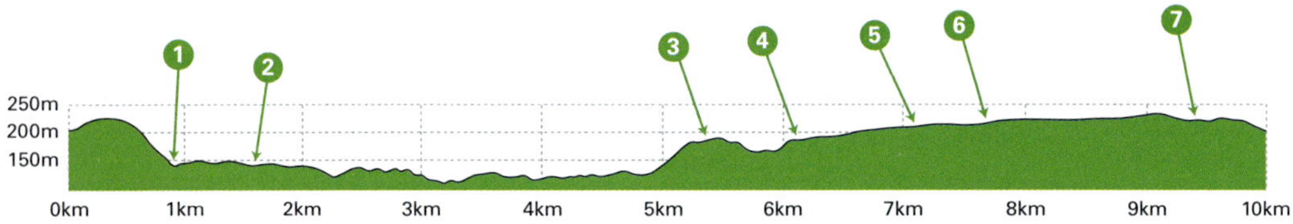

Reigate Hill

horses) are sublime. The woodland clearing with two 'wingtip' benches is a memorial to the nine crew of a USAF B17 'Flying Fortress' which crashed here in 1945. The final landmark is Reigate Fort, built in 1898 to keep French armies out of London (you can enter and run the ramparts!). Note the microcosmic stuff, too. The meadows you run through are home to the Adonis blue butterfly and the rare meadow clary, a plant with tall spikes of blue flowers.

Route description

START Leave the car park to the W by crossing Reigate Hill Footbridge across the A217. Follow the North Downs Way bridleway 350m to a crossroads and turn left (downhill). Descend steeply (there is a choice of footpath or bridleway) until you reach the A217 road. Turn right and follow the road 40m to where a bridleway track leads off on the right. Take this. ❶ Follow the bridleway for 700m along a track behind houses, ignoring any turn-offs leading uphill. When you reach a 'Pilgrim's Way' sign, the bridleway becomes a footpath and you have escaped Reigate; continue ahead. ❷ Follow the footpath W along the

Reigate Hill

base of the ridge and woodland (after 1.3km it becomes the NDW), ignoring any side turns. After 3.3km a track joins from the left (Buckland Lane) and the footpath becomes a byway which heads steeply uphill. Ascend along the byway to a crossroads with a bridleway, at the top of the hill. ❸ Turn right (E) onto the bridleway, follow this winding through the woods. After 750m a bridleway turns off left, take this. ❹ Follow the bridleway along the ridge top for 900m to where a footpath track crosses the bridleway, just after reaching large houses. Turn left onto this. ❺ The footpath track leads into woods. After 200m, a bridleway crosses the footpath, turn right onto this. Follow the bridleway through the woods, crossing two tracks, until it merges with the NDW. ❻ Follow the NDW bridleway E for 1.7km along Colley Hill, with the option to explore the grassy trails which are parallel on the right. When you see Reigate Fort (earthworks) on the righthand side of the NDW, cross the stile on the right before it. ❼ Follow the path which leads below the ramparts until it joins a bridleway. Turn left (uphill) onto the bridleway and ascend to a crossroads with the NDW bridleway. Turn right onto the NDW bridleway, it leads back to the car park.

Trip planning

The car park is reached by following the A217 uphill out of Reigate and turning right onto Wray Lane at a roundabout. It is free to National Trust members (i.e. not to everyone else) and there is a café here. It fills quickly at weekends, in which case head to the NT's Margery Wood car park KT20 7BT / TQ 245 527. This is only two kilometres away, reached by crossing the M25 and taking the first left onto Margery Lane. To access the route, follow the path leading south out of the back of the car park; it crosses the M25 and joins just before ❼, after 350m.

Other routes

Across Wray Lane from the car park, the NDW passes through Gatton Park, which was landscaped in the

Inglis Memorial, Colley Hill

Thistle Hill

Conybury Hill

Reigate Hill

Pilgrim's Way

eighteenth century by Lancelot 'Capability' Brown (see page 280). About half of the park is administered by the National Trust and the trails here are well worth exploring to extend your run by a few kilometres, or as a separate shorter outing. The public bridleway which ascends through the private part of Gatton Park allows for a loop route and gives great views of the landscaped lakes. Look out for the Millennium Stones near top of the bridleway, a stone circle erected in the year 2000.

See Route 63 for info on the NDW to the west of this route.

Other areas worthy of trail exploration in the vicinity include Reigate Heath and Reigate Park (both, unsurprisingly, in Reigate) and Walton Heath and Banstead Heath on the far side of the M25, accessible from this route by two footbridges.

Reigate Hill Fort

Events

The Reigate Priory Park 10K is held in the centre of Reigate; runners complete multiple laps of the park.
Hermes Running's North Downs Marathon and Half Marathon traverse repeatedly along the NDW between Reigate Hill and Box Hill.

View from Colley Hill

65 Happy Valley

Distance	9km (5.5 miles)	Ascent	175m (590ft)
Map	OS Landranger 187 OS Explorer 146		
Navigation	●●●	Many paths, but all pretty much heading in the same direction …	
Terrain	●●●	Some rough and rutted sections, a few short climbs	
Wet feet	●●●	The fields near Chaldon can get claggy	
Start / Finish	Farthing Downs north entrance on Ditches Lane CR5 1AA / TQ 300 588		

Pristine downland trails on London's fringes

This beautiful trail run with its classic winding trails and idyllic countryside is only partly in Surrey; most of it spills over into the London Borough of Croydon. We hope you'll forgive us for sneaking it into the book! It is included here as a trail run which is immediately accessible from the Transport for London network (reached in 25 mins from London Bridge Railway Station!) and more importantly, because it's just lovely. While running, the sole clue that you are in London is a distant glimpse from the highest point of the Shard and the Gherkin.

Farthing Downs (the northerly part of this route) and Happy Valley (the southerly part) are part of the South London Downs National Nature Reserve, only established in 2019. They are designated as an SSSI on account of being the *'most extensive area of semi-natural downland habitats remaining in Greater London'*. These pristine grasslands haven't been ploughed since Roman times, and are interspersed with some

65 Happy Valley

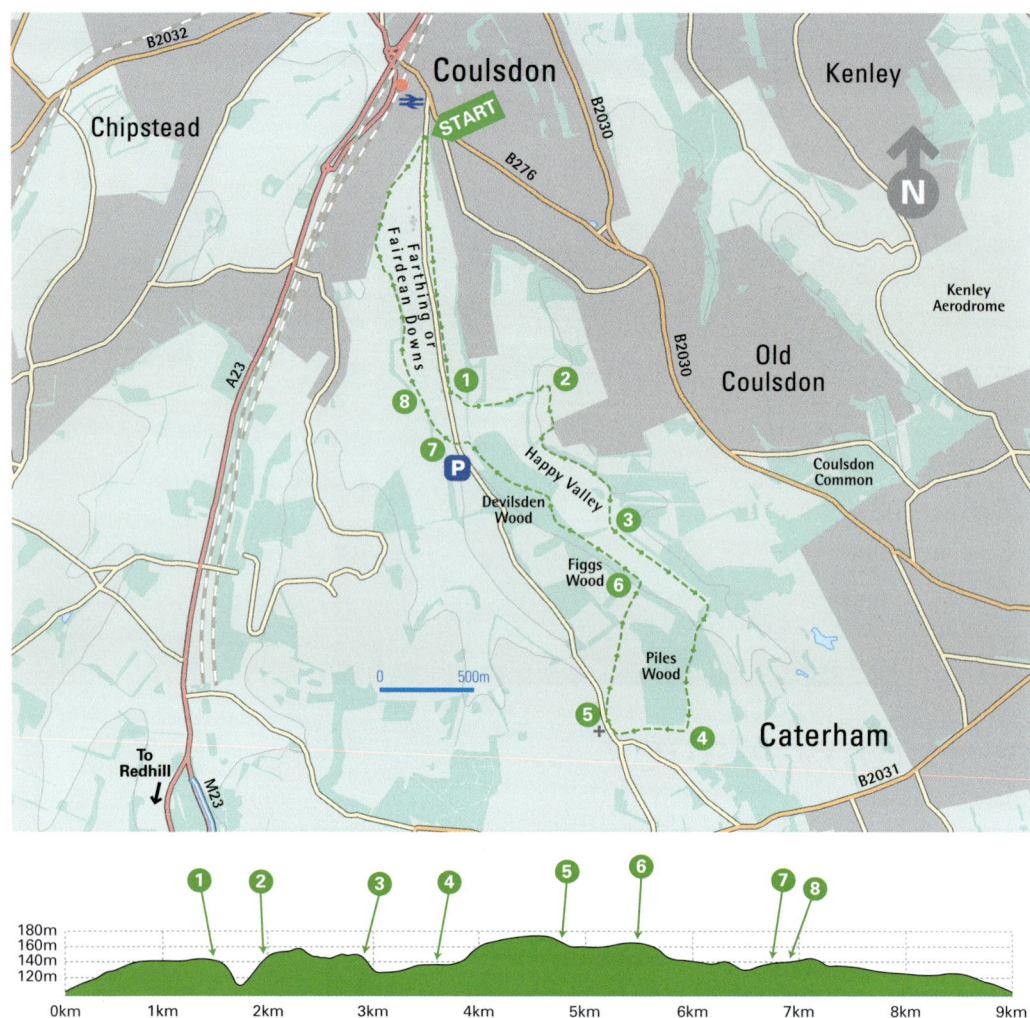

glorious woodland which will provide welcome shade on hot days. Trails and paths riddle this landscape, which is simply a delight to explore via trail shoe. Relish, especially if your journey began on the Tube!

Route description

START From the entrance gate on Ditches Lane (just past the black 'Farthing Downs' sign), follow the path which leads S (uphill) paralleling the lane on the left-hand side. Follow this path along the top of Farthing Downs for 1.3km to a gate, where you'll see a car park ahead. ❶ Pass through the gate and look for a crossroads with a bridleway. Turn left and follow this bridleway (Drive Road) into trees and steeply downhill, following signs for 'Happy Valley'. After reaching the valley floor, continue ahead on the bridleway, steeply uphill again. Ignore the junction with a footpath near the top of the climb after 200m; continue another 100m to where a footpath track turns off on the right; take this footpath. ❷ After 200m, having passed Tollers Design Centre, you reach a children's play area. Turn right (downhill) onto the footpath directly before this. The footpath descends into woods and forks after 100m; take the left fork. Follow this footpath

Happy Valley

Farthing Downs

Drive Road

for 400m along the edge of woods, until it turns uphill and away from the open fields into the woods. At this point, turn right and descend to the floor of the valley (Happy Valley). ❸ When you reach the valley floor, turn left (SE) and follow the permissive bridleway (horseshoe sign) along the valley. After 600m, the bridleway reaches a crossroads. Turn right (uphill) onto the bridleway leading uphill, signposted 'Leazes Ave'. Climb on the bridleway; after 700m it becomes a track and a footpath leads off on the right, signposted 'Chaldon Church'. Turn right onto this footpath. ❹ Follow the footpath along the edge of two fields. After 400m you reach a lane (Church Lane), turn right onto this. After 120m on the lane (and after passing the church), you reach a footpath on the right, signposted 'Happy Valley'. Turn right onto the footpath. ❺ Cross two large fields, following the footpath. After 800m the footpath leads into woods and reaches a junction; turn left onto the permissive footpath, signposted 'Farthing Downs'. ❻ Follow the footpath (which contours along the valley side) ahead (NW), ignoring any side turns leading steeply up- or downhill. After 500m the footpath forks, take the right fork (which leads slightly downhill). After another 700m, you reach buildings; pass these and turn left (uphill) to the car park. ❼ Pass through the car park and leave it beside the large black 'City of London' sign, cross the gravel path behind it and head NW (downhill) following the obvious path across the grass. ❽ 150m from the car park, the path passes through a gate in a fence and then contours N along the boundary of Farthing Downs. 1km from the car park, you cross trails leading downhill to an exit from Farthing Downs, keep contouring N. 1.8km from the car park, the path ends at Ditches Lane, where you started.

65 Happy Valley

The view from Farthing Downs

Trip planning

If you are approaching by train, the start point is 400m from Coulsdon South Railway Station. At the station, cross the tracks via the footbridge (to the side which is opposite the railway station buildings) and follow the path onto Reddown Road. Turn left and follow Reddown Road 120m to a T junction with the B276 Marlpit Lane. Turn right (uphill) onto Marlpit Lane and then immediately turn off right onto Downs Road. After 100m Downs Road splits into Downs Road and Ditches Lane, which run parallel; follow Ditches Lane. When you see a gate across the lane and a black 'Farthing Downs' sign, you've reached the start.

The number 60 bus runs from Croydon Railway Station and stops beside the junction for Downs Lane.

If arriving by car, Farthing Downs Car Park CR5 1AA / **TQ 301 571** on Ditches Lane is the place to start, at ❼ on the route. The car park is free and open from 7.30am to around dusk. There are toilets and information boards at the car park. If you're coming via the M25, turn off at Junction 7.

Other routes

Most of Farthing Downs is Access Land, and Happy Valley has a particularly dense network of footpaths ... so, explore at your leisure!

If you want to extend your explorations further afield, the London Loop (see below) is probably your best starting point. The LL passes through Farthing Downs (bizarrely, by the road) and Happy Valley, before heading north-east across Coulsdon Common and Kenley Common, which are also part of the National Nature Reserve. It is about 22km from the Farthing Downs car park to Hayes Railway Station, most of which is common, park and woodland.

Heading west, the LL passes back through Coulsdon before emerging onto the Banstead Downs, which are pleasant enough but dominated by a golf course.

Happy Valley

Events

In the summer, South London Harriers organise a series of three informal 10km trail races over Farthing Downs and Happy Valley.

Trail running in Greater London

If you live in our nation's capital, you are never far in distance or time from a fantastic wild place to trail run, outside the city; this book is proof of that. However, there are plenty of decent spots to trail run within London itself. The most obvious are the eight Royal Parks, of which Richmond, Bushy and Greenwich offer the best rough trails. 1000-hectare Richmond Park is the largest, with the 12km (and rather hilly) Tamsin Trail following the perimeter,

Farthing Downs

and numerous other possibilities within the interior. Bushy Park beside Hampton Court is the second largest at 445 hectares and Greenwich Park is much smaller but notably hilly with fantastic views from near the Royal Observatory. Less-groomed trails can be found on Wimbledon Common (the perimeter is about 10km) and Hampstead Heath (6km perimeter). Both are over 300 hectares in size, with the latter being notably rougher and muddier, along with having the better views (from Parliament Hill).

The Thames Path National Trail (see page 120) of course passes through, although it is almost all surfaced (and busy with pedestrians) once you reach central London. East of the Thames Barrier (where the TP ends), bleak Rainham Marshes Nature Reserve on the north bank are possibly the wildest spot in Greater London; on foot, they are best reached from Purfleet station in Essex.

Three long-distance trails are definitely worth investigating; the London Loop, Capital Ring and Green Chain Walk. The **London Loop** circumnavigates London anti-clockwise from Erith to Coldharbour, starting and finishing beside the Thames Estuary. The route does an impressive job of linking up countryside around the capital's fringes, all within the M25. Highlights include Farthing Downs (Route 65) and Enfield Chase. The 126km / 78-mile **Capital Ring** follows a far more central loop, linking up parks and commons; those who have completed it say that is it undoubtedly an urban route, unlike the LL which is more mixed. The greenest part is the south-east segment. Echoing that, the 64km / 40-mile **Green Chain Walk** is a network of trails through green spaces across south-east London, from the Thames to Nunhead Cemetery. There is excellent information available online about London's public green spaces, e.g. the Transport for London website. A number of guidebooks also thoroughly cover London's running possibilities.

65 Happy Valley

Farthing Downs

Appendices

Resources

Public transport
Traveline – timetables and journey planner for bus, rail, coach, and ferry services in the UK *www.traveline.info*
National Rail Enquiries – train times *www.nationalrail.co.uk*
Bus times and schedules – *www.bustimes.org*
Google Maps Transit – useful journey planner *maps.google.com/landing/transit/*

Car journey planning
Google Maps *www.google.com/maps*
Bing Maps *www.bing.com/maps*
Traffic England – up to date information on closures, roadworks and traffic jams *www.trafficengland.com*

Weather
UK Met Office – general and upland area forecasts *www.metoffice.gov.uk*
Metcheck – general forecasts *www.metcheck.com*
Magic Seaweed – surf forecasts and reports, useful for checking sea conditions before coastal runs *www.magicseaweed.com*

Accommodation
Visit England – national tourist information organisation with information on travel, accommodation and places to visit *www.visitengland.com*
Visit South East – regional tourist information *www.visitsoutheastengland.com*
Tourist information centres – contact information *www.visitengland.com/plan-your-visit/tourist-information-centres*
Many regions and communities have their own websites with details of local accommodation and businesses.

Mapping

Paper maps
Ordnance Survey – 1:50,000 Landranger and 1:25,000 Explorer maps *www.ordnancesurvey.co.uk*
Harvey maps – 1:40,000 British Mountain Maps, 1:25,000 Superwalker maps for popular areas and National Trail Maps *www.harveymaps.co.uk*

Appendices

Mapping software

Software such as Memory Map or Anquet Maps allows users to look at Ordnance Survey Maps and plot routes on their home computers. Runners with GPS devices can download plotted routes to their devices or upload recorded routes; *www.memory-map.co.uk www.anquet.co.uk.*

There are also many online-only applications. Some websites such as *www.gmap-pedometer.com* provide simple interfaces which enable users to plot and download their own routes. Online communities store large databases of public routes uploaded by their members. Many require you to join their service and / or download and install their app on your computer or mobile device. These communities include Ordnance Survey OS Maps (their previous Getamap service has discontinued) *https://osmaps.ordnancesurvey.co.uk/osmaps/*, Strava *www.strava.com*, Garmin Connect *https://connect.garmin.com/en-US/*, GPS routes *www.gps-routes.co.uk* and MapMyRun *www.mapmyrun.com/gb/*.

Online grid conversion tools convert grid references into post codes for use with sat navs., such as *www.gridreferencefinder.com*

Access

The Countryside Code gives guidance on responsibilities for those who visit and those manage the countryside *www.gov.uk/government/publications/the-countryside-code*.

Detailed guidance on Rights of Way and access to the land is available from *www.gov.uk/topic/outdoor-access-recreation/rights-of-way-open-access*.

Natural England's website gives details of Open Access and CRoW land where you can roam freely *www.openaccess.naturalengland.org.uk*.

Running clubs

There are running clubs all across the region packed with enthusiasts of all abilities. Joining a club is a great way to motivate yourself and also become a better runner, while also making friends and discovering new routes. Find a local club through the searchable map on the England Athletics website *www.englandathletics.org* or from other online sources such as *www.goodrunguide.co.uk/ClubFinder.asp*. Specialist running shops often organise group runs or can provide contact details for local clubs and groups. Every club is different so it is worth enquiring about the running speed of club runs, coaching sessions and the club's emphasis on road, off-road and social activities.

Run Together is a recreational arm of English Athletics with groups all over the country. Run Together aims to make walking and jogging accessible to everyone including absolute beginners *www.runtogether.co.uk*.

Orienteering combines running with navigation and is a good way to develop the skills needed for more remote off-road runs. Find a club or local events by contacting British Orienteering *www.britishorienteering.org.uk*. The South East Orienteering Association *www.seoa.org.uk* organise a busy calendar of events across the region.

Appendices

Trail races

Trail races are increasing in number, both in absolute terms and relative to the number of road events. Their listings are available online at websites such as *www.tra-uk.org*, *www.runnersworld.co.uk*, *www.runabc.co.uk*, *www.findarace.com* and *www.fellrunner.org.uk*.

Numerous trail marathons and ultra-marathons take place in the region, some extending over multiple days. The 100 Marathon Club list most events *www.100marathonclub.org.uk*.

The Long Distance Walkers Association (LDWA) run numerous 'Challenge' events which are entered by runners (don't be fooled by the 'walkers' title, these events can get quite competitive!). The Challenge events offer very cheap but well organised trail runs. The LDWA's events are listed on their website *www.ldwa.org.uk* and also in their member's handbook. Membership is not usually necessary to join their events. Adventure Races and other endurance events which combine running with other outdoor activities are growing in popularity. A good source for event ideas is the Sleep Monsters website *www.sleepmonsters.com*. Parkruns *www.parkrun.org.uk* are a fast-growing phenomenon! These free, weekly 5km runs are held in numerous locations and are a great way to develop confidence in running and to track personal progress. There are also a number of 2km junior parkruns, open to 4–14-year olds. However, many feature tarmac or other hard surfaces.

Training, coaching and guiding

Most clubs organise training sessions as well as social runs. These usually include activities such as hill reps or fartleks. Many coaches work with clubs and it is also possible to hire personal coaches for individuals or small groups.

Confident and accurate navigation only comes through practice, but the basic techniques can be taught on courses intended for orienteers or hill walkers. Suitable courses are run by a number of outdoor centres within the region. A useful instructional tool is *Mountain and Moorland Navigation*, Kevin Walker, Pesda Press 2016 ISBN 9781906095567.

New route ideas

Books and magazines

Trail Running is published quarterly and is the only UK magazine dedicated to off-road running.

Although there are limited trail running guidebooks for the UK at present (and none previously aimed at this region), books and other information aimed at walkers and mountain bikers can be useful sources of ideas for new routes. Outdoor shops, bookshops and tourist information centres usually sell a range of such guidebooks.

Appendices

Online communities and databases
Online communities (see Mapping) can provide ideas of where other people go running in particular areas. Many online communities or route databases intended for walkers and mountain bikers are also useful for trail and hill runners. New websites for runners, walkers and bikers appear all the time so an internet search is the best way of finding suitable sites.

Further information
Tourist information centres and other visitor centres often have free leaflets describing local walking routes. Many of these are also available online through local or national websites.

Forestry England *www.forestryengland.uk*, the rebranded Forestry Commission, promote trail running and offer suggestions for routes on their land (see page 160).

National Trails *www.nationaltrail.co.uk* invariably offer fantastic route opportunities. The websites for each trail include ideas for shorter routes which utilise the trail. The five National Trails in the South East (England Coast Path, North Downs Way, Ridgeway, South Downs Way, Thames Path) are all described in this book. Many other long-distance trails are outlined (see page 75).

The Long Distance Walkers Association (LDWA) *www.ldwa.org.uk* are an excellent source of information for waymarked or named long-distance routes which do not have National Trail designation.

Acknowledgements

Many thanks to Susie Allison, whose outstanding guidebook *Scottish Trail Running* (Pesda Press 2017 ISBN 9781906095628) provided both the inspiration and the model for both this volume and its companion volume *South West Trail Running*. Thanks to also Franco Ferrero at Pesda Press, Vicky Barlow for her great design work, Heather Hall and Ros Morley for their meticulous proofreading and Don Williams of Bute Cartographic for the stunning maps.

All manner of friends came along and ran with me during the research for the book. Cheers for your help all, you are all great company and make the miles so much easier.

Index

Symbols
3 Castles Ultramarathon 102
50-mile Surrey Tops 301, 311
1066 100 Ultramarathon 254
1066 Country Walk 254

A
access land 21
Active Training World 196
Alfriston 258
Allington Castle 243
Alum Bay 25
Alum Bay Chine 27
Amberley 289, 291, 292
Andover Trail Events 96
Appuldurcombe Down 38, 40
Appuldurcombe House 37, 40, 280
Arun River Marathon 293
Ascot Racecourse 97, 101
Ashdown Forest 245, 259, 262
Ashdown Forest Centre 259, 261, 262
Ashridge Estate 170
Asplins Head 198, 200
Audley End 192
Austen, Jane 86
Autumn 100 110
Avebury 111, 113, 114, 115

B
Bablock Hythe 130
Bacchus Marathon, Half Marathon and 10K 317
Baker Barracks 285
Banstead Downs 326
Banstead Heath 322
Barbury Castle 113, 114
Basildon Park 110
Basingstoke and Mid Hants AC 90
Battle Abbey 254
Battle of Britain Memorial 221, 223, 224
Beachy Head 245, 255, 257, 258
Beachy Head Lighthouse 256
Beachy Head Marathon, Half and 10K 258
Beacon Hill 80, 87, 89, 90
Bearsted 229, 231
Beaulieu 58
Beaulieu Heath 55, 56, 57, 58
Belle Tout Lighthouse 255, 256
Bembridge 5 48
Bembridge Down 45, 46
Bembridge Fort 47
Bembridge Harbour 47
Bembridge Windmill 47
Bembridge Youth and Community Centre 48
Benfleet 15 196
Berkhamsted Common 170
Berks, Bucks and Oxon Wildlife Trust (BBOWT) 95, 103, 130
Berkshire 91
Berkshire Bubs 135
Berkshire Downs 91
Berkshire Loop 156
Betsom's Hill 165
Beyond Events 58
BHF Blenheim Palace Half Marathon, 10K and Family Fun Run 134
Bignor 293
Birchington 220
Birling Gap 255, 256, 258
Bisham Abbey 118
Bisham Church 118
Black Down 165, 267, 281, 284
Blackdown Hill Challenge 284
Blackgang Viewpoint 33, 35
Blackheath Common 306
Blackheath Forest 306
Blenheim 7K 134
Blenheim Palace 121, 131, 133, 280
Blenheim Park 132, 134
Boddington Hill Fort 159
Bonchurch Down 37
Bonchurch Landslip 43
Botley Hill 165
Bourne End 118, 119
Bowcombe Down 30
Box Hill 313, 316
Bracknell Forest Runners 102
Bracknell parkrun 102
Brading Marshes RSPB reserve 46, 47
Bradwell Shell Bank 204
Bradwell Waterside 203
Bridge End 135, 137
Brighstone 32
Brighstone Forest 29, 30, 32
Brighton and Hove 265
Brighton Trailblazer Run 266
Broadhalfpenny Down 73
Broadwood's Folly 314, 316
Brockenhurst 55, 58
Brook Down 30
Broomway 197, 200
Broughton 80, 82
Brown, Lancelot 'Capability' 134, 277, 280, 322
Broxbourne 182
Buckinghamshire 147
Buckler's Hard 58
Bucks Epic Trail 10K 160
Burghclere 89, 90
Buriton 290
Burley 59, 60, 61, 62
Burley Beacon 59
Burnham-on-Crouch 201
Bushy Park 327
Butser Hill 68, 69, 70, 165
Butser Hill Challenge 70
Butser Hill National Nature Reserve 68

C
Camber 250
Camber Castle 247, 249
Camber Sands 249
Camp Hill Clump 261
Canary Trail Events 317
Capital Ring 75, 327
Carisbrooke 29
Carisbrooke Castle 29, 32
Carnarvon Mausoleum 88
Castle Hill 135, 137
Castle Hill Iron Age hillfort 59
Castleman's Corkscrew 59, 62
Centurion Running 110, 120, 142, 146, 160, 228, 232, 294
Cernes Farm 242, 243
Chalk, The 48
Challenge Running 110
Chanctonbury Hill 165
Chanctonbury Ring hillfort 273, 275
Chartwell 236
Chattri Memorial 266
Chawton 86
Chequers 153, 155
Chichester Harbour 267
Chichester Harbour Race 288
Chiddingfold 299
Chiddingstone Castle 239, 241
Chidham 287
Chilly Hilly 28
Chiltern Chase 142
Chiltern Hills 143, 147, 152, 171
Chiltern Hills AONB 121, 152
Chiltern Marathon Challenge Event 152
Chiltern Ridge 50km Ultra Trail 160
Chilterns Gateway Centre 171, 173
Chilterns Kanter Challenge Event 170
Chiltern Society, the 156
Chiltern Way 75, 145, 146, 150, 151, 152, 156, 174
Chiltern Wonderland 50 110, 142, 146
Chimney Meadows 127
Chimney Meadows Nature Reserve 127, 129, 130
Chingford 188
Chislet Marshes 217
Chitty Chitty Bang Bang 152
Chrishall Common 165
Christmas Common 145, 146
Churchill Exhibition 134
Churchill, Winston 131
Cissbury Ring hillfort 273, 275
Clarendon Marathon 82
Clarendon Palace 77, 79
Clarendon Way (CW) 49, 75, 77, 78
Cliveden Estate 120
Coastal Trail Series (CTS) 215, 258
Cockley Hill 64
Cock Marsh 118, 119, 120
Colley Hill 319, 321
Column of Victory 133, 134
Combe Gibbet 93, 94
Combe Gibbet to Overton Race 96
Compton Beauchamp 126
Coneycroft Valley 84
Constable, John 205
Cookham 120
Cookham Bridleway Circuit 120
Cookham Dean 117
Cookley Green 145
Coombe Hill 153, 155
Coombe Hill Fell Race 156
Coombe Manor 228
Coopers Hill 63
Coulsdon Common 326
Countryside Code, The 21
county tops (highest points) 165
Crookham 106
Crowborough 165
Crowthorne 101, 102
Croydon 323, 326
Cuckmere valley 255
Culver Cliff 45
Culver Down 47

D
Dallington Forest 244
Danbury Country Park 196
Dark Series 70
Day's Lock 135, 136
Deal 215
Dedham 207
Dedham Vale 205
Dedham Vale AONB 183, 205, 208
deer 236, 237
Dengie Marshes 204
Dengie Peninsula 201
Detling 231, 232
Devil Run, The 301
Devil's Challenge 294
Devil's Chimney 41, 43
Devil's Dyke 269, 271
Devil's Dyke Viewpoint 269, 271
Devil's Kneading Trough 225
Devil's Punch Bowl 297, 299
Ditchling 265
Ditchling Beacon 165, 245, 263, 266
Dorchester 135, 137
Dover 215, 224
Dover Castle 212, 214
Dover Patrol Monument 212
Downland Challenge 266
Downland Devil 9 276
Downland Trail (DT) 68, 69, 70
Downs Link 75, 306
Downs Link Ultra 306
Downton Abbey 87
Drayton Beauchamp 164
Droxford 73, 74
Druid's Challenge 115
Dungeness 250
Dunsmore 155
Dunstable Downs 171, 172, 173
Dunstable Downs Challenge 174
Dunstable Road Runners 174
Duver 47
Duver Dash 48
Duxford Ford 129
Dyke Hills 135, 136

E
Earth Trust 136, 137
Earth Trust Centre 137
Eastbourne 258
East Cliff and Warren Country Park 221
East Cowes 44
East Sussex 245

333

Index

Ecclesbourne Glen 252
Edburton Hill 270, 272
Edenbridge 239, 240, 242
Eden Valley 209, 239
Eden Valley Ultra Trail 243
Eden Valley Walk (EVW) 239, 240, 241, 242, 243, 258
Ellesborough 156
Endurance Life 215, 258
England Coast Path (ECP) 75, 220, 221
Epping Forest 183, 185, 188, 192
Epping Forest Gateway 188
Epping Forest Visitor Centre 186, 187
Essex 183
Essex Cross Country 10K Series 196
Essex Way 75, 188, 205, 208
Ewhurst Windmill 309

F
F3 Events 102
Fairlight 252
Fairlight Glen 252, 253
Fan Bay Deep Shelter 214
Farley Mount Country Park 81, 82
Farley Mount Monument 80
Farthing Downs 323, 324, 325, 326
fastpacking 20
Fell Running Association 40
Fernhurst Recreation Trust 284
ferries, Isle of Wight 28
Fingest 152
Fitstuff G3 Series 306
Five Knolls 171, 173
Flatford 206, 207
Flatford Mill 205
Folkestone 224
Folkestone Warren 221
Ford 292
Fordingbridge 65
Forest 5 102
Forestry England, trail running 160
Foulness Island 197, 198, 200
Founder's Challenge 311
Freedom Racing 284, 306, 311
Frensham Common 300
Freshwater 5K 28
Freshwater Bay 25, 27, 30, 31, 32
Friend's Clump 261
Fulking 272
Fulking Hill 269, 270, 271
Fyfield Down National Nature Reserve 113

G
Gatliff Marathon 243
Gatton Park 280, 321, 322
geology, South East England 48
Gibbet Challenge 96
Gibbet Hill 297, 300
Gills Lap Clump 261
Glatting Beacon 293
Glatting Beacon 5 293
Go Beyond 120
Godshill 65
Golden Hill Country Park 27

Goring 109, 110, 111, 112, 113, 114, 142
Goring Gap 91, 107
Graffham Down 293
Grahame, Kenneth 117
Grand Bridge 134
Grand National 10km Trail Run 276
Grangelands and Rifle Butts Nature Reserve 154
Gravesend 254
Great Brook 127, 128, 129
Great Deep 286
Greater London, trail running 327
Great NorthSouth R#n 36
Great Notley Country Park 196
Great Stones Way 115
Green Chain Walk 75, 327
Greenham Common 91, 103, 105, 106
Greenham Trust 106
Greensand Ridge 209, 233, 267, 301, 307, 312
Greensand Way (GW) 75, 233, 234, 236, 284, 295, 298, 300, 306, 307, 309, 311, 312
Green Way 188
Greenwich Park 327
Grim's Ditch 139, 141, 142
Guildford 303

H
Haddington Hill 157, 160, 165
Hadleigh Castle 183, 193, 195
Hadleigh Country Park 193, 195
Hadleigh Marsh 194
Hainault Forest 192
Hambleden 120
Hambledon 72, 73, 74
Hampshire 49
Hampshire and Isle of Wight Wildlife Trust nature reserve 86
Hampshire Downs ridge 87
Hampshire Hobbit 90
Hampstead Heath 327
Hampton Ridge 63, 64, 65, 66
Hamstreet 312
Hangers, the 84
Hangers Way (HW) 75, 86, 284, 289, 293
Hangover 5 Fun Run 276
Hankley Common 300
Happy Valley 323, 325, 326
Harrietsham 232
Harting Trail Race 293
Haslemere 283, 284, 297, 298, 299, 300, 312
Haslemere Border AC 301
Hastings 245, 254
Hastings Country Park 251, 252
Hastings Country Park Visitor Centre 253
Hastoe Hill 162, 165
Hatfield Forest 183, 189, 190, 191, 192, 280
Hatfield House 175, 176, 177, 178
Hatfield Park 147, 175, 176, 178

Havant 292
Hay Wain, The 205
Head Down 35
Heartbreaker Marathon 66
Henley Half Marathon and 10K 120
Henley-on-Thames 120
Henley Trail Run 120
Hermes Running 322
Herne Bay 220
Hertfordshire 147
Hever 241, 242
Hever Castle 239, 241
Highclere Castle 87, 89, 90
Highclere Castle 10K 90
Highclere Estate 49, 88, 280
High Weald AONB 209, 239, 244, 245, 262
High Weald Landscape Trail 244
hillforts 276
Hilly Half Marathon 266
Hindhead Common 300
Hit the Trail Running 232, 243
Hollingbourne 229, 231, 232
Holmbury Hill 307, 308, 309, 311
Holmbury Hill hillfort 309
Holmwood 307, 310
Home Park 102
Hoy's Monument 33, 34
Humanity Direct Tring Ultra 164, 170
Hundred Acre Wood 259
Hungerford 95, 96
Hurley Lock 120
Hurst Castle 51, 53, 54
Hurtwood 307, 308, 311
Hurtwood 50k Trail Ultra 311
Hylands Park and House 196

I
Ibstone Circle 152
Ibstone Common 151
Icknield Way (ancient route) 152, 167, 170
Icknield Way Path (IWP) 170
Icknield Way Trail (IWT) 75, 155, 170, 174
Ightham Mote 233, 234, 236
Inglis Memorial 319
Inkpen 95
Inkpen Hill 95, 96
Inkpen Wild Walk 95
Isle of Thanet 217
Isle of Wight 23, 28
Isle of Wight AONB 23, 36
Isle of Wight Challenge 44
Isle of Wight Coastal Path (IOWCP) 26, 33, 36, 42, 44, 46, 75, 220
Isle of Wight Fell Running Championship Series 40
Isle of Wight Festival of Running 28, 48
Isle of Wight Owl and Falconry Centre 40
Itchen Navigation Heritage Trail 82
Ivinghoe 169
Ivinghoe Beacon 167, 169, 170, 174

J
Jack and Jill windmills 265
John Clarke Memorial Fell Race 188

K
Kenley Common 326
Kennet and Avon Canal 96, 106
Kent 209
Kent 50 Mile Endurance Run 220
Kent Downs AONB 209, 215, 225
Keyhaven 52, 53, 54
Keyhaven and Pennington Marshes Reserve 51, 53
King Manor Hill 79
Kingsclere 96
Kingsdown 212, 214, 215
King's Somborne 80, 82
Kingston Great Common National Nature Reserve 59
Kintbury 95
Kintbury 5 96
Knacker Cracker 316
Knole House 233, 234
Knole Park 233, 234, 235, 236
Knole Run 237

L
Lambourn 126
Lambourn Downs 126
Landslip, The 41
Langdon Hole 213
Lardon Chase 107, 109
LDWA 62, 115, 152, 170, 192, 215, 237, 317
LDWA Challenge Event 243, 301, 311
Lea Valley Walk (LVW) 182
Lechlade 130
Lee Valley 179, 182
Lee Valley Country Park 179, 182
Leith Hill 165, 307, 308, 309, 311
Leith Hill Half Marathon 311
Leith Hill Tower 308, 310
Lenham Cross Winter Marathon 232
Liddington Castle 126
Limerstone Down 32
Liss Runners 293
Little Wittenham 136, 137
Little Wittenham Wood 135, 137, 138
London 2 Brighton Challenge 266
London Loop (LL) 75, 326, 327
Longmere Point 286, 287
Long Walk, The 99, 101
Long Woodland Trail (LWT) 68, 69, 70
Look Out Discovery Centre 100, 102
Lough Down 107, 109
Lower Cadsden 155
Luccombe Chine 42
Luccombe Down 37, 39, 42
Lurgashall 280
Lymington 27, 55, 57, 58
Lymington-Keyhaven Nature Reserve 51

Index

M
Maidstone 229, 231
Maidstone Riverside 10k and 10m 232
Maplin Sands 197
Marilyns 165
Marker Point 286
Marlborough, Duke of 131
Marlborough Running Club 115
Marlow 118, 119
Marsh Farm Country Park 196
Martello Tower 222
Maverick Original Buckinghamshire Event 156
Maverick Original Oxfordshire Race 146
Maverick Race 62, 70, 266, 293, 311
Mayland 204
Maypole, the 198
Medway Estuary 243
Medway Valley Walk 243
Meon, River 71, 73
Meon Valley Trail (MVT) 71, 73, 74
Mickleham 315
Mid-Essex Casuals 208
Mid-Sussex Marathon Weekend 266
Milford on Sea 54
Milne, A.A. 259
Mole Gap 313
Monarch's Way (MW) 71, 72, 74
Mongewell Woods 139, 140
Moonlight Challenge 220
Mother Dunch's Buttocks 135
Mottistone 32
Mottistone Down 32
Mottistone Estate 32
Mountain and Moorland Navigation 18
Mouth 2 Mouth Marathon 293

N
National Trails, South East 75
National Trust, trail running 317
Natural History Museum (Tring) 161, 164
Natural History of Selborne, The 83
navigation 17
NDW50 232
NDW100 228, 232
Needles Battery 27
Needles Half Marathon 28
Needles Landmark Attraction, the 27, 31, 32
Needles, the 25, 29, 30
Nell Gwyn's Monument 161
Newbridge 130
Newbury 96, 103
Newbury AC 90, 106
New Forest 59, 62
New Forest, access 66
New Forest Challenge 62
New Forest Marathon 58
New Forest National Park 49, 62, 66
New Forest race 62

New Forest Runners 58
New Forest Stinger 66
New Forest Ten 58
New Forest Trail 58
Newlands Corner 303, 305, 306, 316
Newport 29, 31, 32
Newtown River 28
Nice Work 160, 196, 250
Niton 35
Noah's Challenge 208
Noar Hill 83, 85, 86
Norbury Park 313
North Chiltern Trail 156
North Downs 209, 301
North Downs Marathon and Half Marathon 322
North Downs Ridge 50k 306
North Downs Way (NDW) 75, 224, 226, 228, 229, 231, 232, 295, 305, 306, 314, 315, 316, 320
North Sea 197
North Wessex Downs AONB 49, 87, 90, 91, 121
Nutley Windmill 261

O
Oakhaven Hospice 58
Oakhaven Ten 58
Odiham Castle 102
Old Winchester Hill 71, 73, 74
Original Surrey event 311
Orion Harriers 188
outdoor access 21
Overton Harriers 96
Oxford 130, 138
Oxfordshire 121
Oxfordshire Epic 10k 134
Oxfordshire Way (OW) 134, 145

P
PB Race Events 237
Pegwell Bay 220
Penshurst 243
Penshurst Place 239, 241
Pen-y-Bos 281
People's Forest, the 188
Perching Hill 270
Petersfield 284, 289, 290, 292, 293
Petworth House 278, 280
Petworth Park 267, 277, 278, 279, 284
Pevensey 254
Pilgrim's Challenge 232
Pilgrim's Way 231, 232, 304, 319, 320
Pilot Hill 96, 165
Pitch Hill 307, 309, 311
Pitton 79, 82
Polesdon Lacey estate 313, 316
Poynings 272
Pulpit Hill 153
Punchbowl Marathon 301
Pyle Hill 106

Q
Quarry Wood 117, 118
Queen Elizabeth Country Park 67, 70

Queen Elizabeth Olympic Park 182
Queen Elizabeth parkrun 70
Queen Elizabeth's Hunting Lodge 188
Queen Elizabeth Spring Marathon and Half 70

R
Race to the King 294
Race to the Stones 115
Ragnar White Cliffs 215
Ranmore Common 313, 316
Reculver 219, 220
Reculver Country Park 220
Reculver Towers 217, 219
Reigate Fort 320, 321
Reigate Hill 319
Reigate Priory Park 10k 322
Reynards Hill 307, 309
Richmond Park 327
Ridgeway 40 115
Ridgeway Challenge 115
Ridgeway (map) 114
Ridgeway National Trail (RNT) 75, 111, 112, 113, 115, 121, 124, 125, 126, 139, 140, 141, 142, 152, 154, 155, 160, 163, 164, 167, 168, 170
Ridgeway Relay 115
Ridgeway Run 170
Riding and Running 232
River Blackwater estuary 201
River Crouch estuary 201
River Cuckmere 255, 258
River Eden 241
River Kennet valley 91, 94
River Lea 147, 175
River Lee Regional Park 182
River Medway 239, 241
River Meon 71, 73
River Meon Marathon 75
River Mole 313, 314, 315
River Newtown 28
River Rother 248
Rivers Eden 239
River Stour 206
River Test valley 96
River Thames 91, 117, 120, 121, 127, 129, 136, 137, 142
River Wantsum 217, 219
River Windrush 127, 128
River Yar 25
River Yar estuary 28, 46
ROAM 639 Trail 300
Rochester Castle 243
Roc Newbury 10K 106
Romney Marsh 250
Rotary Blenheim 10K and 5K Run 134
Round Hill 135, 137
Royal Military Canal 250, 253
Royal Windsor 10K River Trail Run 102
Royal Windsor Half Marathon River Trail Run 102
Roydon Woods Nature Reserve 56
RUAlive Trail Run 284
Runaway Racing 160, 243

RunBelievable 262
Run Events 70
Run Fest 182
Run Hadleigh Park 196
Run London Epping Forest Trail 10k 188
Run Nation 188
Runner of Azkaban 106
RunThrough 106
Run West Berks 96
Rural Running Events 75
Ryde Harriers 28
Rye 249
Rye Ancient Trails 30k & 15k 250
Rye Harbour 245, 247
Rye Harbour Nature Reserve 247, 249
Rye Heritage and Information Centre 249

S
Saffron Walden 192
Salisbury 81, 82
Salisbury Cathedral 77, 78
Salomon's Memorial viewpoint 313, 314
Salt Marsh Ultra 204
Samphire Hoe Country Park 224
Sandwich 215
Saturn Running 106
Saxon Shore Seaside Series 224
Saxon Shore Way (SSW) 75, 213, 215, 218, 220, 252, 253, 254, 258
Saxons, Normans and Vikings Marathons 220, 224
Seaford 258
Seaford Head Nature Reserve 258
Second Wind Running 70, 96
Selborne 83, 86
Selborne Common 83, 85, 86
Selborne Hill 83
Serpent Trail 75, 280, 284, 293, 300
Serpent Trail Races 284, 301
Sevenoaks 233, 235
Sevenoaks 7 237
Sevenoaks AC 237
Sevenoaks Circular 237
Sevenoaks School 237
Seven Sisters 245, 255, 258
Seven Sisters Country Park 257
Shamley Green 300, 307, 310
Shanklin 41, 43, 44
Shanklin Down 37, 39, 42
Shifford Island 127, 130
Shifford Lock Cut 127, 129, 130
Shoreham 272
Shoreham Woods 10K 237
Sinodun Hills 135
Skirmett 152
Smugglers 10K 220
Smugglers Trail 204
Snow Hill 99, 101
Solent 25, 51
Solent Way 55, 57, 58, 75, 220, 287

335

Index

Soup Run 48
South Coast Challenge 294
South Downs 269
South Downs National Park 49, 84, 245, 267, 272
South Downs Relay 294
South Downs Way 100 294
South Downs Way (map) 294
South Downs Way (SDW) 69, 70, 71, 72, 73, 74, 75, 82, 256, 257, 258, 270, 272, 275, 276, 289, 291, 294, 306
Southern Extension 156
Southern Multisports 293
South Foreland Lighthouse 211, 213, 214
South London Downs National Nature Reserve 323
South London Harriers 327
South West Trail Running 90, 96, 106, 115, 120, 126, 170
Sporting Events UK 220
St Boniface Down 37, 39, 41, 43, 165
St Catherine's Down 33, 34
St Catherine's Oratory 33
St Catherine's Point Lighthouse 33, 35
Stenbury Down 38
Step Up 4 Good 10K 106
Steyning 275, 276
Steyning Stinger Marathon / Half Marathon 276
St Lawrence 204
St Leonards Forest 244
St Margaret's Bay 211, 212, 214
St Martha's Hill 303, 304
St Martin's Down 37, 39
Stonor Park 149, 150, 152
Stour Valley Path 75, 205, 208
Stour Valley Walk 220
St Peter-on-the-Wall, chapel of 201, 203
St Peter's Way Ultra 204
Streatley 109, 110, 138
Surrey 295
Surrey Hills AONB 301
Surrey Hills Challenge 317
Surrey Hills Challenge Ultra 301
Surrey Slog Half Marathon 311
Sussex Border Path (SBP) 75, 244, 284, 288
Sussex Trail Events 266, 288, 293, 306
Sussex Wildlife Trust 249
Swinley Forest 97, 102
Swinley Park 97, 100

T

T184 120
Tapnell 10K 28
Temple 119
Temple Island 120
Temple Lock 117
Temple of the Winds 281, 282
Temple Trail 120, 146
Tennyson Down 25, 31
Tennyson Heritage Coast 36
Tennyson, Lord 29
Tennyson Monument 25, 30, 31
Tennyson Trail 29, 30, 32
Test Valley 49, 77
Test Way (TW) 75, 96
Testway Ultra 96
Thames Challenge 120
Thames Estuary Path 196
Thames Path 100 120
Thames Path National Trail (TP) 75, 110, 117, 119, 120, 128, 130, 137, 138, 142
Thames Ring 250 110
Thames Trot Ultra 120
Thames Valley Orienteering Club 138
Thatcham Nature Discovery Centre 103, 104, 105, 106
Thorndon Country Park 196
Thorney Island 267, 285
Three Castles 30 243
Three Castles Path (TCP) 75, 82, 97, 99, 102
Three Forests Way 75, 188, 192
Three Forests Way Challenge Event 192
Three Forts Marathon / Half Marathon 276
Thurnham Castle 230, 231
Thursley Common 300
ticks 16
Tonbridge 239, 241, 242, 243
Tonbridge Castle 239, 240, 241
Totternhoe Knolls 171
Totton Running Club 66
Tough Runner UK 134, 160
Toys Hill 236
Trail Running Association 115
Trail Running Festival (Boxhill) 316
Trail Running Sussex 262
Tring Park 161, 162, 164
Tring Running Club 156, 170
Trust10 Trail Run 174
T Series Racing 120
Turville 149, 150, 151, 152
Two Tree Island 196

U

Uffington Castle 113, 123, 124, 126
Uffington White Horse 123
UK Running Events 288
UK Ultra Distance Trail Running Championship 115
Ultra Challenge 266, 294
Ultrarunning Ltd 120
Ultraviolet 102
Undercliff 41

V

Vanbrugh, Sir John 134
Vanguard Way 75, 243, 244, 258, 262
Ventnor 38, 40, 41, 43
Vereley Hill 59, 61
Viking 100 Endurance Run 220
Virginia Water 102

W

Wade Marsh 217
Wakering Stairs 198, 200
Walbury Camp 94
Walbury Hill 91, 93, 95, 96, 165
Wallingford 141
Wallingford Thames Run 142
Walmer 215
Walton Heath 322
Wantage Monument 113
Wantsum Channel 217
Wantsum Walk 220
Warburg Nature Reserve 143
War Down 67
Warren Glen 252, 253
Warren, The 221
Water of Life Marlow to Henley Half Marathon and 10K 120
Watership Down 96
Watlington Hill 143, 146, 152
Watlington Runners 146
Watlington XC 10k 146
Wayfarers 100k 96
Wayfarer's Walk (WW) 71, 73, 75, 87, 89, 96
Wayland's Smithy Long Barrow 123, 125, 126
Weald Challenge 262
Weald Country Park 196
Weald, the 239, 244
Wealdway 75, 236, 243, 244, 258, 262
Week Down 38
Wendover Woods 147, 157, 158, 159, 160
Wendover Woods 50 160
Wendover Woods Autumn Festival 160
Wendover Woods Night 50 160
Wendover Woods Spring Festival 160
West Berkshire Living Landscape 103
West Cowes 44
Westerham Heights 165
West High Down 31
West Meon 74
West Sussex 267
West Thorney 286
West Wight Sports and Community Centre 28
West Wight Three Hills 28
Wheatham Hill 86
Whipsnade Zoo 174
Whitecliff Bay 47
White Cliffs Challenge 215
White Cliffs Country Trails 215
White Cliffs of Dover 209, 211
White Cliffs Visitor Centre 211, 213, 214
White, Gilbert 83, 86
Whitehorse Hill 113, 123, 126, 165
Whiteleaf Cross 153, 156
Whiteleaf Hill 153, 155
White Mark, the 143
Whitfield Sewer 217, 219
Wickham 74
Wild Walks 106
Wimbledon Common 327
Winchester 49, 78, 81, 82
Winchester Cathedral 77, 81, 82
Winchester Great Hall 102
Wind in the Willows, The 117
Windover Hill 258
Windsor 101, 102
Windsor Castle 91, 97, 99, 102
Windsor Great Park 97, 101, 102
Winnie-the-Pooh 259
Winnie-the-Pooh Weekend 262
Winterfold Hill 307, 309
Winter Hill 91, 117, 119
Winter Tanners Challenge Event 317
Witchfinder Trail 208
Witley 297, 298, 299, 300
Wittenham Clumps 135, 137
Woodmill 82
Woodstock 133
Woolstone 125, 126
Wormley 298, 300
Wormsley Estate 152
Worsley Monument 38, 40
Worsley, Sir Richard 40
Wroxall 40
Wye Crown 225
Wye Downs 225
Wye Nature Reserve 225, 227

X

XNRG 115, 164, 170, 232, 294

Y

Yarborough Monument 45, 47
Yar Estuary 28, 46
Yarmouth 25, 27, 28

Z

Zig-Zag Path 83, 84